Twilight of the Mission Frontier

Twilight of the Mission Frontier:

Shifting Interethnic Alliances and Social Organization in Sonora, 1768–1855

by

José Refugio de la Torre Curiel

Stanford University Press
Stanford, California

and

The Academy of American Franciscan History
Berkeley, California
2012

Library of Congress Cataloging-in-Publication Data

Torre Curiel, Jose Refugio de la.
  Twilight of the mission frontier : shifting interethnic alliances and social organization in Sonora, 1768–1855 / by Jose Refugio De la Torre Curiel.
    p. cm.
  Includes bibliographical references and index.
  ISBN 978-0-8047-8504-4 (hardcover : alk. paper)
  1. Missions—Mexico—Sonora (State)—History—18th century. 2. Missions—Mexico—Sonora (State)—History—19th century. 3. Franciscans—Mexico—Sonora (State)—History—18th century. 4. Franciscans—Mexico—Sonora (State)—History—19th century. 5. Indians of Mexico—Missions—Mexico—Sonora (State)—History—18th century. 6. Indians of Mexico—Missions—Mexico—Sonora (State)—History—19th century. 7. Social structure—Mexico—Sonora (State)—History—18th century. 8. Social structure—Mexico—Sonora (State)—History—19th century. 9. Sonora (Mexico : State)—Ethnic relations—History—18th century. 10. Sonora (Mexico : State)—Ethnic relations—History—19th century. I. Title.
  F1346.T67 2012
  305.800972'17–dc23

                                                      2012022744

Stanford University Press
Stanford, California

To Rosy, Mariana, and Diego

CONTENTS

ILLUSTRATIONS

Abbreviations

AFPM, AQ	Archivo Franciscano de la Provincia de Michoacán, Fondo Archivo de Querétaro, Celaya, Mexico
AGES	Archivo General del Estado de Sonora, Hermosillo, Mexico
AGI	Archivo General de Indias, Seville, Spain
AGN	Archivo General de la Nación, Mexico City
AHMNAH, FF	Archivo Histórico del Museo Nacional de Antropología e Historia, Fondo Franciscano, Mexico City
AHNM	Archivo Histórico Nacional, Madrid
AHZPFSFSM	Archivo Histórico de Zapopan, Provincia de los Santos Francisco y Santiago de México, Zapopan, Mexico
AMH	Archivo de la Mitra de Hermosillo, Hermosillo, Mexico
ARAG	Archivo de la Real Audiencia de Guadalajara, Guadalajara, Mexico
BL	Bancroft Library, Berkeley, California
BNFF	Biblioteca Nacional de México, Fondo Franciscano, Mexico City
BNM	Biblioteca Nacional de Madrid
BPEJ, CM	Biblioteca Pública del Estado de Jalisco, Colección de Manuscritos, Guadalajara, Mexico
Fr. MCC	Fray Marcellino da Civezza Collection (microfilm in Bancroft Library)
MNM	Museo Naval de Madrid
RAH	Real Academia de la Historia, Madrid
RBP	Real Biblioteca de Palacio, Madrid
UAL	University of Arizona Library, Special Collections, Tucson, Arizona

ACKNOWLEDGMENTS

While preparing this book I had the opportunity to share valuable ideas and moments with many people to whom I owe a deep debt of gratitude. From the beginning I received generous support from William Taylor, Jennifer Spear, and Robert Middlekauff, who helped me put my initial ideas into perspective and made important comments and suggestions on an earlier version of the manuscript presented in 2005 as my doctoral dissertation in the Department of History at the University of California, Berkeley. Since then, Professor Taylor has followed closely the evolution of this work. His respectful, critical but supportive, tone in dialogues with others interested in the historiography of the colonial period in Latin America, and the acute attention he devotes to the experiences, practices, and aspirations of many and varied historical subjects—both individually and collectively—opened a path that, while often difficult, provides comfort to those who travel it. I have striven to keep my research on this trail but, of course, any deviation is my sole responsibility. I thank Professor Taylor especially for his encouragement at those times when the pressure to finish the manuscript threatened to overwhelm other fundamental aspects of my life.

Various sections of the book benefited from comments by several colleagues. I am grateful to all for their criticisms and suggestions though, of course, all meanderings along or around the topics and issues discussed reflect my own decisions and free them from responsibility for the final result. I wish to express my sincere gratitude to Chantal Cramaussel, Salvador Álvarez, Mario Alberto Magaña Mancillas, Cynthia Radding, Robert H. Jackson, Salvador Bernabéu, Rose Marie Beebe, Ivonne del Valle, Jessica Delgado, Karen Melvin, Kristin Huffine, and Julia Sarreal. I am also indebted to the Seminario de Instituciones Novohispanas, which gave me the opportunity to share my ideas on frontier societies with other scholars and enrich my study with their timely comments. These academic exchanges deepened the bonds of friendship I share with that seminar's current members: Marina Mantilla Trolle, Ignacio Almada Bay, Rafael Diego-Fernández, Gilberto López Castillo, Isabel Marín Tello, María del Valle Borrero Silva, and Isabel Scott Palma.

Steve Hackel, Robert Senkewicz, Susan Deeds, William Taylor, and two anonymous readers generously devoted their time to reading the entire text. Their comments proved useful in refining it and detecting topics that required revisions and greater precision. I thank them all for their interest in this dialogue, and hope that the arguments presented here do justice to their suggestions.

In addition, I am indebted to the institutions that provided support during my research and writing. First, I thank the Academy of American Franciscan History for its interest, from the outset, in encouraging the publication of this book, and for the funding that allowed me to present successive versions in a series of fruitful seminars. Special thanks to Jeffrey Burns, director of the Academy of American Franciscan History, for his patience, kindness, and understanding, which helped me reach this goal. In Mexico, the SEP-CONACyT Fund for Basic Scientific Research provided resources that made it possible to broaden the scope of my work in 2008–2009 (project number 79262). At the archives and libraries listed in the abbreviations section, the staff responsible for the respective collections were most helpful in facilitating the working materials I required. Without their kind assistance and broad-based knowledge, my visits to those repositories would not have been nearly as productive as they proved to be.

Also, my gratitude goes out to the Department of History at the University of Guadalajara, especially Lilia V. Oliver Sánchez and David Carbajal López, who received me there and at key moments provided assistance so that I could fulfill my teaching responsibilities without impeding progress in my research. During the final phase of the writing process, El Colegio de Jalisco offered a place where I could reorganize my materials and thoughts and thus meet the deadline established by the editors.

The culmination of this project would not have been possible without the valuable support of Paul Kersey, who translated most of the text into English. Over the years, my visits to his Language Laboratory at El Colegio de Michoacán have been learning experiences that go beyond the professional sphere. He is a true friend who always receives me warmly. Also, amid the pressures of this long journey, the friendship and hospitality of Walter Brem and Cathy Scheiman ensured that my travels included a comforting reception where I felt like family. In Camilo Trumper and Celso Castilho I found two lifelong friends who helped me negotiate my transit through two cultures in the best terms imaginable.

Finally, the support and understanding of my family brought me to this moment, as they constantly encouraged me, even when that meant spending more time at my desk and less time at the playground. A humble way of beginning to repay this debt is by dedicating this book to them and expressing my unconditional love for them.

INTRODUCTION

Although we speak of the 'Spanish mission' or the 'mission system',
in reality each mission recorded a distinct, even diverse, history.
The networks of missions in different regions and in different epochs
may have been analogous, but they were certainly not the same.[1]

In general terms, most modern analysts of the transformation of mission communities in northern New Spain agree that by the late eighteenth century, mission towns had entered a period of change that disrupted local economies, affected communal land tenure systems, and accentuated local patterns of miscegenation and Indian mobility.[2] In some cases, narratives on the transformation of land tenure systems speak of a gradual transfer of control over productive resources from communal to private ownership, emphasizing

---

[1] Charles Polzer, *Kino. A Legacy: His Life, His Works, His Missions, His Monuments* (Tucson: Jesuit Fathers of Southern Arizona, 1998), 127.

[2] Cynthia Radding, *Las estructuras socioeconómicas de las misiones de la Pimería Alta, 1768–1850* (Hermosillo, Sonora: Instituto Nacional de Antropología e Historia, 1979), 12–15; Kieran McCarty, *A Spanish Frontier in the Enlightened Age: Franciscan Beginnings in Sonora and Arizona, 1767–1770* (Washington, DC: Academy of American Franciscan History, 1981), 5–10; Patricia Escandón, "Los problemas de la administración franciscana en las misiones sonorenses, 1768–1800," in *Actas del IV Congreso Internacional sobre los Franciscanos en el Nuevo Mundo* (Madrid: DEIMOS, 1992), 290–91; Miguel León Portilla, "El periodo de los franciscanos, 1768–1771," in *Panorama histórico de Baja California*, ed. David Piñera Ramírez (Tijuana: Universidad Autónoma de Baja California, Universidad Nacional Autónoma de México, 1983), 117–25; Patricia Escandón, "La nueva administración misional y los pueblos de indios," in *Tres siglos de historia sonorense (1530–1830)*, ed. Sergio Ortega Noriega (Mexico City: Universidad Nacional Autónoma de México, 1993), 333–34; Ignacio Almada Bay, José Marcos Medina Bustos, and María del Valle Borrero, "Hacia una nueva interpretación del régimen colonial en Sonora: Descubriendo a los indios y redimensionando a los misioneros," *Región y Sociedad* 19, special issue (2007): 237–65; Ignacio Almada Bay, "La descomposición de las misiones en las provincias de Sonora y Sinaloa, 1690–1767: Un acopio de factores internos y externos a la Compañía de Jesús," in *Misiones del Noroeste de México: Origen y destino 2005*, eds. José Rómulo Félix Gastelum and Raquel Padilla Ramos (Hermosillo, Sonora: Fondo Regional para la Cultura y las Artes, Consejo Nacional para la Cultura y las Artes, 2007), 169–88.

the impact of such evolution upon Indians' social organization.[3] Other explanations address the same process in terms of long-held disputes over the control of mission resources, prompted by the avarice of settlers and royal officers, thus portraying the missions as arenas of permanent political conflict.[4]

Regarding production, commerce, and the growth of non-Indian populations in the vicinity of mission towns, various case studies point out the deterioration of mission productive systems and "the expansion of the *vecino* economy,"[5] which ultimately altered the economic relationship between Spanish and Indian settlers in frontier societies.[6] After the expulsion of the Jesuits, one author has noted, mission communities started to deteriorate since the consequences of this measure were "a decline in discipline, control and attention to the needs of both Spanish settlers and congregated Amerindians," increased incursions of Spanish settlers upon Indian villages, widespread desertion of Indians from mission towns, and increased conflicts over the appropriation of Indian labor.[7] In this context of gradual decline, one historian has noted, the demise of the mission regime was inevitable: First, it was doomed because it controlled the available land and workforce without reporting any profits to the Crown, and second, it was a burden to the colonists' interests. Consequently, all efforts made by the Franciscans to retain control of the missionary districts "proved useless."[8]

REASSESSING THE MISSION CRISIS

In the late colonial period, mission regimes indeed faced various symptoms of crisis; however, if we are to understand how mission structures responded to

---

[3] Cynthia Radding, *Wandering Peoples: Colonialism, Ethnic Spaces, and Ecological Frontiers in Northwestern Mexico, 1700–1850* (Durham, NC: Duke University Press, 1997), 171–93; Saúl Jerónimo Romero, *De las misiones a los ranchos y las haciendas: La privatización de la tenencia de la tierra en Sonora, 1740–1860* (Hermosillo: Gobierno del Estado de Sonora, 1995), 123–35.

[4] Félix D. Almaraz, *The San Antonio Missions and Their System of Land Tenure* (Austin: University of Texas Press, 1989), 6–19; Félix D. Almaraz, "Franciscan Evangelization in Spanish Frontier Texas: Apex of Social Contact, Conflict and Confluence, 1751–1761," *Colonial Latin American Historical Review* 2, no. 3 (1993): 253–87.

[5] Ross Frank, *From Settler to Citizen. New Mexican Economic Development and the Creation of Vecino Society, 1750–1820* (Berkeley and London: University of California Press, 2000), 119–25.

[6] Susan M. Deeds, *Defiance and Deference in Mexico's Colonial North: Indians under Spanish Rule in Nueva Vizcaya* (Austin: University of Texas Press, 2003), 131–89.

[7] Oakah L. Jones, *Nueva Vizcaya: Heartland of the Spanish Frontier* (Albuquerque: University of New Mexico Press, 1988), 177.

[8] Juan Domingo Vidargas, "Sonora y Sinaloa como provincias independientes y como Estado Interno de Occidente: 1821–1830," in *Tres siglos de historia sonorense (1530–1830)*, ed. Sergio Ortega Noriega (Mexico City: Universidad Nacional Autónoma de México, 1993), 435.

this situation we must keep in mind that such a critical phase was neither per-
vasive nor completely irreversible. California, for instance, was a notable exception regarding this scenario of material decline during the late eighteenth century. In fact, these missions actually developed self-sufficient agricultural
operations that in some cases even came to supply settlements of Spanish soldiers and settlers.[9] In similar vein, as this study shows, Franciscan missions in
Pimería Alta (Sonora) experienced a conspicuous, though brief, material
rebirth and new flourishing amid a general trend of mission decline in the late
eighteenth century.

It is clear that in the latter half of the eighteenth century, different missions
responded in distinct ways to the challenges they were facing. What is less evident is why some of them adapted better than others to that process, and why
some contemporary studies of the resulting transformations give accounts of
mission breakdown while others describe consolidation of mission projects.

Questions such as these first led me to inquire into the nature of the mission complexes in Sonora. After an earlier research endeavor had touched,
albeit tangentially, on the presence of the Franciscans in northern New Spain,
I became intrigued by an apparently simple question: How can we explain the
failure of the Franciscan missions in that region?[10]

This query, as I have now come to understand it, is not correctly formulated in this way, nor should it be articulated as such in other mission contexts.
Rather, the fundamental issue is to understand how the internal components of
each mission complex were modified in a context marked by the gradual consolidation of other forms of Spanish settlement.

Based on a close examination of demographic, cultural, economic, and
institutional variables, and through a comparative study of two mission districts
in Sonora, this study portrays the late colonial mission as an institution embed-
ded in complex social structures. Originally designed as an institution of religious indoctrination and political control, the Spanish mission also served specific social functions, such as reorganizing Indian communities along the lines
of the corporate structures of the Spanish *pueblo*, linking the Indians with a
number of aspects of European material culture, and mediating the contact
between Indians and Europeans. However, as this study contends, during the

---

[9] Steven W. Hackel, "Land, Labor and Production: The Colonial Economy of Spanish and
Mexican California," in *Contested Eden: California before the Gold Rush*, eds. Ramón Gutiérrez and
Richard J. Orsi (Berkeley: University of California Press, 1998), 116.

[10] José Refugio de la Torre Curiel, *Vicarios en entredicho: Crisis y desestructuración de la
provincia franciscana de Santiago de Xalisco, 1749–1860* (Zamora: El Colegio de Michoacán,
Universidad de Guadalajara, 2001), 319–44.

late colonial period the mission's ability to fulfill those functions was challenged by the consolidation of Spanish haciendas and villages.

In writing this narrative on the demise of the mission frontier in Sonora, I tried to be attentive to the roles that individuals from various groups played in the transformation of local societies, as I was interested in exploring the cultural exchanges taking place in those settings. However, now that I look back, I realize that without neglecting my original goals, a great deal of attention was placed on the contradictions, paradoxes, and tensions revolving around the Franciscan friars in Sonora. I would like to think this book contributes to an ongoing conversation on the ways in which power relations were created and contested in frontier societies. Thus, missionaries are prominent figures in this analysis because I am persuaded that there is much to be said about the decline of mission structures from a perspective focused on the internal differences, daily conflicts, and institutional struggles those individuals faced. When possible, this conviction brings into the larger picture the ways in which other individuals responded to the deterioration of mission administration.[11] Such a framework retains a close connection with my understanding of the mission as one of the many layers shaping frontier societies. Thus, to gain a more precise image of the changes and continuities this book deals with, a discussion of the concept of "mission" and the roles of missions is in order.

ON THE WRITING OF MISSION HISTORY

How are we to conceive of a mission? What elements should be taken into account to characterize the mission frontier? These two questions are the cornerstone of this work. They are pertinent because they encapsulate many analytical and narrative differences that have marked mission historiography. It must be pointed out, however, that mission historians seldom consider this conceptual precision to be among their main concerns. This area of study cur-

---

[11] I find Gil Pujol's characterization of political history in this respect is particularly insightful, as some of my interests are included in what he considers an expansion of this field: "government and informal politics, institutions and rituals, biography and prosopography, decision making and grass-roots politics, taxation and clientelism, elite formation and popular politics, microphysics of power and non-coercive forms of domination, revolution and negotiation, political culture and language, are some of the arenas this expansive political history has appropriated." Xavier Gil Pujol, *Tiempos de política. Perspectivas historiográficas sobre Europa Moderna* (Barcelona: Universitat de Barcelona, 2006), 13. On the same subject, see Elisa Cárdenas Ayala, Erika Pani and Alicia Salmerón, "Nuevas tendencias en la historia política," *Takwá, Revista de historia* 10 (2006): 103–26.

rently centers, as Susan Deeds has observed, on attempts to understand from various perspectives the cultural changes and exchanges that took place at the missions.[12] Today we ask about the experiences of the actors involved in this history and try to find explanations through multidisciplinary approaches, preferably using a language recognizing the role of marginal actors in challenging the forms of power that influenced their daily life.[13]

However, precision in defining the mission experience has not accompanied this favorable evolution. For the past few decades, conceptions of this historical entity have been linked, to a greater or lesser degree, to one of three frames of reference. First is the posture identifying missions with the initial stage of a process of instruction that begins with the missionaries' earliest penetrations into non-Christian areas and culminates with the creation of parishes.[14] The second vision comes from the tradition that highlights the role

[12] Susan Deeds, "Pushing the Borders of Latin American Mission History," *Latin American Research Review* 39, no. 2 (2004); 220.

[13] In a sense, the direction that mission studies has recently taken is symptomatic of "the return to the philosophy of the subject" and the "return to the political," which inspire one of the leading forms of history writing. Roger Chartier, "The World as Representation," in *Histories: French Constructions of the Past*, eds. Jacques Ravel and Lynn Hunt (New York: New Press, 1995), 545–49.

[14] The first person to propose this functional classification of the missions was Robert Ricard who, in 1933, suggested distinguishing the missionary establishments in New Spain according to their formal characteristics and the relations they maintained with the process of expanding the regular clergy in the sixteenth century. According to Ricard, the complexes established in proximity to an administrative center that also served to consolidate the Spanish presence in a pacified territory were identified as missions of *occupation*; others, more isolated and that accompanied early incursions into untamed territories, were called missions of *penetration*, while those that served as bridges among different mission complexes or nuclei were considered *liaison* points. Robert Ricard, *La conquista espiritual de México: Ensayo sobre el apostolado y los métodos misioneros de las órdenes mendicantes en la Nueva España de 1523–1524 a 1572* (Mexico City: Fondo de Cultura Económica, 1986), 157. Although this scheme has been widely discussed and applied in studies of central New Spain, it has also served as a framework for certain analyses of the northern frontier. George Kubler, *The Religious Architecture of New Mexico: In the Colonial Period and Since the American Occupation* (Albuquerque: University of New Mexico Press, 1972), 17; Ramón A. Gutiérrez, *When Jesus Came, the Corn Mothers Went Away: Marriage, Sexuality and Power in New Mexico, 1500–1846* (Stanford, CA: Stanford University Press, 1991), 74. In more recent times, certain historians have examined the issue of the maturity of the mission settlements and their relation to the occupation of space by highlighting—in terms distinct from those used by Ricard—the evolution of the mission presence in three successive phases, which they have labeled emergence, consolidation, and crisis. Sergio Ortega Noriega, "El sistema de misiones jesuíticas, 1591–1699," in *Tres siglos de historia sonorense (1530–1830)*, ed. Sergio Ortega Noriega (Mexico City: Universidad Nacional Autónoma de México, 1993), 53–61; Ana María Atondo and Martha Ortega, "Entrada de colonos españoles en Sonora durante el siglo XVII," in *Historia general de Sonora*, vol. 2, ed. Sergio Ortega Noriega (Hermosillo: Gobierno del Estado de Sonora, 1996), 79; Escandón, "Los problemas de la administración," 277–78. In another context, Almaraz revised this idea and

of the mission as an enclave of Spanish dominion, and as one of the "frontier institutions" established to sustain the Spanish presence on the edges of the empire.[15] Third, the recent focus on culture has come to terms with a perspective that sees the mission as a process of social change constructed, rejected, or suffered by the indigenous peoples in the context of colonial dom-

---

proposed that "in theory, the mission was a transitory medium with a projected lifespan of twenty years, the equivalent of one generation. The sequence of development involved five stages: i) 'mission', the commitment to fulfill an objective; ii) 'reduction', congregating Indians in a suitable location; iii) 'conversion', formal religious instruction; iv) 'doctrine', the acceptance and observation of Spanish Christianity; and, v) 'parish and town', the political recognition of a locality's religious and civil status." Almaraz, *The San Antonio Missions*, 2. For Charles Polzer, the evolutionary process of the mission had three stages: "entrance," "conversion," and "doctrine," followed by a phase of secularization that resulted in conversion of missions into parishes. Cited in David Weber, *The Spanish Frontier in North America* (New Haven, CT, and London: Yale University Press, 1992), 400.

[15] In Bolton's classic formulation, seeing the mission as a "frontier institution" meant analyzing it from a political perspective and emphasizing its objectives: to convert, protect, and civilize the Indians in order to incorporate them into Spanish society as subjects and taxpayers. In this view, the missions emerged as dependencies of the Crown and Church, designed to Christianize, extend, sustain, and civilize the frontier. Herbert E. Bolton, "The Mission as a Frontier Institution in the Spanish-American Colonies," *American Historical Review* 23 (1917): 42; Herbert E. Bolton, *The Spanish Borderlands: A Chronicle of Old Florida and the Southwest* (New Haven, CT: Yale University Press, 1921). The intellectual origins of this clash between civilization and savagery are found in Frederick Jackson Turner, "The Significance of the Frontier in American History," in *Where Cultures Meet: Frontiers in Latin American History*, eds. David Weber and Jane M. Rausch (Wilmington, DE: Scholarly Resources, 1994), 1–18. For an analysis of the evolution of Bolton's ideas, see John Francis Bannon, *The Spanish Borderlands Frontier, 1513–1821* (Albuquerque: University of New Mexico Press, 1974); and David Weber, "John Francis Bannon and the Historiography of the Spanish Borderlands: Retrospect and Prospect," in *Myth and the History of the Hispanic Southwest*, ed. David Weber (Albuquerque: University of New Mexico Press, 1988), 55–88. Examples of this use of the concept of mission are Henry Dobins, *Spanish Colonial Tucson: A Demographic History* (Tucson: University of Arizona Press, 1976), 6; John Francis Bannon, "The Mission as a Frontier Institution: Sixty Years of Interest and Research," *Western Historical Quarterly* 10 (1979): 303–20; McCarty, *A Spanish Frontier*; Almaraz, *The San Antonio Missions*, 1–7; Weber, *The Spanish Frontier*, 111–12; and David Weber, *Bárbaros: Spaniards and Their Savages in the Age of Enlightenment* (New Haven, CT, and London: Yale University Press, 2005), 6. In Mexican historiography, this position is seen in such works as Vito Alessio Robles, *Coahuila y Texas en la época colonial* (Mexico City: Editorial Porrúa, 1978), 352; Luis Arnal, "Las fundaciones del siglo XVIII en el noreste novohispano," in *Arquitectura y urbanismo del septentrión novohispano*, ed. Luis Arnal Simón (Mexico City: Universidad Nacional Autónoma de México, 1999), 7–55; Martha Ortega Soto, *Alta California: Una frontera olvidada del noroeste de México, 1769–1846* (Mexico City: UAM Iztapalapa, Plaza y Valdés Editores, 2001), 33–41; and José Antonio Cruz Rangel, *Chichimecas, misioneros, soldados y terratenientes: Estrategias de colonización, control y poder en Querétaro y la Sierra Gorda, siglos XVI–XVIII* (Mexico City: Secretaría de Gobernación, Archivo General de la Nación, 2003), 11.

ination. This process is now analyzed from the point of view of the indigenous peoples themselves.[16]

These approaches have produced studies with divergent interpretations of the mission experience as they emphasize, respectively, the missionaries' evangelization program, the members of the conquering society and their actions in the evolution of colonial societies, and indigenous groups' responses to forms of the Spanish presence and dominion. This thematic specialization, however, confirms the complexity of the questions I have posited, as each area of interest has proposed a characterization of the mission complexes that reflects its specific analytical focus.

Thus, for example, the term "mission" has been used to refer to a site (an architectural complex), a space (the set of relations and meanings recognized at that site), and a process (the historical evolution of the community). Likewise, studies of mission history show a clear tendency toward thinking—atemporally—that missions can be understood by analyzing just one or two of their functions. Hence, we find discussions of missions as religious-economic institutions, economic-religious establishments, congregations, and places of confinement.

Furthermore, the *quid* of how the mission is perceived depends on its predominant function as perceived by various authors. Some offer their particular view of the mission by evaluating the activities of missionaries and Indians and arguing that they were communities established primarily for the purpose of religious conversion. Several writers agree that the secondary purpose was to produce goods and subjugate the local Indians.[17] Others suggest that the order

---

[16] The bibliography on this topic is abundant. Here, I refer the reader only to studies I consider emblematic of specific issues. On mechanisms of ethnic resistance and the reconstitution of indigenous groups in mission zones, see Gutiérrez, *When Jesus Came*; Radding, *Wandering Peoples*; and Deeds, *Defiance and Deference*. On the multiple meanings of the confluence of space and identity in the California missions, see Lisbeth Haas, *Conquests and Historical Identities in California, 1769–1936* (Berkeley: University of California Press, 1995); and Steven Hackel, *Children of Coyote, Missionaries of Saint Francis: Indian–Spanish Relations in Colonial California, 1769–1850* (Chapel Hill: University of North Carolina Press, 2005). Important examples of analyses of indigenous religiosity in the mission context can be found in William L. Merrill, *Rarámuri Souls: Knowledge and Social Process in Northern Mexico* (Washington DC: Smithsonian Institution Press, 1988); Cynthia Radding, "Crosses, Caves, and Matanchines: Divergent Appropriations of Catholic Discourse in Northwestern New Spain," *The Americas* 55, no. 2 (1988): 177–203; James Sandos, *Converting California: Indians and Franciscans in the Missions* (New Haven, CT, and London: Yale University Press, 2004).

[17] Escandón, "Los problemas," 290–91; Edward Spicer, *Los yaquis: historia de una cultura* (Mexico City: Universidad Nacional Autónoma de México, 1994), 31; Radding, *Wandering Peoples*, 67–68; Mario A. Magaña, *Población y misiones de Baja California: Estudio histórico-*

of priorities was different. They see the mission as a demographic complex
devoted mainly to ensuring agricultural self-sufficiency and the production and
exchange of goods.[18] At one point it was widely accepted that the missions
were essentially congregations of Indians[19] arrayed in architectural complexes
differentiated according to their degree of urbanization.[20] In another perspective, they were treated as imposing "apparatuses of enculturation," similar to
prisons or plantations and set up to transform the Indians into Catholic peasants.[21] But perhaps the clearest example of what I argue here is the following
description from a recent case study of Lower California: "The missions were
. . . in a few words, *pueblos de indios* administered by missionaries."[22]

Given this panorama, one may ask if it is worthwhile to try to bring some
kind of conceptual order or systematization to the topic of the mission as a

---

demográfico de la misión de Santo Domingo de la Frontera: 1775–1850 (Tijuana: El Colegio de la
Frontera Norte, 1998), 59; María del Valle Borrero Silva, *Fundación y primeros años de la gober-
nación de Sonora y Sinaloa, 1732–1750* (Hermosillo: El Colegio de Sonora, 2004), 43; Sandos,
Converting, 11; Robert Jackson, *Missions and the Frontiers of Spanish America* (Scottsdale, AZ:
Pentacle Press, 2005), 23.

[18] With respect to the Jesuit missions in Sonora, Sergio Ortega states that they were "indigenous communities with a solid economic base; that is, they produced for their own subsistence and
in sufficient quantities to prepare for times of hunger. This Jesuit conception of the model of
indigenous community or 'mission' was oriented to forming a community closed to contact with
the Spanish." Ortega Noriega, "El sistema de misiones," 53–54. Chantal Cramaussel portrays the
missions in Nueva Vizcaya as centers that supplied labor for the mines, haciendas, and ranches
throughout a vast zone of Spanish settlement. Cramaussel, *Poblar la frontera: La provincia de
Santa Bárbara en Nueva Vizcaya durante los siglos XVI y XVII* (Zamora: El Colegio de Michoacán,
2006), 55–81.

[19] Jones, *Nueva Vizcaya*, 90–91; Luis González Rodríguez, *El noroeste novohispano en la
época colonial* (Mexico City: Miguel Ángel Porrúa, Universidad Nacional Autónoma de México,
1993), 219–22; Jesús Franco Carrasco, *El Nuevo Santander y su arquitectura*, vol. 1 (Mexico City:
Universidad Nacional Autónoma de México, 1991), 124–45; Salvador Álvarez, "La misión y el
indio en el norte de la Nueva Vizcaya," in *Misiones para Chihuahua*, ed. Clara Bargellini (Mexico
City: Editorial México Desconocido, Grupo Cementos de Chihuahua, 2004), 28–31. At some
point, the idea of the mission-congregation itself becomes confusing: "[The term 'mission'] may
indicate a simple ecclesiastical incursion into the lands of the pagans or a material establishment
among them; that is, the church built . . . to indoctrinate the surrounding population. If they actually worked with catechumens, they tend to be called 'live missions'; at times the terms 'mission'
and 'doctrine' are used indistinctly, occasioning much confusion." Guillermo Porras Muñoz,
Iglesia y Estado en Nueva Vizcaya (1562–1821) (Mexico City: Universidad Nacional Autónoma de
México, 1980), 191.

[20] Gutiérrez, *When Jesus Came*, 74.

[21] Kent G. Lightfoot, *Indians, Missionaries, and Merchants: The Legacy of Colonial Encounters
on the California Frontiers* (Berkeley: University of California Press, 2005), 50, 62–66.

[22] Ignacio del Río, *El régimen jesuítico de la Antigua California* (Mexico City: Universidad
Nacional Autónoma de México, 2003), 12.

historical construction. Some may assert that any attempt to define the mission more exactly is a waste of time, given the range of features that characterized those establishments along the frontiers of the Spanish empire. Finally, one could argue that defining the object is less important than understanding its functioning. I argue, however, that confronting this problem is a *sine qua non* requirement for understanding and explaining the cultural exchanges and ways of life of any social entity. While it is necessary to discover and explain the meanings of the actions of social subjects, it is also, Geertz suggests, necessary to succeed in inscribing the conceptual structures of those meanings in an analytical system to explain their true connection with the society where they take place.[23]

To begin responding to the problem of conceptualizing the missions in simple and clear terms, a suitable starting point would seem to be a recent reflection by Salvador Álvarez concerning the missions in Chihuahua. Álvarez comments that the mission "necessarily evolved at the rhythm imposed by the advancing presence of a new colonial society in those territories, while, at the same time, the mission itself became one of the elements driving that advance."[24] This means that only to the degree in which we clarify the principles upon which this relation of interdependence was based will we be able to understand the rhythms of evolution of the societies that populated the Spanish empire's frontiers. The fragmentary arguments advanced up to now have yielded similarly partial fruits, so it now behooves us to work with global visions based on a fair appreciation of the components of the societies studied.

One guiding principle of this work, then, is to recognize that despite affinities in the diverse initiatives that the members of the religious orders shared, no one single mission project was uniformly representative of northern New Spain.[25] The response by different Indian populations, the circumstances of the geographical environment, and different logistical and material bases those religious institutions had at their disposal constitute just three of the factors imprinting upon each mission district its own vital rhythm that was distinct from those of neighboring jurisdictions.

---

[23] Clifford Geertz, *The Interpretation of Cultures* (New York: Basic Books, 1973), 27–28.
[24] Álvarez, "La misión y el indio," 67.
[25] "Nowhere at any time was there a uniform mission system," Polzer, *Kino*, 127.

CHANGES IN THE MISSION'S SOCIAL FUNCTIONS:
THE SONORAN CASE

In the face of the complexity shown up to this point, the present study contends that the mission was conceived, first and foremost, as a dynamic form of Spanish settlement, that is, as a process which begins with the creation and appropriation of space by a group of social actors, and then unfolds over time in multiple ways depending on the varying meanings the actors confer to such space and as a result of the reassessment and modification of the social functions attached to that space.[26]

In the interests of clarity, I define my understanding of the mission's "social functions" as follows: congregating dispersed populations, reorganizing Indian communities along the lines of the corporate structures of the Spanish *pueblo*, promoting religious conversion, facilitating cultural exchanges, securing new territories, settling formerly transient groups, warding off the territorial ambitions of other nations, producing foodstuffs for internal consumption and local markets, activating local economies, and supplying labor are some examples of the functions that the mission performed at different places and times.[27]

In the long run, the decline of the mission as a form of colonization and settlement derived from the interplay of social structures such as the influence

---

[26] José Refugio de la Torre Curiel, "Decline and Renaissance Amidst the Crisis: The Transformation of Sonora's Mission Structures in the Late Colonial Period," *Colonial Latin American Review* 18, no. 1 (2009): 53. For a comparative study on mission frontiers, see José Refugio de la Torre Curiel, "La frontera misional novohispana a fines del siglo XVIII: Un caso para reflexionar sobre el concepto de misión," in *El Gran Norte Mexicano: Indios, misioneros y pobladores entre el mito y la historia*, ed. Salvador Bernabéu Albert (Seville: Consejo Superior de Investigaciones Científicas, 2009), 285–330.

[27] When speaking of "functions," I mean some of the processes that the mission explicitly intended to embrace. While certain other developments also set in motion in the context of mission life did constitute part of mission history, they were not specific goals of this form of colonization. This issue has been sufficiently addressed by David Sweet in an article on the impact of missions on Indian societies. David Sweet, "The Ibero-American Frontier Mission in Native American History," in *The New Latin American Mission History*, eds. Erick Langer and Robert H. Jackson (Lincoln and London: University of Nebraska Press, 1995), 7–46. In Kubler's formulation, a mission should be defined by the set of actions that was taking place in that community: "The care of the sick and poor in the pueblos entailed a reorganization of the tribal economy. Livestock, new crops, and European methods of cultivation were introduced. Scattered Indians were brought to live together in new settlements. . . . Instruction was given in many different crafts, as well as in reading, writing and music. The entire settlement, with all these activities, with its church and conventual buildings, was the mission." Kubler, *The Religious Architecture*, 7. In my case, I emphasize the significance of those processes that include the particular actions addressed by Kubler.

and consolidation of non-Indian settlements around the missions, the rejection or acceptance of the mission regime by local Indians, the administrative models implemented by the friars, and the interaction of mission economies and local markets.[28] Over time, the evolution of these structures kept the mission from fulfilling its social functions, a phenomenon that also accounted for the consolidation of other forms of Spanish settlement.[29] In most cases, the question as to why mission districts evolved in distinct ways reflected the priority placed on one or more of these specific functions. Moreover, the fact that mission history has been written in so many ways reflects, at least in part, the emphasis that historians have placed on a certain function or set of functions.[30]

This diversity of parameters partially explains the difficulty involved in assessing whether one mission (or set of missions) was more successful than some other. It would be risky, indeed, to state that any specific mission district ever succeeded in all of its functions at any given time, and I am not sure that any mission complex ever achieved full success in all of its functions at the same time.

In pondering the mission in these terms, I allude to a mission frontier defined not only as a bulwark of Spanish settlement, nor as the backdrop of histories of exploitation and marginalization. I conceive of this type of frontier as one of the most active zones of contact in the context of New Spain, as "places where cultures contend with one another and with their physical environment to produce a dynamic that is unique to time and place."[31] This entails thinking of the mission frontier as *both* place *and* process, as "zones of historical interaction," or as battlegrounds where "power was constantly being contested or negotiated," as Donna Guy and Thomas Sheridan stated.[32]

---

[28] Some of these processes are also identified by Almada, Medina, and Borrero in "Hacia una nueva interpretación," 239–50.

[29] This argument was outlined in De la Torre Curiel, "Decline and Renaissance," 51–73.

[30] Thus, for example, the mission has been presented as an instrument of conquest and colonization meant to promote the Hispanization of Indians and the transition from subsistence economies to market-oriented communities. Radding, "Las estructuras," 1–10. It has been portrayed as a project with three objectives: religious conversion, economic sufficiency, and control of Indian populations. Escandón, "Los problemas," 290–91; Spicer, *Los yaquis*, 31; Radding, *Wandering Peoples*, 67–68; Sandos, *Converting*, 11. In addition, there is the congregational perspective, which conceives of the mission as a congregation destined to supply labor for Spanish haciendas and ranchos. Cramaussel, *Poblar la frontera*, 60, 95; Jones, *Nueva Vizcaya*, 90–91; González Rodríguez, *El noroeste novohispano*, 219–22; Del Río, *El regimen*, 12.

[31] David Weber and Jane M. Rausch, "Introduction," in Weber and Rausch, eds., *Where Cultures Meet*, xiv.

[32] Donna Guy and Thomas Sheridan, "Introduction," in *Contested Ground: Comparative Frontiers on the Northern and Southern Edges of the Spanish Empire*, eds. Donna Guy and Thomas Sheridan (Tucson: University of Arizona Press, 1998), 10–15.

Thus, the mission frontier I explore in this study is both the site where
Spaniards and Indians confronted and interacted with each other, primarily
through the mission town, and a process that mutually modified the ways of
the other through the activities of mission life.

A NOTE ON CULTURAL EXCHANGES

The transformation of daily life in small communities—such as the ones
shaping Sonora's northern frontier—was part of the evolution of the mission's social functions. In fact, this book explores the emergence of new
forms of interaction between mission Indians and other residents as a fundamental condition in the mission's loss of prominence in New Spain's northern frontier. Indians' roles within colonial society developed in various direc-
tions before the mission's social functions were superseded. In some cases,
religious specialists arose from among the catechumens (students of basic
Catholic doctrine) once the Franciscans were unable to staff the missions;
and in Ópata country, Indians gradually abandoned communal work in mission lands as farming and ranching on nearby haciendas proved more attractive for them.

My analysis of these and other forms of interaction and cultural exchanges
taking place on the Sonoran frontier benefits from previous discussions fram-
ing such developments in terms of assimilation,[33] or acculturation and adapta-

---

[33] In his study on Nueva Vizcaya, for example, William Griffen defined the relations between
Indians and Spaniards in terms of different "contact social units," using a model of cultural assimilation characterized by "the introduction of many innovations in material culture, techniques, and
thought patterns that began to skew the socio-cultural systems of the Indians." William B. Griffen,
Indian Assimilation in the Franciscan Area of Nueva Vizcaya (Tucson: University of Arizona Press,
1979), 108–10.

[34] The term "acculturation" gained currency after the publication of Redfield, Linton, and
Herskovits' "Memorandum," in which they defined it as "those phenomena which result when
groups of individuals having different cultures come into continuous first-hand contact, with sub-
sequent changes in the original cultural patterns of either or both groups." Robert Redfield, Ralph
Linton, Melville J. Herskovits, "Memorandum for the Study of Acculturation," *American
Anthropologist* 38, no. 1 (1936): 149–52. In Edward Spicer's view, acculturation occurred in the
Spanish Borderlands when "fairly uniform Spanish cultural influences affected native cultures."
Spicer, "Spanish-Indian Acculturation in the Southwest," *American Anthropologist* 56, no. 4
(1954): 663. On a classic discussion on the understanding of the results of cultural interaction in
Mexican Anthropology see Gonzalo Aguirre Beltrán, *El proceso de aculturación* (Mexico City:
Universidad Nacional Autónoma de México, 1957). For Robert Haskett and John Kicza, acculturation would occur once the Indians were exposed to European material culture and customs, as
they would soon decide to adopt these new elements because of their usefulness and convenience
and because they were compatible with their established way of life. Robert Haskett, "Coping in

tion processes,[34] emphasizing the advantages and disadvantages Indian groups found in their interaction with Spaniards over time. Some insights come from authors addressing the same issue from the perspective of ethnic reconstitution.[35] However, this narrative's main concepts come from different sources since my interest on cultural change is circumscribed to explaining the ways in which Indians and missionaries negotiated their place in local society in the context of declining mission structures.

According to Margaret Connell Szasz, cultural change required the lives that it touched to become "repositories of two or more cultures" and intermediaries between them or "cultural brokers."[36] In the Sonoran context, this process of mediation occurred when Indians participated in "the culture of the other" as interpreters, spiritual intermediaries, and as part of local political, economic, and military hierarchies. But it also took place when missionaries' identities and intellectual frameworks were challenged by the Sonoran frontier

---

Cuernavaca with the Cultural Conquest," in *The Indian in Latin American History: Resistance, Resilience, and Acculturation*, ed. John E. Kicza (Wilmington, DE: Scholarly Resources, 2000), 93–137; Kicza, *The Indian*, xxi. For a similar use of the term in the context of the California missions, see Lightfoot, *Indians, Missionaries, and Merchants*. In a recent study, Susan Deeds understands adaptation and resistance as thoughtful choices; in her study on Nueva Vizcaya she posits what she calls "mediated opportunism," "a framework tailored to understanding how material and mental barriers limit the capacity for change." Deeds, *Defiance and Deference*, 6.

[35] Marcello Carmagnani, *El regreso de los dioses: El proceso de reconstitución de la identidad étnica en Oaxaca* (Mexico City: Fondo de Cultura Económica, 1988). In the Sonoran case, Cynthia Radding identifies this process using the concept of ethnogenesis, "the birth or rebirth of ethnic identities in different historical moments." Ethnogenesis occurred when the Ópata Indians settled the "colonial pact" through which they negotiated their allegiance to king and church in exchange for protection and support. It also occurred when the Indians used colonial institutions (tribunals, judges, etc.) to respond to Spaniards' encroachments on their lands, thus defending what they saw as their "ethnic spaces." In the long run, such processes led to the redefinition of cultural identities among Indians, as they gradually participated "in their own subjugation by legitimating the intrusion of those very institutions into their ethnic polities." Radding, *Wandering Peoples*, 8, 12–13.

[36] Margaret Connell Szasz, ed., *Between Indian and White Worlds: The Cultural Broker* (Norman and London: University of Oklahoma Press, 1994). Kessell has approached this process through the example of the interaction of Pueblo Indians and Spaniards in New Mexico, showing that Spanish-speaking Pueblo Indians were as important as Pueblo-speaking Spanish colonists in the cultural transformation of both groups. Kessell focuses on the role of certain Indians and *métisse* who were designated to deal with the Spaniards, to act as translators for them, or to help the missionaries in their activities. John L. Kessell, "The Ways and Words of the Other: Diego de Vargas and Cultural Brokers in Late Seventeenth-Century New Mexico," in Szasz, ed., *Between Indian*, 25–43. For a study of Indians who acted as cultural mediators in areas other than diplomacy, see the work on Algonquians in New England by Nancy L. Hagedorn, "Faithful, Knowing, and Prudent: Andrew Montour as Interpreter and Cultural Broker, 1740–1772," in Szasz, ed., *Between Indian*, 44–60.

and had to act as mediators between Franciscan institutional constraints and local residents' attitudes towards missionary work.[37]

In this book the idea of cultural mediation is also related to the concept of cultural transfer or transculturation[38] as a means to elucidate the interaction between Indians and Spaniards in Sonora. Cultural exchanges in this area occurred in a context of mutual influences that allowed Indians and Spaniards, colonizers and colonized, and people in different situations within the colonial society to assert themselves and acquire elements pertaining to "the other."[39] Under these circumstances, as Mary Louis Pratt has suggested, peoples from contact zones "are constituted in and by their relations to each other . . . in terms of co-presence, interaction, [and] interlocking understandings and practices."[40]

ON THIS BOOK'S STRUCTURE

This study's premise is that the consolidation of Spanish settlements in the province of Sonora in the final decades of the colonial period modified the social function of the missions, a process that becomes visible in the demographic recomposition of the mission districts, in the cultural transformation of the various people who resided in the missions, and in adjustments in the missions' economic and administrative structures.

The Sonoran case was chosen for this study because after the expulsion of the Jesuits the missions in the Pimería Alta, the Opatería, and the Pimería Baja

---

[37] William Hart observes that a person changes one's identity according to one's needs or those of others with whom one is in contact in a given situation: one may need to wear the clothes of "the other," speak the *lingua franca*, adopt the other's religion, and take a spouse of the other's race or ethnicity—all of which are examples that constitute what Hart calls "situational ethnic identities." William B. Hart, "Black 'Go-Betweens' and the Mutability of 'Race,' Status and Identity on New York's Pre-Revolutionary Frontier," in Cayton and Teute, eds., *Contact Points*, 88–113.

[38] Fernando Ortiz, *Contrapunteo cubano del tabaco y el azúcar* (Havana: J. Montero, 1940); Yolanda Fletcher, *Transculturación, historia y literatura en América Latina* (La Paz, Bolivia: Facultad de Humanidades y Ciencias de la Educación, Universidad Mayor de San Andrés, 1999); Mary Louise Pratt, *Imperial Eyes: Travel, Writing and Transculturation* (London and New York: Routledge, 1992).

[39] Laurier Turgeon, "From Acculturation to Cultural Transfer," in *Transferts culturels et métissages: Amérique / Europe, XVIe–XXe siècle*, ed. Laurier Turgeon (Québec: Les Presses de l'Université Laval, 1996), 36–37; Dean R. Snow, "The Mohawks and Europeans: Cultural Exchange amidst Conflict," in Turgeon, ed., *Transferts culturels*, 271–77; Barbara Ganson, *The Guaraní under Spanish Rule in the Río de la Plata* (Stanford, CA: Stanford University Press, 2003).

[40] Pratt, *Imperial Eyes*, 7.

regions were assigned to two Franciscan institutes, which despite their close proximity developed divergent forms of interaction with local population. The Colegio de Querétaro—whose missionaries are hereafter referred to as Queretarans—and the Guadalajara-based Province of Santiago de Xalisco—point of origin of the missionaries here identified as Xaliscan—administered the missionary districts here analyzed, which provide clear comparisons of consolidation of Spanish settlements, Indian raids, economic pressures, and other processes affecting the missions in diverse ways, depending on a combination of factors (including geography, proximity to Spanish settlements, ups and downs of Franciscan administration, and submission of the Indian population to the mission regime).

With regard to the temporal limits of this work, the expulsion of the Jesuits in 1767 is an obvious starting point for narratives on the Franciscan period in Sonora. The closing date of 1855 may seem arbitrary for the entire province of Sonora, since the Franciscan presence in Pimería Alta ended almost a decade earlier. However, this year marks the Franciscans' departure from their last Sonoran missions.[41]

Since the construction-appropriation of space is a central element in this story, the first chapter analyzes how various narratives concerning the Sonoran landscape reflected distinct perceptions of space along New Spain's frontier. The creation-appropriation of space is examined in this chapter from three perspectives: the missionaries' view, the vision of Crown officials, and the perception of Indian groups. While elaborating this dialogue among different narratives, the text also examines the features of the geographical regions, and the natural resources of the highlands and desert, as well as their biotic communities.

The population trends in the mission districts of the province of Sonora from 1767 to 1850 are analyzed in Chapter 2 on the basis of a series of *padrones* (census lists) and other kinds of reports. The data available show a gradual decline of the Indian population in the Sonoran missions that coincided with a steady increase in the number of Spaniards. The population figures and trends discussed confirm the findings of several authors who have approached this issue, but also offer new insights into the influence the defensive war against rebel Indians had on the native population in the missions, the reconfiguration of ethnic spaces in Sonora, and the Hispanization of local Indian groups.

---

[41] By that time, of course, the mission at San Xavier del Bac had been annexed by the U.S. government as part of the lands acquired through the Gadsden Purchase (1853).

The cultural transformation of the mission Indians is discussed in Chapter 3. Drawing on the texts of several anthropologists and ethnohistorians, I discuss the various approaches and concepts used in attempts to understand how Indian groups coped with the influence of other cultures. Special consideration is given to the evolution of the concept of acculturation, to debates on change and persistence in Indian societies, and to the current use of the concept of transculturation to highlight how cultures influence each other in contact situations. The Sonoran experience is analyzed here through the lens of the transculturation perspective as I attempt to explain the demise of the mission regime not as the result of an economic crisis, but as a manifestation of the maturing relationship between Indians and the rest of Spanish—and later Mexican—society. This mutual transformation of Indian and Spanish cultures took place at various levels, but in this chapter I pay specific attention to changes in native religious practice and material culture (food, clothing, housing, and farming tools and techniques), and to what I call patterns of indigenous migration and emerging pluriethnic mobility.

Chapter 4 is devoted to an examination of the commercial network that linked the mission districts of Sonora with merchants in central Mexico. Using the account books of a merchant established in Arizpe (Sonora), I reconstruct the routes and mechanisms driving the captive commerce that controlled the frontier economies in New Spain. The aim of this chapter is to show that contrary to traditional interpretations, Sonora's economy in general, and that of the missions in particular, were not involved in a capitalist market economy but formed part of a captive system characterized by the ample profit margins that sellers attained through multiple mechanisms for extorting money and labor from workers and end consumers. This chapter is closely related to Chapters 5 and 6, which link more traditional topics involved in the socioeconomic transformation of the province of Sonora (such as land, Indian labor, and financial hardships on the missions), to the limitations of the system of captive commerce discussed in the previous chapter, and to the evolution of the internal regime of the Sonoran mission districts.

CHAPTER 1

Representing the Sonoran Landscape: Geographical Descriptions of Sonora in the Eighteenth and Nineteenth Centuries

In northwestern Mexico, between 27 and 33 degrees north latitude and 113 and 108 degrees longitude, a number of mountain ranges are covered with thin layers of snow in winter. Amid these *cordilleras*, streams and rivers have cut a series of fertile valleys of varying dimensions along the way to the Gulf of California. Then, beyond the foothills and descending toward the northeast, is the majestic and daunting desert.

Comprising the modern state of Sonora and southern Arizona, this area corresponds to what was known in the eighteenth and part of the nineteenth centuries as the provinces of Ostimuri and Sonora, which belonged to the Gobernación de Sonora. Located in the southeastern portion of what is now Sonora, the province of Ostimuri occupied the territory bordered to the north by the Yaqui River, to the south by the Mayo River and to the west by the Sierra Madre.[1] It was in the southwestern section of the present state of Sonora, along the lower course of the Yaqui River, that the Yoeme (Yaqui) people lived, a group of cultivators who had successfully rebuffed the Spanish military advance in the sixteenth century and by the early seventeenth century determined the way in which the Jesuit missionaries would be admitted into their territory.[2] Beyond the Yaqui River lay the vast expanse of the province of Sonora,[3] bordered on the north by the Pima, Pápago, Cocomaricopa, and Yuma Indian nations inhabiting the alluvial plains of the Gila and the Colorado Rivers.

---

[1] Peter Gerhard, *La frontera norte de la Nueva España* (Mexico City: Universidad Nacional Autónoma de México, 1996), 327.

[2] Edward H. Spicer, *Los yaquis, historia de una cultura* (Mexico City: Universidad Nacional Autónoma de México, 1994), 13–31.

[3] The colonial provinces of Sonora and Ostimuri comprise the current Mexican state of Sonora. To avoid confusion, in the text I use the term *province* of Sonora (or Sonora) to refer only to the territory located north of the Yaqui River (not including Ostimuri province), as was the custom during the period of study. In contrast, when the Franciscan Province of Xalisco is

The southern limit of the province was clearly defined with the Yaqui River being recognized as a natural border, although during the colonial period there were different versions and conflicting opinions as to the exact location of the northern frontier of Sonora. Some people held that the province ended with the missions in Pimería Alta, while others argued that the territory included the settlements along the banks of the Gila River.[4]

On the basis of this territory's characteristics, we can speak of two large geographical zones and five ecological niches north of the Yaqui River. Using a south–north division, to the west lies the arid zone of the desert composed of the Gulf Coast and the Lower Colorado Valley, and to the east, there is a second zone composed of the sierra, the Sonoran plains, and the Arizona highlands (or *altiplano*).[5] In the following and later chapters, descriptions focus on the three latter areas.

The San Miguel, the Sonora, and the Oposura Rivers all descend from the Sierra Madre in Sonora to irrigate the Tacupeto, Mátape, and Oposura valleys,

---

mentioned, *province* refers to one of the religious entities involved in missionary work in Sonora. Note that in the first case *province* relates to territory, whereas the second case refers to an institution. See the Glossary.

[4] For example, in 1730 the Jesuit Cristóbal de Cañas noted 33 degrees latitude as the limit of Sonora bordering on New Mexico. This observation coincided with the limits recognized by the Jesuit Juan Nentuig and the Franciscan friar Antonio Barbastro, although these two observers indicated that the Gila River constituted the limit of Sonora. This coincidence can probably be attributed to the fact that both the Franciscans and the Jesuits proposed on several occasions the idea of advancing the mission frontier as far as the Gila River. In contrast, for Fray Antonio de los Reyes, the missions in Pimería Alta marked the northern boundary of Sonora: "Commonly, Sonora is understood as the entire extension of its government from the Cañas River at 23 degrees to the missions of Pimería Alta at 32 [degrees]." He also specified the limits that did not form part of the territory of Sonora: "the gentile nations of the Gila and Colorado Rivers." Cristóbal de Cañas, *Estado de la Provincia de Sonora*, published in González Rodriguez, *El noroeste*, 492. Barbastro's opinion can be seen in his *Informe* (1793) published by Lino Gómez Canedo, *Sonora hacia fines del siglo XVIII* (Guadalajara: Librería Font, 1971), 49–91. On Nentuig, see *Provincia de Sonora*, MNM, *Virreinato de México*, vol. I, exp. 2. The document referred to does not mention the author's name; however, with the exception of the data on the geographical situation of Sonora and certain other passages, the text coincides almost in its totality with the information presented by Nentuig in his *Descripción geográfica natural y curiosa de la provincia de Sonora* (1763). This fact leads me to think that the document found in the Museo Naval may be a copy of a summary of the *Rudo ensayo* augmented by Nentuig at a later date, or simply a synthesis of his completed work with additional notes. The quotation from De los Reyes is in Fray Antonio de los Reyes, *Noticia de la California, Sonora, Nueva Vizcaya, y Nuevo México, en cuyos territorios se han de fundar las Custodias de Misioneros de Propaganda Fide*, BNM, Ms. 2550, 4.

[5] Richard Felger, "Investigación ecológica en Sonora y localidades adyacentes en Sinaloa: Una perspectiva," in *Sonora: Antropología del desierto. Primera reunión de Antropología e Historia del Noroeste*, ed. Beatriz Braniff (Mexico City: Instituto Nacional de Antropología e Historia, 1976), 27; Robert C. West, *Sonora: Its Geographical Personality* (Austin: University of Texas Press, 1993), 2–9.

among others, during the rainy season. These rivers mark the transition from the region dominated by valleys to the foothills. In the valleys, the annual precipitation of 400 millimeters (15.8 inches) makes rain-fed agriculture possible; these conditions made the plains of Sonora the main site for the establishment of Spanish settlements in that region in the colonial period.

To the east of this river system, precipitation increases along with the elevation of the sierra, attaining a maximum of 600 millimeters (23.6 inches) in the highest places. In some places, such as Bacadehuachi in the easternmost part of Sonora, the sierra attains an altitude of 2,500 meters (8,200 feet) above sea level. In this forested zone, pasturelands are more abundant, and pine, oak, and poplar trees, as well as shrubs typical of temperate to cold climates are common. The variety of local fauna, including such species as deer, squirrel, rabbit, beaver, and bear, contributes to the richness of this biotic community.[6]

Located at the northwestern edge of the Sonoran desert, the Arizona highlands offer a succession of streams and marshlands that allowed both the indigenous population and Spanish settlers to develop subsistence agriculture, despite the significant inconvenience of the region's freezing temperatures, which do not occur in other areas of the province.

The Lower Colorado Valley[7] is the most arid, desert-like region of the area under study. Its most important features are the Altar Desert and the lowlands that border the Colorado River.[8] In this desert area, rainfall and temperatures show the most drastic variations in all of Sonora. Annual precipitation fluctuates from 30 to 300 millimeters (1.2 to 11.8 inches), and temperatures are high during the day but very low at night.[9] In spite of these conditions, at certain times it was possible to irrigate crops in the lowlands of the Altar River (Map 1.1).

A NOTE ON THE IDENTIFICATION OF THE INDIAN GROUPS IN SONORA

A major problem posed by the geographic descriptions in the primary sources for this chapter is that European observers frequently misunderstood

---

[6] Beatriz Braniff, *La frontera protohistórica Pima-Ópata en Sonora, México*, vol. I (Mexico City: Instituto Nacional de Antropología e Historia, 1992), 22–24, 55–57; West, *Sonora*, 4–6.

[7] This valley includes five microregions in terms of its specific flora and fauna and distinct patterns of human occupation: the Colorado River Delta, the marshes around the coast of the Gulf of California, the Altar Desert, the "Great Desert," and the Pinacate area.

[8] Felger, "Investigación ecológica," 28–41; Gerhard, *La frontera norte*, 345–47.

[9] Braniff, *La frontera*, 57. The mean annual rainfall in this area is less than 250 millimeters (10 inches). West, *Sonora*, 7.

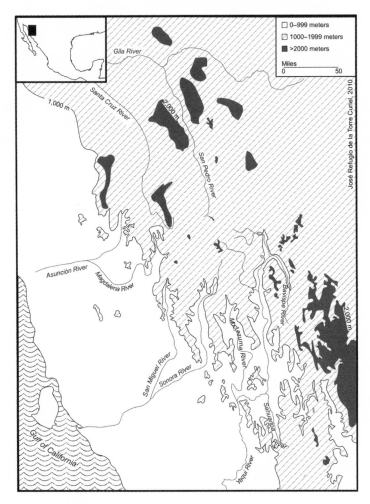

MAP 1.1. Topography of Sonora province

the spatial distribution of Indian groups and their ethnic affinities, which explains the plethora of names used to describe single groups such as the Pima (referred to as Gileños, Piatos, Soba, Sobaipuris, Pápagos, or Pimas Altos, depending on the location of their households). For clarity's sake it is necessary to explain the use of diverse tribal names in this work. Although some colonial manuscripts identify as Nevomes the aboriginal inhabitants of the territory located between the western margins of the Yaqui River and Seri country in the proximities of the Gulf of California, this name disappears after 1680 and the

Indian residents of the area are referred to simply as Pima Bajos; for this reason, the Indians of that zone are identified in this work as Pima Bajos, and their territory is called Pimería Baja. Next to this area was the Ópata region or Opatería, the central and easternmost section of Sonora that was occupied by three separate yet closely related Indian groups (Ópatas, Eudeves, and Jovas) generally described as Ópatas due to the marked affinity among their languages and cultural traits.[10] In this work, each individual group is mentioned using its own name; with regard to their territory, I adhere to the traditional practice of calling this area the "Opatería."

The vast region north of Cucurpe and south of the Gila River was generally identified in colonial records as Pimería Alta, while the western section of this territory, near the point where the Colorado River joins the Gulf of California, was called Papaguería. In both cases, the geographical regions involved were named after the Indian groups that occupied them. In the strict sense, both Pima Altos and Pápagos were members of the same Indian nation (Pima) and shared certain cultural features (e.g., language and religious views), but were differentiated because of their adaptation to the ecological zones of the Gila River and the Arizona Desert, respectively. Since the late seventeenth century, the Jesuits, and at a later date the Franciscans, directed their efforts to the Pima in the mission district of Pimería Alta. Pápago Indians visited the missions on a seasonal basis, but it was not until the late eighteenth century that the original Pima residents of the missions were replaced by the Pápagos due to high mortality rates of the aboriginal Pima population in the mission communities.

Since the mid-nineteenth century, and especially after the Gadsden Purchase (1853), the differences between these groups became accentuated due to the influence of two contrasting sets of neighbors. The territory of the Gila River people was on the route of gold prospectors, hunters, other groups of itinerant Americans, and American soldiers fighting the Apaches, all of which led the Pima population to adopt the language and other characteristics of American society. The Pápagos remained culturally attached to the Altar Desert and closely related to those of their kin living on the Mexican side of the border. As one author puts it, the Gila River people "adopted American names and clothing, and in 1871 they already attended an American school. Meanwhile, the Pápagos spoke Spanish if they had to speak a language other than theirs; they wore Mexican shawls, and considered the Altar Valley as the birthplace of their

---

[10] Jean B. Johnson, *The Opata: An Inland Tribe of Sonora* (Albuquerque: University of New Mexico Press, 1950), 8–9.

culture."[11] In recent times, the Gila River people and the Pápagos have vindicated these historical processes by adopting official names consistent with them; thus, the former (historically identified as Pima Altos) refer to themselves as Akai O'odham (River People), while the Pápagos call themselves Tohono O'odham (Desert People). Throughout this work, the names Pima Altos and Pápagos are used as is consistent with the historical records.

THE CREATION OF SPACE

The purpose of discussing the different ecological niches in Sonora is not just to present the setting in which the events analyzed in this study took place. As the title of this chapter suggests, narrated here is the story of a great transformation: the history of how, toward the end of the eighteenth century, the province of Sonora, an enormous expanse along the so-called "missionary frontier" of New Spain, became a zone distinguished by two contrasting landscapes—the dominions of the Spanish villas and ranches together with the towns of the more Hispanicized Indian peoples, and, in the northern reaches, the series of "frontier missions." In approaching this transformation from the perspective of territorial change, the purpose is to transcend the limits of classic geographical description and consider the Sonora territory as a set of changing scenarios in which the relations between people and their environment were in a process of constant redefinition. This, in the words of Esteban Barragán, leads us to acknowledge that the "spatial forms and social structures are amalgamated and changing: if the valorization of the elements—resources—contained in a geographical space change or are exhausted, the social structure, and the spatial valorization are transformed."[12]

However, comprehending the constant redefinition of the Sonoran scenery presents the challenge of making sense out of the relationship between the location and the appropriation of a landscape, a relation that leads us to the debate between "place" and "space." In this attempt to capture the geography of Sonora through the written testimonies of bishops, missionaries, and functionaries of the Spanish Crown, many questions arise as to the object represented in the sources and the personal situation of those witnesses who walked upon the scenario described in their accounts. One recurring practice in the

---

[11] Ruth Underhill, *Biografía de una mujer pápago* (Mexico City: Secretaría de Educación Pública, 1975), 42.
[12] Esteban Barragán López, "Formas espaciales y procesos sociales en la Sierra del Tigre," *Relaciones* 85 (2001): 128.

analysis of these chronicles, reports, and memoirs consisted of thinking about the territorial dimension as a multitude of independent fragments or as an imperfect mold into which these several parts have been joined, although without ever losing sight of the landscape itself as the setting of human events. It is important to separate the author's personal view from the idea of places as compartmentalized parts of space, and space as a frame containing networks of places because, like J.B. Jackson and William Taylor, the author is rather more inclined to approach the study of place and space by emphasizing the forms in which the interaction between people and environment is lived.[13] It is this perspective that gives rise to the notion in which the landscape is seen as a consequence of the interaction between subject and environment, as a result of repeated experiences, or as a creation of the senses. It is as a human construct and a product of personal experience with the environment that the landscape must be understood, as W.J.T. Mitchell suggests, "not as an object to be seen, or a text to be read, but as a process by which social and subjective identities are formed."[14] In this spirit, the chronicles and reports concerning Sonora gathered together in this chapter are analyzed not only as discursive expressions that look to legitimize a given situation, but also as cultural practices containing individuals' ways of appropriating, creating, disarticulating, and characterizing Sonora. In this respect, Sonora is here analyzed as an idea in transformation in order to explain why certain observers constructed their ideas about this region focusing on local people, settlements, or geography.[15]

[13] John Brinckerhoff Jackson, *A Sense of Place, a Sense of Time* (New Haven, CT, and London: Yale University Press, 1994); William Taylor, "Short Journeys to Sacred Places: Devotional Landscapes and Circulation in Colonial Mexico" (Travis-Merrick Lecture, University of Oklahoma, Norman, Oklahoma, October 27, 2005). This discussion echoes in several ways debates on the definition of region that have developed over the last two decades in Mexico and Latin America. Given the disjunction among defining regions as "hypotheses to be proven," "categories of analysis constructed by the researcher," and "geographical expressions of exchange networks," it seems to me to be more appropriate to think of regions in terms of lived places; that is, as the territorial expression of the interaction of individuals among themselves and with their environment. For a general synthesis on this subject, see Eric Van Young, ed., *Mexico's Regions: Comparative History and Development* (San Diego: Center for U.S.-Mexican Studies, 1992), 3–9.

[14] W.J.T. Mitchell, *Landscape and Power* (Chicago: University of Chicago Press, 1994), 1.

[15] In reaching this understanding of landscape, I have been aided by Ann Bermingham, "System, Order, and Abstraction: The Politics of English Landscape Drawing around 1795," in Mitchell, *Landscape*, 77–101; Elizabeth Helsinger, "Turner and the Representation of England," also in Mitchell, *Landscape*, 103–25. In a sense, my analysis of Sonora's representations draws inspiration from Harley's understanding of maps as social constructions of the world and as rhetorical images to be understood in their own context. J.B. Harley, *The New Nature of Maps: Essays in the History of Cartography* (Baltimore: Johns Hopkins University Press, 2001). Another important contribution in this respect is Barbara Mundy's work on New Spain's early maps: "For New Spain

The interests and convictions of these documents' authors determine the quality of the information presented and the choice of words and tonalities that obscure or give color to their accounts. In this context, these sources do not allow a reliable reconstruction of the cultural expressions of those groups who left no written records concerning their past. Hence, in this section the history of the Indians and the anonymous settlers of Sonora are not addressed. The analysis of complementary sources in later chapters will present a more complete framework of the participation of these groups in the transformation of the society of New Spain. Addressed here, in contrast, is the way in which the prejudices and personal affectations filling so many pages of reports and geographical descriptions can be used to document the discursive transformation of the "idea of Sonora."[16]

For ecclesiastical writers (in this case, bishops and Jesuit and Franciscan missionaries), as well as for the soldiers and officials of the Crown, Sonora meant distinct realities over time, which can be seen in the various representations of that province penned by such a vast array of authors. The inhabitants, settlements, geography, climate, and economic activities, as well as the forms of coexistence of diverse human groups, are recurring themes in these descriptions and reports. What is by no means uniform, however, is the agency that these aspects take on in one epoch or another, or what these informants have to say about it. Thus, for example, the fears and concerns of the Jesuits with respect to the magical and supernatural universe that distinguished the indigenous populations are not echoed in the descriptions elaborated later by the Franciscan missionaries, as they were more concerned with attacks by the Apaches and expansion into new missionary territories. By the same token, the wealth of notes about the people who lived in the sierras and valleys found in early descriptions of Sonora were

---

to be mapped, it needed to be imagined. How did this act of imagining come about? . . . In looking at the Relaciones Geográficas . . . [it can be found that] 'New Spain' was beginning to make itself felt in the indigenous imagination. [During the sixteenth century] 'New Spain' filtered through to its indigenous inhabitants in the ways that Spanish colonists looked at the landscape and through the exercise of power by the viceregal government, the embodiment of New Spain. Official power made itself felt in possessing the landscape, at least implicitly, and then giving it away with land grants. It also asserted itself in renaming communities with names that were represented in alphabetic script, thereby undermining local representations of the landscape, which formerly were able to capture space with a net of their own toponyms." Mundy, *The Mapping of New Spain: Indigenous Cartography and the Maps of the Relaciones Geográficas* (Chicago: University of Chicago Press, 1996), 214–15.

   [16] I have borrowed this expression from Edmundo O'Gorman, whose brilliant study discusses the evolution of the "idea of America." O'Gorman, *La idea del descubrimiento de América* (Mexico City: Universidad Nacional Autónoma de México, 1976).

the precursors of serious reflections from later epochs concerning the problems of the layout of the places in which those people lived.

In this thematic diversity, four aspects can be clearly identified because they appear often in practically all testimonies evaluated here. They will serve as the guiding axes of this analysis: (1) the characterization of the Sonoran settlers, (2) the criteria for regionalization and division of the province, (3) the influence of geographical conditions (climate, soil erosion, fluctuations in precipitation) on the planning and permanence of populations, and (4) the nature of the coexistence of the colonists there. To better appreciate the ways in which both the representations of the Sonoran landscape and the province itself changed, available testimonies are grouped into three periods: from the early eighteenth century to the Indian uprisings of 1740, from the recomposition of Sonora to the expulsion of the Jesuits in 1767, and from the reorganization of the ecclesiastical jurisdictions to the final days of the Franciscan administration.

THE EARLY EIGHTEENTH CENTURY

In 1687, missionaries of the Society of Jesus succeeded in gaining a foothold in Pimería Alta when they established New Spain's northernmost missions (Map 1.2).[17] Their arrival in Pimería Alta marked the culmination of an important phase of expansion that allowed them to establish colleges and missions under their auspices from the villa of San Felipe and Santiago in Sinaloa as far north as Tucson. To ensure a better spiritual and material administration of their mission establishments, the Jesuits organized this territory into four rectorates or administrative units.[18] Each one came under the direction of a priest-rector who, in turn, answered to the authority of the father provincial . During the early years of mission organization in Sonora, it was a common practice for the Jesuits themselves, or a visiting priest on his triennial inspection, to send reports back to their superior in Mexico City concerning the condition or status of those missions. However, after 1721, the general of the Jesuits in Rome decreed that such reports be remitted to Rome by a father visitor every six years, together with more detailed news on the state of the missions and the number of settlers, among other matters deemed sufficiently important to be included.[19]

---

[17] In that year, Eusebio Kino founded the Dolores mission, a site that would serve as the platform for later establishments in Pimería Alta. Gerhard, *La frontera norte*, 350; Ortega Noriega, "El sistema," 61.

[18] Rectorado de Nuestra Señora de los Dolores, Rectorado de San Francisco de Borja, Rectorado de San Xavier, and Rectorado de los Santos Mártires de Japón.

[19] González Rodríguez, *El noroeste novohispano*, 460–61.

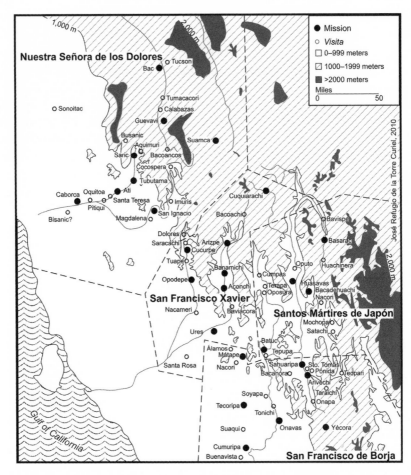

MAP 1.2. Jesuit rectorates in Sonora, ca. 1700

Following these orders, the priests Daniel Januske (1723) and Cristóbal de Cañas (1730) drafted voluminous descriptions of Sonora that highlight different aspects of the province, according to the experiences of each author. These records provide the source for the following descriptions of Sonora.

In 1723, the four rectorates of Sonora contained a total of twenty-seven missions, made up of sixty-four pueblos "and a few ranches," in which an estimated 15,000 to 16,000 people resided.[20] This population could be divided

---

[20] Daniel Januske, *Breve informe del estado presente en que se hallan las misiones de esta Provincia* [de Sonora] (1723), AGN, Archivo Histórico de Hacienda, leg. 278, exp. 2.

roughly into two main groups: the mission Indians and the so-called *vecinos*. With respect to the first group, Januske's report is not particularly forthcoming, as this priest limited himself to commenting only upon general matters specified by his superiors. Nonetheless, certain occasional references to the Indians' occupations and activities are suggestive of reaccommodations of the commercial and work relations in Sonora, in addition to indicating the cultural transformations these changes involved. Together with demographic data and his report on the variety of languages spoken (Pima, Ópata, Eudeve, Jova, and even Tarahumara) in those missions, Januske added his personal impression of how the Indians led a lifestyle of almost total abandonment to indolence and cravenness, a condition supposedly endemic to their kind. However, on the margins of this disparaging image a few commentaries reveal complex processes of change within the indigenous population. Those of Batuco, for example, are described as "avaricious for [money] to spend on dress and *fiestas* in which they are most splendid." This greed, Januske affirms, was born of many seasons that men from Batuco had spent in the nearby mines, or even in mines as far afield as Chihuahua, Parral, and Sombrerete. Just like their counterparts in Batuco, Indians from Opatería and Pimería Baja regularly left their homes to work in local mines, having been "enticed away" by the Spanish. Described by Januske as "sinful greed," this need and urge of the Ópata and Pima Indians to find a better-compensated alternative to their agricultural activities was spurring an accelerated process of cultural change among these groups that, by the 1730s, had carved out an active zone in which seasonal laborers moved between Sonora and Chihuahua.

In contrast to his few comments concerning mission residents, Januske's report devotes considerable space to the characteristics of the *vecinos* living in the surrounding area. Those not subject to the mission regime and whom he identified as "the great obstacle" impeded the missions from flourishing. He divided the *vecinos* into four groups. The first included the captains of the presidios, the *alcaldes mayores* (district governors), and other legal officials (*justicias*). The second consisted of miners and merchants. The third included "Spaniards, ranchers, and other poor folk." The fourth and final contingent was the most numerous, as it included "*coyotes*, mulattoes, and other filth of the earth that roam around these parts with no other occupations than gambling, stealing, harassing women, sewing discord, and committing other misdeeds proper to their low station." The rhetoric of the time obliged the missionaries to express the dangers that awaited the souls of those Indians who lived continually with Christians of such dreadful countenance. Januske contributes to this literature and is by no means hesitant to denounce the "disturbance" that the *vecinos* represented for the mission regime, as in "the meager or null assistance that one finds in Spanish justice" to allow the missions to fulfill their spiritual and temporal (worldly) duties. In addition, the existence of a seigneurial regime beyond Jesuit control was soundly condemned as an excess of the *vecinos*, who impeded the Indians from returning to their homeplaces once they entered into their service, "because either the justices themselves receive them in their service, or [they] allow others to shower them with clothes [purchased on] credit that they have to pay for with their personal services," thus imposing debts on them that were passed on from father to son. Januske's list of complaints and offenses ends, finally, with "the scant veneration for the ecclesiastical state that usually exists in this province," and "the great liberty given to the Indians in many work crews."

The Sonora described by Januske was a representation of what this missionary perceived around him and simultaneously that which the religious institution to which he belonged wished to see.[21] Although it is true that his text contains evidence of undeniable realities, such as Indian mobility, it was designed to present a view of mission districts that would be much better off without the intrusion of the Spanish *vecinos*, that is, the celebration of a Jesuit Sonora.

Januske's report describes the geography of the Sonora missions by following the limits of each of the four rectorates described therein. However, a careful reading discerns in this report two distinct geographies. The first, consciously delineated, was formed by the four rectorates, the territorial division imposed by the Jesuit administration. The second geography, only intimated by Januske but of greater importance for the present study, contains a tacit recognition of the existence of zones whose topography, climate, and soil composition varied so enormously that it was possible to characterize Sonora as a "highly intemperate" area, in which "totally distinct climates are found at very short distances" (Map 1.3). With small variations, these ways of perceiving space correspond to the ecological niches mentioned above. Thus, Pimería Alta and, above all, the area around the Altar River were described in 1723 as "perhaps the most fertile of the entire *visita*," well-suited for cultivation, but limited by the extreme heat of Caborca and the excessive humidity and cold of Dolores. In the south of Sonora province, along the frontier with Ostimuri,

---

[21] As Ivonne del Valle has clearly demonstrated, such ambiguity was a central component in Jesuit chronicles on New Spain's frontier regions. Individual Jesuit writing practices, she argues, were mediated by "ideological, cognitive, and affective implications," and by the interests of the specific readers they were writing for, which determined what individual chroniclers decided to include or exclude in their accounts. Ivonne del Valle, *Escribiendo desde los márgenes: Colonialismo y jesuitas* en el *siglo XVIII* (Mexico City: Siglo XXI, 2009): 27–28.

MAP 1.3. *Plano Corographico e Hydrographico de las tres provincias de Sonora, Ostimuri y Sinaloa*, by Francisco Álvarez Barreiro, 1727 (Source: AGI, Mapas y Planos, Mexico 123)

what stands out is the area identified as the cattle-raising region of the Mátape River, near Mátape and Tecoripa. The land in this zone, generally inadequate for agriculture "because of the aridity, the lack of irrigation and the scarcity of water over many years," was better suited for raising livestock. Another area was defined along the approach to the sierra by way of Sahuaripa and Ónapa in the Tacupeto Valley, also a zone of scant agricultural yields "because often, all or a very large part, of [the harvests] are lost due to excessive water and hail," although quite appropriate for ranching, as Januske affirms when he points out that the Indians who lived there were better at "cowhand activities than farming." In the heart of Opatería, between the San Miguel and the Sonora Rivers, what stood out were the fertile valleys whose excellent soils—in the case of Ures—or the introduction of irrigation systems at places such as Arizpe, produced excellent harvests of corn and wheat. Finally, in the highlands of the sierra where the Oposura and the Santa María Rivers are formed, one finds the best agricultural terrain. There were very good lands between Cuquiarachi and Huásavas that, with abundant irrigation, produced "the high fertility that, in [the midst] of this province's barrenness, succors a large part of her."

Around 1728, Sonora was devastated by a measles epidemic. According to calculations by the Jesuit Cristóbal de Cañas, as a result of the disease the population of Sonora decreased to approximately 12,132 inhabitants in 1730, almost 4,000 less than in 1723, a decline of some 25 percent.[22] Despite this substantial change in the number of inhabitants, what apparently did not change was the indifference with which the indigenous groups of those environs were generally described. For Father Cañas, for example, the only difference between the so-called *naturales* (natives) of Sonora and the Indians of other areas of New Spain was their language: "[These] Indians are just like the others in the kingdom in color, nature, capacity and indolence. They wandered around naked in ancient times but now are decently dressed."

A secondary effect of the tremendous impact of disease in Sonora would be a redrawing of the missions' map in certain regions. In Pimería Alta—the zone worst hit by the recent epidemic—some pueblos disappeared entirely, while others were reduced to modest ranches.[23] Thus, for example, and according to a report by Cristóbal de Cañas in 1730, the Tubutama mission district lost two of its villages (*pueblos de visita*), while the settlements belonging to the

[22] AGN, Historia, vol. 16, ff. 139–60. The document has neither a signature nor an exact date of elaboration. In a detailed study of this text, Luis González Rodríguez concludes that the author is, in effect, the Jesuit Cristóbal de Cañas. González Rodríguez, *Etnología y misión en la Pimería Alta, 1715–1740* (Mexico City: Universidad Nacional Autónoma de México, 1977), 265–304.

[23] During this period the mission district of Cucurpe began to be considered as part of the territory of Pimería Alta. Given its geographical location near the sources of the San Miguel River, Cucurpe pertained to the set of mission districts of the San Miguel and Sonora Rivers that made up the San Francisco Xavier rectorate (geographically and ethnographically speaking, part of Opatería). This may have been due to an error by the *visitador* to those missions, or perhaps because in 1730 the conditions at Cucurpe were similar to those of the northernmost missions in Sonora. In any case, by that year, according to Cristóbal de Cañas, Pimería Alta had gained ground by pushing its limits a few leagues south of Dolores—its traditional boundary—to include Cucurpe. By 1744, during the visit of Father Juan Antonio de Baltasar, Cucurpe was included once again in the San Xavier rectorate. *Visita de la provincia de Sonora. . .* , in *El Noroeste de México: Documentos sobre las misiones jesuíticas, 1600–1769*, eds. Ernest J. Burrus and Félix Zubillaga (Mexico City: Universidad Nacional Autónoma de México, 1986), 171.

mission at Caborca were described in that same year as simple ranches "that are not yet pueblos."

On the one hand, Cañas's allusion to disease as the main cause of the population decline of this epoch reveals that the most formidable enemy Sonoran settlers faced at the time was neither the Apaches nor the local unsubjugated tribes. Rather, it was disease—real or imagined—that constituted the plague afflicting the province, and, to a certain extent, also characterized part of the period before the Indian uprisings of the 1740s.[24]

In effect, the vulnerable physical condition of the Indians and Spaniards was a predominant theme of the concerted efforts to sustain the Spanish presence in northern New Spain after the turn of the eighteenth century. The recent epidemics had affected the indigenous population of Sonora with special virulence, a situation that was made even worse by the precarious hygienic conditions in which the residents of some missions were living.[25] It should not be thought, however, that conditions were any better for the region's other residents. Although they were able to escape the worst effects of the common illnesses in the province, the constant fear of knowing they were potential targets of Indian vengeance, together with the maladies related to poor diet and the arduousness of adapting to extreme climatic conditions, all combined to claim many lives. As far as Cristóbal de Cañas was concerned, the deaths of Jesuit priests were very often the result of perverse machinations by Indians who reviled the missionaries. According to him, missionaries faced a combination of mortal consequences made up of the Indians' desire for vengeance and their frightening knowledge of "curses and poisonous herbs" that caused "the indefinable illnesses that some priests suffer, the acute, continuous pain caused by some occult spell because, as the [missionaries] ate from the hands of the Indians [who] are so familiar with these highly poisonous herbs, they live under the constant threat of revenge."[26]

Indian vengeance was a terrible thing, indeed. As Carlos de Rojas mentioned in 1744, the Jesuits were concerned about it because it was evil inspired by the devil.[27] It was precisely Satan himself who had inspired a

---

[24] Ignaz Pfefferkorn, *Descripción de la provincia de Sonora* (Mexico City: Consejo Nacional para la Cultura y las Artes, 2008), Chapter 9, 200–10.

[25] Robert Jackson, "Demographic Change in Northwestern New Spain," *The Americas* 41, no. 4 (1985): 462–79; Radding, *Wandering Peoples*, 116–17.

[26] Cañas, *Estado de la provincia*, 500.

[27] Carlos de Rojas, *Misión de Nra Sra de la Asunción de Arispe*, or "Descripción de Arispe," BL, M-M 1716:41. Bernd Hausberger, "La vida cotidiana de los misioneros jesuitas en el noroeste novohispano," *Estudios de Historia Novohispana* 17 (1997): 76–78. For this reason, says Pfefferkorn, some Indian groups in Sonora referred to the devil as *muhaptura*, the killer. Pfefferkorn, *Descripción*, Chapter 10, 213.

"wizard" (*hechicero*) from Cuquiarachi to attack Father Marcos de Loyola and injure his nose, "from which, to the astonishment of all those present, the Father expelled some hairy worms that ate his nose and reduced it to such a lamentable state." It was without a doubt the devil, Rojas thought, who had inspired this sorcerer to attack Loyola from a cave, using "a doll dressed as a Jesuit with a thorn thrust through its nose," as came to light some time later when the attacker confessed to his crime. Cañas himself had succumbed to such a spell, as in his later years he suffered from "swelling in his legs that . . . left him unable to walk." In Father Rojas's view, Sonora provided a stage for an ongoing struggle against the devil. The omnipresence of evil reinforced the central arguments that justified the Jesuit missionary project: It was necessary to free the Indians from their captivity and show them the road to salvation, an enterprise in which the Jesuits were to wield the weapons of the faith.

These last examples, taken from the 1730s and 1740s, are indicative of various ways in which the Jesuits strove to understand the geographical environment and its occupants. On the one hand, a clear notion is gained of the differences in the composition of the mission territories, their potential, and their disadvantages for agriculture and ranching, as well as their situation with respect to Spanish settlements. In rather stark contrast to this expressed need to become more familiar with the landscape, the image of the Indian nations that these early reports construct is based on very different precepts. Born of an ambivalent relationship established in distinct terms for the Indians and the new colonists, this image was a product of the conclusion of the first cycle of the history of Sonora's missionary districts. As the close of the seventeenth century brought to an end the phase of mission expansion led by Eusebio Kino and his companions in Pimería Alta, in subsequent decades the mission districts first turned inward, where they discovered their most significant challenges, rewards, and problems. The largest threat to the permanence of the missions was still not the hostility of the Apaches; rather, during this epoch of consolidation, the task that genuinely worried the missionaries was that of distinguishing between good and evil among the people surrounding them. If the missionaries had time to find the devil at home it was because their attention was focused on the interior of their communities. The Indian uprisings of the 1740s would teach the Spanish population that great peril was walking among them, although as we shall see in the following section, the true enemy had nothing to do with supernatural entities, but was very much of this world and clearly determined to reclaim it.

THE EFFECTS OF PEACE IN THE MID-EIGHTEENTH CENTURY

For the Spanish authorities of Sonora, the years between 1720 and 1740 represented a period of relative peace, disturbed only by "sporadic attacks by the Seris on Spanish populations."[28] Although it is true that Indian uprisings and the threat from indigenous groups not yet brought under Spanish control were a constant potential danger for the northern provinces, it should be pointed out that the peril was not permanent, and periods of peace allowed settlers to devote their time to daily activities both inside established villages and beyond the protection they offered.[29] The reports cited thus far correspond precisely to this period, characterized as it was by a truce granted by the Indians of the interior (Yaquis and Seris) who up to that time represented the most imminent threat to settlements in Sonora.

As the 1740s began, however, a series of rebellions by these two groups ushered in a prolonged period of concern for domestic security. As a result of both the intensity of the Indians' forays and the orientation of defensive measures adopted by Sonora's colonial administration, the ways of perceiving and occupying space subsequently underwent radical transformations.

Motivated in part by the 1740 rebellions, but perhaps even more by the need to bring the administration of the northern provinces into line with the canons of a more centralized regime, the visit by José Rodríguez Gallardo to Sonora and Sinaloa in 1748–1749 is of special importance, as it constituted the first moment in which the administrative, logistical, and structural problems of Sonora were analyzed as a whole.[30] As a result of this analysis, the image of Sonora projected by the *visitador* revealed structural deficiencies impeding the consolidation of Spanish settlement in the frontier area. One important aspect

[28] Martha Ortega Soto, "La colonización española en la primera mitad del siglo XVIII," in Ortega Noriega, *Tres siglos*, 213.

[29] Chantal Cramaussel, *La provincia de Santa Bárbara en Nueva Vizcaya* (Chihuahua: Universidad Autónoma de Ciudad Juárez, 1990), 45.

[30] The objective of Rodríguez Gallardo's visit was to restore order to the provinces of Sonora and Sinaloa—which comprised the *gobernación* of the same name—after the divisions caused by the administration of the outgoing governor, Agustín de Vildósola. Upon relieving Vildósola of his post, Rodríguez Gallardo was put in charge of the administration of those provinces until the arrival of the new governor, Diego Ortiz Parrilla, in 1749. Rodríguez Gallardo became convinced that the problems affecting that area of the viceroyalty were a product of a defective mechanism of land adjudication and appropriation—which explains his desire to prevent the *composiciones* from allowing the *pueblos de indios* to occupy large extensions of land, and his insistence that only by granting lands to new settlers would it be possible to pacify and sustain those provinces. María Luisa Rodríguez-Sala, *Los gobernadores de la Provincia de Sonora y Sinaloa, 1733–1771* (Culiacán: Universidad Autónoma de Sinaloa, 1999), 125–38.

of his commentaries is that neither the geography of Sonora nor the characteristics of its inhabitants was presented as the cause of the region's woes. Unlike
so many other observers, the purpose of Rodríguez Gallardo's writings was not
to denounce groups of people considered responsible for the misfortunes that
affected them.

In a first glimpse of Sonora and Sinaloa, the *visitador* perceived "provinces
rich in their interior, peaceful in appearance, populated in name only, governed
not as they should be but as their own constitution allows, and in a word, fragile and plentiful in and of themselves."[31] As far as this commentator was concerned, it was clear that the ruination of the northwestern reaches of the
viceroyalty was due to four causes: restrictions impeding maritime trade, colonization policies based on congregations of Indians that did not include
encomiendas or the creation of Spanish settlements, the scarcity of money, and
the disproportionate extension of the territory.[32] Of special interest here is the
emphasis that Rodríguez Gallardo placed on planning the colonization of
Sonora in the mid-eighteenth century. After dividing the population into two
large groups—Indians and Spaniards—he began to offer his impressions as to
the characteristics of the former. He felt that Yaquis and Ópatas were worthy
of praise as the "most cultured nations" of the province, as they were "lovers
of good dress, more inclined to work, and much more sociable than other
Indians." The Yaquis, Gallardo wrote, "are a generous, magnanimous people,
high-thinking [and] much inclined to religion." In contrast, the Seris and
Apaches were portrayed as warlike tribes who laid waste to the territory and did
not allow the consolidation of Spanish colonization.

This comparison of the Yaquis and Ópatas had a very important implica-
tion. Traditionally, the latter group had earned the highest praise from the
Spanish, but in this report it is the Yaquis who attracted the attention of the
royal official. It must be remembered that this visit occurred while Sonora was
still trying to recover from the 1740 rebellion, and in this context Gallardo's
report sought to underline the best features of the Yaquis and the Yaquimi in
order to promote a new settlement policy oriented toward Spanish penetration
into that area. To reinforce this thinking, the *visitador* presents the Sonoran

[31] José Rodríguez Gallardo, *Informe que el visitador general de la Sinaloa y Sonora hace en
cumplimiento de su obligación*, 1750, AGN, Provincias Internas, vol. 29, exp. 6, ff. 396–440.

[32] For a more detailed analysis of Rodríguez Gallardo's comments and their influence on José
de Gálvez's policies on New Spain's northern provinces, see José Refugio de la Torre Curiel, "El
Crisol del Reformismo: Sonora en la víspera de la visita de Gálvez y Beleña," in *Manifiesto de
Eusebio Bentura Beleña*, ed. Ignacio Almada Bay (Zamora: El Colegio de Michoacán, Universidad
de Guadalajara, El Colegio de Sonora, 2006), 43–67.

landscape as a territory shared by Indians and Spanish in which the latter should enjoy complete freedom to settle near Indian dwellings so that both groups could benefit from their proximity, as had occurred in other areas and above all in central New Spain.[33] In order for the image projected by the *visitador* to materialize, it was necessary to attend to the spirit of the Laws of the Indies (Leyes de Indias) that spoke of the division between Indians and Spanish because, in Rodríguez Gallardo's opinion, the separation contemplated therein was designed to protect the Indians from "restless, bad-living men, thieves, gamblers, [and] vice-ridden, lost souls." These restrictions, the *visitador* pointed out, should not be understood as rejecting contact between Indians and Spanish, as there were many good people in both groups who were needed to aid in the conversion of the Indians and in sustaining the frontier. It was necessary to liberate the Spanish population from limitations that for so long had discouraged the colonization of the most promising lands:

> Some Spaniards would live in towns, even without lands. . . . [S]ome do not live there due to repugnance, others for resentment or fear that the Leyes de Indias would literally descend over them. . . , and for one reason or another, they look upon the towns as if they were a foreign country in which one would need a certificate of naturalization, while others look upon them as enemy country.

In this context, and by the mid-eighteenth century, the lands between the Yaqui River and Pimería Alta were presented as the most promising areas for Spanish settlement in Sonora. From the perspective of this royal functionary, molded by Western notions of property and land use, Sonora provided a multitude of unoccupied territories available to be distributed among those willing to settle there. Undertaking a "formal redistribution [of land] to settlers by assigning them pasturelands and fields" would be the best way to populate Sonora, given that a person without "a lot, or field or pasture can hardly be called a resident or settler, nor is he such." It was precisely this lack of landowners that impeded mining from attaining greater prosperity because, as Rodríguez Gallardo also recognized, despite the abundance of mineral wealth in Sonora,

---

[33] Rodríguez Gallardo's ideas on settlement policies were not far removed from reality. Though he does not express it textually, his proposal was equivalent to uniting the *encomiendas*, the mining districts, the missions, and the Spanish *villas* in one interdependent complex. In other places, this complex had guaranteed the consolidation of Hispanic colonization. See, for example, the detailed study by Chantal Cramaussel, in which she analyzes the way in which these components were related in the province of Santa Bárbara (Nueva Vizcaya) over a period of almost an entire century. Cramaussel, *Poblar la frontera*, 55–81.

exploitation was not possible because the support of an agricultural population was lacking.[34] Guided by his conviction of the need to foster this type of colonization, in 1748, Rodríguez Gallardo pushed for land redistribution among the colonists of the San Miguel de Horcasitas presidio, at the moment in which this presidio was being moved from Pitic to a new site near Pópulo.[35]

The failure of settlement policies in Sonora had affected not only the consolidation of productive activities but also opened the door to incursions by enemy Indians: "The settlement and infestation by Sonora's enemies," he wrote, "is because there are no settlers." Such was Rodríguez Gallardo's response to the widely diffused idea that "the sparse settlement of Sonora is due to the [Indian] enemies."

To what point did this analysis of the situation in Sonora in the eighteenth century reflect reality, and to what degree was it the product of Rodríguez Gallardo's bias against the existing administrative system? On the one hand, the *visitador*'s conclusion that the regime of land adjudication limited the potential of mineral exploitation, agriculture, and ranching arose from a deep knowledge of the vices of colonial administration. On the other, although Sonora had no population centers that could compare with the main cities and villas of Nueva Vizcaya or Nueva Galicia, Rodríguez Gallardo's impression that the province was unpopulated was not entirely accurate. Given the geographical characteristics of Sonora, most congregations of Indians, as well as a large proportion of Spanish settlements (villages, mining districts), had been established in the valleys between the San Miguel River and the border with Nueva Vizcaya in the Sierra Madre, or in the area of the Yaqui River in Ostimuri. In fact, in the 1740s, the Jesuits themselves had confirmed the maturity of Spanish colonization in this region by proposing that the missions of Ostimuri be ceded to the Diocese of Durango. Curiously, the argument used to justify this transfer was not that of the Indians' "perfect understanding" of Christian doctrine, but rather the habitual communication that they sustained with the Spanish population: "These missions [of Ostimuri] are surrounded by small mines and,

---

[34] This observation by the *visitador* confirms Salvador Álvarez's thesis that in the settlement of New Spain the consolidation of agricultural colonies established the bases that allowed mine-related settlements to flourish. This view challenges the traditional opinion that it was the mining activity that preceded and even spurred agricultural settlement. Salvador Álvarez, "Colonización agrícola y colonización minera: La región de Chihuahua durante la primera mitad del siglo XVIII," in *El septentrión novohispano. Ecohistoria, sociedades e imágenes de frontera*, ed. Salvador Bernabéu Albert (Madrid, Consejo Superior de Investigaciones Científicas, 2000), 78.

[35] Juan Nentuig, *El rudo ensayo: Descripción geográfica, natural y curiosa de la provincia de Sonora, 1764* (Mexico City: Instituto Nacional de Antropología e Historia, 1977), 79.

almost in their midst, is the parish of Río Chico. They hold few people and are set up to treat with the Spanish, especially the miners; so it could be that they would not feel the change too deeply."[36]

On the basis of a series of reports gathered in 1752–1753 by the governor of Sonora, Diego Ortiz Parrilla, the administrative map of the province can be reconstructed to allow us a better appreciation of the problems broached by Rodríguez Gallardo two years earlier (Map 1.3).[37]

Map 1.4 reveals a fundamental problem of Spanish settlement in Sonora in particular and, more generally, throughout northwestern New Spain. The consolidation of the Spanish presence in these zones was not accomplished by establishing interdependent population nuclei connected by ongoing, expeditious contacts. In contrast, what appears in these settings is a series of human settlements with networks of exchange limited by the geographical setting, the absence of efficient systems of communication, and the hostility of enemy groups.

The concentration of Spanish settlements and Indian pueblos in the mountain valleys was the most visible feature of this atomization of Spanish colonization in Sonora, although it was not the only aspect that explained this area's precarious circumstances. There, as in other frontier societies, both Indian and non-Indian establishments shared common spaces, but in comparison with other regions in Sonora they became entangled in serious conflicts over the use of material and human resources (especially land and Indian labor).[38]

These farming and ranching operations faced an additional difficulty: The missions claimed rights over surrounding lands and even over distant plots. The

[36] Juan Antonio Baltasar to Cristóbal de Escobar y Llamas, n.d. (*ca.* 1743), in Burrus and Zubillaga, *El Noroeste de México*, 164.

[37] Diego Ortiz Parrilla, *Informe general de Sonora*, San Miguel de Ures, October 22, 1753, Bancroft Library, M-M 500. This report specifies Sonora's localities, the distances from one place to another, and the names of the principal *vecinos* of the major mining districts and haciendas. The descriptions presented here were solicited by Ortiz Parrilla in late 1752 from the *tenientes de alcalde mayor* (district governors' deputies) in Sonora. Map 1.3 is based on the *Plano de la provincia de Sonora* elaborated by Juan Nentuig in 1762. I use this map because it shows the location of most of the towns, villas, and ranches described in the reports compiled by Ortiz Parrilla, and because it was produced around the time of those reports.

[38] Take, for example, the case of the province of Santa Bárbara where *encomiendas*, mines, haciendas, and missions were articulated through the utilization of common resources. Cramaussel, *La provincia de Santa Bárbara*. A discussion of the functions of the congregations of Indians that the Jesuits and Franciscans set up between the Concho and Florido Rivers occupies a special place in Cramaussel's analysis. In addition to their religious purposes, these establishments provided labor for the nearby haciendas and mines. In this sense, the mission complemented the occupation of a settled area that had been dominated by *estancias* and mining districts since the mid-sixteenth century.

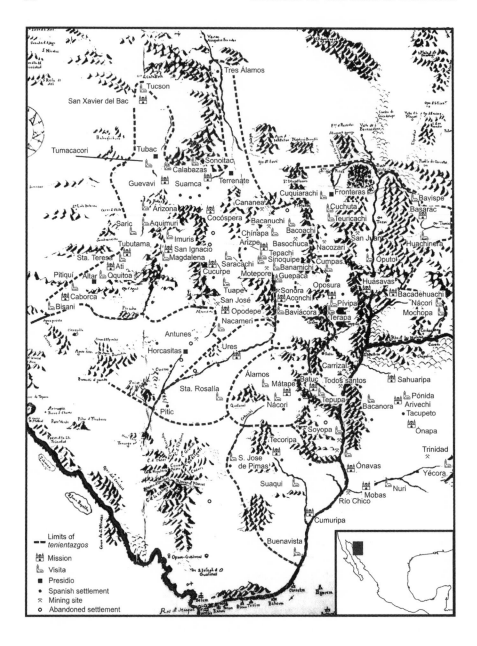

MAP 1.4. Administrative map of Sonora, 1753 (Adapted from Nentuig, 1762, *Plano Corográfico de la Sonora y Pimería: Provincias de la América Septentrional. . .* , original in British Museum)

TABLE 1.1. Types of settlements in Sonora, 1753

	Towns	Mines	Ranches and haciendas	Abandoned settlements
Horcasitas	2	1	1	6
San José de Gracia	4	6	5	
Mátape	4	3	17	2
Ventana	6	2	4	3
Tepache	5	3	6	1
Oposura	3	1	7	8
Nacozari	9	2	3	7
Corodehuachi	4			
Motepore	10	5	4	12
Concepción	1	1	3	3
Soyopa	1	3	4	
Opodepe	4	1	10	1
Pimería Alta	21	2	14	3
TOTAL	74	30	78	46

Source: BL, M-M 500.

resulting situation was the concentration of land in the hands of the mission towns, which limited Spanish access to territorial property because, with the exception of a few wealthy persons involved in ranching and mining, the only option available to the less wealthy or poor settlers was to become tenant farmers dependent on the Jesuit missions.

The district of Mátape offers the case that best exemplifies this situation, due to the importance of the ranches established there. According to the report by the *teniente de alcalde mayor* in residence there, in 1752 his jurisdiction comprised four pueblos, three mines, seventeen ranches, and two haciendas.[39]

This predominance of ranches in the sierra terrain of Mátape was associated with the importance of cattle raising in the region. At that time, ranches in Mátape sent herds of as many as 2,000 to 3,000 head of cattle to Nueva Vizcaya, which established it as the principal cattle market in Sonora.[40] Behind the image of the economic bonanza that these figures might suggest, however, lurked the problem of land tenure. In the canyon formed by the Mazatán and the Batuco Sierras, the largest landowners were the mission towns of Mátape,

[39] BL, M-M 500.
[40] *Informe de Enrique Grimarest al virrey Revillagigedo*, Álamos, July 31, 1792, AGN, Historia, vol. 72, f. 310.

Nacori, and Alamos. In some cases, the lands that these missions claimed as their own were more than seven leagues distant, as occurred, for example, in the settlement of Las Cuevas, where Mátape reserved a "canyon of crags [with] abundant water." Somewhat less frequently, mission towns also considered as part of their dominions lands with poorly defined boundaries such as valleys or sierras, such as the lands located between Quisuani, Cobachi, and the intersection of the Mátape and Aivino Streams, sites cultivated by "the occupants of those terrains with the blessing of the ministers, as continues to occur today"—that is, as tenant farmers.

The reports presented by Governor Ortiz Parrilla in 1753 indicate that as far as the Spanish settlers in Sonora were concerned, territories north of the Yaqui River did not form a compact unit, but instead included at least three zones of colonization whose geographic features and demographic composition marked the intensity and character of the contact between Indians and Spaniards. The first of these was the farming and ranching corridor formed by the Sonora and Mátape Valleys, characterized by available irrigation systems along the banks of the Sonora River and by the abundant pasturelands and watering holes of the Mátape Valley. The availability of these resources explains why this zone became the most heavily populated area in Sonora and why it was the region that more readily overcame the uprisings of the Seri and Pima Indians, at least in comparison to Ostimuri.

The second zone was the sierra belt in the eastern part of the province, whose proximity to the so-called "sierras of the Apaches" made it quite unattractive to potential Spanish settlers and exposed the mission towns to the attacks of enemy Indians. This frontier, in turn, comprised two regions differentiated by the frequency and intensity of Apache incursions. On the one hand, the corridor formed by the Tepache and Oposura Valleys extending through Nacozari as far as the Fronteras presidio, comprised a succession of high valleys containing a few ranches, mines, and missions, where a constant, cyclical occupation, and abandonment of populated zones occurred because of the "great danger from Apache enemies." Another zone of colonization was located to the east of the Huásavas Sierra, following the line of the river of the same name, between Bacadehuachi and Babispe, although the Spanish presence there was practically nonexistent. In the roughest terrain of the sierra lived the Ópatas and Jovas, who were charged with defending the region against the Apaches in their capacity as "warriors against said enemy," as they were described by the *teniente* of Tepache.

Third, and finally, to the north of the agricultural and ranching valleys, with the ancient town of Dolores as its entry point, was the territory known as Pimería

Alta, characterized, according to one of Ortiz Parrilla's informants, as having "several unpopulated areas because it was located along the Apache frontier."

In the previous testimonies there is a marked insistence on two premises influencing the view held by the Spanish population with respect to the province of Sonora. From the civil authorities' point of view, the tragedy of Sonora was its abundance of empty spaces, that is, the existence of lands without owners according to Western concepts of property and land use. With respect to the local Indian population, the Spaniards made a basic distinction between the warlike tribes, on the one hand, and those subject to Spanish dominion, on the other. This utilitarian perspective served to justify the extermination of the Seri and Apache Indians as well as the condemnation of the Yaquis and Pimas due to the precarious character of the peace reached with them at various times.[41] In this same discourse, the subjected Indians appear in the testimonies of the era's civil authorities as a heterogeneous mass whose most important feature was their serving as laborers in the mines and on the ranches or as soldiers employed to defend the northern frontier and protect travelers.

This way of perceiving space contrasted with the posture that the Jesuits had promoted up to the 1760s. According to their descriptions, the geographical environment and the native population were a single integrated entity, at least in terms of the space they inhabited. From the perspective of those missionaries, it was important to present this province as a coherent whole, populated by a succession of Indian nations well disposed to receiving the word of God. In this way they could reinforce the image of Sonora as a compact missionary district subject to the administration of the Society of Jesus. Faithful to this tradition, the last eighteenth-century Jesuit description of Sonora presents the area as part of the enormous territory "from Culiacán to San Javier del Bac and Tucson" that the Jesuits had conquered "for the church and for the Catholic monarchy . . . with no more cost to the royal treasury than that of its stipends."[42] Taken as an isolated text, this description of Sonora by Juan Nentuig offers a rich ethnographic and geographical panorama that transmits both the observations of one particular missionary as well as the prejudices of an entire epoch in general. In this sense, the work is, as one of the editors wrote, "one of the most complete and richest colonial treatises on a territory and its inhabitants and on missionary work."[43] Placed in this context, the text

---

[41] Juan de Pineda, *Informe que en el año de 1763 hizo Don Juan de Pineda al virrey de Nueva España*, RBP, II/2824, *Miscelánea de Ayala*, vol. X.

[42] Nentuig, *El rudo ensayo*, 41.

[43] Margarita Nolasco, Teresa Martínez, and América Flores, "Introducción" to Nentuig, *El rudo ensayo*, 5.

can be understood as part of a proposal designed to remedy "the decline of the missions" and the slow progress of Spanish colonization in the region.[44] It is an evaluation of the status of Sonora's population, its resources, and the possibilities it offered to extend Spanish dominion even farther north. From this perspective, Nentuig's text bears comparison to the proposals previously elaborated for the same purpose by governors and *visitadores*, despite the fact that while they all dealt with basically the same problems, the starting point and conclusions of Nentuig's analysis present important contrasts.

According to this Jesuit's vision, the Sonoran province comprised four areas of indigenous settlement: Pimería Alta; Pimería Baja; the sierra inhabited by the Ópatas, Jovas, and Eudeves; and the lowlands where the Seris dwelt. While the first zone held out the promise of good agricultural yields, there was also the inconvenient fact that it was not yet fully under Spanish control. The Pimería Baja and the sierra regions were not conducive to successful agricultural settlements, although this disadvantage was compensated to a degree by the possibility of putting Indian labor at the disposal of new residents. The western portion of the province, in contrast, was still dominated by the Seris, a fact that made any attempt at Spanish settlement futile.[45]

Unlike the description offered by Governor Ortiz Parrilla, Nentuig presents the mission towns and *not* the Spanish villas as the main form of occupation in the Sonoran landscape. It was by virtue of this difference that Nentuig could argue that the heart of Sonora was indeed sufficiently populated, although still vulnerable to incursions by Indian enemies. Thus, for example, when he writes about the Ópatas, Eudeves, and Jovas, he asserts that:

> The Indians that make up these three nations populate most of Sonora from well within the sierra; the limits of their territories are . . . the desert towns of Nátora, Arivetzi, Bacanora, Tonitzi, Soyopa, Nácori, Álamos, part of Ures, Nacameri, Opodepe, Cucurpe towards the west; [and] from there [to] Arispe, Chinapa, Bacoatzi, Cuquiaratzi, as far as Babispe to the north.[46]

---

[44] Nolasco, Martínez, and Flores, "Introducción," 5. According to Ivonne del Valle, Jesuit chronicles aimed at documenting Sonora's grandeur in order to attract the attention of the authorities of New Spain and persuade them to rectify the "erring colonial policies" that kept Sonora from prospering. Valle, *Escribiendo desde los márgenes*, 134.

[45] The heart of this zone was made up of the mountain ranges described by Governor Ortiz Parrilla "that trace a line through what we properly call the middle of the province of Sonora from west to east, from the town of Nácori . . . to the *villa* of San Miguel. [There] are six that make up [together] with a certain part of the Sierra Madre . . . a kind of staircase that as it recedes from said Sierra Madre and approaches the coast, tends also to lose bulk and elevation." Nentuig, *El rudo ensayo*, 50.

[46] *Ibid.*, 76.

Upon writing of the Lower Pimas, he portrays a more compact set of towns:

[Therefore], I say that the towns of the Lower Pimas are like [the] landmarks of this province, because from Taraitzi to Cumuripa, Onapa, Nuri, Movas and Ónabas they [extend] to the south; from Cumuripa, Suaqui, San José de Pimas, Santa Rosalía, Ures and Nacameri to the east [which] is the frontier with the Seris.[47]

In contrast, Nentuig presents Pimería Alta as an open space that, while certainly occupied by the Upper Pima Indians, was insufficiently populated:

The Upper Pima Indians occupy the entire territory from Cucurpe through Santa Ana, Caborca, to the sea, from east to west and south [to] north[.] [A]ll the land from said mission . . . as far as the Colorado [River] . . . extends from northeast to southwest some 130 leagues and from east to west in some places 60 [leagues], [and] in others less or more [up to] as many as 130 leagues. The truth is that in all of this vast space there is much unpopulated [land], . . . [such as] salt marshes . . . and because most of [this space is] . . . inhospitable due to the severe scarcity of water and the barrenness of the land. . . . [A]ll the long trek from Caborca to close to the mouth of the Colorado River . . . is almost all sandbanks and moors with little water, which is found almost exclusively along the coast.[48]

It was in this latter area that Nentuig suggested carrying out a new expansion stage of Spanish settlement. Occupying the northernmost frontier of Sonora was necessary, he argued, both to "repopulate unpopulated stretches" as well as to "advance settlement right up to the very backs of the enemies."[49] Only the effective occupation of those territories would allow the Spanish to abandon the fruitless offensive war that they were waging against Indian enemies and to contemplate a defensive one.[50]

Nentuig's perception of the Sonoran landscape was influenced by the cultural matrix in which he had been trained, the prejudices of the Spanish world with respect to Amerindian cultures, and his interest in keeping those mission districts in the hands of the Society of Jesus. With respect to the forms in which the first two aspects influenced the Jesuit's rhetoric, a few exemplary studies

---

[47] *Ibid.*
[48] *Ibid.*, 77.
[49] *Ibid.*, 100.
[50] *Ibid.*, 116.

trace through the Biblical and Medieval traditions the sources providing the
followers of St. Ignatius with their frames of reference for interpreting the
world.[51] Here, for the moment, the utilitarian character of the Jesuit narrative
is discussed to emphasize the contradictions between two ways of understanding and planning for the Spanish presence in Sonora.

Together with Nentuig's identification of the zones inhabited by the Pima,
Seri, Ópata, Eudeve, and Jova Indians, his *Descripción Geográfica* contains a
second criterion concerning the zoning of Sonora: the opposition between the
sierra—where the principal missionary districts and the most important Spanish
settlements were located—and the open spaces on the periphery of that zone—
which Nentuig presented as the area in which any new attempts at colonization
should be concentrated. This way of imagining the landscape does not seem to
correspond well with conventional analyses of tensions between Jesuits and
Spanish colonists, in which the clergy eagerly sought ways to keep the *vecinos*
as far away as possible from their missions and to systematically block their
access to mission land. What emerges, rather, seems to be an attempt to guarantee the presence of a controlled Spanish population around the mission
towns, perhaps with an eye to establishing a defined group of tenant farmers
and others who would become consumers of mission products, while simultaneously offering peripheral areas around the mission districts for Spanish colonization. "To repopulate that which is deserted and to push settlements right
up to the enemies' backs," synthesizes this program for the preferential assig-
nation of spaces for colonization.

In contrast to this view, Sonora's civil authorities (from José Rodríguez
Gallardo through Diego Ortiz Parrilla and up to Juan de Pineda) perceived the
local geography in very different terms. The descriptions analyzed in the above
paragraphs coincide in the idea of first settling the heart of the province—precisely the area that Nentuig proposed for repopulation—that had not been systematically colonized as the civil authorities had projected.

Spatial Organization Projects in the Second Half of the Eighteenth Century

The presence of the Jesuits and their unwillingness to renounce their control of Spanish settlement patterns in Sonora translated into a relative impasse

---

[51] Guy Rozat, *América, imperio del demonio* (Mexico City: Universidad Iberoamericana,
1995), 61–62; and by the same author, *Indios imaginarios e indios reales en los relatos de la conquista de México* (Mexico City: Tava Editores, 1993).

in realizing the projects described thus far in this chapter. With the expulsion of the Jesuits in 1767, however, a new stage in the history of Sonora began[52] in which several aspects of Spanish-American political and ecclesiastical structures would be reformulated, together with forms of occupying and socially organizing space in the area previously assigned to the Society of Jesus.[53] The most significant visible expressions of these two processes in Sonora were the arrival of the Franciscans in 1768 to take over the missions administered up to that time by the Jesuits; the creation of new political, military, and ecclesiastical jurisdictions; and the intensification and diversification of contact between Indians and Spaniards that became possible once the restrictions imposed by the Jesuits were lifted. The importance of these processes in transforming Sonora will be taken up in later chapters. What commands interest at this point is elucidating the relationship between, on the one hand, the implementation of new socioreligious programs in the province, the increasing mobility of Sonora residents, and the conflicts between the Franciscans and the diocesan clergy and, on the other, the discursive re-elaboration of the ideas defining Sonoran space after 1767.

From the moment of their arrival in Sonora, the Franciscans from the Colegio de Querétaro and the Province of Santiago de Xalisco[54] perceived, in

---

[52] On the expulsion of the Jesuits from Sonora and New Spain, see Polzer, *Kino. A Legacy*, 106–109; Alberto Francisco Pradeau, *La expulsión de los jesuitas de las provincias de Sonora, Ostimuri y Sinaloa en 1767* (Mexico City: Antigua Librería Robredo, 1959); Andre Jansen, "El virrey Charles de Croix y la expulsión de los jesuitas de Mejico en 1767," *Hispania: Revista Española de Historia* 36 (1976): 321–54; John L. Kessell, *Spain in the Southwest: A Narrative History of Colonial New Mexico, Arizona, Texas and California* (Norman: University of Oklahoma Press, 2002), 253–62; Salvador Bernabéu Albert, *Expulsados del infierno: el exilio de los misioneros jesuitas de la península californiana, 1767–1768* (Madrid: Consejo Superior de Investigaciones Científicas, 2008), 69–82; Priestley, *José de Gálvez*, 211–13. For a more detailed analysis on the expulsion of the Jesuits in the Americas, see Magnus Mörner, *The Expulsion of the Jesuits from Latin America* (New York: Knopf, 1965).

[53] In the province of Sonora in particular, this rupture profoundly disturbed the terms of what Cynthia Radding has called the "colonial pact" through which the Indians negotiated their subordination to the Crown and the church in exchange for protection and assistance. Radding, "Cultural Boundaries between Adaptation and Defiance: The Mission Communities of Northwestern New Spain," in *Spiritual Encounters: Interactions between Christianity and Native Religions in Colonial America*, ed. Nicholas Griffiths (Lincoln: University of Nebraska Press, 1999), 116–35. In spite of these changes, some authors contend, the expulsion of the Jesuits from Sonora "was not a catastrophe for mission Indians." Almada, Medina, and Borrero, "Hacia una nueva interpretación," 250.

[54] The Colegio de Querétaro and the Province of Santiago de Xalisco were the two Franciscan entities responsible for the administration of the missions in Sonora after 1767. The Colegio de Querétaro's backgrounds are to be found in the Congregation for the Propagation of the Faith—*Propaganda Fide*—founded in 1622 by Pope Gregory XV in an attempt to promote a

addition to the precarious material conditions of their missions, a social order in which the barrier between mission towns and non-Indian locales was disappearing rapidly and permitting ever greater mobility between the two. Referring to this circumstance with a heavy heart, an anonymous Franciscan from Querétaro stated in the census (*padrón*) of 1768 at the mission of Cucurpe, that it was impossible to calculate the number of "*vecinos* and those who are called 'of reason'" who reside there "because they do not recognize any hometown, and wander about wherever it pleases them."[55]

This missionary's comments were symptomatic of the new reality of the mission establishments, because according to new royal dispositions, Franciscan authorities had agreed not to intervene in the "civil interaction" between Indians and Spaniards,[56] but to limit their activities to the spiritual domain. In another context, this testimony was related to the categories of identification used by the clergy to describe the Sonoran milieu. Unlike the Jesuit epoch, when notions of open and inhabited spaces permeated writings on Sonora, for the post-1768 era, several texts written by clergy and civil authorities reveal a new referential orientation dominated by the problem of defining precisely which parts of Sonora constituted territories appropriate for the conversion of souls and which ones could already be considered

---

better instruction and preparation for missionaries. Sixty years later, on March 12, 1682, the Minister General of the Franciscans authorized fray Antonio Linaz to establish in New Spain a seminar modeled according to the spirit of this Congregation. This project came to life in 1683 with the founding of the Colegio de Querétaro, the first institution of this type in the Americas. Félix Sáiz, "La expansión misionera en las fronteras del imperio español: Colegios misioneros franciscanos en Hispanoamérica," in *Franciscanos en América*, ed. Francisco Morales (Mexico City: Conferencia Franciscana de Santa María de Guadalupe, 1993), 188–90; Isidro Félix Espinosa, *Crónica de los Colegios de Propaganda Fide de la Nueva España* (Washington, DC: Academy of American Franciscan History, 1964); Antolín Abad Pérez, *Los franciscanos en América* (Madrid: Mapfre, 1992), 88–89. The Franciscan Province of Xalisco was not a geopolitical entity, but a conglomerate of convents, *doctrinas*, and missions, under the spiritual direction of a superior or minister provincial. It was created in 1607, after the minister general of the Franciscan Order and a provincial chapter approved the segregation of 32 convents from the Franciscan Province of San Pedro y San Pablo de Michoacán. De la Torre Curiel, *Vicarios en entredicho*, 24–25.

[55] AFPM, AQ, Letter K, leg. 14, no. 7.

[56] *Instrucciones dadas por el Discretorio del Colegio de Querétaro a los misioneros destinados a Sonora, 4 de agosto de 1767*, AFPM, AQ, Letter K, leg. 14, no. 3. One of the points of this *instrucción* informed the missionaries that by order of the king they could not deprive the Indians of "civil treatment, communication, trade, and residence with the Spanish," and that if they encounter grave inconveniences that impede the Christian doctrine in the customs, instruction and assistance of the Indians, they were not to use means of correcting them other than the notification they were to give to the father president so that he may "procure their goodly pacification with those chiefs without causing any judicial clamor."

Christianized zones. As the reader will see below, defining space in these terms implied not only the delicate task of judging the degree of acceptance of Christianity among the Indians, but also belied the fact that the underlying interest was to justify the implementation of diverse settlement projects.

A report on the geography of Sinaloa and Sonora, written for the purpose of demonstrating the need to establish *cajas reales* (royal treasuries) in El Rosario and San Antonio de la Huerta, is the earliest example of this dualist vision of Sonora.[57] Drafted in 1772, this report presented a general panorama of the sites of the principal mines and extolled the fertility, the "very healthy temperament," and the great mineral wealth of the valleys located in the central and southern portions of the Sonoran province.[58] The document also praised that area's intermountain valleys, "named according to the localities that the Spanish established therein, such as the Sonora, Santa Ana, Tepache, and Ruipa Valley[s], where [one] also finds a fair number of Indian towns that up to a short time ago were missions."[59] What draws our attention to this particular idea of Sonora is the exclusion of Pimería Alta, an area populated by yet un-Christianized Indians where, at that time, the Spanish presence was still quite modest. The Sonora of this report, therefore, is the Hispanicized Sonora.

The emphasis this author places on the fact that in the southern part of the province the natives were no longer "mission Indians" was part of a program that sought to narrate the progressive consolidation of Spanish colonization in Sonora. The most revealing feature of this report is its affirmation that the Indian pueblos in this Hispanic Sonora no longer pertained to the missions. It is meaningful because by 1772 the only *secularizations*[60] of missions in Sonora proper (not including Ostimuri) were the cases of Oposura and Batuc. In that same year, the missions of the Yaqui River had been assigned on an interim basis to the clergy of the Diocese of Durango, although they conserved their status as missions and, moreover, were located in Ostimuri. Thus, the question arises: Why were they at such pains to affirm that the towns north of the Yaqui River were no longer missions? The answer is probably to be found in the fact that the author is not referring to the juridical status of those towns, but to the fact that *in practice* one could observe the greater assimilation of Pimería Baja

---

[57] There had been a *caja real* in Álamos since 1769, though it was later moved to El Rosario.

[58] *Descripción sucinta de las Provincias de Culiacán, Sinaloa y Sonora*, Mexico City, November 1, 1772, BNM, MS 19266. Although the document does not bear any signature, there are reasons to think that the author is Fray Antonio de los Reyes, as most of the issues discussed in this text are further developed by De los Reyes in his writings.

[59] *Descripción sucinta*, BNM, MS 19266.

[60] See Glossary.

and Opatería to the patterns of civility and religiosity that the Spanish identi-fied as characteristic of what they called "life in society."

The writings of Fray Antonio de los Reyes, a missionary from the college of Querétaro and, later, Sonora's first bishop, confirm the essence of this discursive re-elaboration. On several occasions, reports of de los Reyes have been inter-preted as proof positive of the crisis that affected the mission regime in Sonora and as testimony to the consolidation of his political career in close association with José de Gálvez.[61] In contrast to this view, however, by studying these records as a whole, carefully tracing their internal evolution, and placing them in dialogue with other contemporaneous sources, it becomes possible to pro-pose a different vision of the province of Sonora in the late eighteenth century.

In his first known work on Sonora, signed on April 20, 1772,[62] de los Reyes begins his description of the territory by mentioning the paradox most frequently cited by analysts of the problems of northern New Spain: the con-trast between the region's enormous riches and the ruin of its population cen-ters. To explain this contrast, de los Reyes, as did many of his predecessors, took up the theme of the invasions of Indian enemies and the small number of permanent settlements. Although he agreed with many earlier commentaries on these points, he attributed a rather different meaning to the problems they enunciated. The low number of permanent towns and their ineffective organi-zation and government are the main topics of his 1772 report, as he not only proposes attracting new settlers to the province, but also distinguishes in detail among the types of existing localities, the characteristics of the colonized zones, and the structural problems of the towns and mining districts.

To begin with, de los Reyes presents a general characterization of both the missions and the Spanish settlements. The problem with the Spaniards, he wrote, was that upon their arrival in Sonora they thought only of amassing for-tunes in mining and so were predisposed to migrate as soon as local mining resources began to run out.[63] In these circumstances, the friar wrote, "they

---

[61] Albert Stagg, *The First Bishop of Sonora: Antonio de los Reyes, OFM* (Tucson: University of Arizona Press, 1976).

[62] This report, dated in Mexico City, was addressed to Viceroy Antonio María Bucareli. AHMNAH, FF, vol. 66 ff. 52–61. In the Archivo General de Indias, there is a copy of this report ordered by de los Reyes himself in 1777. Due to a scribe's error, the title of the copy bears the date of April 20, 1774. AGI, Guadalajara 586.

[63] De los Reyes's comments indicate that these prospectors' willingness to migrate was one of the causes of Sonora's lack of permanent Spanish settlements, however, the opposite situation might apply to the Sonoran case. Consider that most of these prospectors' activities were not sup-ported by an agricultural base of their own, which prevented them from getting supplies and food-stuffs at reasonable prices. Most of these miners could not afford investing in the technology they

form their mines and towns at such a low cost and subsistence that at the first opportunity that arises they abandon them with no difficulty or loss." Itinerant by necessity, the Spaniards and castes in the province soon became a problem for Indians and the friars, as they would attempt to establish residence in the missions. The critique that this missionary presents in his narrative of these problems centers on the temporary nature of Spanish settlements, while intimating that forcing them to establish fixed residence would contribute to improving Sonoran society.

The situation of the Indian towns was more complex. On this point, the missionary orients his observations toward demonstrating that because of the precarious material conditions of Indian dwellings, the missions could hardly be considered true population centers:

> In material terms, the mission towns are formed and arranged against all rational political and civil society. The dispersed dwellings [are] made of mud and straw, very small and with no partitions [between them]; have no furnishings or rational comforts, [the Indians] sleep on the floor, or perhaps on a skin or mat; their [populations] are not numerous, some have eighty to one hundred families, others from thirty to fifty, and some ten to twelve.

According to de los Reyes, in 1772 Sonora consisted of a collection of poorly formed towns, of "no utility to our beloved Sovereign or to the nation as a whole." Moreover, Sonora's government lacked any kind of coherent structure because governors typically delegated most of their responsibilities in the *alcaldes mayores* they appointed. These officials chose their own lieutenants, who in turn were aided by a number of deputies (*comisarios*). Thus, de los Reyes concluded, the result was a chaotic government structure in which these officials acted "as they please."[64]

Improving this disorder would require the "re-establishment" of those towns, that is, a re-ordering to include all three types of settlement or local-

---

needed to extract ore from deep deposits for the same reason, deciding to move forward to other mining sites instead. Álvarez, "Colonización agrícola," 73–108. On the Sonoran economy, see Chapter 4.

[64] In this respect, de los Reyes backed up Gálvez's criticism to the same government structure: "Most of the alcaldes are men of meagre intelligence, who do not know how to assist the viceroy; they devote their energies to acquiring riches, and their lieutenants in the smaller towns only render the evil more widespread. Some alcaldes are honest, but overwhelmed with debts; most of them think it proper to appropriate the tributes, of which the king receives only half what he should." The remedy, Gálvez suggested, was to establish the intendancy system in New Spain. Herbert Ingram Priestley, *José de Gálvez: Visitor-General of New Spain (1765–1771)* (Berkeley: University of California Press, 1916), 290.

ity existing in the province. First, the "new establishments or conversions of the infidels" destined to "convert the beasts into rational [beings]" would be the responsibility of the missionaries, who would use "the most educated and conscientious Indians for political and civil government; these towns must constitute a territory barred to Spaniards, who would not be allowed to settle within a perimeter of four leagues." Second, in the oldest pastoral territories—*antiguas doctrinas*—the Indians possessing greater familiarity with Christian doctrine and proven ability to cultivate wheat and corn opened up three important possibilities: eliminate community life, distribute land among them, and begin to charge them parish fees. Third, and finally, all Spaniards would be obliged to "settle and reside in the few towns that currently exist."

Although the 1772 report does not specify the geographical distribution that de los Reyes had in mind while writing of these three kinds of localities, in a later document he clearly identifies Pimería Alta as the zone devoted to "converting the savages." The ancient *doctrinas*, meanwhile, were those that occupied both the zone of Opatería and that of Pimería Baja, although de los Reyes refers to the entire area as simply Pimería Baja.[65]

By July 1774, in a missive sent to Viceroy Antonio Bucareli, this missionary from Querétaro added new elements to the division of the territory of Sonora that he had developed previously.[66] The friar's map of the "new" and old zones of evangelization was complemented on this occasion by a description of what residence in these different areas meant as far as social relations were concerned. In the ancient *doctrinas*, where proselytizing was undertaken in 1609, as de los Reyes noted,[67] the Indian population had begun to show a certain indisposition with respect to the work of the missionaries and was being increasingly attracted to interact with other sectors of the Spanish population. In Opodepe, for example,

---

[65] *Noticia de la California*, 6. This document has no date, but I am inclined to think that it was written *circa* 1776–1777 as it presents a general description of the provinces of northern Mexico at a time when the possibility of creating several missionary *custodias* there was being discussed.

[66] Fray Antonio de los Reyes, *Memorial y Estado Actual de las Misiones de la Pimería Alta y Baja: Presentado al Exmo Sor Virrey Frey Dn Antonio María Bucareli y Ursua, en 6 de julio de 1774*, AGI, Guadalajara 586.

[67] *Ibid*. In another document, de los Reyes indicates that it was around 1610 when the first missionaries entered Pimería Baja. *Noticia de la California*, 6. His mention of this date refers to the entry of Franciscans from New Mexico into northern Opatería in 1610. According to Gerhard, the earliest permanent Spanish occupation in this area dates from 1617, when the Jesuits arrived in Cumuripa and Tecoripa. Gerhard, *La frontera norte*, 347.

The Indians say they are of the Eudeve and Ópata nations, but in truth they are a confusion and mixture of Spanish, mulattoes, coyotes and other castes. . . . [T]hey pretend to be Indians so that the [local] priest will not ask them to pay or charge them for [parochial] fees . . . but they have no desire to be governed as Indians or to obey the corrections and council of their missionary.[68]

Although Indian languages still predominated in Pimería Baja and Opatería, de los Reyes argued that in general those Indians "understand and speak the Spanish language." Finally, this missionary made it clear that in this area, Indian demands to be released from the mission regime and freed from the communal work and services it imposed upon them were becoming increasingly insistent. In fact, by petitioning that they be "removed from the government of the mission," those Indians were seeking to be "treated as *gente de razón*."

In Pimería Alta, however, the panorama was quite different. Despite almost an entire century of religious presence, very little had been accomplished in terms of establishing Christianity and the Spanish language among the Indians.[69] For the missionary from Querétaro, Pimería Alta was synonymous with pristine lands whose inhabitants still lived in complete barbarism. In contrast to his treatment of the other zones of Sonora in his report, when de los Reyes spoke of Pimería Alta he concentrated his attention on the infinite bounty of the land and the rustic nature of its inhabitants. The entire territory of Pimería Alta, he wrote, "is very fertile and suitable for cultivating all kinds of crops [and] for raising and exploiting all manner of European fruits and trees; it rains and snows [there] in the winter and, in all respects, the climate and temperament are very similar to those of Spain." When he focused his comments on the inhabitants of this region, however, the narrator's admiration turned to contempt as he criticized their spiritual condition, characterized as "more doleful than that of the barbarians and gentiles of the frontier," and expresses the revulsion he felt towards the physical appearance of the Pimas as follows:

They are generally corpulent, above average height, with ferocious faces and features. . . . [T]hey know no shame or modesty, living totally naked wearing

---

[68] De los Reyes, *Memorial y Estado Actual*.

[69] In the *Memorial* of July 6, 1774, de los Reyes states that missionary work in Pimería Alta dated from 1668, although in the *Noticia de la California* he indicates that it was around 1680 when the first missionaries entered those lands. Fray Francisco Antonio Barbastro, on the other hand, affirms that it was perhaps in 1687 when predication began in this area. Gómez Canedo, *Sonora hacia fines*, 52. Gerhard also points to 1687 as the year that Eusebio Kino arrived in Pimería Alta to establish mission Dolores. Gerhard, *La frontera norte*, 347.

only a loincloth, they use large bows and arrows [made of] reeds . . . and these represent all their furniture and utensils. Some women paint their hands, arms and chest. . . , they are very dirty, savage and horrible to behold.

De los Reyes thus ushered in a phase in which the occupation of the north-ernmost reaches of Sonora began to be considered in a different way. In his writings one discovers the transition from a Sonora seen as a missionary fron-tier to a Sonora that harbors a series of frontier missions in the region most exposed to incursions by the Apaches. This Franciscan's insistence in pointing out the differences between the patterns of occupation in Pimería Alta and the territory formed by Pimería Baja and Opatería was part of this new perception of space; but there was also a second feature that was symptomatic of this trans-formation of the Sonoran landscape. In his memorial of 1772, de los Reyes wrote of "new establishments or conversions of the infidels" that were to be set up in Pimería Alta. Five years later, when he presented a copy of this document to the Consejo de Indias, he replaced this phrase with the term "frontier mis-sions," thus changing the point of reference from the inhabitants of those places to the localization of that series of missions.[70] Behind this change in his representation of the mission landscape in Sonora was an attempt to explain that most of Sonora was a province in which the population participated fully in the Christian doctrine and that only an appendage of that territory—"the frontier with the gentiles"—was still a zone of living conversion.

In essence, de los Reyes's description of Sonoran geography reflected pre-cisely what the ecclesiastical and civil authorities perceived in those areas, that is, a territory in need of political reform and divided according to the antiquity of participation in Christianity and the level of integration of Hispanic culture into local traditions. However, the scenario that de los Reyes presented differed substantially from other contemporaneous testimonies in both its image of the inhabitants and in its basic intention to divide the territory into two regions.

De los Reyes believed it important to present the Sonoran stage in dual-istic terms in order to promote a plan designed to reform the colonization and spiritual administration of the province. Strengthening the authority of the recently appointed intendant of Sonora,[71] establishing the Diocese of Sonora

---

[70] The 1777 copy in AGI, Guadalajara 586.

[71] On January 15, 1768, José de Gálvez and Viceroy Carlos Francisco de Croix signed a plan for the establishment of intendancies in New Spain. Based on the results of diverse types of inten-dants in France, Spain, Havana and Louisiana, Gálvez and Croix believed this system would con-tribute "to the rehabilitation of the country by the betterment of civil and economic government of the provinces." Priestley, *José de Gálvez*, 289–92. According to that plan, eleven intendancies

in 1779,[72] and choosing de los Reyes as its first bishop were the initial steps toward the realization of his project of reorganization that would soon be reinforced by the creation of the Franciscan custody of San Carlos de Sonora in 1783. As a result, the local missionaries would be subject to the authority of Sonora's bishop, who in turn would foster the intendancy's reformist policies among his parishioners. The spirit of the new order projected by de los Reyes also required that the territory of the ancient *doctrinas* would be subject to a new organization granting greater freedom to those Indians who progressed from catechists to tributaries and then to parishioners—that is, those who would be obliged to pay religious fees. The incorporation of the barbarous north into this scheme would have to wait for a future phase.[73]

With respect to Pimería Alta, the zone of new conversions, Fray Francisco Garcés offered an image different from that narrated by de los Reyes. Sent by the Colegio de Querétaro in 1768 to serve in those missions, Father Garcés devoted much of his ministry to visiting the distant lands around the Gila and the Colorado Rivers in order to become familiar with the Indian nations that inhabited them. In contrast to the Jesuit project of advancing toward the Gila River to establish a new missionary district there,[74] Garcés's idea of occupying

---

would be needed for New Spain—a general intendancy in Mexico City and the others in the viceroyalty's provinces. Although the king approved the plan in 1769, the system was not fully implemented in New Spain until 1786 with some modifications. Twelve intendancies were then established, and Arizpe was ratified as the administrative center of Sonora's intendancy. Áurea Commons, *Las Intendencias de la Nueva España* (Mexico City: Universidad Nacional Autónoma de México, 1993), 1–26. The Intendancy of Sonora was, in fact, created before 1786. In practice, Eusebio Bentura Beleña acted as the first intendant of Sonora—Intendente de Real Hacienda—between June 1769 and April 1770, although his appointment was not ratified by the king. The first official intendant of Sonora, Pedro Corbalán, was appointed in 1770. De la Torre Curiel, "El Crisol," 63.

[72] The idea of creating the Diocese of Sonora had been broached originally in 1768 by José de Gálvez, who considered it a fundamental part of a program for the administrative reorganization of northwestern New Spain. In addition to the need to create that diocese, Gálvez also projected the creation of a *comandancia general* that would group the northern provinces together under the military command of one man. After discussing both ideas with Viceroy Marqués de Croix, the two men agreed to suggest to the king that the seat of these new instances be located in Arizpe. In order for the town and mission of Arizpe to become the seat of these two powers, the king issued a decree on July 6, 1780 granting it the title of city. *Consejo de 23 de septiembre de 1780*, AGI, Guadalajara 372. Despite orders that the bishop reside in Arizpe, de los Reyes found it more convenient to live in Ures. The episcopal seat was later moved to Culiacán.

[73] Despite Bishop de los Reyes's efforts to put his plans into practice, the strong opposition of the missionaries led by Fray Francisco Antonio Barbastro and the low viability of several of his proposals impeded the materialization of the ideal of a more urban and ordered society. The bishop's death in 1787 and the suppression of the *custodia* in 1791 sealed this chapter.

[74] Since Kino's time and the first forays into Pimería Alta, the intention had always been to reach the Gila River. Roughly between 1730 and 1750, the Jesuits in the missions of Pimería Alta,

this area actually formed part of an imperial strategy designed to link New Mexico with Sonora and California.[75]

In this context, the issues that orient Garcés's writings emerge from his goal to discover the nature of the frontier with the "gentiles" and to decide how it should be settled by the Spanish in order to achieve its effective incorporation into the king's domains. The first problem is approached only indirectly in his texts, as Garcés describes the skills of the inhabitants of that area and the forms of organization that he encountered during his travels there. Unlike the image of barbarism that de los Reyes had presented earlier, Father Garcés offers a more favorable portrait that extols the Pimas for their willingness to serve the Spanish "as older Christians would" and emphasizes such elements as agriculture, industry, dress, and trade, all of which constituted essential components of Spanish notions of civility:

> All of these peoples have large fields of wheat, some of corn, cotton, squash, and other crops with well-formed trenches for irrigation, with fields divided by common fencing and those of different owners separated with private ones. These Indians dress in cotton clothes that they make, or clothes of wool from their sheep, or brought from Moqui country.[76]

Beyond the lands of the Pimas around the Gila River, Garcés found these same features of industry and people's openness to receiving Christianity among the Opa, Yuma, Cajuenche, Cucapá, Jamajabe (Mojave), and other nations who lived in the territory between Sonora and California. Although divided by ancestral rivalries, Garcés believed it would be feasible to congregate these nations into a single enormous mission district guarded by a pair of presidios as, in effect, he proposed to Viceroy Bucareli in one of his reports. By presenting the frontier as a field open to new conversions, Garcés subsumed the individuality of each tribe in order to unite them in the evangelization program that he would

---

including Jacobo Sedelmayer, actively promoted this project and went so far as to offer the missions of Ostimuri to the Diocese of Durango in order to advance to the Gila River. The project had been authorized by royal decrees of November 13, 1744 and December 4, 1747, but was not implemented due to the Pima uprising of 1751. The issue would not be taken up again until the time of Fray Francisco Garcés. Burrus and Zubillaga, eds., *El Noroeste de México*, xv–xvi, 163–64, 211–16.

[75] Francisco Garcés, *Diario de Exploraciones en Arizona y California (1775–1776)*, ed. John Galvin (Malaga: Editorial Algazara, 1996), xi–xii. Garcés's proposal in this area was to found missions in the Gila River basin and establish a line of presidios between them and the Apache territory to better defend the new conquests. Fray Francisco Garcés to Fr. José del Río, San Xavier del Bac, March 8, 1771, AFPM, AQ, Letter K, leg. 14, no. 6.

[76] *Diario de exploraciones,* 19.

propose almost from the beginning of his assignment to Sonora. Showing little concern for the features proper to each one of the tribes that he encountered on his travels, this missionary seemed to be content to confirm the presence of external traits that evidenced the viability of establishing new missions.

Garcés's death, and those of other Franciscans at Río Colorado in 1781, would demonstrate to the believers in this missionary utopia that the frontier was neither peaceful nor particularly well-disposed to receiving Christianity.[77] Despite this setback, the missionaries from Querétaro maintained their conviction for several decades that because of its inhabitants' traits, the northern reaches of Sonora might well comprise the New Jerusalem to revitalize their proselytizing mission in New Spain. If Bishop de los Reyes had discarded Pimería Alta (due to the supposed lack of civility of its peoples) in order to concentrate his efforts on Opatería and Pimería Baja, the Franciscans from Querétaro took advantage of this territorial separation to carry out their Colegio's socioreligious project of occupying the area around the Gila and the Colorado Rivers.[78] During this stage, it fell to Fray Diego Miguel Bringas de Manzaneda[79] to promote this expansion by taking advantage of those Indians' good disposition:

---

[77] Fray Diego Miguel Bringas de Manzaneda, *Sermon que en las solemnes honras celebradas en obsequio de los VV. PP. Predicadores apostólicos, Fr. Francisco Tomás Hermenegildo Garcés, Fr. Juan Marcelo Díaz, Fr. José Matías Moreno, Fr. Juan Antonio Barreneche, misioneros del Colegio de Propaganda Fide de la Santa Cruz de Querétaro. . .* (Madrid: Imprenta de Fermin Villalpando, 1819).

[78] In this venture, the evangelical ideal was accompanied by the ambitious project of the Colegio de Querétaro and certain viceregal authorities to finally unite the frontier of New Spain all the way from New Mexico to Alta California. In such project, consolidating the Spanish dominion over northern Sonora was the key element: If they did not take advantage of the local Indians' willingness to receive the Spaniards they would run the risk of losing that strategic pass to the Apaches. The missionaries from Querétaro knew the importance of the role that their Colegio could play in this enterprise and insisted on the need to win over the gentiles for the province of Sonora right up to the end of the viceregal period. From 1800 to 1804, the Colegio de Querétaro continued to promote the cause of founding five missions among the Pimas Gileños to the archbishop of Mexico and the viceroy. In this cause, Fray Diego Bringas de Manzaneda was the representative of the Colegio and the principal promoter of expansion into Pimería Alta. AFPM, AQ, Letter K, leg. 18, no. 37.

[79] A Franciscan born in the mining district of Álamos (Sonora), son of a Spanish merchant. He was the chronicler of the *Colegio de Propaganda Fide de la Santa Cruz de Querétaro* and, in 1795, was sent as *visitador* to the missions in Pimería Alta to reform their mode of government. That same year, he was named *procurador apoderado* (procurator) of the Colegio de Querétaro to promote the founding of new missions along the Gila and Colorado Rivers. Some of his writings as *procurador* (including some materials cited in this chapter), were translated to English and published in Daniel S. Matson and Bernard L. Fontana, eds., *Friar Bringas Reports to the King: Methods of Indoctrination on the Frontier of New Spain, 1796–1797* (Tucson: University of Arizona Press, 1977).

The Gileños . . . are diligent, given to work, they live from their industry, cultivate their fields, and . . . with the crude work of [cultivating] their lands with
stakes, they make them produce harvests of a variety of grains, [including]
corn, wheat, beans, and other vegetables that the Spanish cultivate. They also
cultivate cotton and know how to spin and weave it, which gives them such
succor that many of them walk about decorously dressed. The skins that they
know how to soften skillfully, the cotton fabrics and their grain harvests, is the
sum total of the form of trade they have with us and with some of the nearby
gentiles. . . . Their towns are firmly established . . . [and] their fields are metic-
ulously and solidly fenced and worked with devotion.[80]

In his defense of this project, Father Bringas took up the distinction
between a Christian Sonora and the frontier area using the pro–Pimería Alta
perspective to favor the interests of his colegio. For Father Bringas, the notion
of frontier missions emerged not only because of the location of those settlements beyond the reach of Spanish dominion but, more importantly because
they were inhabited and surrounded by "many heathens."[81]

Bringas's objective in his insistence upon demonstrating that the
Queretaran missions in Sonora were indeed of a frontier nature because of their
location, the tribes residing in and surrounding them, and their dedication to
propagating the faith, was to convince the monarch to support that institution's expansion towards the Gila and the Colorado Rivers and of the need to
maintain the governing regime of the ancient missions.[82] The map that this
missionary drew in 1795 offers a visual synthesis of his reasoning. In the center
of his drawing, Bringas placed the zone inhabited by the Pápagos (Papaguería),
an extensive area between the Altar River and the confluence of the Gila and
the Colorado Rivers, flanked to the east and south by the line of Queretaran
missions. By placing his college's missions precisely in this marginal situation,
Bringas managed to create the effect that those establishments were sur-

---

[80] Fray Diego de Bringas to the commander of the Internal Provinces, Chihuahua, March 7,
1796, AFPM, AQ, Letter K, leg. 18, no. 27.

[81] Fray Diego de Bringas to the king, 1796, AFPM, AQ, Letter K, leg. 18, no. 25, paragraph 21.

[82] This "ancient method of government" was the one established in the Jesuit period, when
the missionaries were in charge of both the spiritual and temporal administration of the missions.
In contrast to this form of government, in other mission areas the friars had been separated from
the administration of mission properties and limited to participating in the control and discipline
of the Indians. Indeed, the failure of the Queretaran missions in Yuma territory in 1781 was due,
as Father Bringas argued, to the fact that they had been founded in 1779 on the basis of the
maxims of this new method of government, and not in accordance with the "method accredited
by experience and good results." *Informe de fray Diego Bringas*, paragraph 64.

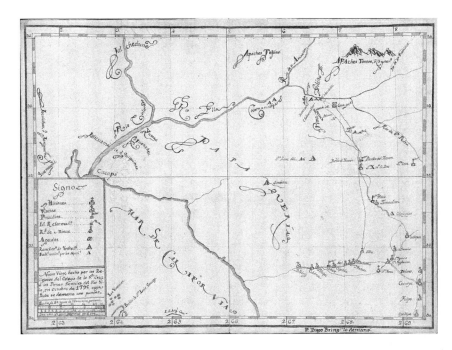

MAP 1.5. New Spain's northwestern frontier by Fray Diego de Bringas, 1795 (Source: Fr. Diego de Bringas, Nuevo Viaje hecho por los Religiosos del Colegio de la Santa Cruz a los Pimas Gentiles del Rio Gila. . . , original in Harold B. Lee Library, L. Tom Perry Special Collections, Map Vault Mss 30)

rounded by Pimas, Pápagos, and Apaches. But, more importantly, they represented a setting in which the Papaguería appeared to be a virgin territory for Spanish expansion to the northwest, a fact that would facilitate communications with Alta California (Map 1.5).

A halfway point between de los Reyes's contempt and the utopian vision of the missions by Garcés and Bringas is found in the writings of Fray Francisco Antonio Barbastro, a missionary with strong links to both the Colegio de Querétaro and the Sonoran missions. During the phase in which his influence over the organization of the Queretaran missions in Pimería Alta was greatest,[83]

[83] We can distinguish three periods of Fray Antonio Barbastro's tenure in Sonora, stages in which he experienced a different approach to the province of Sonora and that translated into distinct concerns and ways of relating to his environment. Here, I focus on his characterization of Sonora while he was president of those missions, after dissolving the custody of Sonora in 1791. Barbastro's missionary career began in Sonora around 1773, when he was assigned to the mission

Barbastro pointed out the differences between the mission districts of Pimería
Alta and Pimería Baja in terms not only of the maturity of their respective doctrinal programs, but principally as a function of their demographic composition, productive dynamics, and forms of government.

Unlike the local custom of dividing the area between the Altar and the
Gila Rivers into Papaguería and Pimería Alta, Barbastro defined the entire
region as simply Pimería Alta, "because all of its inhabitants, both Christian
and gentile, are of the [Pima] nation."[84] Thus defined, the Pimería was not
only the territory in which the Pima missions were located, but also the homeland of both the Christian and gentile Pimas who lived in northern Sonora. It
was clear to Barbastro that notable differences existed between this area and
Pimería Baja, evidence of two processes of colonization opposed in both conception and execution.

The climate of Pimería Alta could be extremely cold or hot, conditions that
caused life-threatening diseases.[85] Also latent along that frontier was the
Apache threat, although these factors had not prevented the missions from
making certain inroads in terms of the materials used in the construction of
people's houses and in the spiritual improvement of the Indians. In fact,
Barbastro was by no means hesitant to point out that things were actually
going much better in Pimería Alta than in the missions located in outlying areas
or *tierra afuera*:

---

at Ures, though he was later transferred to Tubutama. In 1777, he was named president of the
Queretaran missions in Sonora and in 1783 rose to the position of vice-custos of the Sonoran custody. While occupying these posts he was in charge of the organization and government of the missions; this was Barbastro's most important phase of epistolary activity and the period in which he
wrote the most voluminous and important texts concerning his trajectory. Toward 1795, however,
his star began to fade as he was mentioned in rumors of abuse and mismanagement of the missions
and had to confront the distrust of the discretory of the college and the scrutiny of Father Bringas,
who was sent *ex professo* to determine the state of the missions in Pimería Alta. From that time until
his death in Aconchi in 1800, Barbastro devoted his time to defending his administration in Sonora
and to promoting the Franciscan Third Order that he had founded in the town of Aconchi. For a
biography of Father Barbastro, see Gómez Canedo, *Sonora hacia fines*, 9–18; Fray Juan Domingo
de Arricivita, *Crónica seráfica y apostólica del Colegio de Propaganda Fide de la Santa Cruz de
Querétaro*, Part Two (Mexico City: F. de Zúñiga y Ontiveros, 1792); and the collection of
Barbastro's letters in AFPM, AQ, Letter K, leg. 16, 2nd portion.
    [84] Gómez Canedo, *Sonora hacia fines*, 51. Beyond the linguistic affinity cited by Barbastro as
a defining element in Pimería Alta, there were important links between the arid landscape and the
inhabitants of that region. James Griffith has shown that for the Tohono O'odham (Pimas) local
topography had a special meaning in religious terms; spirituality, Griffith writes, was the "key link
between people and places." James Griffith, *Beliefs and Holy Places. A Spiritual Geography of the
Pimería Alta* (Tucson: University of Arizona Press, 1992).
    [85] Gómez Canedo, *Sonora hacia fines*, 57.

All of the missions and annexed towns have communal oxen and all of the utensils needed to cultivate the land. . . . [A]ll the towns and missions have quite decent churches. . . , they have been introduced to the use of mortar and brick that the Indians did not know and have erected *a fundamentis* with these materials[, including] . . . various [churches] with beautiful domes, like something never before seen, not only in Pimería but even throughout Sonora, causing admiration and stimulating people to praise God.[86]

If the solidity of those sacred buildings was such that it deserved comment, the security provided by the houses of Indian families was also a motive for satisfaction for Barbastro. In contrast to the image of those ranches that de los Reyes had formed years earlier, when he criticized them as being little more than a "poorly formed tangle of branches," Barbastro presented an image of settlements designed to resist the severe conditions of the frontier: "The Indians live in houses of adobe with doors, and many have locks with keys, [while] others close the door using a stick in the form of a brace that they know how to make. All the towns that are more open to enemy invasions are surrounded by walls. . . ."[87]

Barbastro attributed these advances to the fact that the missions in Pimería Alta had conserved "the old government," that is, communal property and labor to which they added a supply system of merchandise from Mexico City supervised by the Colegio de Querétaro itself. However, in accordance with the recommendations of de los Reyes, the ancient administrative regime had been eliminated in Pimería Baja and, from that moment forward, according to Barbastro,

> [t]he Ópatas make every effort to ensure that the minister does not learn of their sins. . . . They hear it said and have learned that the priest is there only to celebrate Mass and to confess, that he has nothing to do with them, and other similar things. Thus it is that they work only two half-days and however they want, that they wander around anywhere they please with nothing to tie them down, because it is said that they are free, not slaves.[88]

Barbastro concluded that conditions in Pimería Baja had deteriorated because the old method of government had been replaced. In the missions of Pimería Alta, in contrast, "the method is conserved, and with the method what is there is maintained."

---

[86] *Ibid.*, 54, 61.
[87] *Ibid.*, 56–57.
[88] *Ibid.*, 72.

Apparently, Barbastro's argument was not just the product of empty rhetoric with which he was attempting to defend his performance as the director of those missions, as his detractors adduced. In fact, the intendant of Sonora himself, Enrique Grimarest, seemed to share Barbastro's thoughts, as shown by a report sent to Viceroy Revillagigedo in 1790 that ratified the division of Sonora in two zones administered by "methods of government" that produced different results. Although he does not explicitly mention Pimería Baja and Opatería, the intendant indicated that those missions in which the mode of government employed by the Jesuits had been altered and the communal regime abolished indeed faced imminent ruin. So serious was the situation that it was urgent to proceed with secularization. In Pimería Alta, however,

> [t]he priests from Queretaro have maintained [the Indians] dedicated and in good order, their churches in a regular state of decency, and the properties [they] administer well-arranged, so it seems to me that it would not be convenient to make changes; for if they have not prospered more it has been without question due to the continuous hostility of the Apache[s]. . . .[89]

With the end of the colonial period, the differences that had emerged between the populations of Pimería Alta and central Sonora in previous decades became even more acute. As the independent governments made their presence felt, support for mission programs was drastically reduced and the privileges that the *pueblos de indios* had enjoyed were curtailed due to the prolonged conflicts among various parties at both the national and state levels of government.

By 1835, it had become clear that in Sonora the fiscal and administrative disorder of the new Mexican nation had impeded the consolidation of settlement projects in Pimería Alta, Pimería Baja, and Opatería. Moreover, in addition to the problems that the recently formed government had inherited from the previous regime, new conflicts arose around such issues as the incorporation of certain Indian groups as citizens of the new nation-state and the redistribution of communal lands.[90] That year, an experienced soldier from Sonora, Ignacio Zúñiga, wrote a summary of the decadent aspect that Sonora had acquired in recent times, in which he confirmed that the two zones of settlement mentioned above were more distant than ever before in terms of the

---

[89] Report by Enrique Grimarest to Viceroy Revillagigedo, Arizpe, August 16, 1790, BNFF, 35/771. This account was solicited by the viceroy on January 5, 1790, to corroborate the situation described by the bishop of Sonora, Fray Antonio de los Reyes, in his report dated September 15, 1784.

[90] Radding, *Wandering Peoples*, 171–207.

character of their inhabitants, the solidity of their towns, and the essence of the problems that assailed them.[91]

In central Sonora, the idea of the existence of Opatería was rapidly diluted by the growing number of nonindigenous people who settled there and by drawn-out conflicts over land. As far as Zúñiga was concerned, the region that other observers had identified as Opatería was then perceived as a collection of towns inhabited by "another one of the subject tribes," that were to be found "disseminated in the main, central part of the state, in its most densely populated and richest parts."[92] However, it was not just that such a particular geographical entity had disappeared from the perspective of people like Zúñiga. The Ópata nation itself was acquiring new traits as a result of its contact with other groups: "The spirit of union that once distinguished the Ópatas has ended; and the addictions and vices that emanate from the contact and the mixing with other races have gained an invincible ascendancy in their morale.... [M]ost of them dress as do the *gente de razón*, whose manner they adopt without rejection."[93] In these places, most of which were no longer under the direction of Xaliscan missionaries, a substantial number of *vecinos* lived among the Indians, a situation provoking an unending chain of conflicts over the usurpation of land and the thorny problem of determining which people had rights to the land to be redistributed after the communal properties were broken up. Many towns, Zúñiga wrote, "either have no Indians of pure origin, or those who would pretend to be so are not Indians at all, or . . . [the Indians] are so few and of such small numbers that it would be unjust and prejudicial for them to accumulate land in their hands."[94]

In Pimería Alta, in contrast, the towns maintained the juridical status of missions. It was there that "[the] most backward [Indians] in terms of the development of their abilities and those who have least acquired the uses of the *gente de razón*" were to be found.[95] Except for the towns of Imuris, San Ignacio, and Magdalena, cultural change in Pimería Alta was barely visible to Zúñiga, who was of the opinion that those settlements had known better times before Mexican Independence, when Indian *justicias* were in office and their properties were managed by the friars. It was only in Imuris, San Ignacio, and Magdalena where one could find a "respectable neighborhood" that had pros-

---

[91] Ignacio Zúñiga, *Rápida ojeada al estado de Sonora: Dirigida y dedicada al Supremo Gobierno de la Nación por el Lic. . .* (Mexico City: Imprenta de Juan Ojeda, 1835).

[92] *Ibid.*, 52.

[93] *Ibid.*, 55.

[94] *Ibid.*, 54.

[95] *Ibid.*, 59.

Map 1.6. *Mapa del Departamento de Sonora* by E. Varga de Dèèsi, 1855

pered through trade in flour and cattle, which promised to make the secularization of those missions viable.

The rest of Pimería Alta should continue as mission territory, Zúñiga suggested, as a means to strengthen Sonora's defense against the Apaches.[96] However, this part of Zúñiga's idea did not last very long. By 1855, when the last Franciscans left Sonora, a number of ranches and new villages surrounded

---

[96] *Ibid.*, 21, note 19. "The conservation of the missions or towns between or around the presidios is of great importance . . . as there are always in each one a respectable number of armed warriors that would come very opportunely to the defense of the country; and that also [functioned] as supply points for the presidios. . . . For these reasons, the Spanish government provided with magnificence for the establishment of these colonies that have been administered with zeal and wisdom by the missionaries from Querétaro."

the northernmost old mission towns, thus representing the dominant feature in the construction of a new Sonoran landscape (Map 1.6).

THE REINVENTION OF SONORA

The texts summarized in this chapter demonstrate the wide variety of ways in which witnesses from different epochs narrated what they considered the most important features of their milieu and the principal challenges imposed on them. It is true that these accounts conceal the deeds and thoughts of many people, that is, those who were unable to make their impressions reach the main circles of the viceregal government. Nevertheless, upon analyzing these sources in their totality, certain patterns appear to indicate what might have been the way in which diverse sectors of the Sonoran population were integrated or distanced by factors yet to be explained.

The chronicles and reports portraying the Sonoran landscape show that the province's transformation in those texts derived from the confluence of diverse projects emanating from different personal and community circumstances. To affirm that the ongoing reinvention of Sonora was a product of the frontal collision between the interests of missionaries and civil colonists would be tantamount to ignoring the experiences that each particular witness lived in different moments. The richness of the Sonoran landscape's evolution during the final years of the colonial period does not rest on the changes that one personage or another might have influenced. Instead, biases, intellectual acumen, and corporate interests are represented in the processes of change. As addressed in the following chapters, this is not just a history of certain changes in Sonora; it is the history of different groups of people caught up in a context of change.

From the earliest Jesuit reports examined here up to the final references to mission administration in Sonora, it is possible to identify three major cycles in the contact between Indians and Spaniards: (1) the opening up of new spaces for settlement, (2) the evangelization of local Indians, and (3) the cultural transformation of Indians and Spaniards. It is important to clarify here that the identification of these processes in no way assumes that they occurred in chronological order. Quite the contrary—what the sources discussed here reveal is that although there may well have been phases in which all three processes were present at the same time, it is evident that each one had special relevance in certain contexts. To mention one example: In the early eighteenth century, the primordial concern of recent arrivals in Sonora was to define the zones of occupation in order to bring to fruition different settlement projects, a phenomenon that found expression in the duality between "open" and "populated" spaces analyzed above. The arrival of the Franciscans in Sonora, the creation of the diocese of the same name, and discussions of reforms of the method of mission government presupposed, in contrast, successive moments for the evaluation of the advances of Christianity and the heightening of the distinction between Christians and "gentiles." At the close of the colonial era, discussion centered on integrating local ethnic groups into Hispanic-Mexican society and exploiting the dualism between groups that were integrated into national life and those still in the process of assimilation.

During the final decades of the eighteenth century, the distinction between Pimería Alta and adjacent areas was made more evident than ever before. In fact, Sonora ceased to be a mission frontier in its totality and began to be imagined by its inhabitants as a province whose northern border happened to house a series of frontier missions. This great transformation confirmed that the Sonoran landscape was constructed and lived from diverse personal situations.

An essential question related to this development is why, upon the arrival of the Franciscans, did the occupation of Sonoran territory no longer seem to be a motive for conflict between Spaniards and Indians? How is the coincidence between this apparent truce and the important gap found in the chronology of land grants in Sonora between the mid-eighteenth and early nineteenth centuries to be understood? Another relevant point is to understand the exact significance of assigning mission towns to the category of Christian or gentile in the late eighteenth century, and whether this interest in classifying the Indians was related to what Salvador Álvarez has identified as the transformation of indigenous populations from conquered to tributary towns, which led up to their consolidation as Indian towns (*pueblos de indios*).[97] Finally, what was the impact of disputes over land tenure and the demographic recomposition of the Indian communities upon widening the membership of the citizenry in the early nineteenth century? In order to understand the dimensions of these reaccommodations during the Franciscan period, in the following chapters four lines of inquiry are taken up to evaluate the demographic, cultural, economic, and institutional changes in the three mission zones described herein (Pimería Alta, Pimería Baja, and Opatería).

---

[97] Salvador Álvarez, "El pueblo de indios en la frontera septentrional novohispana," *Relaciones* 95 (2003): 115–64.

CHAPTER 2

Population Trends in the Mission Districts of Sonora

> While the aboriginal cultural pattern of the area south of the Pápago may never be known with any detailed accuracy, one fact is immediately apparent in nearly every group within the boundaries. This is the overwhelming Hispanicization that has significantly remade the cultural complexions and even influenced the physical types of these people.[1]

For several decades now, many recognized scholars have focused their research efforts on establishing reasonable calculations of the size of the aboriginal population in the Americas at the moment in which they came into contact with the European conquerors, and on determining the fate of those groups in the centuries that followed. With reference to northwestern New Spain, studies by Sauer and Gerhard suggest that at the moment of contact the population living between the Yaqui and the Gila Rivers had reached perhaps 85,000 to 125,000 inhabitants.[2] From the sixteenth century on, the series of epidemics caused by Euro-Asiatic diseases (smallpox, measles) that raged through central Mexico drastically reduced the number of inhabitants in northwestern New Spain as well. Following the trade routes introduced by the Spanish, and the patterns of movement of certain indigenous groups and European explorers, those epidemics led to the demographic collapse and social disintegration of the northwestern peoples.[3] The decline of Indian pop-

---

[1] Thomas B. Hinton, "Southern Periphery: West," in *Handbook of North American Indians: The Southwest*, vol. 10, ed. Alfonso Ortiz (Washington, DC: Smithsonian Institution, 1983), 318.

[2] Gerhard gives the lowest figure, *La Frontera Norte*, 310; Carl Ortwin Sauer, *Aboriginal Population of Northwestern Mexico* (Berkeley: University of California Press, 1935), 5.

[3] Robert H. Jackson, *Indian Population Decline: The Missions of Northwestern New Spain, 1687–1840* (Albuquerque: University of New Mexico Press, 1994), 3; Daniel T. Reff, *Disease, Depopulation and Culture Change in Northwestern New Spain, 1518–1764* (Salt Lake City: University of Utah Press, 1991), 98, 102–19.

ulations in northwestern New Spain has largely been associated with a combination of epidemics and conditions imposed by mission life.[4]

Some studies have also focused on new forms of social organization and the increasing mobility that indigenous peoples developed during the colonial period.[5] This last framework is here explored in an attempt to expand our understanding of the complexities of demographic change in frontier societies. In the Sonoran case, in addition to the abovementioned causes of population loss, emphasis is put on the human costs of seasonal migrations, wars against Indian rebels, and Indian attacks on mission towns.

The objective in this analysis comprises not only determining the causes of the indigenous population decline, but, in addition, elucidating what happened to those Indians who managed to survive the epidemics, rigors, and privations that were endemic to colonial society.

Any study of demographic change in the Franciscan mission districts of Sonora depends primarily on two types of documentary sources: ecclesiastical records (baptisms, marriages, and burials), and population counts (*padrones*) that various authorities, both civil and ecclesiastical, generated periodically. In the specific case of Sonora, data of the first type for most mission towns have disappeared and complete series that have been preserved are indeed rare in number. The scanty nature of these sources has not, however, prevented some authors from succeeding in establishing the rhythms of population change in certain communities of northwestern New Spain.[6] As if the scant or fragmentary nature of these sources were not problematic enough, such records present an additional difficulty, which is especially important in the context of frontier societies. Because of their very nature, such sources were incapable of capturing the magnitude of the migratory movements characterizing those societies, phenomena that can be appreciated much more clearly in formal pop-

[4] Sherburne Cook, *The Extent and Significance of Disease among the Indians of Baja California from 1697 to 1773* (Berkeley: University of California Press, 1935); Cook, *The Conflict between the California Indians and White Civilization* (Berkeley: University of California Press, 1976); Sauer, *Aboriginal Population*, 12–13. Robert Jackson has argued that factors both biological and nonbiological contributed to such changes, attributing them primarily to the following causes: disease, poor hygienic conditions, stress of mission life, and the decline in women's fertility. Henry Dobyns, in turn, adds that those alterations were exacerbated by "the depredations of hostile Indians (Seri, Pima, Apache) or . . . pressures of the increasing numbers of Spaniards in the area." Robert Jackson, "Demographic Change in Northwestern New Spain," *The Americas* 41:4 (1985): 462–79; Jackson, *Indian Population Decline*, 55–56; Henry Dobyns, *Spanish Colonial Tucson: A Demographic History* (Tucson: University of Arizona Press, 1976), 133–38.

[5] Reff, *Disease*, 244–49; Spicer, *Los Yaquis*, 7, 20–31.

[6] Dobyns, *Spanish Colonial Tucson*; for Opatería, Cynthia Radding has analyzed changes in family structures in *Wandering Peoples*, 103–68.

ulation counts. Although their elaboration was seldom based on systematic or uniform practices, the series of censuses and head counts that have survived to the present have the advantage of offering a broader view that allows us to isolate, at least in general terms, certain moments of demographic growth or decline. Although it is true that these sources lack the degree of precision required to carry out detailed analyses of population phenomena such as birth indices, death rates, or marriages, they suffice to exemplify and allow a comparison of more general demographic trends over large geographical areas. For all of these reasons, this chapter presents a comparative review of the available population censuses and head counts from mission districts located in the Pimerías and Opatería. The purpose is to pinpoint the zones and moments in which demographic changes affecting the Indian population took place in those mission districts. This analysis, then, provides a point of reference for the explanation of several other processes related to the decay of the Franciscan mission regime in Sonora.

THE FRANCISCAN MISSIONS IN SONORA AFTER 1767

After the expulsion of the Jesuits, the Indian populations in the mission districts of Pimería Alta, Pimería Baja, and Opatería experienced a steady decline. At the same time, however, the records clearly reflect a continuous increase of residents of Spanish extraction and of people from other population groups (especially mestizos and blacks). These tendencies were not uniform throughout these three districts, because such factors as epidemics, raids by rebel Indians, regional variations in Franciscan administration, and indigenous mobility affected each mission complex in varied ways and degrees.

In order to analyze demographic change in these mission districts, data from the 1765–1850 period have been carefully examined and compared. Specifically, this examination is based on the following sources: ninety population counts (*padrones*) covering the years 1766, 1768, 1774, 1783, 1784, and 1795; and eleven population lists compiled by mission districts for the years 1765, 1774, 1794, 1799, 1802–1819, and 1850.[7]

Analyzing these sources was anything but unproblematic. Of the ninety censuses mentioned above, only thirteen that correspond to 1766 and ten from

---

[7] The difference between these two sets of sources consists in the fact that the population lists only indicate the number of residents for individual towns or mission districts without any additional information. The population counts or *padrones*, in contrast, offer more detailed data about one or more of the following: number of members of each family, age, gender, ethnicity, occupation, and names of the residents of individual towns.

1768 include detailed information on the number of families, the number of members per family, and the name, age, and sex of each person. The other sixty-seven only identify ethnic composition and indicate the number of families that lived in each town. The criterion used to convert data on families into the actual number of inhabitants posits an average of four individuals per family. This figure appears most consistently in the records that the missionaries themselves used to elaborate some of the censuses examined herein.[8]

Unfortunately, many population lists drafted by the friars combined the data that refer to individual *pueblos de visita* with the global information on their corresponding *cabeceras*. This circumstance led to expressing the results of the analyses of those sources in terms of mission districts (*i.e.*, *cabecera* plus *visitas*). Nonetheless, when the information available allows it, data for individual towns will be presented.

Pimería Alta

According to recent estimates of the population of Pimería Alta in the late seventeenth century, approximately 8,600 Indians resided there. However, a population count in that region ordered by José de Gálvez around 1768 indicates that only 2,018 Indians and 178 Spanish settlers were living in Pimería Alta. Almost a century later, José Francisco Velasco, a retired politician who devoted part of his life and fortune to the compilation of statistics for northern Mexico, indicated that those proportions had been radically inverted, and that Pimería Alta had become a predominantly Spanish area.[9]

Jackson's estimates indicate a gross population decline of 54 percent between 1519 and 1700, that is, a reduction from 50,000 to 23,000 people in the Pimería Alta. This second figure dropped to 4,000 Indians living in the same area by 1760.[10]

While the population figures available for Pimería Alta certainly confirm the demographic decline established in the literature on this topic, they also allow us to appreciate the timing of certain phenomena associated with population change

---

[8] This conversion factor is lower than the one used by Carl Sauer (6 persons per family) in his estimates of this area's aboriginal population, which is clearly too high for the population in the sixteenth century. Peter Gerhard, meanwhile, based his calculations on a conversion factor of 3.8 persons per family. Sauer, *Aboriginal Population*, 2; Gerhard, *La Frontera Norte*, 485, note 28.

[9] Jackson, *Indian Population Decline*, 57; José Francisco Velasco, *Noticias Estadísticas del Estado de Sonora* (Hermosillo: Gobierno del Estado de Sonora, 1985), 142.

[10] Jackson, *Indian Population Decline*, 57.

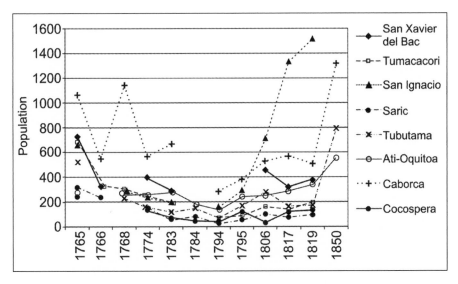

GRAPH 2.1. Population trends in Pimería Alta: total population, 1765–1850 (Source: Table 2.1)

in this area. Table 2.1 and Graph 2.1 demonstrate reduction of the total population in the northern reaches of Sonora, a tendency that reached its lowest point around 1794 (perhaps 1,002 inhabitants), before entering a period of sustained recovery that extended through at least the first half of the subsequent century.

In this particular context, however, certain elements suggest that these demographic changes in Pimería Alta cannot be attributed solely to factors such as disease or falling birth rates brought on by psychological factors. Those tendencies must also be considered in terms of, for example, the cost in human lives that local groups had to pay as a consequence of late eighteenth-century military campaigns.[11] In many cases, Indian allies were uprooted from their towns, enlisted as soldiers, and killed in such military campaigns. Likewise, no available figures represent the number of Indians who did not return due to a wide variety of other reasons.

The mission Indians in Pimería Alta participated in military actions against the Apache and Seri Indians. In January 1780, for example, Pima Indians

[11] In that period, "war rather than pacification had become the prevailing mode of subduing intractable nomads." Weber, *The Spanish Frontier*, 214. For a more detailed analysis of the war against rebel Indians in northwestern New Spain, see the section entitled "Pluriethnic bands in Sonora" in Chapter 3.

TABLE 2.1. Population of mission districts in Pimería Alta, 1765–1850

	1765–1766		1766	1768	1772	1774			1779			1783		
	I	S	I	n	n	I	S	n	I	S	n	I	S	n
San Xavier	399	—	187	166	260	160	0	160	—	—	—	132	40	172
Tucson	331	—	139	—	n.d.^a	239	0	239	—	—	—	112	4	116
N	730	—	326	—	—	399	0	399	—	—	—	244	44	288
Guevavi^b	111	172^c	—	54	86^d	—	—	—	—	—	—	—	—	129
Tumacácori	199	—	82	70	93	98	19	117	—	—	—	117	12	—
Calabazas	116	—	93	77	64	138	0	138	—	—	—	63^d	—	—
Sonoitac	91	—	95	110	94^d	—	—	—	—	—	—	—	—	—
San Ignacio	98	131^e	—	149	148	128	16	144	—	—	—	96	60	156
Imuris	326	—	—	40	39	30	0	30	—	—	—	16	—	—
Magdalena	107	—	—	92	86	57	10	67	—	—	—	28	—	—
N	531	—	—	281	273	215	—	—	—	—	—	140	—	—
Saric	212	—	136	—	137	157	7	164	236	4	240	68	4	72
Aquimuri	67	—	82	—	58^d	—	—	—	—	—	—	—	—	—
Busanic	41	—	24^d	—	—	—	—	—	—	—	—	—	—	—
Tubutama	368	—	—	166	176	96	19	115	96	56	152	40	36	76
Sta. Teresa	156	—	—	62	52	49	0	49	60	0	60	44	—	—
N	524	—	—	228	228	145	19	164	156	56	212	84	—	—
Ati	142	—	—	146	137	96	0	96	164	0	164	76	4	80
Oquitoa	131	—	—	127	106	105	52	157	196	40	236	127	76	203
N	273	—	—	273	243	201	52	253	360	40	400	203	80	283
Caborca	556	—	302	564	632	211	25	236	292	20	312	232	56	288
Pitiqui	269	—	132	310	360	202	8	210	272	28	300	179	61	240
Bisanig	241	—	117	271	271	122	0	122	172	0	172	138	4	142
N	1,066	—	551	1,145	1,263	535	33	568	736	48	784	549	121	670
Cocospera	133	—	—	—	110	133	9	142	—	—	—	68	8	76
Suamca	114^d	—	—	—	—	—	—	—	—	—	368	—	—	—
Altar^g	—	—	—	—	—	—	—	—	—	—	—	—	—	—
Terrenate^g	—	411	—	—	—	—	—	—	—	—	—	—	—	—
Tubac^g	—	421	—	—	—	—	—	—	—	—	—	—	—	—

TABLE 2.1. (continued)

	1784			1794	1795			1802			1806		1817		1819		1850
	I	S	n	n	I	S	n	I	S	n	I	S	I	S	I	S	n
San Xavier	93	13	106	—	121	56	177	363	37	400	—	—	—	—	—	—	—
Tucson	—	82	—	—	77	—	—	—	—	—	414	44	287	37	318	62	—
N	—	95	—	—	198	—	—	—	—	—	—	—	—	—	—	—	—
Guevavi[b]	—	—	—	—	—	—	—	—	—	—	—	—	—	—	—	—	—
Tumacácori	53	—	—	69	87	32	119	76	102	178	83	80	105	35	123	73	—
Calabazas	—	—	—	—	—	—	—	—	—	—	—	—	—	—	—	—	—
Sonoitac	—	—	—	—	—	—	—	—	—	—	—	—	—	—	—	—	—
San Ignacio	103	80	183	109	38	134	172	108	48	156	—	—	—	—	—	—	949
Imuris	11	—	—	—	—	21	—	—	—	—	—	—	—	—	—	—	—
Magdalena	28	—	—	51	49	51	100	—	—	—	108	609	36	1,300	49	1,470[f]	896
N	142	—	—	—	—	206	—	—	—	—	—	—	—	—	—	—	897
Saric	48	32	80	40	45	17	62	25	5	30	25	80	25	55	19	81	—
Aquimuri	—	—	—	—	—	—	—	—	—	—	—	—	—	—	—	—	—
Busanic	—	—	—	—	—	—	—	—	—	—	—	—	—	—	—	—	—
Tubutama	19	—	—	29	40	95	135	41	68	109	—	—	—	—	—	—	800
Sta. Teresa	34	—	—	38	26	7	33	—	—	—	66	207	35	130	28	150	—
N	53	104	157	67	66	102	168	—	—	—	—	—	—	—	—	—	—
Ati	37	—	—	40	32	—	—	—	—	—	—	—	—	—	—	—	—
Oquitoa	29	—	—	99	57	156	213	113	149	262	106	146	126	163	144	194	—
N	66	112	178	139	89	—	—	—	—	—	—	—	—	—	—	—	560
Caborca	71	—	—	125	145	35	180	—	—	—	—	—	—	—	—	—	610
Pitiqui	123	—	—	60	63	12	75	—	—	—	—	—	—	—	—	—	—
Bisanig	138	—	—	100	118	11	129	—	—	—	—	—	—	—	—	—	—
N	332	24	356	285	326	58	384	—	—	—	—	—	—	—	—	—	709
Cocospera	48	—	—	45	68	64	132	417	75	492	422	114	393	175	362	149	—
Suamca	—	—	—	—	—	—	—	69	80	149	20	16	87	36	103	36	—
Altar[g]	—	—	—	—	—	—	—	—	—	—	—	—	—	—	—	—	—
Terrenate[g]	—	—	—	—	—	—	—	—	—	—	—	—	—	—	—	—	—
Tubac[g]	—	—	—	—	—	—	—	—	—	—	—	—	—	—	—	—	1,009[h]

NOTES TO TABLE 2.1.

Note: Blank cells indicate abandoned towns; an em dash is used when sources do not include data on a particular town.

I, Indians; S, Spaniards (includes *gente de razón* and castes); *n*, total population (I + S); *N*, population of mission district (*cabecera* and *visitas*).

a "More than two-hundred families."

b Around 1774 the *cabecera* of this mission was transferred to Tumacácori.

c *Gente de razón* living at Guevavi, Santa Bárbara, and Buenavista.

d Abandoned as a result of Indian raids.

e *Gente de razón* in Santa Ana.

f Includes three ranches and five towns of Spanish residents.

g Presidio.

h Includes Tucson.

Sources: 1765–1766 in Pedro Tamarón y Romeral, *Viajes pastorales y descripción de la Nueva Vizcaya* (Madrid: Aguilar, 1958), and Hubert H. Bancroft, *History of the North Mexican States and Texas*, vol. 1 (New York: Bancroft Company, n.d.), 563; 1766 in AGN, Archivo Histórico de Hacienda, leg. 17, exp. 31; 1768 in AFPM, AQ, Letter K, leg. 14, no. 7; 1772 in BNFF, 32/663; 1774 in AGN, Californias, vol. 39, exp. 2; 1779 in Roque de Medina's inspection to Altar presidio, AGI, Guadalajara 272; 1783 in AGI, Guadalajara 348; 1784 in BNFF, 34/759; 1794 in AGN, Misiones, vol. 2, exp. 2, and AGN, Provincias Internas, vol. 5, f. 365; 1795 in AFPM, AQ, Letter K, leg. 18, no. 17; 1802 in AGI, Mexico 2736; 806 in BNFF, 37/829; 1817 in AGN, Misiones, vol. 3, exp. 3; 1819 in AGN, Misiones, vol. 3, exp. 36; 1850 in *Memoria en que el gobierno del Estado Libre de Sonora da cuenta de los ramos de su administración...* (Ures: Imprenta del Gobierno del Estado a cargo de Jesús P. Siqueiros, 1850).

from San Xavier del Bac were recruited to accompany Pedro de Allende, captain of the presidio at Tucson, in his forays against rebellious natives (called *mariscadas*). At the end of that year, some sixty Desert Pimas who lived in Pitiquito, Caborca, and Bisanic appeared beside Pedro Tueros, captain of the presidio at Altar, in a campaign against the Seris.[12] A report dated June 30, 1781, tells us that forty-four of them returned home.[13] In the 1780s, the company of Pima Indians from San Ignacio proved to be one of the most valuable auxiliary units to participate in defending the inhabitants of Santa Ana, Real de la Cieneguilla, and the presidio at Altar, and even pursued the Apaches into the far-off sierra.[14] Although official reports indicate that the defense mounted by the Pima Indians from San Ignacio was usually effective, the latter were not always blessed with good fortune, as described in the following note dated 1785:

[12] AGI, Guadalajara 271.

[13] *Ibid.*, Guadalajara 267.

[14] *Ibid.*, Guadalajara 518, Guadalajara 520.

On January 11th, the Apaches stole 50 animals from the area around . . . San Ignacio where the company of Pima Indians was formed. Pursued by [the Pimas] [through] dispersals and skirmishes, [the Apaches] lured them into a major ambush in which 18 were made victims of their inconsideration. . . , [O]n the [12th] [the Apaches] repeated the [damage] once again by stealing 125 head of cattle from the mission.[15]

Unfortunately, there is no way of calculating with certainty the cost in human lives for the population of Pimería Alta that resulted from, first, attacks by rebel Indians, and, second, the military campaigns sent out to combat them. Nevertheless, the demographic records surviving from around the time that this policy of offensive warfare ended indicate a gradual population recovery among the people of Pimería Alta. Graph 2.2 demonstrates that in the late 1780s and early 1790s, the population of the area began to show an upward tendency, a process coinciding in time with peace negotiations between the Apaches and the authorities of the Comandancia General of the Internal Provinces. By 1786, Commander Jacobo Ugarte y Loyola was promoting the relocation of Apache families to Bacoachi, and from that time forward, the offensive war gave way to attempts at negotiating a series of accords with those Indians.[16] In addition to that policy, the late 1790s witnessed a new resolve in Franciscan efforts to establish Pápago Indians on the missions located in that region, which up to then had been inhabited predominantly by Gila River Pimas.

The change in ethnic composition confirms the recovery of indigenous population numbers as reflected in the censuses that date from the same period. Mission districts such as San Xavier del Bac and Tumacácori are examples of this process because, while the 1784 census describes residents there as Pima Alto Indians, the population count of 1795 identifies the inhabitants of both districts as predominantly Pápagos, with only a few Pima Altos.[17] Despite this late eighteenth-century recovery, the early years of the nineteenth century once again saw the population of the mission districts in the Pimería Alta decline.

At that time, only San Xavier del Bac and Caborca managed to sustain a resident Indian population of perhaps two hundred to three hundred individuals, while all other towns there saw their numbers fall to only a handful of families. A document from 1845 states that "Bisani, a *visita* of Caborca, has no

---

[15] *Ibid.*, Guadalajara 520.

[16] *Ibid.*, Guadalajara 521. AGN, Provincias Internas, vols. 225 and 234, contain accounts of the resources destined for the families of Apaches who settled in Bacoachi between 1787 and 1791.

[17] BNFF, 34/759; AFPM, AQ, Letter K, leg. 18, no. 17.

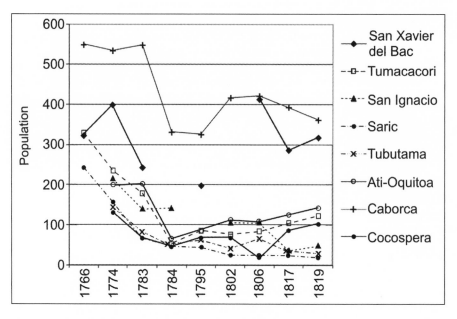

GRAPH 2.2. Indian population per mission district in Pimería Alta, 1765–1819 (Source: Table 2.1)

indigenous families. . . , Pitiquito [has] eight [or] ten families, and Oquitoa the same number. Saric has none, as it is depopulated."[18]

   Parallel to these movements among the indigenous peoples, the late eighteenth and early nineteenth centuries also witnessed a sustained—though generally modest—increase in the non-Indian population of Pimería Alta (Graph 2.3). One exception was the mission district of San Ignacio, where the non-Indian population increased from 80 in 1784 to 1,470 in 1819. Although data from 1850 do not specify the ethnicity of those inhabitants, it is not unreasonable to assume that most of the district's 2,732 inhabitants were either recently arrived settlers who had been drawn to the zone by the growing availability of mission lands in the 1820s and 1830s, or descendants of the Spanish population already registered there in the early nineteenth century.

---

[18] Velasco, *Noticias Estadísticas*, 129.

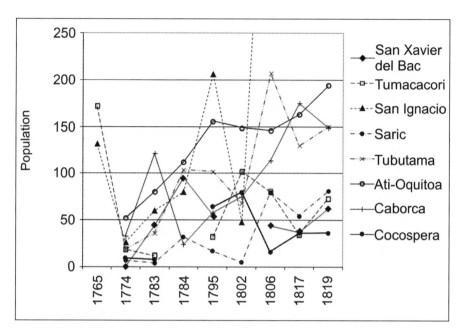

GRAPH 2.3. Hispanic population per mission district in Pimería Alta, 1765–1819 (Source: Table 2.1)

PIMERÍA BAJA

Thanks to its location in the southeastern part of Sonora, where the Yaqui River to the south formed a natural corridor between the desert and the sierra, the Pimería Baja region was one of the earliest zones of Indian–Spanish contact in Sonora. As early as 1619, the Jesuits had begun their missionary labor in this area, finding upon their arrival just over ninety Indian villas or towns.[19]

The territory to the north of the Yaqui River between the Gulf of California and the Sierra Madre was home to two indigenous groups marked by contrasts. On the one hand, there were the Seri Indians, a nation of nomadic gatherers and fishermen whose lands covered the westernmost part of Sonora along the coastline of the Gulf of California between the mouths of the Mátape and the Concepción Rivers.[20] From very early times, the Seris had rejected the Spanish presence in their territory and they tenaciously resisted cultural assim-

[19] Sauer, *Aboriginal Population*, 24; Ortega Noriega, "El sistema de misiones," 61.
[20] Thomas Bowen, "Seri," in Ortiz, *Handbook*, 230–37.

ilation throughout the colonial period. To the east of Seri territory lived a group that the Spanish identified as "Nevome" until 1678. Thereafter they were known as Pima Bajos.[21] At the time of Spanish contact, the Pima Bajo Indians inhabited the valleys of the Sierra Madre Occidental between Yécora and Tutuaca, including pueblos located along the middle reaches of the Yaqui River and the region around the confluence of the Sonora and the San Miguel Rivers.[22] Unlike their Seri neighbors, the Pima Bajos showed little reluctance to participate in the agricultural and mining activities of the Spanish settlers or to involve themselves in the Jesuit mission regime. By 1619 they were supervised by Jesuit priests in the mission districts of Ures, Cumuripa, Tecoripa, Ónavas, Movas, and Ónapa, and in the pueblo of Nacameri, which pertained to the *cabecera* of Opodepe in Opatería. According to estimates by Campbell W. Pennington, Pimería Baja was at that time inhabited by perhaps six thousand Indians who spoke the Nevome language, although Spicer posits that the Pima Bajo population in the nine Jesuit mission districts totaled only slightly more than four thousand in 1678.[23]

The growing influx of Spanish settlers into Pimería Baja in the early years of the seventeenth century, and their constant attempts to secure Indian land and labor, triggered serious tensions among missionaries, colonists, and Indian residents leading to recurring episodes of violence. Indeed, the Seri rebellions of 1725, 1749, 1760–1764, and 1766–1768, as well as the Pima Bajo uprisings that broke out in 1737 and 1751, constituted one of the most serious problems in Indian–Spanish relations in the entire area.[24] Nonetheless, despite the latent peril of Indian uprisings, by 1769 the non-Indian population in the region had climbed back to around eight hundred inhabitants.[25]

Although the Jesuit regime had succeeded in keeping the Spanish population away from their mission districts, in the years after the expulsion of the

[21] Campbell W. Pennington, *The Pima Bajo of central Sonora, México* (Salt Lake City: University of Utah, 1989), 1–6.

[22] Timothy Dunnigan, "Lower Pima," in Ortiz, *Handbook*, 218.

[23] Pennington, *The Pima Bajo*, 32–37, especially 36; Edward Spicer, *Cycles of Conquest: The Impact of Spain, Mexico and the United States on the Indians of the Southwest, 1533–1960* (Tucson: University of Arizona Press, 1962), 89.

[24] Ortega Soto, "La colonización española," 208–16; José Luis Mirafuentes Galván, *Movimientos de resistencia y rebeliones indígenas en el norte de México (1680–1821)* (Mexico City: Universidad Nacional Autónoma de México, 1989), 17–60.

[25] Spicer, *Cycles of Conquest*, 89. According to reports by José Francisco Velasco, in that year the non-Indian population of Pimería Baja included perhaps 192 settlers, though Peter Gerhard claims that this population may have reached 7,000 in the 1760s. Velasco, *Noticias estadísticas*, 141; Gerhard, *La Frontera Norte*, 353.

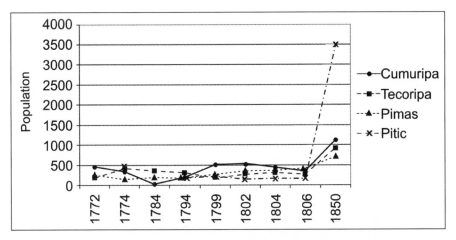

GRAPH 2.4. Population of selected mission districts in Pimería Baja, 1772–1850 (Source: Table 2.2)

Society of Jesus (1767) the Indian population began to decrease rapidly as a result of epidemics, rebellions, and, above all, ongoing assimilation into the Spanish domain. The data available to document this are synthesized in Table 2.2 and Graph 2.4.

These charts present information from the Ures, Onavas, Cumuripa, Tecoripa and Ónapa mission districts (the latter of which was secularized in 1767), to which the new missions at San José de Pimas and El Pitic would be added in 1771 and 1773, respectively.[26] The figures presented in these charts are lower than those compiled by other authors because they include only the mission districts of Pimería Baja, and do not take into account the population that resided in mining centers, haciendas, and villages located beyond the reach of missionary administration.[27]

The establishment of missions at San José de Pimas and El Pitic in the early 1770s marked an attempt by viceregal authorities to concentrate the Seri Indians in places where they could be monitored more closely and assimilated into Spanish society. Despite their best efforts, however, the people they

[26] Data for the town of Nacameri (Pimería Baja) have been included in this and subsequent sections because the reports by Franciscan friars added the population there to that of Opodepe (Eudeves and Ópatas), the *cabecera* of the mission of the same name.

[27] In his calculations of the Indian population of Pimería Baja in general, Gerhard estimates that from 1765 to 1800 the group declined from 3,500 to just 1,800 individuals. Gerhard, *La Frontera Norte*, 352.

Table 2.2. Population of mission districts in Pimería Baja, 1765–1850

	1765–1766	1768	1772	1774			1775			1784			1794		
	I	I	n	I	S	n	I	S	n	I	S	n	I	S	n
Onavas	520	532	530	595	8	603	599	0	599	350	—	—	—	—	—
Tonichi	372	396	398	296	17	313	296	17	313	210	—	—	—	—	—
Soyopa	221	209	213	177	34	211	177	34	211	126	0	—	—	—	—
Cumuripa	180	102	136	82	0	82	83	0	83	28	0	28	—	—	—
Buenavista[a]	299	163	327	188	80	268	188	64	252	—	—	—	—	—	—
Suaqui[b]	—	—	—	—	—	—	—	—	—	—	—	—	—	—	—
N	479	265	463	270	80	350	271	64	335	—	—	—	150	49	199
Tecoripa	210	158	135	155	28	183	156	28	184	110	48	158	—	—	—
Suaqui	391	83	62	220	0	220	224	0	224	206	0	206	—	—	—
N	601	241	197	375	28	403	380	28	408	316	48	364	—	—	—
San José de Pimas	190	267	276	160	0	160	172	0	172	208	12	220	234	78	312
Ures	236	278	317	267	99	366	347	150	497	316	>280	>596	170	20	190
Sta. Rosalía	53	100	99	92	14	106	98	15	113	62	0	62	—	—	—
N	289	378	416	359	113	472	445	165	610	378	>280	>658	—	—	—
Pitic	—	—	—	452	39	491	601	38	639	—	—	—	193	9	202
Omapa	33	—	—	—	—	—	—	—	—	—	—	—	—	—	—
Taraichi	50	—	—	—	—	—	—	—	—	—	—	—	282	12	294
Yécora	—	—	—	—	—	—	—	—	—	—	—	—	—	—	—
N	—	—	—	—	—	—	—	—	—	—	—	—	—	—	—
Nacameri (visita of Opodepe)	113	—	34	49	290	339	48	294	342	19	>320	>339	—	—	—
Buenavista[d]	—	—	—	—	—	—	—	—	—	—	—	—	—	—	—

Table 2.2. (continued)

	1799			1802			1803			1804			1806			1850
	I	S	n	I	S	n	I	S	n	I	S	n	I	S	n	N
Onavas	—	—	—	—	—	—	—	—	—	—	—	—	—	—	—	1,093
Tonichi	—	—	—	—	—	—	—	—	—	—	—	—	—	—	—	683
Soyopa	—	—	—	—	—	—	—	—	—	—	—	—	—	—	—	511
Cumuripa	68	92	160	—	—	—	—	—	—	—	—	—	—	—	—	626
Buenavista[a]	—	—	—	—	—	195	320	291	611	57	398	455	45	313	358	—
Suaqui[b]	201	163	364	—	—	326	—	—	—	—	—	—	—	—	—	500
N	269	255	524	—	—	521	—	—	—	—	—	—	—	—	—	—
Tecoripa	135	70	205	—	—	287	—	—	—	—	—	—	—	—	—	921
Suaqui																
N	—	—	—	—	—	—	—	—	—	—	—	—	—	—	—	—
San José de Pimas	177	75	252	—	—	287	131	150	281	128	191	319	102	170	272	726
Ures	—	—	—	—	—	364	198	165	363	201	166	367	174	213	387	3,767
Sta. Rosalía																
N	—	—	—	—	—	—	—	—	—	—	—	—	—	—	—	—
Pitic	214	0	214	—	—	155	163	0	163	165	0	165	184	0	184	3,503
Omapa																
Taraichi	64	0	64	—	—	69	—	—	—	—	—	—	—	—	—	—
Yécora	76	22	98	—	—	87	127	27	154	97	25	122	82	0	82	201
N	—	—	—	—	—	—	—	—	—	—	—	—	—	—	—	—
Nacameri (*visita* of Opodepe)	44	319	363	—	—	423	—	—	—	—	—	—	—	—	—	1,567
Buenavista[d]	—	—	—	—	—	—	—	—	—	250	927	1,177	—	—	—	—

[a] Sometime after 1783 Buenavista was separated from the Cumuripa mission district. The *capellán* (parish priest) of the recently founded presidio at Buenavista took charge of local residents' religious instruction.

[b] Once a *visita* of the Tecoripa mission, Suaqui was annexed as a *visita* of Cumuripa after dissolution of the San Carlos de Sonora custody.

[c] Abandoned as a result of Indian raids.

[d] Presidio.

I, Indians; S, Spaniards (includes *gente de razón* and castes); *n*, total population (I + S); N, population of mission district (*cabecera* and *visitas*).

Sources: See Table 2.1; 1765–1766 in Bancroft, *History of the North Mexican States*, vol. 1, 572–76; 1768 in AFPM, AQ, Letter K, leg. 14, nos 7–8; 1775 in Fr. MCC 201, exp. 5; 1799 in BNFF, 36/802; 1802 in AGI, Mexico 2737; 1803 in BNFF, 36/815; 1804 in AGI, Mexico 2736; data on Buenavista presidio (1804) in BNFF, 31/644.

Note: Blank cells indicate abandoned towns; an em dash is used when sources do not include data on a particular town.

brought together in those two missions did not remain for very long. In fact, what most characterized the Seri Indians in these zones was their back-and-forth movement between their original territory and the mission towns, and not their permanent residence in the latter. Their rejection of the mission regime, zeal to preserve their autonomy, and desire to flee from the yoke imposed by the living conditions in the missions led to frequent escapes from those two places. One such incident—the most important one to appear in the records—took place in Pitic in the early 1780s in reaction to an outbreak of smallpox that had decimated the local population. By mid-1781, such occurrences had become such a concern to local authorities that the commander general of the Internal Provinces reported to the court of Madrid that one of the most urgent matters those territories faced was that "the Seri Indians of Pitic continue to die of smallpox."[28] In the aftermath of the epidemic, the residents of Pitic who had survived became convinced they were no better off in the mission than they would be in the coastal mountains, so by early 1784 they had abandoned the mission:

> On the night of [February] nineteenth, the Seri Indians who were there fled from Pitic, leaving behind all they had. In the morning, the troops followed them, but brought back only two boys, who had been abandoned as they could not [run] away. . . .[29]

Although this mission was re-established at a later date, the number of Seri Indians residing in Pitic (even short term) never returned to levels of the early 1770s (about 450 people). Similar to the situation at Pitic, the indigenous population of other mission districts in Pimería Baja also experienced a gradual decline in clear contrast with an increase in the number of Spanish and other non-Indian settlers (Graphs 2.5 and 2.6). Demographic change in this zone is exemplified by the mission districts of Cumuripa, Tecoripa, and San José de Pimas, where by 1774 the Indian population had dropped by 805 individuals and then by 318 more by 1806. According to the conservative estimate of a contemporary official, by 1850 only 30 or 40 indigenous families remained in those mission districts,[30] while, again in stark contrast, the non-Indian population living in those same mission districts had increased from 108 to 696 in the 1774–1806 period.

---

[28] AGI, Guadalajara 267.
[29] Report by Felipe de Neve, Arizpe, April 5, 1784, AGI, Guadalajara 518.
[30] Velasco, *Noticias Estadísticas*, 129.

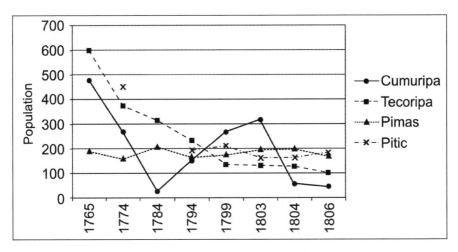

Graph 2.5. Indian population of selected mission districts in Pimería Baja, 1765–1806 (Source: Table 2.2)

In addition to these demographic changes that clearly reveal the decline of the Indian population and an increase in the numbers of nonindigenous residents, certain towns in Pimería Baja apparently experienced a process of ethnic recomposition in the late eighteenth century.

Apache raids, Indian uprisings, and epidemics had led the missionaries, on various occasions, to move groups of families or even entire populations from one site to another, thus altering the map of the traditional territories that at one time pertained to the various Indian peoples. One noteworthy case is Nacameri, a town of Pima Bajo Indians whose population was identified as Eudeve in the 1784 report of Bishop de los Reyes, which, in addition, makes no mention whatsoever of the previous residents.[31] It is not clear whether the town of Soyopa was originally a Eudeve or Pima Bajo community. Pennington is inclined to accept the first hypothesis, although some censuses (e.g., 1774 and 1784) identify the local population there as Pima Bajo. He holds that it was originally a Eudeve settlement that had absorbed some Pima Bajos. Leaving this discrepancy to one side, it is known that by 1793 Soyopa was

[31] Pennington affirms that at the time of Indian–Spanish contact, Nacameri was inhabited by the Pima Bajo. *The Pima Bajo*, 9. The 1774 census cited in Table 2.2 mentions only Pima Bajo, while the 1784 population count and the list of missions compiled by Viceroy Revillagigedo in 1793 allude only to Eudeves. Conde de Revillagigedo, *Informe de las misiones, 1793* (Mexico City: Editorial Jus, 1966), 34.

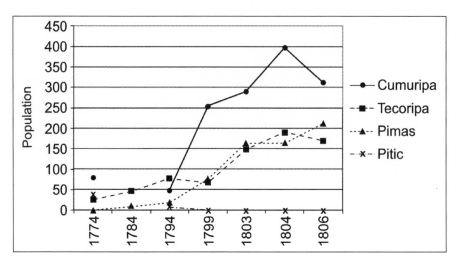

GRAPH 2.6. Hispanic population of selected mission districts in Pimería Baja, 1774–1806 (Source: Table 2.2)

clearly Eudeve.[32] It seems that up to the seventeenth century Nuri was associated with the Cahita towns of northern Sinaloa, but during the eighteenth century the Pima Bajos displaced the original inhabitants there or reoccupied this place, because by 1793 Nuri was reported as a locale populated by Pima Bajos.[33] After the Jesuit exodus, several Ópata families were settled in Ures. They appear in the records from 1774, 1784, and 1793, although there are indications that they abandoned the town definitively in 1795.[34] These population shifts, together with those that took place in Opatería in the same period are presented at the end of this chapter in Maps 2.1 and 2.2.

OPATERÍA

In the strict sense of the term, the mountainous portion of the area of Sonora located east of the San Miguel River and north of Pimería Baja did not constitute a bounded territory, nor was it identified by its inhabitants as a common ethnic space. Rather, three different ethnic groups (Jovas, Eudeves, and Ópatas) coexisted there in zones of occupation that could still be distin-

[32] Pennington, *The Pima Bajo*, 28.
[33] Revillagigedo, *Informe*, 33; Pennington, *The Pima Bajo*, 25.
[34] BNFF, 36/800; Revillagigedo, *Informe*, 34.

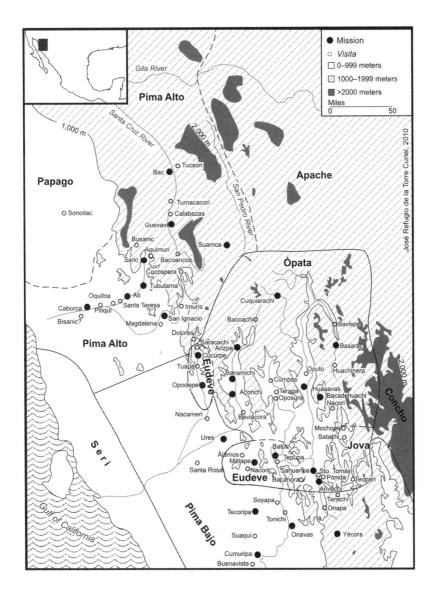

MAP 2.1. Distribution of ethnic groups in Sonora, ca. 1700 (Adapted from Pennington, *The Pima Bajo*, n.p., and West, *Sonora*, 17)

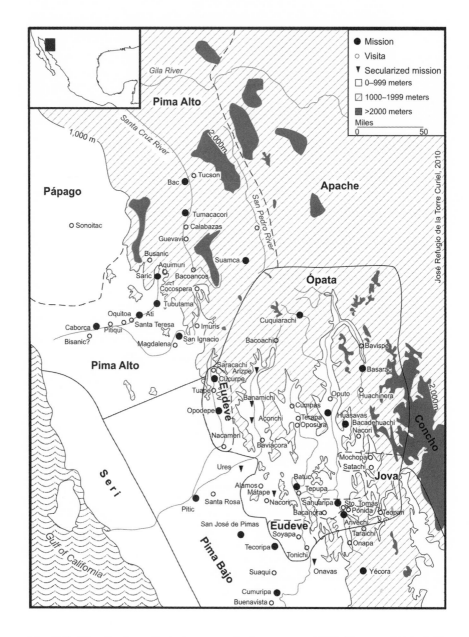

MAP 2.2. Distribution of ethnic groups in Sonora, ca. 1795 (Source: Table 2.3)

guished until at least the mid-eighteenth century.[35] The linguistic affinity among these peoples, plus the fact that by the early nineteenth century the Jovas and Eudeves seem to have become assimilated with other populations, have led to the common practice of identifying this territory as a zone of Ópata occupation, often called Opatería.[36] To the southeast of this zone, in the ravines found between the Yaqui and the Aros Rivers, Jova Indians inhabited small *rancherías* , whose numbers in the early eighteenth century have been estimated at 5,000.[37] Separated from this zone by a small valley west of the Sahuaripa River, a number of Eudeve settlements were located "in the head-water areas of the Mátape and the Junta Rivers, along the southern course of the Moctezuma River just before it joins the Yaqui River, and along the Yaqui River north of Tonichi."[38] A second Eudeve cluster of villages was located north of Opatería, along a portion of the San Miguel River, between Opodepe and Saracachi (see Maps 2.1, 2.2, and 2.3).[39] According to Sauer's estimates, the indigenous population of Opatería proper and the two Eudeve clusters may have been as high as 60,000 in the early seventeenth century, although more conservative estimates put it at around 20,000.[40]

From very early times, the mountain valleys of the areas discussed in this section had been one of the most attractive zones for establishing Spanish settlements. This circumstance, added to the evident disposition of the local

---

[35] By mentioning only Jovas and Ópatas, Sauer gave rise to the modern use of equating Eudeves and Ópatas as a single group. Sauer, *Aboriginal Population*, 26–29. Hinton identifies the Eudeves as a subgroup of the Ópatas, differentiated only by minor linguistic variations, while considering the Jovas an "intermediate people . . . identical to the Opatas." Hinton, "Southern Periphery: West," 320–22.

[36] The censuses from the early nineteenth century are revealing with respect to the possible mixing of Jovas and Eudeves with other groups. For example, the censuses of 1803 and 1806 mention only Ópatas, Pimas, and Seris as residents of the missions in the area. BNFF, 36/815; BNFF, 37/829. According to Sauer, the Jovas "were being absorbed by the Ópata at the time the Jesuits came into the country." Sauer, *Aboriginal Population*, 26. Cynthia Radding suggests that the gradual "disappearance" of the Jovas in the late colonial years may have been due to several factors: "A small minority may have taken an Ópata identity; some may have joined the growing mass of *naborías* and *mestizos* who labored in the mines and haciendas; and still others may have adopted the nomadic life of the Apaches." *Wandering Peoples*, 150.

[37] Sauer, *Aboriginal Population*, 26.

[38] Pennington, *The Pima Bajo*, 16.

[39] Sauer states that this region was inhabited by Ópatas and makes no mention of Eudeves. Carl Sauer, *The Distribution of Aboriginal Tribes and Languages in Northwestern Mexico* (Berkeley: University of California Press, 1934), 48. Ethnographic studies in recent decades have established that the area of interest here was inhabited by three different peoples of the Uto-Aztecan family, thus refuting the idea that the Jovas and Eudeves were subgroups of the Ópatas. Pennington, *The Pima Bajo*, 16–18; Braniff, *La frontera*, vol. I, 162; Radding, *Wandering Peoples*, 24.

[40] Sauer, *Aboriginal Population*, 29; Hinton, "Southern Periphery: West," 320.

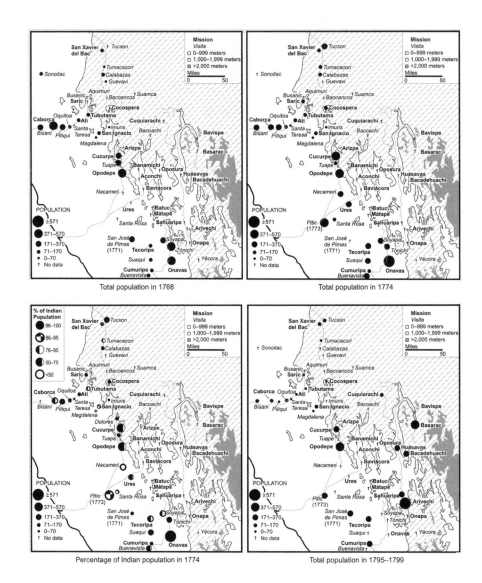

MAP 2.3. Population growth in Sonoran missions, 1768–1799

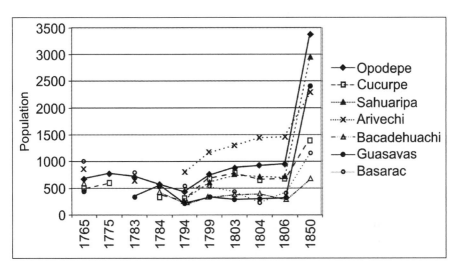

GRAPH 2.7. Total population of selected mission districts in Opatería, 1765–1850 (Source: Table 2.3)

Indians to cooperate with the new settlers, contributed to Opatería becoming the site of perhaps the most intense and long-lasting interethnic contacts in Sonora. Table 2.3 and Graphs 2.7 and 2.8 show the rapid increase of Spanish and other non-Indian colonists in the mission districts of this zone, and improve understanding of the factors that drove the transformation of the mission regime in the nineteenth century. Unlike other mission districts, the primary cause of the Indian population's decline in Opatería was a process of miscegenation that emerged as a result of, on the one hand, the proximity of nonindigenous groups to Indians and, on the other, the inclination of the Ópata, Jova, and Eudeve peoples to adopt Spanish ways and customs. As a congressman from Sonora observed in 1822, the number of Ópatas was "notoriously shrinking, and humanity cannot find solace in the fact that this reduction [in numbers] stems from their mixing with other castes."[41]

Due to their location in the roughest terrain of the Sonoran sierra and consequent vulnerability to repeated attacks by Apaches, the mission districts of Baserac, Bacadehuachi, and Huásavas showed rapid decline of the indigenous population (Graph 2.9). The Indian population at Baserac, for example, suffered a severe collapse: 87.3 percent between 1783 and 1786, from 801

[41] Juan Miguel Riesgo, *et al.*, *Memoria sobre las proporciones naturales de las provincias internas occidentales* (Mexico City: Imprenta de D. José Ramos Palomera, 1822), 50–51.

Table 2.3. Population of mission districts in Opatería, 1765–1850

	1765–1766		1766			1775			1783		
	I	S	I	S	n	I	S	n	I	S	n
Opodepe	413	—	—	—	—	300	140	440	288	80	368
Nacameri	113	—	—	—	—	48	294	342	30	320	350
N	526	153[f]	—	—	—	348	434	782	318	400	718
Cucurpe	141	—	—	—	—	300	108	408	—	—	—
Tuape	173	—	—	—	—	158	0	158	—	—	—
N	314	188	—	—	—	458	108	566	—	—	—
Sahuaripa	140	—	154	18	172	—	—	—	119	204	323
Sto. Tomás	—	—	60	12	72	—	—	—	114	—	—
Teopari [a]	121	—	106	4	110	—	—	—	—	—	—
N	—	52	320	34	354	—	—	—	—	—	—
Arivechi	112	—	247	199	446	—	—	—	236	152	388
Bacanora	163	—	187	173	360	—	—	—	112	184	296
Pónida	131	—	—	>200[b]	—	—	—	—	—	—	—
N	406	44[b]	—	>572[b]	—	—	—	—	—	—	—
Batuco	210	—	229	159[c]	388	—	—	—	—	—	—
Tepuspe	163	—	170	0	170	—	—	—	—	—	—
N	373	30[d]	399	159	558	—	—	—	—	—	—
Bacadehuachi	208	—	—	—	—	—	—	—	80	—	—
Nácori chico	208	—	—	—	—	—	—	—	—	—	—
Mochopa	183	—	—	—	—	—	—	—	—	—	—
N	599	—	—	—	—	—	—	—	—	—	—
Arizpe	393	—	354	93	447	—	—	—	—	—	—
Chínapa	296	—	339	84	423	—	—	—	—	—	—
Bacoachi	92	—	117	54	171	—	—	—	—	—	—
Aconchi	205	—	—	—	—	—	—	—	283	22	305
Baviácora	294	—	—	—	—	—	—	—	247	56	303
N	499	—	—	—	—	—	—	—	530	78	608
Mátape	114	—	—	—	—	—	—	—	124	52	176
Álamos	113	—	—	—	—	—	—	—	120	—	—
Nácori grande	108	—	—	—	—	—	—	—	72	28	100
N	335	—	—	—	—	—	—	—	192	—	—
Guásavas	205	—	266	18	284	—	—	—	187	10	197
Óputo	221	27	193	0	193	—	—	—	152	—	—
N	426	—	459	18	477	—	—	—	339	—	—
Basarac	546	—	—	—	—	—	—	—	323	—	—
Guachinera	200	—	—	—	—	—	—	—	162	—	—
Bavispe	259	—	214	0	214	—	—	—	316	—	—
N	1,005	—	—	—	—	—	—	—	801	—	—
Banamichi	158	—	246	8	254	—	—	—	—	—	—
Guépaca	129	—	177	0	177	—	—	—	—	—	—
Senoquipe	134	—	223	8	231	—	—	—	—	—	—
N	421	—	646	16	662	—	—	—	—	—	—
Cuquiárachi	115	—	52	12	64	—	—	—	—	—	—
Cuchuta	73	—	29	10	39	—	—	—	—	—	—
Teuricachi	82	—	61	0	61	—	—	—	—	—	—
Oposura	205	—	170	130	300	—	—	—	—	—	—
Cumpas	116	—	106	171	277	—	—	—	—	—	—
N	321	1,266[f]	276	301	577	—	—	—	—	—	—

Table 2.3. (continued)

	1784			1794			1799			1802
	I	S	n	I	S	n	I	S	n	n
Opodepe	137	100	237	—	—	—	286	120	406	456
Nacameri	19	>320	>339	—	—	—	44	319	363	423
N	156	>420	>576	341	96	437	330	439	769	879
Cucurpe	92	232	324	—	—	—	254	261	515	836
Tuape	63	0	63	—	—	—	199	0	199	293
N	155	232	387	230	40	270	453	261	714	1,129
Sahuaripa	102	—	—	—	—	—	81	420	501	146
Sto. Tomás	—	—	—	—	—	—	116	0	116	156
Teopari[a]	93	—	—							
N	—	—	—	71	197	268	197	420	617	302
Arivechi	43	—	—	—	—	—	123	534	657	894
Bacanora	—	—	—	—	—	—	157	161	318	416
Pónida	22	—	—	—	—	—	191	0	191	—
N	—	336	—	464	343	807	471	695	1,166	—
Batuco	134	—	—	—	—	—	—	—	—	—
Tepuspe	73	—	—	—	—	—	—	—	—	—
N	207	308	—	—	—	—	—	—	—	—
Bacadehuachi	218	—	—	—	—	—	99	65	164	169
Nácori chico	116	—	—	—	—	—	112	22	134	105
Mochopa	107	—	—	—	—	—	48	0	48	58
N	441	24	465	173	51	224	259	87	346	332
Arizpe	—	—	—	—	—	—	—	—	—	—
Chínapa	—	—	—	—	—	—	—	—	—	—
Bacoachi	78	80	158	—	—	—	49	397	446	566
Aconchi	230	—	—	—	—	—	—	—	—	—
Baviácora	116	—	—	—	—	—	—	—	—	—
N	346	640	986	—	—	—	—	—	—	—
Mátape	170	—	—	—	—	—	—	—	—	—
Álamos	111	—	—	—	—	—	—	—	—	—
Nácori grande	93	—	—	—	—	—	—	—	—	—
N	374	320	694	—	—	—	—	—	—	—
Guásavas	170	—	—	—	—	—	184	13	197	192
Óputo	145	—	—	—	—	—	139	0	139	120
N	315	240	555	198	34	232	323	13	336	312
Basarac	142	—	—	—	—	—	215	25	240	260
Guachinera	78	—	—	—	—	—	128	0	128	148
Bavispe	—	—	—	—	—	—	106	50	156	147
N	—	—	—	381	124	505	449	75	524	555
Banamichi	111	—	—	—	—	—	—	—	—	—
Guépaca	67	—	—	—	—	—	—	—	—	—
Senoquipe	120	—	—	—	—	—	—	—	—	—
N	298	>320	>618	—	—	—	—	—	—	—
Cuquiárachi	—	—	—	77	15	92	—	—	—	—
Cuchuta	—	—	—	—	—	—	—	—	—	—
Teuricachi	—	—	—	—	—	—	—	—	—	—
Oposura	202	—	—	—	—	—	—	—	—	—
Cumpas	130	—	—	—	—	—	—	—	—	—
N	480[g]	440	920	—	—	—	—	—	—	—

Table 2.3. (continued)

	1803			1804			1806			1850
	I	S	*n*	I	S	*n*	I	S	*n*	*n*
Opodepe	—	—	—	—	—	—	—	—	—	1,815
Nacameri	—	—	—	—	—	—	—	—	—	1,567
N	334	543	877	364	565	929	378	580	958	—
Cucurpe	—	—	—	—	—	—	—	—	—	—
Tuape	—	—	—	—	—	—	—	—	—	—
N	376	371	747	331	332	663	378	300	678	1,435
Sahuaripa	—	—	—	—	—	—	—	—	—	2,340
Sto. Tomás	—	—	—	—	—	—	—	—	—	621
Teopari[a]										—
N	89	668	757	190	537	727	241	461	702	—
Arivechi	—	—	—	—	—	—	—	—	—	1,190
Bacanora	—	—	—	—	—	—	—	—	—	692
Pónida	—	—	—	—	—	—	—	—	—	411
N	712	587	1,299	509	938	1,447	518	940	1,458	—
Batuco	—	—	—	—	—	—	—	—	—	1,050
Tepuspe	—	—	—	—	—	—	—	—	—	—
N										
Bacadehuachi	—	—	—	—	—	—	—	—	—	530
Nácori chico	—	—	—	—	—	—	—	—	—	142
Mochopa	—	—	—	—	—	—	—	—	—	—
N	268	115	382	280	125	405	201	102	303	—
Arizpe	—	—	—	—	—	—	—	—	—	1,491
Chínapa	—	—	—	—	—	—	—	—	—	—
Bacoachi	60	531	591	423	530	953	458	564	1,022	1,145[e]
Aconchi	—	—	—	—	—	—	—	—	—	1,427
Baviácora	—	—	—	—	—	—	—	—	—	1,475
N	—	—	—	—	—	—	—	—	—	—
Mátape	—	—	—	—	—	—	—	—	—	1,062
Álamos	—	—	—	—	—	—	—	—	—	883
Nácori grande	—	—	—	—	—	—	—	—	—	582
N	—	—	—	—	—	—	—	—	—	—
Guásavas	—	—	—	—	—	—	—	—	—	2,412
Óputo	—	—	—	—	—	—	—	—	—	—
N	224	73	297	216	81	297	247	80	327	—
Basarac	—	—	—	—	—	—	—	—	—	517
Guachinera	—	—	—	—	—	—	—	—	—	100
Bavispe	—	—	—	—	—	—	—	—	—	543
N	336	108	444	178	64	242	102	286	388	—
Banamichi	—	—	—	—	—	—	—	—	—	1,186
Guépaca	—	—	—	—	—	—	—	—	—	1,524
Senoquipe	—	—	—	—	—	—	—	—	—	537
N										
Cuquiárachi	—	—	—	—	—	—	—	—	—	—
Cuchuta	—	—	—	—	—	—	—	—	—	—
Teuricachi	—	—	—	—	—	—	—	—	—	—
Oposura	—	—	—	—	—	—	—	—	—	2,447
Cumpas	—	—	—	—	—	—	—	—	—	1,309
N	—	—	—	—	—	—	—	—	—	—

Table 2.3 (continued)

Note: Blank cells indicate abandoned towns; an em dash is used when sources do not include data on a particular town.

[a] Abandoned as a result of Indian raids.

[b] Including *gente de razón* living in the valley of Tacupeto.

[c] *Gente de razón* living in the valley of Batuco (San Francisco, Santa María, and other rancherías).

[d] *Gente de razón* living in four settlements: Realito, La Mesa, Chihuahua, and Todos Santos.

[e] Includes Fronteras.

[f] Includes seven settlements: Conadepa, Jamaica, Yécora, Toiserobabi, Tombabi, Pinipa, Tepachi.

[g] Includes Terapa and Tepache.

I, Indians; S, Spaniards (includes *gente de razón* and castes); *n*, total population (I + S); N, population of mission district (*cabecera* and *visitas*).

Sources: See Table 2.2; 1766 in AGN, Archivo Histórico de Hacienda, leg. 17, exp. 24 and 31.

Indians to just 102. Figures for Bacadehuachi indicate a decline of 54.5 percent between 1784 and 1806, from 441 to 201. In Huásavas, meanwhile, the population decreased by 47.3 percent between 1766 and 1806, from 469 to 247. This tendency toward reduced Indian numbers in the final decades of the eighteenth century was less pronounced in Cucurpe (17.3 percent) and Sahuaripa (7.3 percent), while in the 1774–1806 period, the Indian population had recovered somewhat in Opodepe (8 percent increase), and in Arivechi (19.3 percent increase), although the latter was likely attributable to the influx of new mission Indians.

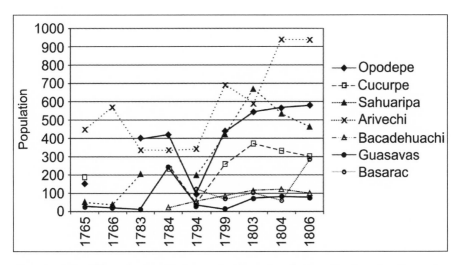

Graph 2.8. Hispanic population of selected mission districts in Opatería, 1765–1806 (Source: Table 2.3)

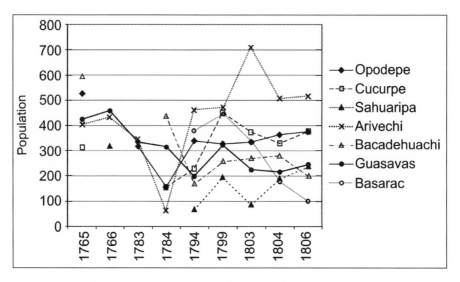

GRAPH 2.9. Indian population of selected mission districts in Opatería, 1765–1806 (Source: Table 2.3)

The sum of the tendencies in Indian and Spanish population changes in Opatería had cultural consequences of tremendous importance for the Ópata Indians. It is estimated that by the early 1850s, the various dialects of their language had disappeared. In the words of Thomas Hinton, the nineteenth century "saw the demise of the Ópata culture and the assimilation of the group."[42] The correlations among such cultural transformations, the demographic changes outlined above, and the dismantlement of the Franciscan mission regime form the focus of the following chapters.

[42] Hinton, "Southern Periphery: West," 321.

CHAPTER 3

Changes in the Lifeways of Indian Towns

After a lifetime devoted to crisscrossing the varied landscapes of Sonora on horseback and on foot, at times as a soldier, captain of a presidio, military judge, and even as a congressman and senator for the state, by 1835 Ignacio Zúñiga was highly qualified to give an account of the transformations during the last years of the colonial period through the advent of political independence. For Zúñiga, along with other members of Sonora's governing elite, it was important to emphasize the new terms upon which the relationship between certain indigenous peoples and the rest of Sonoran society was being erected.

> In other times, the Ópatas were considered apt to serve only as soldiers, as there was no other need and no other idea [that] fit into the narrow-minded politics of the viceregal government. . . . Today, everything has changed for them and ourselves [as] there is now a reciprocal interest between the government's commitments . . . and the demands of our new political situation that [the Indians] be of greater use to us, something that should work in favor of a reform of those tribes, who wish to attain their own well-being. . .[1]

Zúñiga's description of the redefinition of the Ópatas' role in early nineteenth-century Sonora derives from a utilitarian cultural perception marked by the prejudices that typified the mestizo society of the epoch. However, it also contains an observation that should not be dismissed out of hand. Many aspects of life among Indians and Spanish settlers had changed—"for them and for us"—as Zúñiga wrote, and each was seeking new ways of making sense of the relations that linked them at the dawn of the nineteenth century, whether by force, out of necessity, or simple convenience.[2]

---

[1] Zúñiga, *Rápida ojeada*, 58.
[2] A process that reminds us Hart's description of the cultural broker. Hart, "Black 'Go-Betweens'," 90.

Unlike other chapters in this book—in which the analysis focuses on demographic, economic, and administrative readjustments characteristic of the final decades of the mission regime in Sonora—here the discussion turns to the intertwining of three processes of continuity and change hinted at in the quotation from Zúñiga: the cultural transformations accompanying the process of the mission regimes' disintegration in Sonora, the consolidation of Spanish colonization by laypersons, and the adaptation of Indian communities in the face of threats to their survival personified by the arrival of political independence. In other words, this chapter explores the evolution of the symbiotic relation between mission residents and other individuals within Sonoran society during the closing years of the mission regime.[3] As contended in the following pages, that process involved a gradual change in the mission's social functions, which came to be assumed by the Spanish town and the hacienda. But more importantly, it also meant that mission residents' roles in local communities were altered. Indians not only became more actively involved in religious and economic activities that they already performed (acting as religious intermediaries and as workers on nearby haciendas and ranches), but they also switched their work, allegiances, and commitments to individuals outside the mission domain.

As in other contact zones between Indians and Europeans in North America, the Sonoran experience was the result of negotiations involving various historical transformations in process.[4] In order to demonstrate the complexity of this experience, I use the language of cultural transfers, cultural mediators, and changing identities in an attempt to present a dynamic image of the more elusive aspects of Indian–Spanish contact along New Spain's northwestern frontier. Changes in religion, forms of social organization, everyday life are topics analyzed in this chapter. My intention in taking up these scenarios of interethnic contact is to underscore the small-scale stories that are often

---

[3] "The relationship between mission and Spanish society was . . . [characterized] by interdependence and mutual benefits. It was a symbiotic one, so to speak. In exchange for the outstanding aid it got from [colonial authorities] . . . the mission was instrumental in regulating and keeping control over Indian populations that had not been fully assimilated by Spanish colonial society." Álvarez, "La misión y el indio," 35.

[4] In his works on the processes of cultural change in North America in the context of European imperial rivalries, James Axtell portrays the way in which the policies of settlement and the exploitation of natural resources assayed by the English and French propitiated diverse responses on the part of local Indians. The relations between the groups represented in that scenario, Axtell argued, were regulated by a principle of mutual and parallel influences. James Axtell, *The European and the Indian: Essays in the Ethnohistory of Colonial North America* (Oxford and New York: Oxford University Press, 1981); and *The Invasion Within: The Contest of Cultures in Colonial North America* (New York: Oxford University Press, 1985).

obscured behind institutional changes and to see in them the necessary coun-
terpoint to accounts of the demographic, financial, and political crises affecting
the frontier.

LOVING GOD IN INDIAN COUNTRY

In the colorful folklore of Mexico, it is said a person who finds him/her-
self in a tight spot amid adverse circumstances with almost no chance for success can truly appreciate what it means to "love God in Indian country." This
proverb—still common in contemporary Mexico—has a profound historical
backdrop that relates directly to the mission ventures undertaken in many different regions of New Spain. The case of the Franciscan experience in Sonora
perhaps illustrates the proverb's origins because, as discussed in this section,
neither the missionaries' attempts to win new converts among the Indians of
northern New Spain nor Indians' contact with clergymen were free of great
difficulty.

Around 1745, a Jesuit priest who had recently completed his inspection of
the provinces of Sinaloa and Sonora wrote that in the towns of Pimería Alta the
conversion of Indians was progressing slowly, although he found that some
Pima Alto, Sobaipuri and Pápago Indians had been Christianized, "but poorly,
as they conserve many of their heathen and barbarian idolatries."[5] Unlike
parishes in central Mexico, where superstition was one of the problems that
most concerned the clergy, missionaries in the frontier zones found idolatry to
be the main obstacle to Indians' acceptance of the new religion.[6] The precari-
ousness and vulnerability of Spanish settlements along that frontier, together
with the missionaries' own fragile position due to the isolated conditions of
their work, provided neither a stable strategy for counteracting the inclination

---

[5] *Descripción de las provincias de que se compone el gobierno de Sinaloa,* AGI, Indiferente 107,
t. 1. As William Taylor has documented for central Mexico, the recognition of the imperfect reception of Christian doctrine among the Indians by the clergy was a frequent phenomenon that illus-
trated the problems they faced in communicating to the faithful the relationship between the external signs of Christianity and their meanings. Moreover, it reflected the frustration that the clergy
felt upon seeing the external acts of Christianity "taken from their control and put to local uses."
Taylor, *Magistrates of the Sacred: Priests and Parishioners in Eighteenth-Century Mexico* (Stanford,
CA: Stanford University Press, 1996), 48–49.

[6] Taylor explains the difference between these two expressions as follows: "Idolatry and
superstition expressed an official Christian view of what was false in religion. Idolatry was a serious
deviation: rejection of the one, true God by the worship of alien gods, implicitly of Satan.
Superstition was a lesser, venial sin, more the product of ignorance than a willful violation of what
was correct or a rejection of God." Taylor, *Magistrates,* 48.

of the Pima Indians to conserve their animist beliefs and celebrate rituals designed to invoke rains or purify food, nor for diminishing their trust in the curative powers with which certain animals endowed them during their shamans' trances.[7]

For the Jesuits originally and, somewhat later for the Franciscans, the attempt to persuade the Pápago and Sobaipuri Indians to settle in towns and receive the rite of baptism were the first steps toward their eventual conversion. From the missionary perspective, the rite of baptism transformed them into new Christians, but, as experience would soon reveal, the ritual alone did not ensure that the Indians would become good Christian converts because they could so readily relapse into their ancient practices.[8]

In contrast to the situation in Pimería Alta, the opinion concerning the mission towns in Pimería Baja and Opatería was that the Indians there were good Christians known for their loyalty to the king and the Spanish, who showed no tendency toward preserving their ancient cults. It is probable that the opinion voiced by Fray Ángel Núñez (the Xaliscan missionary at Basarac) regarding the religiosity of the Ópata Indians was shared by other clergy as a means of explaining Christianity's apparent progress among those peoples. He was convinced that in antiquity the Ópatas "had had no idolatry at all, as they never recognized or venerated any object as a deity, nor offered sacrifices to any idol, nor had any other God or Deity than the freedom their land offered them."[9]

Given the character of Father Núñez's testimony, it may well be that he, like many of his contemporaries, perceived the problem of religious change among the mission Indians in Sonora in dualistic terms, that is, as a question of good versus bad catechumens, of Christians against pagans, or of those devoted to God and those who did the devil's bidding. At some point in time, the task of religious conversion was indeed approached through the use of this dialectic of opposites, which is implicit in the language of resistance to—and the adoption of—new religions. More recently, however, emphasis has shifted

---

[7] Bernard L. Fontana, "History of the Pápago," in Ortiz, *Handbook*, 137–42; Paul H. Ezell, "History of the Pima," in Ortiz, *Handbook*, 155; Donald M. Bahr, "Pima and Pápago Medicine and Philosophy," in Ortiz, *Handbook*, 193; Louise Lamphere, "Southwestern Ceremonialism," in Ortiz, *Handbook*, 758–62; Ruth Underhill, *Pápago Indian Religion* (New York: Columbia University Press, 1939).

[8] De los Reyes, *Memorial y Estado Actual*. Recent ethnographic evidence shows that from the perspective of the Pimas, baptism did not seem incompatible with native religious beliefs: it was well received and understood as a healing rite, but not as a symbol of religious conversion. Ezell, "History of the Pima," 155; Fontana, "History of the Pápago," 138.

[9] Fray Ángel Antonio Núñez, *Carta edificante histórico-curiosa*, Santa María de Basarac, March 31, 1777, UAL, Special Collections, MS 193.

away from such polarizations as studies have come to focus more on the entire range of responses, which run from outright rejection to total conversion, all of which emerged in the reactions of diverse Indian peoples to such religious projects.[10] Moreover, it is well known that despite indigenous people's efforts to preserve their traditions and customs within the conceptual frameworks of Christianity,[11] religious conversion (nominal or real) implied a high cultural cost for the natives that was visible not only in ritual aspects but also in alterations of their social organization brought about by changes in, or the consolidation of, the functions of men and women within the indigenous communities themselves.[12]

[10] Ramón Gutiérrez's analysis of the attitudes of New Mexico's Indians toward Christian practices and teachings concerning matrimony and sexuality is a good example, as it studies the responses of Indians to these new values as a window that allows him to narrate "a story of contestation, of mediation and negotiation between cultures and between social groups." Gutiérrez, *When Jesus Came*, xvii. In his study of Indian responses to Christianity in the Andes, Nicholas Griffiths discusses four processes that ran the gamut from total rejection of the new faith to complete conversion. Incomplete conversion, he says, was "the most common Native response" to Christianity. Indian behavior, says Griffiths, oscillated among external syncretism (religious practice based on native religion but with active participation only in Christian rites), internal syncretism (practice based on native religion with active participation in both Christian and native rites), compartmentalization (belief in both religions and participation in both rites), and *nepantilism* (the gradual loss or deterioration of the rites of native religions accompanied by a misunderstanding of the new religion). Upon analyzing the case of the Spaniards' violent campaigns to extirpate the religion of the Maya in sixteenth-century Yucatán, Inga Clendinnen finds that the Indians' attachment to their ancient religion and social structures functioned as a means of bringing their traditional way of life parallel to the Spanish system. Nicholas Griffiths, *The Cross and the Serpent: Religious Repression and Resurgence in Colonial Peru* (Norman and London: University of Oklahoma Press, 1995); Inga Clendinnen, *Ambivalent Conquests: Maya and Spaniard in Yucatán, 1517–1570* (Cambridge: Cambridge University Press, 1987).

[11] For the Indians of Martha's Vineyard, says James P. Ronda, Christianity reinforced political and social practices after the influence of the pow-wows declined in the 1640s and 1650s and when a leadership vacuum developed on the island, leaving a void that was filled by Indian pastors. Indian men also promoted Christianity among women as a means of ensuring social cohesion and stability and, in fact, Christian women soon came to represent the model of what "good women" should be: diligent with their husbands, proficient in the performance of household tasks, and counselors to younger women. James P. Ronda, "Generations of Faith: The Christian Indians of Martha's Vineyard," in Peter C. Mancall and James H. Merrell, eds., *American Encounters* (New York and London: Routledge, 2000), 138–60.

[12] For Carol Devens, "[M]en and women diverged in their receptivity to Christianity and how they confronted the changes triggered by European intrusion." Indian women, she affirms, opposed Christianity because conversion meant subordination to men and the imposition of European-defined sex roles. Indian men, in turn, decided to convert to Christianity pragmatically because of its political and economic advantages. In contrast to this position, Nancy Shoemaker argues that such conclusions "presume a linear, assimilationist model of change" and take for granted that Indians interpreted Christianity as did the Europeans. The conversion and exemplary

Without losing sight of the transcendence of these processes as significant individual phenomena, the aim here is to demonstrate their importance as elements in a much more complex network of exchanges and adjustments that involved all groups of the frontier society. The analysis includes various responses by Sonora's Indian populations to the religious programs of both Queretarans and Xaliscans while also providing answers to the following questions: What was the importance of differences of opinion among the clergy as to the best methods of conversion used along the Sonoran frontier? To what degree did the presence or absence of Spanish settlers affect the conversion process? What circumstances explain differences in the systems of offices and responsibilities that were conferred on Indians in the mission districts of Sonora? How did the lay Spanish population participate in the conversion of the Indians to Christianity?

As other authors have pointed out, conversion was a process that began with the rite of baptism, rather than leading to that sacrament.[13] Although conversion has traditionally been defined as a process clearly oriented toward changing people's beliefs or internal conduct, it may also encompass religious practice. As William Merrill suggests, conversion should be understood as a process through which individuals develop shifting connections between their own beliefs and practices and those of others.[14]

The analysis presented here has no pretensions of offering a comprehensive study of the forms of religiosity in northwestern Mexico, as the available

---

lives of Indian women such as Kateri Tekakwitha, contends Shoemaker, show that for the Iroquois, Christianity did not entail the oppression of women. On the contrary, she avers, there were several parallels between Christianity and traditional Iroquois society that accounted for the adoption of the new religion. The Jesuit baptism and the Iroquois requickening ceremony, the predominance in both spheres of certain social organizations, and the significance of female images for both Jesuits and Iroquois speak of the similarities between Christianity and traditional Iroquois practices. Focusing on the late eighteenth-century government programs of "civilization" among the Cherokee, Theda Perdue contends that women welcomed the changes brought by the intervention of Anglo-Americans in their communities. Carol Devens, "Separate Confrontations: Gender as a Factor in Indian Adaptation to European Colonization in New France," *American Quarterly* 38, no. 3 (1986): 462; Nancy Shoemaker, "Kateri Tekakwitha's Tortuous Path to Sainthood," in Nancy Shoemaker, ed., *Negotiators of Change: Historical Perspectives on Native American Women* (New York and London: Routledge, 1995); and Theda Perdue, "Women, Men and American Indian Policy: The Cherokee Response to 'Civilization,'" in Shoemaker, ed., *Negotiators of Change*, 90–114.

[13] William L. Merrill, "Conversion and Colonialism in Northern Mexico: The Tarahumara Response to the Jesuit Mission Program, 1601–1767," in *Conversion to Christianity: Historical and Anthropological Perspectives on a Great Transformation*, ed. Robert W. Hefner (Berkeley and Los Angeles: University of California Press, 1993), 136; Sandos, *Converting California*, xv.

[14] Merrill, "Conversion and Colonialism," 153–54.

sources would not allow such an analysis in any event. It is possible, however, to situate the isolated notes that are available concerning local religious expressions in the context of the many changes that this frontier zone was experiencing in the late colonial period, and, more specifically, during the Franciscan epoch. Religious practices are then perceived as an area of intersection among local traditions and beliefs, the societal projects that the missionaries fostered, and the initiatives adopted by local governments to force Indian communities to adapt to the northward expansion of Spanish and *mestizo* society.[15] To explain how these factors were faced and re-elaborated in the terrain of religiosity, it behooves us to analyze series of testimonies that offer accounts of the problems characterizing the physical and symbolic approximation of not only Indians and Spaniards but also old and new Christians, as well as missionaries and catechumens, and of the relationships between Christian doctrine and local practice, and between religion and social organization at the community level.

THE AMBIGUITY OF LOCATION: LIVING AMONG CHRISTIANS VERSUS BECOMING A CHRISTIAN

One goal of the Jesuit and Franciscan mission enterprises in northwestern New Spain was to congregate the Indians in "true towns" so that they would live in good order (*en policía*), that is, in accordance with European notions of order and sociability. No doubt, in most cases this ideal was in fact realized, despite the precarious living conditions of the Sonoran populace at the time of the expulsion of the Jesuits when the ecclesiastical map of the provinces of Ostimuri, Pimería Baja, Pimería Alta, and Sonora showed thirty-three mission towns (*cabeceras*) and forty-nine satellite villages (*visitas*).[16]

In the years following the expulsion of the Society of Jesus, the spread of Spanish colonization gradually approached those mission towns, and, not long

---

[15] In the sociology of religion, and specifically according to the concept of congregational religiosity, these elements are considered fundamental parts of charismatic domination and its routinization, where, in the final analysis, religiosity is reduced to unequal power relations between the ministerial hierarchy and the mass of believers. Max Weber, *Economy and Society: An Outline of Interpretive Sociology*, eds. Guenther Roth and Claus Wittich (Berkeley and Los Angeles: University of California Press, 1978), 241–49, 1111–23. I distance myself from this posture to consider here the forms of religiosity as a product of the dynamic interlocution among the three groups of actors identified, as I established above in my discussion of the concept of transculturation.

[16] De los Reyes, *Relación clara y metódica*, 1784, BNFF, 34/759. According to the information presented by Juan Nentuig, by 1764, the Jesuits had thirty-one *cabeceras* and forty-two *visitas* in the four rectorates they administered in Sonora (not including the Yaqui River). Nentuig, *El rudo ensayo*, 84–101.

after that, the Indian population was clearly outnumbered by Spaniards and castes. One such case was Arivechi, an ancient Ópata pueblo that by 1799 had 534 non-Indian inhabitants and only 123 Ópatas.[17] The missionaries of the Jesuit period had enjoyed a certain degree of success in keeping the Spanish and caste populations away from their missions, although this reality changed dramatically in the period of Franciscan administration when, even in the towns of Pimería Alta, the most remote area of Spanish colonization, this process of territorial expansion was already well under way in the late eighteenth century, although its major phase of development would not come until the first half of the nineteenth century.

The Indians of northwestern New Spain had gradually become familiar with the realities of living among Christians in accordance with the forms of sociability promoted by the clergy and Spanish settlers (although the religious observances as practiced by those rather unique non-Indian settlers is a matter for debate). The question of whether such proximity contributed to the conversion of the Indians to Christianity was quite another story. It appears that it did not. Not all indigenous groups in Sonora who at some time or another had lived "as Christians" actually converted to Christianity. What was it, then, that allowed certain Indian groups to retain their religious beliefs practically intact while others more readily adopted the religion introduced by the missionaries? What were the basic elements of the process of change impelled by religious conversion in Sonora? The answers to these questions lie, I believe, in the following factors: the intensity of the contact between Indians and Spaniards, the imperfect communication between Franciscans and Indians, the distinct evolution of patterns of indigenous mobility, the fact that some Indians found congruence between certain aspects of Catholicism and their own forms of social organization, and the diverse strategies implemented by Queretaran and Xaliscan missionaries in the districts they administered.

In order to evaluate these factors, it is necessary to circumscribe the analysis to the external aspects of Christianity and indigenous religiosity, that is, to the way in which religion was actually practiced, much as MacCormack and Taylor have done for the cases of the Andes and central Mexico.[18] In the absence of other indicators, the relationship between Christianity and Hispanization, and the celebration of certain rituals combining native elements with features of Christian ceremonialism offer clues to illuminate certain aspects of change in the religious practices of Sonora.

---

[17] Similar cases from the same year are Cucurpe, Bacoachi, and Sahuaripa. BNFF, 36/806.

[18] Sabine MacCormack, *Religion in the Andes: Vision and Imagination in Early Colonial Peru* (Princeton, NJ: Princeton University Press, 1991), 6; Taylor, *Magistrates*, 47–48.

During the Franciscan period, the spiritual status of the Indians of both Pimerías (Alta and Baja) appeared little altered from the condition they had maintained in the Jesuit era. Ten years after their arrival in the Pimerías, the Franciscans from Querétaro recognized that the instruction of the Indians in the catechism was, quite simply, "lagging far behind." It seems that despite being aware of this reality, the friars were unable to agree on the reasons for their slow progress or to find common ground in terms of identifying mechanisms to bring them greater success in this undertaking. Particularly worrisome for the Queretarans was the spiritual condition of the Indians of Pimería Alta: No other Franciscan missionary district in Sonora reflected more clearly the continued existence of ancient native beliefs.[19]

One fundamental problem of the mission programs in Pimería Alta was that both the Jesuits and the Franciscans had attempted to convince the Pápago and Sobaipuri Indians to settle permanently in mission towns, although those peoples' existing social and economic organization was based in part on occupying two distinct dwelling areas in accordance with agricultural cycles and the seasons of the year.[20] The missionaries attempted to limit these patterns of mobility—examined in greater detail below—because they supposed that the Indians followed them in order to continue celebrating their rites beyond the watchful eyes of their friars. This cyclical movement made it practically impossible for the missions in Pimería Alta to bring together a permanent group of catechumens, which would partially explain why the priests' instruction there never advanced beyond a rudimentary level. This problem persisted until at least the late eighteenth century, when more Pápagos began to reside permanently in the Pimería Alta missions, due to the decline of the indigenous population in the mission towns and thanks to the missionaries' "offers of land to till and promises of a more abundant life."[21]

However, in addition to the problems of relocation, serious differences of form and substance also divided the Queretarans with respect to the spiritual attention they provided to the Indians under their charge. In contrast to the precise nature of their instructions concerning the nature of the relations to be maintained among missionaries, Indians, Spanish settlers, and the authorities, the Queretarans received no specific guidelines for the Indians' spiritual administration. In spite of the fact that the evangelization program was left to their

[19] In other regions of Sonora, beyond the area of Franciscan administration, the Yaqui and Seri Indians were the most notable examples of Indian peoples that succeeded in minimizing the impact of Catholicism on their religions.

[20] Bernard L. Fontana, "Pima and Pápago: Introduction," in Ortiz, *Handbook*, 125–33.

[21] Fontana, "History of the Pápago," 138.

own discretion, the Queretaran missionaries adopted a more or less traditional model characterized by the time-honored practices of convening the faithful and organizing prayers at certain times of the day. The customs of the Queretarans included ringing the church bells at dawn to call the people to mass and, with the help of a *mador* (catechism teacher) and two *fiscales*, ensuring that children and unmarried people attended the morning ritual. At the conclusion of mass, all present recited diverse prayers in Spanish led by the missionary. Those rites were repeated as evening fell, when the people also recited the rosary and other prayers. Sunday mass was obligatory for all mission residents, and was often accompanied by the music of harps, violins, and a chorus of Indian women.[22]

Some friars referred to the performance of these rites as "the method" of imparting Christian doctrine in the Sonoran missions. According to missionaries such as Antonio de los Reyes, the Indians' imperfect reception of Christianity via this method was explained by various factors, including the poor urban planning of Indian towns, unsupervised relations between Indians and Spaniards, and lack of a local ecclesiastical authority responsible for monitoring and regulating missionary work. In his opinion, the method employed by the Queretarans was suitable, but achieving the conversion of the Indians required adjusting the structures within which it was applied.

On another mission front, however, the Queretaran "method" was criticized for paying little attention to the possibility that the catechumens did not necessarily share the missionaries' meaning and the significance of Christianity's external manifestations. According to Fray Antonio Barbastro, the problem of "imperfect conversions" among the Indians was not to be attributed to the latter's supposed incapacity; rather, he believed, this was just an excuse used to conceal "the friars' own inconsistency." The real problems, Barbastro continued, resided in the absence of a uniform doctrinal model, in the missionaries' inability to effectively communicate the meaning of a doctrine that they imparted in the Spanish language, and, especially, in their failure to understand the meaning that the Indian converts attributed to the doctrine as they recited it in their native languages. Hence, by 1777, the result of missionary work in the two Pimerías was a cacophonous concert in which a chorus of voices seemed to be all that signaled knowledge of the prayers:

> At some missions they always pray in Castilian; in others one day in Castilian and another in their own language. At some [missions] [they respond to] cer-

---

[22] De los Reyes, *Memorial y Estado Actual.*

tain questions, in others [to] other ones. At some missions they recite the general confession, a long act of contrition, and the rest of the doctrine, the virtues. . . . Prayers in Castilian are commonly led by one *temastián*, but by another in Pima; and what follows from this? That (except for a very few) they do not know how to pray in either Pima or Castilian. . . . Some ministers are convinced that their Indians know how to pray well, because when they pray much noise is heard in the church; and I have been one of them, but upon testing them individually, I found that three-quarters of the Indians knew nothing at all.[23]

Entrusting the recitation of prayers in the Pima language to the *temastianes*, as had been the custom since the Jesuit era, represented a serious risk for the Franciscans because, like the expelled missionaries before them, their lack of proficiency in that language made it difficult for them to know what their catechumens were really saying.[24] Clearly, simple physical proximity was insufficient to forge strong bonds between friars and catechumens.

Although some missionaries seemed quite satisfied with such practices and even took lengths to justify them,[25] others, like Barbastro, pointed out that the lack of vigilance during those incomprehensible prayers could easily allow the Indians to alter them. In fact, he warned, the prayers had become so confusing for the Indians "that not even they can elucidate what they are doing and, as they receive no explanation, this becomes a mode of prayer that not only makes them resemble the parrot . . . [but] may [also] admit errors of which we are unaware."[26] The use of bilingual manuals elaborated by the Jesuits to assist in

[23] Fray Antonio Barbastro to Fray Diego Ximénez, Santa Teresa, May 4, 1777, AFPM, AQ, Letter K, leg. 16, 2nd portion, no. 1.

[24] Carlos de Rojas to Minister Provincial Fray Francisco Ceballos, Arizpe, May 14, 1764, AGN, Archivo Histórico de Hacienda, leg. 17, exp. 8; Manuel Aguirre to Francisco Ceballos, Bacadehuachi, February 18, 1764, AGN, Archivo Histórico de Hacienda, leg. 17, exp. 22.

[25] In 1773, one of the missionaries in Pimería Alta wrote: "The style and method that we have followed from our arrival up to the present is that which is most conducive to conserving these poor folk. As by assisting them with their needs using the common properties which are under his control, the minister assures the permanence of his sons, and through continued teaching . . . [has] achieved sufficient notions of the evangelical truths. . . . [T]hey go to the church twice daily to pray, knowing the entire doctrine in the Castilian language, learned word-for-word by these poor folk through our labor. Every day they recite the Holy Rosary with the minister, [and] sing the *salve* and the *alabado*. They listen attentively to the daily explanation of the mysteries . . . through interpreters, whose method and style seem to be the same as those that the first conquerors observed." Fray José Soler to Fray Romualdo Cartagena, San Diego del Pitiquí, August 12, 1773, Fr. MCC, 201, exp. 28. Similar opinions expressed by Fathers Soler and Juan Díaz, the missionary at Caborca, can be found in Fr. MCC, 201, exp. 3, and 202, exp. 9.

[26] AFPM, AQ, Letter K, leg. 16, 2nd portion, no. 1. Barbastro's impressions were shared with other friars from Querétaro. For example, a series of reports drafted in 1772 by Fathers

preaching among the Indians was not a viable alternative for the Franciscans, as some of them held that the manuals "were not good."[27] Preaching through interpreters was a practice that the missionary at Cocóspera, Fray Francisco Roch, attributed more to necessity than convenience, as in addition to being unreliable it was "most complex and difficult."[28]

The difficulties that the missionaries encountered in explaining Christian doctrine to their catechumens in Pimería Alta required special attention to the way that the Pima Alto Indians responded to mission programs. In conjunction with historical records, certain ethnographic descriptions and oral testimonies can help us to better appreciate how their responses were articulated.

A first indication of the religiosity of the Pimas in the Franciscan period comes from a Queretaran in 1774, who described certain acts that accompanied festive days in Pimería Alta: "In the most classic or festive [days] of Holy Mary they parade through town singing the rosary, and on other days [the Indians] are allowed to dance [and to enjoy] certain innocent diversions and games." Though the friars opposed the Indians' celebrating other kinds of rituals on such occasions, they were obliged to tolerate certain "superstitious dances and [especially] hair dances" to avoid conflicts with the province's civil authorities.[29] Evidence allows us to suppose that those dances continued during the late colonial period, especially because the civil authorities defended them as one of the most effective mechanisms for maintaining peace among the Pima Indians. In 1790, the intendant of Sonora lauded the labors of the Queretarans in Pimería Alta because they conserved the mode of social and economic organization originally established by the Jesuits, thus "keeping those natives in good order and application." Here, the intendant implicitly recognized that the Pimas were still allowed certain "innocent public diversions, especially on the days of the patron saints of the missions *and their religion*, allowing the dances to which they are inclined."[30]

Thus, the Indians convened in the Pimería Alta missions observed the Catholic liturgical calendar while at the same time preserving the observance of

---

Francisco Cordón, José María Espinosa, and José Antonio Caro (missionaries in Opodepe, Cumuripa, and Ónavas, respectively) noted that Indians prayed in Spanish "like parrots," reciting the prayers, but without understanding what they said. AGN, Provincias Internas, vol. 81, exp. 5–17.

[27] AGN, Provincias Internas, vol. 81, foja 177.

[28] *Ibid.*

[29] De los Reyes, *Memorial y Estado Actual.*

[30] Enrique Grimarest to Viceroy Revillagigedo, Arizpe, August 16, 1790, BNFF, 35/771. Emphasis added.

important dates in their own annual cycle, identified by some Spaniards such as Intendant Grimarest as the Pima religion. As Bernard Fontana observes, for the Desert Pimas on those missions,

> important public ceremonies were connected with crops, hunting, warfare, community well-being and, most important of all, "bringing down the clouds." Rain meant life in the desert, and a great deal of religious energy was directed toward invoking that blessing.[31]

Especially important in this "ceremonial cycle" were the *má amaga* (a corn harvest and deer-hunting ritual), the *wi gida* (prayer-stick ceremonies, an early winter harvest rite), the *célkona* (harvest celebration or winter rain dance), and the purification rites required to hunt eagles, go to war, or undertake the journey to bring salt from the Gulf of California. In addition to these autumnal rituals, other important rites included a "naming ceremony" and a rain-making ceremony performed in July every year in which cactus wine was drunk.[32] The reason why the Indians were allowed to celebrate these rituals while also observing Catholic holidays seems to have been certain congruence in the content of the two kinds of rites. Like the Catholic festivities held to celebrate the lives and virtues of the saints and, above all, to ask for their intercession to obtain a favor related to one's personal well-being or that of the community, Pápago ceremonies focused "on how individual men could obtain things upon which the general welfare depended."[33]

This coexistence of Pima ceremonialism and Catholic rites in no way represented a displacement or substitution of the Indians' ancient beliefs. What occurred, in contrast, was what William Merrill identifies as a "selective integration" of certain elements of Catholic ritual into native cultural frameworks.[34]

---

[31] Bernard L. Fontana, "The O'odham," in *The Pimería Alta. Missions and More*, eds. James Officer, Mardith Schuetz-Miller, and Bernard L. Fontana (Tucson: Southwestern Mission Research Center, 1996), 26.

[32] Lamphere, "Southwestern Ceremonialism," 761; Donald M. Bahr, "Pima and Pápago Social Organization," in Ortiz, *Handbook*, 180; James Griffith, "Kachinas and Masking," in Ortiz, *Handbook*, 770–71; Fontana, "History of the Pápago," 140; Underhill, *Pápago Indian Religion*; Bernard L. Fontana, *Of Earth and Little Rain: The Pápago Indians* (Tucson: University of Arizona Press, 1989).

[33] Bahr, "Pima and Pápago," 180.

[34] In addition to religious aspects, this "selective integration" was applied to the adoption of nonreligious elements such as technology, foods, and animal husbandry. Merrill, *Raramuri Souls*, 46–48. Edward Spicer calls this an "incorporative" type of contact. Spicer, "Types of Contact and Processes of Change," in *Perspectives in American Indian Culture Change*, ed. Edward Spicer (Chicago: Chicago University Press, 1961), 530.

Even today, for example, the liturgical year and the annual calendar of Catholic festivities among the Pápagos on the reservation at San Xavier del Bac begins and ends on December 3 with the fiesta of Saint Francis Xavier, an event traditionally associated with the Pima Indians' autumn rituals.[35]

The fiesta of Saint Francis Xavier is by far one of the most important religious celebrations in the area, not only in terms of the number of believers it attracts to the town of Magdalena (Sonora) each year, but also due to the transformations it has undergone over time. Some authors assert that in the early eighteenth century the mission Pápagos in Pimería Alta combined the cult of Saint Francis Xavier (a Jesuit saint) with that of Saint Francis of Assisi (founder of the Franciscan order), as they commemorate the Jesuit saint's feast day on October 4, which is the feast day of Saint Francis of Assisi.[36] The fiesta is still celebrated on that date and the custom to attribute this mixing of dates to the Pápagos remains unchallenged. Nonetheless, there is evidence showing that at least up to the early nineteenth century, the Pápago Indians in the Magdalena area (San Ignacio mission district) celebrated the fiesta of Saint Francis Xavier in early December. A contemporaneous investigation of the excesses committed by Fray Matías Creo, a Queretaran missionary assigned to Pimería Alta, mentions that he participated in the fiestas of Saint Francis Xavier in San Ignacio in December 1814, when, accompanied by two other friars from Querétaro, he took part in a mass celebrated jointly to "please the Indians."[37] It seems to me that the intention of bestowing on this religious practice such respectable antiquity reflects a desire to demonstrate the persistence and profundity of the religious changes introduced by the Jesuits; from a different perspective, it serves as an example to explain the Pápago Indians' ability to fuse these dif-

---

[35] McCarty, *A Frontier*, 132.

[36] Fontana, "History of the Pápago," 141; James Griffith, "Saints, Stories, and Sacred Places," in Officer, *The Pimería Alta*, 98. According to local tradition, the reclining statue of Saint Francis Xavier arrived in Magdalena by accident, as the Jesuit Eusebio Kino had ordered it to be taken to Sonora and deposited at the San Xavier del Bac mission. As local people recount the story, it was later recovered by a group of specialists in architecture and local fiestas, only to be destroyed by anticlerical groups in 1934 and burned in the furnaces at the local brewery, Cervecería Sonora. Buford Pickens, ed., *The Missions of Northern Sonora: A 1935 Field Documentation* (Tucson: University of Arizona Press, 1993), 63–64; Griffith, "Saints, Stories," 98. In fact, the original statue was destroyed by the Seri Indians who attacked the town of Magdalena around 1788, according to an inventory of the properties of the mission of San Ignacio. In the part that concerns the *visita* of Magdalena, this report states: "that church and house were completely ruined since the Seris burned them and destroyed [the statue of] the saint Saint Francis Xavier." The repetition of "saint" comes from the original in Spanish. BNFF, 35/761.

[37] BL, M-A 25:3, document 7.

ferent religious traditions.[38] It is difficult to accept that this change of dates and the linking of the two saints should be attributed to the Pápagos because, as has been shown, in the final years in which those Indians were present in the San Ignacio mission district, that fiesta was celebrated in early December (as it is today among the Pápagos of San Xavier del Bac). No testimonies suggest that this situation changed in the later years of the Franciscan administration of that mission, so it is highly probable that the identification of the image of Saint Xavier with the fiesta of Saint Francis occurred after 1841, when the Queretarans abandoned the region. If this is so, then the fiesta of Saint Xavier as it is celebrated today in the town of Magdalena would be a notable example of transculturation between the Pápagos and the Mexican populace of that part of Pimería Alta. Thus, a celebration originally promoted by missionaries among local Indians was later converted into an indigenous festival and then inherited and modified by Mexican residents in the mid-nineteenth century.[39]

In the Opatería region, in contrast, the study of religious change is elusive due in part to the scarcity of colonial sources and in part to the dearth of ethnographic studies of the Ópata, extinct as an ethnic group in the second half of the nineteenth century. The infrequent references found in eighteenth-century ecclesiastical sources indicate that during the period there was no structured, visible ritual among the Ópatas that the missionaries could have interpreted as an ancient religion, at least not according to European criteria.[40] In 1764, Nentuig stated that he knew of no sacred site or ceremonial object among the Ópatas.[41] Father Ángel Núñez seconded this view in 1777, when he denied the existence of indigenous rituals, although he attributed it to the "apostolic zeal" of the Franciscans who had evangelized that area of Sonora before the Jesuits arrived.[42] In general, the Indians of Opatería, like those of Pimería Baja, were portrayed by the Franciscans replacing the Jesuits as "fairly well instructed" in

---

[38] One opinion characteristic of the first case is that of James Griffith, who sees in this kind of story "evidence that the cultural and religious systems introduced into the Pimería Alta by Eusebio Francisco Kino and his successors are alive and have flourished for more than three centuries." Griffith, "Saints, Stories," 103; James S. Griffith and Francisco Javier Manzo Taylor, *The Face of Christ in Sonora* (Tucson: Rio Nuevo Publishers, 2007). Fontana, "History of the Pápago," 141, for example, would be found in the second case.

[39] It is important to remember in this regard that in the mission district of San Ignacio, in general, and in the town of Magdalena in particular, the indigenous population had been displaced long before the Franciscans abandoned the mission. See *supra*, Chapter 2.

[40] Pfefferkorn, *Descripción*, Chapter 10, 212.

[41] Nentuig, *El rudo ensayo*, 67.

[42] Núñez, *Carta edificante*, 95–99.

Christian doctrine, although their knowledge of Christian precepts was not accompanied by obedience to the missionaries. Throughout the Franciscan period, local residents constantly invoked the decrees of Governor Juan de Pineda that barred the missionaries from using force to make Indians "fulfill their Christian obligations." In these conditions, the Franciscan period in Opatería and Pimería Baja was characterized by the relative freedom that Indians enjoyed to defy ecclesiastical authority and even to flee from the missions. This, in turn, allowed for more frequent contacts with Spanish settlers and with life on the margins of the missions, and offered the Indians a variety of opportunities to practice religious rites that mixed Christian ceremonialism with indigenous elements.[43]

Although it is true that among the Ópatas religious sentiment seems not to have been articulated through any recognizable ceremonialism, at least as far as Spanish society could discern, some sources allow us to identify certain moments in which the need to communicate an emotional state, to celebrate the foundations of their society, or to manifest their hopes for the future, found expression in dance and rites of passage. For the Ópatas, as for other Indian groups, the relationship with the supernatural world was not separate from the way in which humans coexisted with their environment, which explains why each aspect of life was celebrated and commemorated through a series of rites that involved the community as a whole. In this sense, the traditional religion of the indigenous peoples is best defined as a way of life, and not as a kind of cult.

Thus, according to Jean B. Johnson, "the concepts of rain and fertility were important" for the Ópatas, as expressed in a number of rain dances they performed. They also "venerated the sun and the moon as brother and sister respectively. They greeted the new moon by throwing handfuls of pinole in the air. The sun likewise received offerings of pinole when it appeared each morning."[44]

Among the Ópatas, marriage was another special occasion that brought the community together. With the people gathered around the soon-to-be-married men and women, the rite began with the future spouses forming two lines. At a signal giving them a head start the women began to run, followed by the men who tried to overtake them. Each man chose his spouse, reaching out to take her by her left breast as he overtook her, a gesture that confirmed their matrimony. Once the race was over, the community celebrated with a dance, while the newlyweds were accommodated on straw mats where they would pass the night.[45]

[43] De los Reyes, *Memorial y Estado Actual.*
[44] Johnson, *The Opata*, 23, 33.
[45] Nentuig, *El rudo ensayo*, 69.

When deaths occurred among the Ópatas, special attention was paid to those who died in violent accidents, as this might "excite the soul" of the deceased. The custom was to leave the body at the scene of the accident for three days in the hope that its soul would return to it.[46] In 1730 it was reported that the Ópatas believed that

> at death, the souls go to a large lake, on the north shore of which is a little man, a dwarf called *Butza Uri*. He receives the souls, and transports them in a large canoe to the south shore, where a revered old woman called *Hoatziqui* lives. She swallows the souls one by one, save those she finds with painted faces. . . . These she rejects, saying that they are spiny like the cactus, and throws them into the lake. Those [that] she swallows live a life of plenty in her belly.[47]

In everyday life, reciprocity was a fundamental principle of Ópata society, a sentiment expressed in the *dagüinemaca*, a dance with which this nation celebrated the day when they began to fraternize with the Spanish. More than a dance held to commemorate the historical meaning of their alliance with the colonizers, for Ópata society the *dagüinemaca* celebrated the congruence of that pact with their own values. The name of this dance literally means "give to me and I shall give to you" (*dame y te daré*), while the virtues personified in its execution include mutual aid, solidarity, friendship, and gratitude. This dance actually survived the Franciscan period in Opatería. According to the testimony of one nineteenth-century observer:

> The custom is for men and women to dedicate this dance to the person for whom they have high regard. They take the icon of a gift (perhaps a horse, cow, chicken, etc.) and approach the person for whom they feel affection, obliging him/her to dance a turn or two to the rhythm of the music; [this] marks an agreement of alliance and friendship between the two that can only be weakened by death. They call these persons *noraguas*, that is, friends; but they are so sincere and good that an Indian will leave his children and wife for his *noragua* when he learns that he is to undertake a long journey or when he can provide a service.[48]

---

[46] *Ibid.*, 68.

[47] Johnson, *The Opata*, 34. Luis González Rodríguez transcribed the same story—written by Cristóbal de Cañas in 1730—although he identifies the little man as *Butzu Uri*, and refers to the old woman as *Vatecom hoatzi*. The main difference in these two versions of the story is that Johnson states that the people Vatecom hoatzi rejected had the face painted "like the Pima" Indians, while González's transcription does not allude to any ethnic group in this episode. González Rodríguez, *El noroeste novohispano*, 498.

[48] Zúñiga, *Rápida ojeada*, 4, note 2.

Together with this dance, the Ópatas also preserved in the early nineteenth century a second one of a historical character through which they recalled, in the words of one eyewitness, "the journey of the Aztecs and the arrival of Moctezuma, whom they await as the Jews do the Messiah."[49] The *jojo*, as this dance was known, linked Ópata oral traditions with a belief in a more hopeful future, perhaps not in the messianic sense in which Ignacio Zúñiga understood it in 1835, but as a yearning to discover in their ranks someone capable of vindicating the primacy of the Ópatas and carving out a better place for his compatriots in Spanish society.[50]

In addition to these rites that reinforced historical memory, relations of reciprocity, and hope for a better future, the Ópatas also found that certain games and war exercises were effective means of maintaining the internal cohesion of their communities. On Sundays, for example, the townspeople in Opatería were accustomed to playing games such as *guachicori* or *gomi*. To play *guachicori*, the participants were first divided into two sections, each of which named a captain who, leading the men of his group, began a race in which they competed against their opponents to advance two bones that were tied together. During the race, the opposing group tried to take away the bones by hitting the members of the first team with small sticks that all participants carried. The women and others followed the race, cheering on the delegation that represented their sector. *Gomi*, meanwhile, entailed a race in which two or more competitors (always an even number) ran a distance of one or two leagues while pulling two orange-sized wooden balls with one foot. In addition to these games, the Ópatas also practiced the *taguaro*, a representation of battles with the Apaches in which a few residents dressed as Apache Indians pretended to enter the town to steal women and donkeys. As this raiding party was fleeing from the town, the rest of the people gave chase to recover the loot that the Apaches had stolen. Upon returning to the town with the recovered goods and the captured Apaches, the whole group gathered in the square around a tall pole with a *taguaro* (effigy) tied at the top. Then, in front of the *taguaro*, the older folk began to sing accompanied by rattles and the town's warriors

---

[49] *Ibid.*, 7, note 6.

[50] The importance of these claims and the Ópatas' expectation of the coming of this figure were reflected clearly in the rebellions of 1819 and 1824, and in later uprisings following the state governments' policies concerning privatization and redistribution of communal lands expressed in laws 88 and 89 of 1828. On those occasions, the increasing pressure on territorial property led the Ópatas to attempt to wrest control from the state government and propose the creation of autonomous governments that would recognize the privileges that their nation had enjoyed during the colonial period. Vidargas del Moral, "Sonora y Sinaloa," 453.

shot arrows at the *taguaro* while the people cheered or jeered their marksmanship skills.[51]

Campbell Pennington's ethnographic work among the Pima Bajo Indians at Ónavas suggests that in the last decades of the eighteenth—or perhaps early nineteenth—century some of these Ópata traditions were appropriated by the Pima Bajos. Thus, for example, they played *gomi* and a variant of *guachicori*, although Pennington's data indicate that the games were abandoned by the early twentieth century.[52] Among the Pima Bajos, dances focused less on historical elements—their focus among the Ópatas—than on emphasizing the people's relationship with the local fauna and the celebration of specific religious ceremonies. It seems that the evolution of these dances among the Pima Bajo Indians was strongly influenced by contact with other Pima groups, the Yaquis, and the Spanish, as can be deduced from certain affinities in the performance of the dance of the deer and the dance of the *matachines* among the two former groups, and from the identification of these dances with festivals in the Christian liturgical calendar.[53]

In both Opatería and Pimería Baja, the mission experience and contact with the Spanish population had modified such expressions of the lifeways of these local groups. On the one hand, the Christian calendar was superimposed on the annual cycle of indigenous festivities, thus incorporating them into the rituals that accompanied Catholic celebrations. The most notable influence in this respect, however, was the Indians' interaction with the Spanish population that, in the case of the Ópatas, led to the gradual substitution of their historical dances by other kinds of dances. On this point a comment by the missionary at Basarac is illustrative. Ópata traditional dances, he wrote, "are now little used, as today they use, practice and know all the dances of the Spanish."[54]

It is probable that as far as the Ópatas were concerned, the Franciscan presence after 1768 was interpreted as an auxiliary in the celebration of their religious ceremonies more than as the continuation of Jesuit authority and leadership.[55] Unlike the Queretaran missionaries, the Xaliscans, who administered the

---

[51] Zúñiga, *Rápida ojeada*, 6–7, note 6; Núñez, *Carta edificante*, 136.

[52] Pennington, *The Pima Bajo*, 258–59.

[53] *Ibid.*, 248–51.

[54] Núñez, *Carta edificante*, 136.

[55] It is important to situate this affirmation in a more general context. It did not mean that the Indians were not interested in having a missionary, as quite the opposite is demonstrated by the abundance of cases in which they sent representatives to the civil authorities to ask that new missionaries be assigned on those occasions in which due to the death or transfer of previous ministers towns were left unattended for some length of time. There can be no doubt as to the transcendence of ministers in such towns; rather, the question that must be asked is: *Why* were

Opatería and Pimería Baja, found themselves almost from the beginning, as the civil authorities required, bereft of the faculty to scold or punish the Indians or to force mission residents to remain subject to their authority. While the Franciscans came to play important roles in defending communal property and protesting abuses that miners and merchants committed against the Indians, the gap between missionaries and Indians was still wide. This fact can be seen plainly in the Xaliscans' complaints, in which they stated that their Indian charges were not "attracted to the things of the church."[56] The reality of this abyss in spiritual matters between Indians and the region's missionaries during the Franciscan period seems to be confirmed by the repercussions of the missions' secularization in the eighteenth century (Arizpe *ca.* 1779; Banamichi, Aconchi, Mátape, Ónavas, and Ures in 1791), and the gradual withdrawal of the Xaliscans in the early nineteenth century. It should be noted that even when the Diocese of Sonora could not provide secular priests to replace the Franciscan friars, the missions in Pimería Baja and Opatería did not lack the services of spiritual specialists responsible for organizing religious services in their towns. On the contrary, in such locales the missionary was replaced by a member of the community who was invested with the authority to organize residents to continue reciting the prayers and songs they had been taught by their priests and to perpetuate the meaning of the dances and rites of passage they had practiced since ancient times.[57]

CHANGES IN GOVERNING STRUCTURES OF INDIAN COMMUNITIES

In the missions of Pimería Alta and the mission district of Pimería Baja and Opatería, the local population played an active role in promoting religious

---

missionaries important in their communities? As in another section of this study I attempt to respond to this question, I shall only mention certain aspects related to the friars in their capacity as spiritual specialists.

[56] Fray Diego Pozo, *Noticia de las misiones que ocupan los religiosos de la Santa Provincia de Xalisco*, San José de Pimas, June 21, 1795, AGN, Misiones, vol. 2, exp. 2.

[57] One example of this local religious leadership among the Ópatas is found in an account of the pilgrimage from Tuape to the basilica of Our Lady of Guadalupe, in Mexico City, in 1839. In preparation for the trip, and before the pilgrims left for Mexico City, one member of the community, the guardian or *maestro mayor* of the church, organized the recitation of the rosary, the singing of certain hymns, and gave the pilgrims his blessing as they left the town. Dora Tabanico, "De Tuape a la Basílica de Guadalupe," in *Memorias del IV Simposio de la Sociedad Sonorense de Historia A.C.* (Hermosillo: Instituto Sonorense de Cultura, 1993), 134. The active involvement of members of Sonoran communities in the preservation of religious statues and paintings after the Franciscan period deserves special mention in this respect, as Griffith and Manzo have documented. Griffith and Manzo, *The Face of Christ in Sonora*.

activities. In an attempt to avoid problems of miscommunication with their catechumens, the Franciscans in these two districts took advantage of the communities' systems of offices to achieve a more effective evangelization. It is well known that from Jesuit times, missionaries had created a system of social stratification that allowed them to organize the productive activities in their missions, enforce control over the population, and ensure the populace's timely participation in religious events.[58] In the mission districts overseen by Queretarans and Xaliscans, the functions of the *gobernador, alcalde, topiles, capitán,* and *fiscales* were similar,[59] although those of the *mador* and *temastián* differed somewhat. In the Xaliscan missions among the Pima Bajo, Ópata, Jova, and Eudeve Indians, the position of *mador* was equivalent to that of the "teacher of doctrine." In the mornings and evenings he taught children the catechism at the church, while on festival days he instructed adults. In those missions, the *temastián* served essentially as the sexton of the church, entrusted with "caring for the vestry, the vestments [and] the sacred vessels, and cleaning the church and altars."[60] Meanwhile, in Pimería Alta, the *mador* also taught doctrine to children, while adult instruction was entrusted to the *temastián*. In Pimería Alta, this latter official served not only as the sexton of the church, but was also in charge of leading the community in daily prayer and other religious acts. Finally, he was responsible for explaining doctrine to the townsfolk in general and became, in effect, the spiritual specialist in those communities.[61]

[58] Radding, *Wandering Peoples,* 68; Nentuig, *El rudo ensayo,* 103.

[59] According to the *Descripción de Arizpe* attributed to Fray Agustín Morfi, the *gobernador* and *alcalde* were in charge of governing the town's economy, assigning work, and punishing Indians through the *topiles* when the intervention of the Spanish authorities was not required. The *capitán* held the military command when it was necessary to lead campaigns against Indian enemies, while the *fiscales* called the people to mass, religious instruction, and other church-related events. BNFF, 34/733.

[60] There are two different copies of the *Descripción de Arizpe* that provide complementary information on this position. Both the copy in the Biblioteca Nacional de México and the one conserved in the Museo Naval in Spain coincide in affirming that the *mador* was responsible for teaching doctrine to children in the church in the mornings and afternoons, and for ensuring that parents sent their children to those sessions. The copy in the Biblioteca Nacional also indicates that the *mador* could "punish those who failed to attend" the doctrine, while the book in Madrid states that the *mador* and "the teacher of the doctrine" are the same, and that, moreover, he is charged with instructing adults on festival days. BNFF, 34/733; MNM, Virreinato de Mejico, vol. 1, MS 567, doc. 14. Jesuit sources tell us that the *mador* was the primary *fiscal* or missionary's assistant; he could fulfill the functions of the church notary, undertaker, and assistant missionary in all matters related to ecclesiastical services, but could not intervene in teaching the doctrine. The *temastianes,* in contrast, taught doctrine and served as sacristans. Nentuig, *El rudo ensayo,* 103.

[61] AFPM, AQ, Letter K, leg. 16, 2nd portion, no. 1; Fray Juan José Agorreta to Fray Romualdo Cartagena, Dolores del Saric, September 8, 1773, Fr. MCC, 202, exp. 17. In this

Leaving to one side these minor differences between the *temastián* and *mador*, the important issue here is that at the outset of the Franciscan administration of the Sonoran missions, local residents played a predominant role in religious life. The social organization of Indian communities in Sonora had internal hierarchies that, although not equivalent to the scheme introduced by the clergy, did coincide in recognizing that certain members of the community performed functions necessary for the people's material and spiritual life.[62] Despite these early parallels, the later religious history of these two mission districts reveals divergence in the emerging roles of their spiritual intermediaries, due to the distinct circumstances characterizing the mission programs of the friars from Querétaro and Xalisco and especially the different rhythms that marked the consolidation of Spanish colonization in Sonora.

In the last years of the eighteenth century, viceregal authorities (especially the archbishop of Mexico, Francisco Lorenzana) attempted to "stamp out" native languages and promote education and catechism instruction in Spanish, although the Sonoran missionaries still depended on *temastianes* and *madores* to teach catechism in native languages and Castilian.[63] In Pimería Alta, the role of the *temastián* was apparently consolidated in the late eighteenth century. At a time when illness and frequent Apache raids jeopardized those missions, the Franciscans were forced to organize new groups of catechumens from among the Indians living on small ranches dispersed throughout Pimería Alta as a means of ensuring the continuity of their mission projects.[64] In this context, the presence of a *temastián* responsible for explaining doctrine to such recently arrived Pima Indians in their own language continued to be a vital necessity during the Queretaran period in Pimería Alta, although it proved to be a double-edged sword in the local religious context. On the one hand, it served the missionary's ends in such matters as teaching prayers and the external aspects of Christian doctrine, as mission Indians learned to recite "the Lord's Prayer, the Ave María, the Creed, the Salve, the Ten Commandments of God and the church, the Sacraments and the short version of the Catechism by

---

respect, among the Pima Alto Indians, the *temastián* was more similar to that of the Yaqui towns in southern Sonora. Spicer, *Los Yaquis*, 20.

[62] Among the Pápagos, for example, the "wise speaker" (ritual orator) played a prominent role, as did the "keeper of the smoke" (organizer and principal speaker at meetings), the "keeper of the plaited basket" (who was in charge of the group's sacred bundle), and "the one above" (a person with "great man" status). Fontana, "The O'odham," 26.

[63] The reply from the intendant of Sonora, Pedro Corbalán, to Archbishop Lorenzana's initiative, in which he alleges the impossibility of developing such a program in Sonora, can be found in Pedro Corbalán to Tomás de Mello, Real de los Álamos, January 15, 1771, AGI, Guadalajara 338.

[64] AFPM, AQ, Letter K, leg. 18, no. 25.

memory," achievements recognized in the visitations to those missions to evaluate the level of instruction among the Pimas.[65] However, the possibility of preserving native languages allowed the Indians to maintain a high degree of cohesion at a time of severe demographic contraction and territorial displacement (although congregated on missions by the friars, they readily fled if they found their interaction with the clergy and Spanish settlers inconvenient).

It is probable that in Pimería Alta the *temastianes* played a fundamental role in preserving Pima dances and ceremonialism, simultaneously fulfilling the responsibilities of their religious position on the missions as well as certain traditional, native functions. In spite of the fact that the missionaries saw that their catechumens learned the doctrine and precepts of the church, they also observed that the Pima Indians left the missions on certain occasion to visit places they regarded as ceremonial sites, where they participated in ancient rituals. Although everyone knew that such religious survivals were common in all towns in Pimería Alta, nowhere was this more worrisome than in the most remote missions, located far from areas of Spanish colonization. As late as 1831, the Queretarans became alarmed upon receiving news that the Indians around Bisanic still practiced their "dances, songs and other heathen rites" using several "diabolical instruments" that were confiscated and then burned. Another ongoing concern at about the same time involved the Indians living in the San Xavier del Bac mission, who maintained kinship relations with Desert Pimas who had not been congregated on missions. While they were in the mission towns, the residents behaved as Christians, but they left the mission periodically to get together with their relatives and renew their ancient rituals.[66] As miscegenation increased in the towns of Pimería Alta in the late eighteenth century, and as the non-Indian populace began to appropriate more and more of the lands belonging to those towns, the few Pima residents still left in those missions abandoned them in ever greater numbers to return to the desert.[67] There, the re-creation

---

[65] One example is Fray Diego Bringas, *Testimonio de la visita*, 1795, AFPM, AQ, Letter K, leg. 18, no. 17.

[66] Fray Faustino González and Fray Saturnino Arizeta to the commander of the presidio at Altar José Romero, n.p., n.d. BL, M-A 25:5, document 32.

[67] Margarita Nolasco points out that after 1767 the Pápago Indians began to abandon mission towns and return to the desert, though they visited those towns sporadically in the winter. Margarita Nolasco, "Ser mujer pápago," in Underhill, *Biografía*, 19. In the words of a contemporaneous witness, by 1843 in Pimería Alta "due to the lack of religious attention, many Indians have abandoned religious practice, left the missions, and returned to the open desert," quoted in McCarty, *A Frontier*, 92. According to McCarty, the return of the Pimas to the desert was not an indication of an abandonment of Christianity: "When the mission system was in full bloom, and even today, the distant desert villages had and have their tiny chapels for devotion to the saints." *A Frontier*, 134.

of their rituals at traditional ceremonial sites contributed to preserving their culture in a kind of fusion of Catholicism with Pima rites identified elsewhere as
"Sonoran Catholicism."[68]

The changes introduced in the internal government of Indian towns in the
nineteenth century by the early constitutional and republican authorities
favored consolidation of this type of religiosity in Pimería Alta, although the
mechanisms involved were in no way intended to produce that result. The suppression of the *cargos* system or communal offices stipulated in the 1812
Constitution, and the mandatory election of constitutionally approved mayors
(*alcaldes constitucionales*) in each town presupposed a reorganization of the
forms of social control practiced in Indian communities, as the constitutional
mayor would assume the faculties once exercised by indigenous officials. When
that constitution was abolished in 1814, towns in Pimería Alta returned to the
"old method of government," electing Indian governors and other officials as
they had done before.[69] However, the Independence period brought other
changes in the organization of those towns, especially with the 1825
Constitution of the Estado de Occidente (Sonora and Sinaloa), which stipulated that all localities with more than three thousand inhabitants had to elect
town councils (*ayuntamientos*), while smaller towns were to appoint *alcaldes de
policía*. These measures meant, however, that the towns of Pimería Alta faced
the problem of participating in a dual system of government—represented by
the mayor, elected in accordance with the Constitution of 1825, and their own
traditional authorities.[70] Later still, in 1828, the state legislature ratified a law
designed to regulate the internal government of Indian towns. Among many
other things, this law authorized the creation of schools for primary education
(*primeras letras*) where "young people were taught to read, write and count"
and instructed in "the principles of our religion and their civil and political
rights."[71] It also stipulated that the constitutional mayor was to oblige the

[68] Sonoran Catholicism "represented Pápagos' efforts to carry out Christian rituals—complete with homemade chapels and an attendant ceremonial and feasting area adjacent to the
chapels—that they had been taught, only now the teachers were no longer present." Fontana,
"History of the Pápago," 141.

[69] Fray Francisco Moyano to Fray Diego Miguel Bringas, Oquitoa, June 4, 1815, BL, M-A
25:3, document 8; Fray Juan Bautista de Ceballos to Fray Diego Miguel Bringas, San Xavier del
Bac, July 7, 1814, BL, M-A 25:3, document 13.

[70] Juan Domingo Vidargas, "Sonora y Sinaloa," 424–34. Radding, *Las estructuras*, 19; John
L. Kessell, *Friars, Soldiers, and Reformers: Hispanic Arizona and the Sonora Mission Frontier,
1767–1856* (Tucson: University of Arizona Press, 1976), 259–60.

[71] Congreso del Estado de Occidente, *Ley para el gobierno particular de los pueblos de
Indígenas* (Ley 88), article 10, Concepción de Álamos, September 30, 1828, BL, M-M 285:122.

heads of households to send their children to school and ensure that adults attended religious instruction every fortnight.[72] Thus, the new mayor was made responsible for the functions previously assigned to the *mador* and *fiscales*. However, the most important change introduced by the state government in this respect was combining children's education with religious instruction and putting both spheres of activity under the supervision of the Indian teacher (*preceptor indígena*) who was often (as the law contemplated) the town's *temastián*. This situation became even more complicated in that same year when most Queretarans on the missions in Pimería Alta were forced to leave Sonora when the 1828 law ordering the expulsion of all Spaniards was put into effect.[73] With this, the education of the young passed entirely into the hands of the town's Indian schoolteachers.

In 1831, the government of the recently created state of Sonora once again modified the scheme of internal administration for towns in Pimería Alta, through Law 19 (ratified on June 11), which fused the functions of earlier officials (*gobernador, alcalde, temastián*, etc.) in those of the *juez económico* and *alguacil* in each town.[74] The new regulation stipulated that the sole responsibility of the local authorities was to correct and/or punish lesser crimes (concubinage, drunkenness, theft) that went against "morality and social rights," while leaving all doctrinal issues in the hands of the missionaries.

The formal elimination of the position of *temastián* from Indian towns in Pimería Alta took place in the context of the secularization of that society, the consolidation of Spanish settlement, and, above all, the demographic changes that resulted in the progressive Hispanization of the old missions. By 1831, most towns in Pimería Alta were predominantly *mestizo*, and their forms of community organization had come under serious attack by interests that favored privatizing land and doing away with the corporative character of local social organization.

These changes in the internal government structure of the towns facilitated the withdrawal of religious functions from local authorities and deeply affected the forms of expression of local religiosity. As the number of priests in the Pimería Alta region was inadequate in the 1830s and the old system of communal offices had been suppressed, religious practices apparently moved from the public sphere to the domain of home and family, although exceptions could

---

[72] *Ley para el gobierno particular de los pueblos de Indígenas*, article 13, BL, M-M 285:122.

[73] See *infra*, Chapter 6.

[74] Decree no. 19 of the Government of the State of Sonora, June 11, 1831, BL, M-A 25:5, document 68.

be found in communities that still had a substantial indigenous population (San Xavier del Bac, for example).

In Opatería and Pimería Baja, meanwhile, there was a distinct evolution of community participation in the religious domain during the Franciscan period. Six years after their arrival in Pimería Baja, the Franciscans from the Colegio de Querétaro found that those towns' residents were already so deeply involved with the Spanish settlers and so reluctant to accept the rigors of the communitarian mission regime that they decided to withdraw from the missions.[75] Upon turning those missions over to the Franciscans from Xalisco province, the Queretarans argued that the ongoing contact between Indians and Spaniards, together with the former's insubordination to their ministers engendered by those relationships made it impossible to distinguish the missions from parishes administered by secular priests.[76] Although it is true that the Indians in some missions, such as Suaqui, were not well versed in Christian doctrine, Fray Juan Díaz, who visited those missions in 1775, found that residents were, in general, fairly well instructed. In his opinion, comparisons with parishes attended by secular priests were more justified in the cases of missions such as Ónavas, Cumuripa, Tecoripa, San José de Pimas, Opodepe, Ures, and Cucurpe, where the Indians had been "thoroughly separated from their ancient vices and customs," lived, generally, "in good order," and were devoted to agricultural work.[77] Father Díaz extended his praise to include the Opatería region, where religious instruction and the Hispanization of the Indians had progressed to a similar degree.

Once the Franciscans from Xalisco took over all of the missions in Pimería Baja and Opatería in 1775, they introduced a standardized method of distributing the aforementioned community positions in towns there—the importance of the *mador* in spiritual matters within their scheme has been noted. Although the civilian population exercised significant influence in those towns, the *cargos* system that the missionaries controlled maintained a relative balance between the interests of Spanish settlers and the missions. In 1781, however, this scheme underwent important adjustments when the commander general of the Internal Provinces, Teodoro de Croix, issued orders on August 2 that

[75] As the reader will recall, the Colegio de Querétaro was a Franciscan institute dedicated to "propagating the faith" (*propaganda fide*) among the heathen, which was not the situation that reigned in Pimería Baja, given the inhabitants' already considerable degree of integration into Spanish society.

[76] Report of Fray Diego Ximénez to the viceroy, Colegio de San Fernando, December 6, 1774, Fr. MCC 201, exp. 3; BPEJ, CM, book 50, vol. IV.

[77] Díaz, *Copia de la visita*, Fr. MCC 201, exp. 5.

took away the right by religious to punish "the negligent and immoral" in their towns and gave that faculty to the secular authorities. This decree also restricted the practice of using coercive mechanisms to force the Indians to attend religious events and limited the missionaries to reporting such absences to the local justices.[78]

The repercussions of these and other measures on the economic life of the missions have been discussed elsewhere.[79] The intent here is to underscore the implications of their application in the religious milieu of Pimería Baja and Opatería. The reader must keep in mind that the policy of eliminating forms of coercion used to ensure that the Indians to attend religious services was never applied uniformly in the Sonoran mission districts. While it is true that the abovementioned decrees included the missions in Pimería Alta, their application was much reduced there, primarily because everyone recognized the urgent need to keep the Pima Alto Indians on the missions as a means of populating that frontier zone. In Pimería Baja and Opatería, in contrast, the Indians more jealously guarded the material benefits that those measures granted them. As one missionary stated in 1796, the Pima, Ópata, Jova, and Eudeve Indians were at that time "so thoroughly accustomed to the freedom they have been granted . . . that though the form of government be changed in a thousand ways, [it] will never alter the way of life they lead."[80]

Because of the restrictions placed on the use of coercive measures once employed to oblige the Indians to attend mass and religious instruction, the late eighteenth century saw attendance at those services dwindle dramatically. In that period, children and adult women became the protagonists of religious fervor in those regions of Sonora.[81] Reciting and studying the catechism continued to be compulsory for children instructed by a *mador*, who, in all probability, began to be called *maestro* (teacher) by the people after the secularization of the missions. In the absence of a parish priest, he was in charge of caring for the church, teaching children, and organizing religious

[78] Fray George Loreto, *Informe en que se manifiesta el estado en que se halla en lo espiritual esta misión de Sta Ma. Basarac y sus pueblos de visita*, 1796, BL, 71/283m, folder 3.

[79] In concert with the colonial authorities' desire to grant the Indians greater freedom, Teodoro de Croix's decrees were strengthened in 1794 by Pedro de Nava, who eliminated the Indians' obligation to provide personal services. See Chapters 5 and 6.

[80] Fray George Loreto, *Informe*, BL, 71/283m, folder 3.

[81] In his narrative of the disdain with which the residents of Basarac regarded religious matters, Father Loreto mentioned one important exception: "[W]hat I have said of the Indians is not to be understood to include all of them, as there are some very good Christians, though very few. . . , especially among the women, most of whom are assiduous attendees at all church [functions]." Loreto, *Informe*, BL, 71/283m, folder 3.

events.[82] Women, in turn, began to play a more active role as cultural mediators by organizing public ceremonies.[83] One late example of female leadership in religious matters can be seen in the pilgrimage undertaken by the
Ópatas from Tuape to the basilica of the Virgin of Guadalupe in late 1839.
According to local tradition, the women of the community organized this
pilgrimage (clearly an extraordinary act for the time). After convincing their
husbands to accept the idea, they hurried to provision the participants for
this unusual event.[84] In subsequent years, the life of one of those women,
Juliana Cucivichama, was devoted to organizing local religious observances.
Near the end of her days, she was entrusted with the care of the church when
the town's *maestro* died.[85]

CHANGES IN THE EVERYDAY LIFE OF FRONTIER SOCIETIES

Without question, the greatest impact of contact between Indians and
Europeans in North America was the decline of indigenous populations in
ensuing years, due to the elevated mortality caused by European diseases, low
birth rates, the stress engendered by changes in Indian lifestyles, and the
poor sanitary conditions characteristic of the places that the Spanish established as dwellings for the Indians.[86] Literature on this topic is extensive. Part
of it is flawed by a tendency to explain the processes of change that occurred
after the onset of Indian–European contact using a narrative that speaks of
ethnocide or cultural genocide. Contrasting with this vision, there is also a
triumphalist history, one that recounts the saga of the missions' heroic efforts

---

[82] Tabanico, "De Tuape," 134. Among the Rarámuri, even today, there is an official called
mestro (from the Spanish *maestro*, teacher), who leads religious services most of the year. Merrill,
Rarámuri Souls, 43.

[83] The analysis of Indian women's agency as cultural mediators is well represented by Theda
Perdue, *Cherokee Women: Gender and Culture Change, 1700–1835* (Lincoln: University of
Nebraska Press, 1998); Clara Sue Kidwell, "Indian Women as Cultural Mediators," *Ethnohistory*
39, no. 2 (1992); Lucy Eldersveld Murphy, "Autonomy and the Economic Roles of Indian Women
of the Fox-Wisconsin River Region, 1763–1832," in Shoemaker, ed., *Negotiators of Change*,
72–89. See also Eldersveld Murphy, "To Live Among Us: Accommodation, Gender, and Conflict
in the Western Great Lakes Region, 1760–1832," in *Contact Points: American Frontiers from the
Mohawk Valley to the Mississippi, 1750–1830*, ed. Andrew R. L. Cayton and Fredrika Teute (Chapel
Hill and London: University of North Carolina Press, 1998); Natalie Zemon Davis, "Iroquois
Women, European Women," in *American Encounters: Natives and Newcomers from European
Contact to Indian Removal, 1500–1850*, eds. Peter C. Mancall and James H. Merrell (New York
and London: Routledge, 2000), 97–118.

[84] Tabanico, "De Tuape," 134.

[85] *Ibid.*, 133.

[86] See *supra*, Chapter 2.

to convert the Indians to Christianity and incorporate them into models of European civility. The opposition between the "Christophobic nihilist" posture and the "Christophilic triumphalist" perspective, as they have been called, has left little room for a more balanced analysis of the relations between Indians and Europeans in various frontier areas.[87] More recently, studies concerned with the history of subaltern groups have attempted to present a different version by recounting the measures taken by indigenous peoples to preserve and reconstruct their ethnic identities amid conditions of oppression and exploitation that characterized colonialism and the emergence of capitalist societies.[88]

However, beyond these stories of extermination, civilization, or ethnic survival, life along those frontiers presupposed a principle seldom recognized in studies dealing with contact between Indians and Europeans. Due to stagnant or declining population growth, near-absent military defense, harsh environmental conditions, and the ambivalent attitude toward the Spanish presence, frontier life did not grant long-lasting conditions of privilege or deprivation to any particular group, but rather caused all groups of actors to oscillate between situations of relative security and extreme dependence. This study does not idealize life on the frontier. Its aim is to identify the dynamics of Indian–Spanish interaction as aspects of the broader process of colonization. If the exploitation thesis were to be followed, then the separation of the Franciscans from administering mission assets—*temporalidades* or temporalities, as they were called at the time—would suffice to explain the conclusion of the mission period in northern New Spain. However, this fact alone cannot be considered "the cause" of this enterprise's erosion. Rather, it was the ascendancy of Spanish settlers in the latter half of the eighteenth century that eventually made the missions' projects increasingly incompatible with the times.

The study of transformations generated by Indian–Spanish interaction in Sonora has generally centered on broad topics such as religious and demographic change, as well as the transformation of Indians' working conditions. However, interethnic contacts in Sonora also affected less visible aspects of the everyday life of both mission communties and Spanish settlements (those inhabited by "whites," as non-Indian settlers began to be known in the nineteenth century), in ways that have only recently begun to

---

[87] Weber, "John Francis Bannon," 62; Sandos, *Converting California*, xiii-xiv.

[88] In Sweet's words, "This is not to presume that we are able to think as the colonized Native Americans did about their experiences in the missions. It is simply to recast the discussion of mission history in such a way as to make Indian experience rather than missionary experience its subject." Sweet, "The Ibero-American Frontier," 1.

be analyzed.[89] The material culture of both Indians and Spaniards, indigenous horizontal mobility, and forms of socialization and interdependence are just a few of the issues that must be explored in greater detail in order to gain a more complete image of the cultural transfer that characterized life along New Spain's northwestern frontier and that, in general, help us to understand why and how the residents of the missions ceased to be "mission Indians" in the post-1767 period.

Indian and Spanish Material Culture

Among the positive elements that emerged from Indian–Spanish contact several processes compete for primacy, one of which was the introduction of new foods and crops that complemented the Indians' traditional diet and agricultural cycle. For the Indian peoples of Sonora, the arrival of products such as lentils, chickpeas, fava beans, cabbage, onions, leeks, garlic, cowpeas, sugar cane, mustard, anise, mint, pepper, melons, apples, grapes, quinces, peaches, plums, pomegranates, apricots, and figs constituted welcome additions to their diet. Together with these foods, wheat was also very important, as it allowed them to add a winter harvest to supplement their traditional agricultural cycle based on corn, squash, and the giant cactus harvest.[90] In addition to such products, the adoption of agricultural techniques, metal tools, and textiles introduced by the Spanish also contributed to modifying Indian patterns of social organization.[91]

But the Spanish, in turn, also adopted new items, as they learned of a rich variety of natural resources from the Sonoran Indians, most of which were hidden from their view by the desert and the sierra.[92] According to its diverse

---

[89] Studies of sexuality, marriage, and family formation by Radding and Gutiérrez are among the proposals that have attracted the most attention due to their novel character and the interpretative possibilities they offer. Radding, *Wandering Peoples*, 103–68; Gutiérrez, *When Jesus Came*, 227–97.

[90] Thomas Sheridan, "The Columbian Exchange," in Officer and Schuetz-Miller, *The Pimería Alta*, 59; Edward F. Castetter and Willis H. Bell, *Pima and Pápago Indian Agriculture* (Albuquerque: University of New Mexico Press, 1942), 114, 202–207.

[91] Radding, *Wandering Peoples*, 67–75. The *Carta edificante* of 1777 describes the stone axes used by the Ópatas before they became accustomed to using steel ones. Núñez, *Carta edificante*, 136.

[92] In this respect, transculturation processes in Sonora bear comparison to the same kind of contact situation in the Guaraní missions, as analyzed by Ganson: "As part of a process of transculturation, the Guaraní were selective in their acceptance of things European. They chose to adopt what proved to be useful and rejected those things of little value to them. . . . [T]he Guaraní and the Jesuits created a New World culture in the reductions, which resulted from the blending of European and native traditions, diets, medicines, material culture, and technologies." Ganson, *The Guaraní*, 84.

geographical zones, the province of Sonora offered a long list of wild fruits that provided an important source of nourishment for the Indians, and later for the Spaniards. The pitahaya, sahuaro, prickly pear, cholla, nopal, dates, agave, *lechuguilla*, mesquite, *bachata*, *temaqui*, and squash were just some of the fruits and vegetables available to the townspeople of Sonora that were incorporated, sooner or later, into the diet of the Spanish colonists.[93] We know that by 1764 the Indians were selling pitahayas, picked from May to July, to their Spanish neighbors. The agave was so important in Pimería Alta that in certain seasons it was the only wild edible available to Indians and Spaniards alike, while *temaqui*, a whitish tuber, was much appreciated by Indians and "poor Spaniards" alike.[94] However, among the Sonoran populace in general, none of these foods enjoyed the popularity of cured squash, also called *vichicóri* or *vitzicóri*, a "delicious dish" prepared by the Indians that consisted of long strips of dried squash cooked in water.[95]

In addition to the abovementioned food sources, Sonora's flora offered a rich variety of medicinal herbs that the local population used. In his description of Sonora, Nentuig presents a list of thirty-three herbs that alleviated all manner of pains, fevers, urinary afflictions, and even venereal diseases. Although this Jesuit recognized that the Indians discovered applications of such herbs, by 1764 they were being used with skill by "elderly Spanish women [who had] taken over traditional Sonoran healing." In the words of one Franciscan missionary, the Spanish population of Sonora "owe most of their recoveries to the Indians," who knew the secrets of the herbs thanks to "their continued schooling in the mountains."[96] From the miserable dwellings of the presidio troops, to the missionaries' tables, and all the way up to the offices of the local authorities, the indigenous herbal medicine of the Sonoran peoples found in the Spanish populace a broad public in need of remedies to cure mal-

---

[93] Nentuig, *El rudo ensayo*, 58; West, *Sonora*, 9–13; Castetter and Bell, *Pima and Pápago Indian Agriculture*, 100–102; Núñez, *Carta edificante*, 121–23; Johnson, *The Opata*, 10–13.

[94] Nentuig, *El rudo ensayo*, 58–59. The importance of agave as a food is expressed in a military report on the presidio at Fronteras, where it was said that in April 1781 some of the inhabitants had gone out to cut "*mezcales*, the only food that, due to the scarcity of corn, wheat and other kinds of grains, is sustaining the troops and families" of the locality. AGI, Guadalajara 267.

[95] As the missionary at Santa María Basarac observed in 1777, preparing *vichicoris* consisted in the following steps: "after peeling the squash, it is cut in half and left in the open exposed to sunlight. . . . Next, long, thin strips are cut, which are placed under the sun's rays until they dry. Finally, they wind the strips into large balls that are cooked in a little water to obtain the final preserve." Núñez, *Carta edificante*, 121.

[96] Nentuig, *El rudo ensayo*, 61–64; Núñez, *Carta edificante*, 130. In this letter Father Núñez offers a list of ten medicinal herbs that complete Nentuig's earlier account.

adies common to frontier life. Indeed, at one point, an important Spanish official came to depend on such medical care to save his life. According to the testimony of one of his secretaries, during the most critical moments of the fevers and delirium that struck the *visitador* José de Gálvez on his travels through Sonora, some Indian women offered him their knowledge of local medicine.[97]

Of particular importance to the Indians was the introduction of textiles made of cotton and wool, which were transported to the northern provinces by the Jesuits and used, among other goods, as a means of remunerating Indian labor. Because woolen blankets and clothing soon became necessities for the Indians, the Jesuits urgently required that their orders for such merchandise be shipped to the missions punctually at the onset of winter. This, in fact, became a source of missionaries' frequent complaints. They insisted that their orders be sent out from Mexico City in a timely fashion.[98] Some authors argue that these textiles were important among the Sonoran Indians because they provided them with a currency to participate in local markets.[99] However, some evidence suggests the most widespread use of textiles (after their use as clothing of course) emerged when such items came to be recognized as status symbols by Indians and Spaniards. Around 1777, for example, it was said that the Ópatas at Basarac were dressing "in the Spanish style," and were "so fond of dressing well, that any who can do so wears good clothes, including silver accessories." The women from Basarac were particularly attracted to Spanish attire, and "wear many rich *zarazas* and blouses, though the *sarga* is more common."[100]

The prestige that accrued to the blue suit and red sash of the Ópata auxiliary soldiers was another example of this phenomenon: "[T]he suit they most fancy is that of the soldier, and many of them walk about in uniform, buying blue woolen cloth for the *chupa*, to which they add lapels and red cuffs."[101] The conflict between the general of the Ópata nation and the Indian governor of Basarac mission in 1789 is a highly illustrative case of the importance that Sonoran Indians came to attribute to "Spanish-style" dress as a status symbol. During a

---

[97] Almada Bay, *Manifiesto*, 126.

[98] Letter from Manuel Aguirre to Minister Provincial Ceballos, Bacadehuachi, January 7, 1764, AGN, Archivo Histórico de Hacienda, leg. 17, exp. 22; *Método que se ha seguido con las cinco provincias de misiones [jesuitas] que últimamente estaban a cargo del P. Joseph Hidalgo, procurador general de ellas*, 1767, BNFF, 16/301.

[99] My objections to this opinion are expressed in Chapter 4. Here, I limit myself to repeating that textiles cannot be considered as a form of storing wealth or as a substitute for currency, especially under the severe weather conditions of Sonora, which caused these textiles to deteriorate rapidly, thus reducing their value to the detriment of their owner.

[100] Núñez, *Carta edificante*, 138.

[101] *Ibid.*, 139.

visit to the town of Basarac, the Ópata general Ignacio Noperi, though not involved in any commission related to his post, happened to cross paths with the local governor, Francisco Medrano. Both men were dressed in the distinctive garb of their respective positions, with staff of office and hat included. Noperi believed that as he was the general of the entire Ópata nation it was only right that the *gobernador* of the town show him respect by doffing his hat in his presence. As Medrano did not do so, Noperi considered that his authority had improperly gone unrecognized. He proceeded to strike the governor and remove his hat, after which he ordered the residents of Basarac to detain him, remove him from office, and give him a whipping. During the inquiry that followed, it was established that Noperi had clearly exceeded the functions of his office because, as both officials were in the town and Noperi was not carrying out any kind of military action, he should have known that he was, in fact, subject to the authority of the local governor. In the opinion of the intendant of Sonora (the authority responsible for resolving the matter), Noperi's attitude reflected his ignorance of the relative hierarchy of his post and that of Medrano.[102] From a wider perspective, however, it is clear that it was both men's yearning to have their symbols of prestige recognized that led to such confrontations.

In the view of the missionaries and the rest of Sonora's populace, the Ópatas' use of this style of dress was representative of their desire to adopt Spanish appearance and indicative of their progress.[103] Around 1850, for example, a Spaniard in Sonora praised those people for their desire to dress according to "the customs of whites." Among the Ópatas, wrote José Francisco Velasco, "it is uncommon to see them naked or with *zapeta*, as they wear short white pants (*calzones*), shirt or perhaps a long smock (*cotón*) and leather shoes (*tegua*). The women use skirts (*enaguas*), and many tunics, their shawl (*rebozo*), shoes, etc."[104]

Among the Spanish and mestizo population of Sonora, the early decades of the nineteenth century witnessed a boom in ranch-style clothing, especially among those who lived on ranches and haciendas. Depending on the purchasing power of those who hankered for such attire, styles ran from modest to finely decorated garments with a range of options that, as a description from 1843 tells us, included the following features:

---

[102] Pedro Garrido y Durán to Ignacio Noperi, Arizpe, August 11, 1789, BNFF, 35/767.

[103] *Descripción de Arizpe*, BNFF, 34/733. A description of a campaign organized to pursue a group of Apaches in 1768 mentions that "the Indian auxiliaries of the north" (an expeditionary corps that included sixty Indians and forty riflemen) "were given a red headband to distinguish them." AHNM, Clero, Jesuitas, leg. 122, no. 6.

[104] Velasco, *Noticias Estadísticas*, 138.

sleeves . . . often made of fine woolen cloth . . . and cuffs of velvet adorned with fringes of gold and silver and trim of the same material, with a lining of *indianilla* cloth. The short pants [are] also made of fine woolen cloth, velvet or *paño*, adorned with seams and cuffs with braided strands of gold or silver and adornments, [and] buttons of golden or white metal on the closings. . . , the boots are always made of deerskin.[105]

By the mid-nineteenth century it was possible to identify, besides the Indians who had adopted Spanish dress and the people wearing rancher apparel, an undetermined number of vagabonds (*léperos*), that is, Indians and mestizos who meandered through the towns of Sonora in search of any means (licit or illicit) to secure their sustenance. In a later section of this chapter, the population's prejudices against such uprooted folk are discussed. While some contemporaneous observers identified these people as vagabonds, drunkards, thieves, and prostitutes, other witnesses emphasized certain features of dress that they considered common to this floating population. In their opinion, such people could be identified by their lack of attachment to any city or town in the state and by certain features of dress: plain, short cotton pants and a blanket thrown over the shoulder were the distinctive markings of this group, which was at the base of the social pyramid. Differences could also be noted within this sector of the population: "[S]ome are more naked than others, as in everything there are hierarchies." Among the women of this social stratum, their worn knickers, "made of any old cloth," and bare legs, arms and torsos were associated with a dissipated lifestyle. Their clothing included a shawl and shoes "made of satin, silk or some such thing."[106]

During the Franciscan period in Sonora, the space inhabited by the mission Indians also underwent certain transformations that affected primarily the maintenance of church buildings and the structure of their own houses. After the epoch of their foundation, the most important period of construction of mission churches in Sonora came in the late eighteenth century, especially in Pimería Alta. By 1800 the Franciscans from the Colegio de Querétaro and the residents of their missions had reconstructed almost all of the churches in Pimería Alta and equipped them with new wooden roofs or domes, adobe or stone walls, steeples, new façades and, in some cases, luxurious interior adorn-

---

[105] Vicente Calvo, *Descripción política, física, moral y comercial del Departamento de Sonora en la República Mexicana*, 1843, 140–41, BNM, Mss 19637.

[106] Calvo, *Descripción*. . . , 133–134.

ments such as those of San Xavier del Bac and Pitiquito.[107] In contrast, the churches in Pimería Baja and Opatería suffered a gradual deterioration during that period. According to a report by Fray Juan Díaz, by 1797 several were on the verge of ruin. Exceptions were the churches at Tuape, where the Queretarans had done some remodeling before 1774, Nacameri (*visita* of Opodepe), Buenavista (Cumuripa), Santa Rosalía (Ures), and Tónichi (Ónavas), where the missionaries from Querétaro had built new churches before turning the missions over to the Franciscans from Xalisco.[108]

With respect to Indian dwellings, around 1772, Father de los Reyes wrote that they were characterized by their irregular distribution, the fragility of their materials and the simplicity of their construction.[109] In this missionary's opinion, their small straw houses with mud roofs, described as "poorly formed huts . . . with no sign of a town," reflected the Indians' poverty and lack of civilization.[110] This friar's personal attraction to the town of Ures led him to present it as the exception to the rule of the poor material quality of housing in Pimería Baja, as he stated that the constructions there were the best to be found in all of Pimería Baja, because they were "made of adobe or stones and mud, with portals, bowers and fine wood."[111] According to this missionary, Opatería and

---

[107] The reasons for this boom in the material advancement of the churches in this period are discussed in the section entitled "Changes in mission administration and generational crises," in Chapter 5. For now, suffice it to say that in Cocóspera and Magdalena, the reconstruction was finished before 1795, with the conclusion of the work begun by friars Juan de Santiesteban and Pedro Arriquibar, respectively. In Tubutama, Saric, Ati, and Oquitoa, Friars Barbastro and Iturralde had also terminated reconstructions by that date. BNFF, 36/802. In Pitiquito the church was concluded by 1795, with a domed roof, thanks to funding obtained by Fathers Pedro Font and Antonio Ramos from 1780 to 1783. The murals in that building date from the decade 1783–1793. Fr. MCC, 203, exp. 24; Benjamín Lizárraga García, *Templo de San Diego del Pitiquí* (Hermosillo: Gobierno del Estado de Sonora, 1996), 202. The church at San Xavier del Bac was an imposing one after its reconstruction: "[W]ith dimensions of 36 *varas* in length, 8 [*varas*] in width and 22 across, that form two chapels. It is made entirely of cement and brick with its corresponding dome, collaterals and interior adornments of 38 full-sized saints. . . , and a series of angels and seraphims, its façade is very beautiful, its two towers in front, though one is as yet unfinished, its atrium which has 10 *varas* of frontage, with a cemetery on its left also made of brick and cement, of some 30 *varas* in circumference." The cost of this building reached 40,000 pesos. José de Zúñiga, Tucson, August 4, 1804, BNFF, 36/819. An exceptional case was that of the church of Caborca: Due to its location on the banks of the Asunción River (today the Concepción River) it had to be rebuilt on several occasions after flood waters washed away its walls. The building that can be seen today dates from approximately 1803–1809, and shows damage caused by the river. Pickens, *The Missions of Northern Sonora*, 87–88.

[108] Fr. MCC, 201, exp. 5; BNFF, 36/806.

[109] "Las casas dispersas, fabricadas de tierra y paja, muy pequeñas y sin división de viviendas." De los Reyes, *Noticia de las Provincias de Sonora*, AGI, Guadalajara 586.

[110] De los Reyes, *Memorial y Estado Actual.*

[111] *Ibid.*

Pimería Alta offered similar diversity, and the latter was characterized by the traditional homes of the Pápagos that were described brusquely as "simple stick works in the shape of an oven."[112]

The homes in Pimería Alta described in such disdainful terms were, in reality, a notable example of the Indians' adaptation to the difficult conditions imposed by their environment. The traditional round, flat-roofed house of the Pima Indians, known as the *ki*, was made of compacted sticks and mud, materials that were quite suitable for providing shelter from extreme heat.[113] In addition to their functionality for the inhabitants of Pimería Alta, such abodes were also congruent with the patterns of mobility that characterized those Indians. As discussed in the following section, securing their subsistence required the Desert Pimas to change their place of residence on a seasonal basis. This kind of dwelling underwent few modifications during the period under study.[114] What changed was that some Pima Indians in southern Pimería Alta began to construct adobe houses in such places as Imuris, Magdalena, Cocóspera, and San Ignacio, places that in 1778 registered 15, 18, 25, and 34 such homes, respectively, sufficient to house their respective local populations of 30, 67, 142, and 144 inhabitants.[115]

In Pimería Baja and Opatería, the diffusion of adobe houses was also a phenomenon characteristic of the last decades of the eighteenth century, especially in the Opatería, which offered a marked contrast to Pimería Baja in terms of the ratio of homes to inhabitants, as seen in Table 3.1.

With the exceptions of Opodepe, Nacameri, Basarac, and Bacoachi, villages in Opatería registered a more reasonable ratio of adobe houses to families. The figures for Bacoachi reveal discrepancies, as several Spanish and Indian families had been attracted to that town by the tracer mines discovered in the surrounding area. No reason has yet been found to explain why a larger number of adobe houses did not exist in Pimería Baja by 1778, so it may be supposed that the destruction occasioned during raids by the Seri and Pima Indians, or the possible rejection of such dwellings by the Pima Bajo Indians, were involved.

---

[112] De los Reyes, *Relación clara y metódica de todas las misiones*, BNFF, 34/759.

[113] Robert A. Hackenberg, "Pima and Pápago Ecological Adaptations," in Ortiz, *Handbook*, 173.

[114] In 1804, straw huts (*jacales de paja*, or *ki*) were still reported as the dwellings of the Pimas on the outskirts of Terrenate and at the Cocóspera mission. BNFF, 31/644. On the persistence of these constructions among contemporaneous Pimas, see Hackenberg, "Pima and Pápago," 171–77.

[115] I have calculated an average of 4 to 4.5 people per family using the criteria of the missionaries of the time. Data on housing and population are from BNFF, 34/736, and AGN, Californias, vol. 39, exp. 2, respectively.

TABLE 3.1. Ratio of adobe houses to number of families in selected sites, 1774–1778

Mission	Population		Families	Houses	Ratio
	Indians	Spaniards			
Pimería Baja					
Soyopa	177	34	53	15	1:3.5
Cumuripa	82		21	10	1:2.1
Tecoripa	155	28	46	16	1:2.9
Suaqui	220		55	12	1:4.6
San José de Pimas	160		40	12	1:3.3
Ures	267	99	92	18	1:5.1
Santa Rosalía	92	14	27	1	1:27
Opatería					
Opodepe	301	144	111	5	1:22.2
Nacameri	49	290	85	27	1:3.1
Cucurpe	300	108	102	110	1:0.9
Tuape	157		39	52	1:0.7
Basarac	556		164	122	1:1.3
Bavispe	256		64	59	1:1.1
Huachinera	220		55	59	1:0.9
Arizpe	389		97	118	1:0.8
Chinapa	493		123	132	1:0.9
Bacoachi	223		56	35	1:1.6

Sources: BNFF, 34/736; AGN, Californias, vol. 39, exp. 2; Núñez, *Carta edificante*, 118.

According to contemporaneous descriptions, by the mid-nineteenth century single-story adobe houses and wooden roofs had become the most common architectural model among the Indian and mestizo populations of Pimería Baja and Opatería. However, by that time because these structures had been increasingly linked to those segments of the population, the adobe house—once considered preferable to the earlier huts and bowers—had been transformed into a symbol of discomfort and simplicity. Around 1845, the town of Ures, then the capital city of Sonora State, was portrayed in a general description of the state as a lackluster place reflected in the absence of notable public buildings and the poverty of private homes, which were "highly irregular and lacking beauty, and also very weak as are all those made of adobe."[116] In Hermosillo, the one-story adobe houses that predominated in the urban set-

[116] Velasco, *Noticias Estadísticas*, 286.

ting of the adjacent ex-mission of Pitic,[117] and comprised the majority of private homes in that town were described in 1840 as miserable constructions in comparison with the houses of certain well-off families (some of which even had two stories) that were equipped with wide doorways, large windows, and, sometimes, ornamental trim made with limestone.[118]

Frontier Horizontal Mobility

From time immemorial, indigenous groups in Sonora had engaged in specific migration patterns, depending on the particular local configuration of their respective ecological environments, agricultural cycles, hunting and gathering activities, wars, religious celebrations, and exchange relationships with other communities. To this condition, which I call patterns of indigenous migration, the colonial period added what I identify as emerging pluriethnic mobility, a type of horizontal mobility[119] born of the Indian–Spanish relations and characterized by the flow of people of various ethnic groups going back and forth between missions and Spanish villages, town and country, and subjection and defiance to the colonial order. Changes of residence among Indians—especially to towns populated by other ethnic groups—due to such factors as intermarriage, employment, and formation of pluriethnic bands of

[117] In the mid-eighteenth century, the name Pitic identified Don Agustín de Vildósola's hacienda on the site of what is now Sonora's capital city. On that hacienda Vildósola established a garrison (*compañía presidial*) of the same name. On September 5, 1828, a decree issued by the state legislature of the Estado de Occidente renamed the "villa del Pitic," creating the "city of Hermosillo." BL, M-M 285:108. The hacienda, the presidio, and the villa del Pitic shared this name with the mission that had been founded directly to the south of that site, across the Sonora River. José Marcos Medina Bustos, *Vida y muerte en el antiguo Hermosillo, 1773–1828: Un estudio demográfico y social basado en los registros parroquiales* (Hermosillo: Gobierno del Estado de Sonora, 1997), 85–107.

[118] Calvo, *Descripción política*, 124–26.

[119] This concept has been generally applied to studies on migration and occupational changes in contemporaneous societies. However, its emphasis on changes in position without changes in status is useful in my analysis of Sonoran society in the late colonial period. Pitirim A. Sorokin, *Social Mobility* (London and New York: Routledge, 1998), 381–412. S. Patwardhan defined horizontal mobility as the "change from one occupation to another which indicates a change within the field of the same status level rather than strata." Patwardhan, "Aspects of Social Mobility among Scheduled Castes in Poona," in *Urban Sociology in India: Reader and Sourcebook*, ed. M.S.A. Rao (New Delhi: Orient Longman, 1974), 300–31. For an analysis of traditional forms of upward mobility in the colonial period, see Antonio Manuel Hespanha, "Las estructuras del imaginario de la movilidad social en la sociedad del Antiguo Régimen," in *Poder y movilidad social: Cortesanos, religiosos y oligarquías en la península ibérica (siglos XV–XIX)*, eds. Francisco Chacón Jiménez and Nuno Gonçalo Monteiro (Madrid: Consejo Superior de Investigaciones Científicas, Universidad de Murcia, 2006), 21–42.

outlaws and cattle rustlers exemplify these types of movement. To some extent, these processes allowed the Sonoran population to temporarily satisfy their needs for food, employment, and personal well-being, and although they did not represent a way out of poverty or a means to modify the social hierarchy, they offered the local population the opportunity to cope with the Spanish colonial order from diverse places and situations.

In Pimería Alta, earlier migration patterns were reflected in the forms of social organization of the Desert Peoples (Tohono O'odham or Pápagos) and the mechanisms they developed to adapt to that region's distinct ecological niches. Due to the ecological features of Pimería Alta, the Tohono O'odham manifested three different activity and settlement patterns that centered on the availability of foodstuffs. In the extreme western area of Pimería Alta, where the Colorado River flows into the Gulf of California, scanty rainfall (mean annual precipitation of zero to five inches) made agriculture impossible, so the Pápagos of that zone gained their subsistence by food gathering, which meant that they had to roam over large distances. The inhabitants of that region had no fixed settlements, which explains why attempts to adapt them to life at San Marcelo de Sonoita, were never quite successful, and why modern anthropologists often refer to them as the "No Village People." The central zone of Pimería Alta, meanwhile, was originally the territory of the Pápagos, which the Spanish called Papaguería. There, the rainy season allowed the inhabitants to cultivate certain crops, so in the summer months the people relocated to be near their plots, and then returned to their winter camps as the rains drew to an end. The mobility of these "Two-Village People" was one factor that dissuaded the clergy from establishing missions in the area, as they considered its inhabitants to be nomads. Finally, along the courses of the rivers that ran through Pimería Alta there were permanent settlements where other Pimas (the River People or Akai O'odham) practiced a flourishing rain-fed agriculture and benefited from the more abundant local flora and fauna. In this area missionaries established the towns that comprised the center of mission activity in Pimería Alta.[120]

In both Jesuit and Franciscan sources, these people's early patterns of mobility were explained in relation to the agricultural security that the missions in Pimería Alta provided to these denizens of the desert. In 1742, one Jesuit described their seasonal movements as follows:

---

[120] The patterns described thus far constitute the Pimas' modes of adaptation to their geographical milieu according to modern studies by anthropologists interested in Pimería Alta. See Fontana, "The O'odham," 20–23.

At times they [the Pápagos] come to Pimería Alta in great numbers, bringing with them their small children of three or four years of age to be baptized, and they stay on to help the Pimas with their planting and harvests, with no other interest than that of being fed; they also come when the friars call them to build a church or house and work in their own interest.[121]

In the Franciscan period, the Queretarans stationed in Pimería Alta said that "many Pápagos" came to those missions during the wheat and corn harvests, although they returned to their lands as soon as the season ended.[122] One description of Caborca, dated in 1793, underlines the importance of the annual arrival of the Pápago Indians at that mission and its corresponding *visitas* (Pitiquí and Bisanig):

[They come to] visit every year for two or three months in such numbers that I have counted as many as 250 [Indians] including older and younger ones; and the same thing happens in Bisanig, as those Pápagos say that their lands are very arid and bereft of water and, as they have no other occupation they come to these towns to work.[123]

These periodic visits to the missions in Pimería Alta continued in the same way even as late as 1830; the Pimas arrived in winter, only to leave again with the coming of spring.[124] Testimonies such as these have led some authors to argue that the main or general reason that brought the Indians to accept their subjection to the mission regime was precisely this ongoing search for more secure forms of sustenance. The case of the Pápagos, however, offers an important corrective to this view, as it shows that securing food did not, in fact, persuade those Indians to take up permanent residence in mission towns. Quite the contrary—the example of the Desert Pimas demonstrates one way in which certain Indian peoples managed to reconcile the arrival of new forms of colonization with older kinds of relationships between the people and their ecological environment. As we have seen, the Pápagos were accustomed to moving back

---

[121] *Descripción de las provincias de que se compone el gobierno de Sinaloa*, n.d., AGI, Indiferente 107, t. 1, ff. 302–309 v.

[122] Fray Juan Díaz to the discretory of the Colegio de Querétaro, Caborca, August 8, 1768, Fr. MCC, 201, exp. 3.

[123] Fray José Mora, *Plan de la misión de Caborca*, contained in his letter to the intendant of Sonora, dated in La Cieneguilla, June 12, 1793, BNFF, 36/795.

[124] "Indian tribes of the Gila River also arrive here (San Xavier del Bac) in great numbers to pass the lean winter season, but they return home in spring." Fernando María Grande to the governor of Estado de Occidente, Cucurpe, May 25, 1830, cited in Kieran McCarty, *A Frontier Documentary: Sonora and Tucson, 1821–1848* (Tucson: University of Arizona Press, 1997), 23.

and forth between the desert and the river basins (where the Pimería Alta missions were eventually set up), according to the seasons of the year, always taking care to arrive in the latter area around the time of the corn harvest. Although it is true that the founding of the missions in those areas modified this seasonal movement by justifying a second trip by the Pápagos to the missions in Pimería Alta at the time of the wheat harvest in late winter,[125] what is important is that the presence of the mission regime in no way kept the Pápagos from complementing their diet with the sources of food they exploited in their native habitat during the rest of the year. The same author who penned the description of Caborca (1793) cited above suggests this complementarity by pointing out that although the Pápagos did indeed arrive at the missions at harvest time, in the rainy season they cultivated their own fields back in their places of origin.[126]

In addition to these population shifts associated with the search for food, the Desert Pimas also undertook frequent journeys to the area around the Gila and the Colorado Rivers, where they could barter clothes and animals with the Yuma and Cocomaricopa Indians to obtain captive *nijoras* (Apache slaves) whom they would later sell in Spanish towns.[127]

Among the Ópatas, such early migration patterns seem to have been more restricted in their spatial dimension. The forests and intermountain valleys of Opatería offered Indians there sufficient rainfall for dryland and irrigation agriculture, as well as plentiful animals to hunt and wild vegetable products to gather. Thanks to their agricultural self-sufficiency, the Ópatas had no need to undertake extensive migrations such as those described above for the peoples of Pimería Alta. In fact, a Franciscan document from 1777 tells us that in ancient times the Ópata Indians of Santa María Basarac believed that the boundaries of their village extended only one day's walk in each direction, a territory in which no other people lived except the residents of Basarac, and which offered them everything they needed to live.[128]

With the establishment of the mission regime in Sonora, local Indians became involved in other forms of interaction with their environment and with the new settlers who had begun to arrive in the province. As a result, in addi-

---

[125] According to the testimony of Father Barbastro, the visits by the Pápagos to the missions in Pimería Alta occurred twice a year. Fray Antonio Barbastro, *Lista de los religiosos que esta custodia de San Carlos de Sonora tiene empleados en la Administración de las misiones*, Aconchi, November 16, 1791, AGI, Guadalajara 569.

[126] BNFF, 36/795.

[127] AGI, Indiferente 107, vol. 1, ff. 302–309; Teodoro de Croix to José de Gálvez, Arizpe, January 23, 1781, AGI, Guadalajara 267.

[128] Núñez, *Carta edificante*, 94.

tion to their early patterns of migration, new routes of dispersal began to emerge, as did new reasons for following them. Although constrained or controlled by the Jesuit missionaries, the seasonal movements of mission Indians to Spanish population centers in search of work, and the arrival of non-Indian colonists at mission centers marked changes in the orientation of the activities and the rhythm of life of the inhabitants of that frontier. Moreover, these nonviolent forms of population displacement were not the only ones, as the uprisings of the Seri and Pima Indians in the 1750s and 1760s and the growing hostility of the Apaches led to the emergence of a different type of itinerancy, this one personified by pluriethnic bands of outlaws.[129]

When, in 1768, new restrictions were placed on the missionaries' capacity to intervene in local governments in the Pimerías and Opatería, the Indians took advantage of the moment to begin to sell their products and labor outside the confines of the missions, free of any interference on the part of the clergy.[130] In the short term, this process led to the intensification of contact between Indians and Spanish settlers, as well as to an important modification of the dependency relationship that had existed between Spaniards and the mission towns. As a letter dated in 1772 synthesizes, by that time Indian mobility had become a vital cog in the economy of the mining establishments in Sonora, as Indian labor was an essential element in the subsistence of these centers. In the words of the head of the Cieneguilla political district (*partido*), it was of crucial importance for the mines there to maintain a permanent population of Indians who were satisfied and motivated to work:

> [For] if these [Indians] become displeased then all the work would end as they are the ones who search with great zeal for the rich fruits that [the mines] hold.

---

[129] In the beginning, the emergence of such bands was observed with disdain by local authorities who were much more concerned with trying to suffocate attempted rebellions that brought together several peoples and large contingents of Indians. In 1772, the governor of Sonora, Mateo Sastre, praised the campaign that Domingo Elizondo had led against the Seris from Cerro Prieto, though he minimized the fact that some rebels may well have gotten away: "The advantages obtained after the Expedition in these provinces, are that [the Indians] have been almost entirely pacified, as *no great disquiet is caused by the fact that some individual from the surrendered nations* [may] *insult travelers, rob or kill cattle* that [they] may find, as I consider them . . . just vagabonds, outlaws, thieves. . . ." Mateo Sastre to Viceroy Bucareli, San Miguel de Horcasitas, October 14, 1772, AGI, Guadalajara 513. Emphasis added.

[130] "Upon the exodus of the Jesuit fathers, it was told to all the Indians of these provinces that they would be freed from the labors they were forced to provide. . . . Because of that, it is now impossible to sustain the Texas method, or the one that the [Jesuit] fathers used to have, even in the event that such regulations be eliminated." Fray Francisco Garcés to Fray Sebastián Flores, San Xavier del Bac, August 3, 1768, Fr. MCC, 201, exp. 24.

. . . [I]t is the labor of [the Indians] that produces the *royal fifths* and the stability of this new locality, which subsists as long as they are treated with love and looked upon with mercy, because if they leave, then the entire area will immediately be deserted.[131]

Although the inhabitants of the Pimerías and Opatería had worked in the mines since earlier times, their participation had never been as great as in this later stage.[132] According to the same letter, the mining area of Cieneguilla had a population of some 4,000 inhabitants, most of whom (3,000) were Indians from different towns. The problem for the Sonoran miners and prospectors was that it proved difficult to retain Indian labor at the mines, because "as soon as the idea gets into their heads, they tend to parade off in large numbers back to their towns."[133] Information from an 1804 source confirms the persistence of these patterns of displacement towards the mining centers, especially in Ostimuri province. There, for example, the inhabitants of Yécora (fifteen Indian families and four families of other castes) worked at the Guadalupe mine; the residents of Taraichi worked as laborers in nearby towns; those of Arivechi, Pónida, Santo Tomás, Sahuaripa, Bacanora, and Nuri, though also dedicated to agricultural activities, "earn their sustenance as prospectors at the Ostimuri and Trinidad mines." The Indians from Ónavas and Tónichi also combined farming with gold prospecting in the rivers and work in the mines at San Antonio de la Huerta.[134]

The haciendas in the province of Sonora were another destination that attracted a substantial migrant population of extremely diverse origins. One example of this comes to us from the haciendas located near the old mission of Dolores, north of Cucurpe, where the *hacendados* "admit and offer work to all the outlaws and vagabonds who wish to labor there," using them to cultivate their plots and tend their cattle. A report from 1774 cites occasions during which more than thirty couples of Yaquis gathered in the town of Dolores on the pretext of looking for work on local haciendas; although those couples seemed to consist of "publicly recognized" matrimonies, some people believed

[131] Pedro Tueros to Viceroy Bucareli, Cieneguilla, October 16, 1772, AGI, Guadalajara 513.

[132] Due to the limits of this study, I do not discuss the displacement of the Yaquis into Sonora, Chihuahua, and other northern provinces, where they worked in mines and haciendas. Suffice it to say that no other indigenous group from Sonora compares with the Yaquis in terms of the frequency, distance, and duration of their movements for such reasons. On this, see Spicer, *Los Yaquis*, and Evelyn Hu-DeHart, *Missionaries, Miners and Indians: Spanish Contact with the Yaqui Nation of Northwestern New Spain, 1533–1820* (Tucson: University of Arizona Press, 1981).

[133] Pedro Tueros to Viceroy Bucareli, Cieneguilla, October 16, 1772, AGI, Guadalajara 513.

[134] Jacinto Álvarez, Real de Baroyeca, May 18, 1804, BNFF, 36/819.

them to be "almost all made up of Indians who are fugitives from their towns, and . . . women who are unfaithful to their husbands."[135]

One of the most important effects of these emerging patterns of pluriethnic itinerancy was that their dual nature—from missions to the exterior (Spanish towns, other Indian settlements) and *vice versa*—soon brought about a demographic reconfiguration that became visible in both the missions located along the frontier and those established closer to centers of Spanish colonization.[136]

In the second half of the eighteenth century in Pimería Alta, attacks by Apaches, diseases, uprisings, and precarious sanitary conditions caused a severe reduction of the local Indian population. As Fray Diego de Bringas explained in 1795, "the old Indians of the missions have succumbed to the rigors of the sustained hostilities of the Apaches, of disease and also of guns when they have rebelled."[137] Bringas went on to explain that by this later date, mission residents in Pimería Alta were mostly gentile Indians only recently congregated there. In the latter half of the eighteenth century, the decline of the original population along the riverways where the missions in Pimería Alta had been founded had forced the Franciscans to initiate programs designed to congregate Indians from the Desert Pimas who often visited those missions at certain times of the year, as well as Indians from other groups who arrived in those towns as slaves, for purposes of trade, or due to kinship ties. In 1803, the head of the Queretaran missions in Pimería Alta acknowledged the population change that this program had triggered:

> The primitive and radical nation of the Indians at those missions is that of the Pimas; though at present they are thoroughly mixed with the Pápagos who frequently congregate at these towns where there are also various other nations which are called Nijoras, though they are Yumas, Jalchedones, Cahuenes, Cocomaricopas, all of whom speak the Pima language.[138]

In the district of Pimería Baja and Opatería, the demographic rearrangement taking place there in the closing years of the eighteenth century was characterized by the decline of the Indian population (due to miscegenation or dispersal) and the rapid increase in the numbers of nonindigenous residents in the

[135] De los Reyes, *Memorial y Estado Actual.*
[136] See *supra*, Chapter 2.
[137] AFPM, AQ, Letter K, leg. 18, no. 25.
[138] Fray Francisco Moyano, *Noticia de las misiones que ocupan los religiosos del colegio de la Santa Cruz de Querétaro en dicha provincia* [de Sonora]. . . , Oquitoa, May 18, 1803, AGI, Mexico 2736.

missions. The mission at Ónapa provides a clear example of these processes. A 1784 report mentions that this mission's three *visitas* (Taraichi, Yécora, Tacupeto) had been deserted, and that no one knew where the Indian families who had once lived there had gone. At the same time, in Ónapa "a multitude of families of mulattos and other castes have joined the Indians." In Sahuaripa and Arivechi, the arrival of Spaniards and castes in Indian towns and the exodus of Jova and Ópata Indians to live outside the missions were phenomena that had occurred since the expulsion of the Jesuits.[139] By 1797, the situation in Móchopa and Taraichi confirmed this dispersion of the indigenous population. In the words of the friar who inspected the Pimería Baja missions in that year, Móchopa "is a town in name only, which I found ruined and almost deserted," as the local population had dispersed "into the mountains and [other] villages in search of sustenance." In Taraichi, this *visitador* found only five families living in the town "as all the other [Indians] are away, some with women they have stolen, others as servants [leaving], in a word, the town collapsed."[140]

Of course, the abandonment of these mission towns was also due in no small degree to Apache raids. Indian villages like Suamca, Saracachi, Guevavi, and Calabazas were deserted after being attacked and ransacked, and mining centers such as Aguaje, Aygame, San Juan Bautista de Sonora, and Mababi, as well as several haciendas and ranches in Sonora, were also abandoned after the 1760s, when incursions by the Apaches increased in intensity.[141]

Although the Apache peril certainly explains the total and permanent abandonment of those sites, it cannot explain the partial depopulation of other missions or the cyclical movement of mission Indians between their villages and nearby Spanish settlements. The indigenous population's growing lack of conformity to the mission regime and the possibility of finding an alternative to that form of government in Spanish society may serve much better as the reasons for the demographic changes described above. Let us consider from this perspective a complaint presented in 1777 before Juan Bautista de Anza, captain of the Tubac *presidio* by Ópata Indians from several villages. Through the intervention of the Ópata general, Juan Manuel de Varela, they said

> that to the serious detriment of their persons, their women, and children, as well as the few goods they possess, in most of the missions [the missionaries]

---

[139] De los Reyes, *Relación clara*, 1784, BNFF, 34/759.

[140] Fray Juan Felipe Martínez to Commander Pedro de Nava, Ures, June 8, 1797, BNFF, 36/806.

[141] *Noticias separadas que ha adquirido el gobernador de Sonora de otros minerales. . . , desiertos y desamparados por las hostilidades de los indios*, 1761, AGI, Guadalajara 511; BNFF, 32/666.

make them work all the weeks of the year, poorly fed and treated worse with
injurious words . . . , that . . . they are denied the foods they require even on
the few days when [the missionaries] employ them in their service [and] that
of the motherland and of the king, in pursuing their enemies. That [the
Indians] are treated in the same way when they accompany their Captain for
the same purposes.[142]

Whether fictitious or real, these accusations by the Ópatas spurred by the
privations they experienced in mission towns did indeed reflect their disinterest in continuing to live under the mission regime. In this context, the real possibility that Indians (especially in Opatería) would "simply leave without saying
a word to the governor of the town or the father minister" and take jobs as servants or fieldworkers for "entire years" constituted the most important factor
behind the emerging patterns of mobility described herein.[143]

Interethnic Alliances in the Transformation of Sonora's Northern Frontier

This emerging mobility had two faces that the Spanish authorities in northwestern New Spain found enormously difficult to cope with. As noted above,
this itinerancy gave Indians the opportunity to find alternative means of subsistence and thus escape from the pressures that the mission regime imposed on
them, while at the same time providing Spanish colonists with a way of securing sufficient workers for their varied enterprises and projects. On the other
hand, this constant transit of Indians from one place to another constituted a
serious concern for the security of Sonora's inhabitants, as the bands of Indian
rebels that frequently perpetrated assaults along the roads or in the towns took
advantage of this movement when they were detained by local authorities:
They would simply allege that they were just simple Indians who were making
their way to some mine or hacienda in search of work. It was precisely for this
reason that in 1769, during his visitation to Sonora, José de Gálvez had
ordered local authorities to prohibit Indians, mestizos, and members of other
castes from abandoning their place of residence for any reason unless they were
carrying a certificate issued by the local authorities or their missionary that
accredited "their affiliation, character, state, wife and family." During the same
visit, Gálvez also ordered that any official, hacienda owner, or administrator

---

[142] BNFF, 34/734.
[143] *Padrón de San Miguel de Ures*, 1772, AGN, Provincias Internas, vol. 81, exp. 7.

who knew about an Indian that disobeyed this disposition should denounce him to local authorities so that he could be apprehended.[144] Those local authorities, of course, saw very clearly that it would be exceedingly difficult to tell the difference between an Indian walking about in search of work and a simple vagabond, outlaw, or bandit. Equally evident was the fact that in the prevailing circumstances, the need for people to move from place to place was one of the visible expressions of certain forms of socialization that put the Spanish authorities' control of Sonora in jeopardy. Let us now move on to examine the nature of these and other forms of interaction among the various groups who were by then living in Sonora.[145]

PLURIETHNIC BANDS IN SONORA

In a report sent to the Ministry of the Indies in Spain in 1778, Commander Teodoro de Croix expressed pride in his soldiers' actions after a successful confrontation with a band of Seri Indians that for some time had been harassing missions and Spanish settlements in Pimería Alta and a large area of central Sonora. After detailing the band's atrocities, de Croix described the counteroffensive launched by his troops. He was especially satisfied

> because one of the dead was the Pima rebel [known as] 'Juan el Cocinero', who had joined the Seris and was used to seduce them and those of his own nation. He was the oracle of both [groups] and perpetrator and cause of most of the deaths and devastation that Pimería Alta has suffered in the past five years.[146]

The incident recounted by de Croix reveals the pluriethnic nature of the rebel Indian bands that rose up to torment the province of Sonora. This particular case highlights the influence exercised by a Pima Indian at the helm of a group made up mostly of Seris, and generically identified with the latter ethnic group. Also significant is the nickname of the band's leader, *el cocinero*

---

[144] The 1769 disposition was reiterated in the royal order dated March 14, 1786, issued by José de Gálvez to the viceroy of New Spain. It commanded the viceroy to instruct the interim commander general of the Internal Provinces to reissue the 1769 order. Viceroy Conde de Gálvez did so on September 15, 1786, by instructing Commander Jacobo Ugarte y Loyola accordingly. AGI, Guadalajara 406.

[145] The following discussion on Apache raids in Sonora had been partially outlined in José Refugio de la Torre Curiel, "'Enemigos encubiertos': Bandas pluriétnicas y estado de alerta en la frontera sonorense a finales del siglo XVIII," *Takwá* 14 (2008): 11–31.

[146] Teodoro de Croix to the Ministry of the Indies, Valle de Santa Rosa, February 15, 1778, AGI, Mexico 2462.

("the cook"), which may refer to the trade he plied in his home village, but also reflects the degree of identification that some members of such bands maintained with local villages.

The case of Juan "the cook" was no isolated incident. In 1776, the presidio at Janos was attacked by an Apache band led by a Spaniard, who had been captured by Apaches shortly before. At one point during that attack, this captive found himself face to face with one of his own relatives, an uncle who implored that his life be spared. The Spanish-turned-Apache raider replied that "he had no other uncle or father than the mountain" and proceeded to slay his relative.[147] Two years later, in early 1778, a band of Apaches set upon the presidio at Santa Cruz. The military report on that raid stated that during the skirmish "José Elías was seen among the Indians." Elías had been a resident at that presidio, but "had gone over to . . . [the Apaches] in the previous year of 1777 and has been the cause of this damage."[148] In another incident, a group of more than three hundred Indians attacked the people of Cucurpe as they were out working in their cornfields, killing forty-five people, and taking another forty-four women and children as prisoners. According to the testimony of one survivor, the attackers had spared the life of the missionary (who at the time of the skirmish was also out in the fields), "because the captive who commanded them so ordered."[149] Several witnesses confirmed that "the captive" who led the Apaches in the attack on Cucurpe was none other than a local resident named José María, the son of one Eugenio Gómez, who had been taken captive by the Apaches some time before.[150] But José María was not the only non-Apache who was active in this band; once freed in exchange for some clothes and tools, the prisoners taken by the "Apaches" led by José María in Cucurpe "adduced that most of the aggressors were captive Pimas, Ópatas, Yaquis, *gente de razón*, some Seris and only a few Apaches."[151] Given their composition and knowledge of the terrain and towns, these pluriethnic bands[152] (normally identified simply as

---

[147] Núñez, *Carta edificante*, 127.

[148] Teodoro de Croix to José de Gálvez, Chihuahua, June 29, 1778, AGI, Guadalajara 276.

[149] Teodoro de Croix to the Ministry of the Indies, Arizpe, June 30, 1781, AGI, Guadalajara 267.

[150] The final reference that I have to the activities of José María finds him as part of a group of Apaches that accepted peace in Bacoachi on November 7, 1786. On that date, José María González arrived with fifteen people from the Peñascosa sierra (near the presidio of Santa Cruz), including two nieces and one daughter of the Apache captain Chiquito. AGI, Guadalajara 521.

[151] AGI, Guadalajara 521. According to a report by the commander general of the Internal Provinces, all attacks by the Apaches included "many Pimas *gileños* and Pápagos *cimarrones*." Joseph Antonio Rengel, Chihuahua, November 1, 1784, AGI, Guadalajara 520.

[152] The term "pluriethnic" was not used in this period, although diverse testimonies make it clear that the Sonoran populace knew that the bands were not made up of people from a single

Apaches[153] or Seris in most of the literature on this topic), possessed an extraordinary capacity to move, disperse, and then coalesce once again. It was well known, for example, that the raids perpetrated by such bands declined once the harvest seasons ended, and that they were rarely seen in the villages again until it was time to bring in new harvests.[154]

How were such bands formed? What internal mechanisms brought about the coming together of people from such diverse backgrounds? Some observers, including Commander Felipe de Neve, believed that they were just groups of "sloths, vagabonds, outlaws and undesirables" accompanied by "many Indian fugitives from their villages and missions," who carried out their robberies and killings while dressed as Apaches. According to one missionary in Opatería, these bands emerged from among the "mass of idlers and vagabonds that . . . live in indolence, leaving their miserable families in total abandonment, need and privation," persons who because of their dissolute lifestyle were easily captured or recruited by the Apaches. By the mid-nineteenth century, people who had abandoned their homes and come together to roam through the state of Sonora, were described as *léperos* (vagabonds, loafers) who "abhor any kind of work and give themselves up to idleness," living by fraud, gambling, and often "pillaging and theft."[155] In other cases, opinions on this subject were less visceral and emerged from a closer observation of the conduct of such bands. In 1787, Commander General Jacobo Ugarte attributed this problem in the towns and haciendas of Sonora to the presence of "covert domestic enemies," that is, individuals who served as spies and auxiliaries for the Apaches, transmitting

---

ethnic background. In a recent demographic study, David Carbajal López uses this adjective to refer to the families whose members had been identified during their lives with different ethnic categories in the sacramental records, a result of phenotypical differentiations made by the priests involved. Carbajal López, *La población en Bolaños, 1740–1848: Dinámica demográfica, familia y mestizaje* (Zamora: El Colegio de Michoacán, 2009).

[153] According to Chantal Cramaussel, the word *apache* was first used to identify the peoples living east of the Pueblo Indians near New Mexico. However, during the eighteenth century, Spanish officials extensively documented the presence of Apaches throughout large portions of northern New Spain, which Cramaussel suggests, should be understood as a loose usage of the term (including various ethnic groups within this category) rather than a "sudden and unexpected expansion of a nomadic group of people." Chantal Cramaussel, "Los apaches en la época colonial," *Cuadernos del Norte* 21 (1992): 25–26. Apparently, the Spaniards borrowed the term from the Maricopas "in whose language it signifies enemy." Joseph Amasa Munk, *Southwest Sketches* (New York: G.P. Putnam's Sons, 1920), 217.

[154] AGI, Guadalajara 267.

[155] *Bando* issued by Felipe de Neve on December 10, 1783, prohibiting Indians from leaving their towns without a certificate from their priest or local justice. AGI, Guadalajara 406; Núñez, *Carta edificante*, 127; Calvo, *Descripción*, 132.

timely notification and news as to what was going on, in addition to guiding or aiding them in their forays and attacks.[156]

Identifying the Apaches' allies, however, does little to explain the circumstances and motivations that led them to participate in such dangerous undertakings. In order to understand the general context of these developments, we must consider the evolution of imperial policy as it related to the defense of New Spain's northern frontier, as well as the reasons for the Apaches' southward displacement.

Since the creation of the Comandancia General de las Provincias Internas in 1776,[157] and under the aegis of bureaucrats and reformers who sought to strengthen the Spanish presence on the empire's peripheries, Commander General Teodoro de Croix attempted to increase both the number of troops and the financial resources assigned to northern New Spain.[158] The reports that de Croix—the first Spanish officer in charge of the Comandancia General— received from the Internal Provinces, and then forwarded on to the court of Madrid, constituted a clear justification of his intention to deploy an additional force of two thousand men along the frontier.[159] Thus, by the 1780s viceregal

---

[156] This list was included in the *bando* in which Ugarte y Loyola conceded a general pardon to "the prisoners for high treason and collaboration with the enemies that were hidden, absent, or fugitives from their towns." Chihuahua, January 4, 1787, AGI, Guadalajara 406.

[157] Gálvez and Croix projected the creation of the comandancia (January 23, 1768) as an autonomous government aimed at promoting the Internal Province's economic growth and improving the efficiency of the region's defenses and administration. Although the plan was approved by the king, it was not implemented until José de Gálvez assumed the position of secretary of the Indies in 1776. "The Comandancia General was semi-autonomous at best. Although independent of the viceroy in theory . . . [it] remained within the Viceroyalty of New Spain, and its commander in chief was required to keep the viceroy informed of his activities and he depended on the viceroy for supplies." The first commander general was Teodoro de Croix, and his jurisdiction included the Californias, Sonora, Sinaloa, Nueva Vizcaya, New Mexico, Texas, and Coahuila. Weber, *The Spanish Frontier*, 224–25. See also, Priestley, *José de Gálvez*, 293–95; Mario Hernández Sánchez-Barba, *La última expansión española en América* (Madrid: Instituto de Estudios Políticos, 1957), 114–32; Luis Navarro García, *Don José de Gálvez y la Comandancia General de las Provincias Internas del Norte de Nueva España* (Seville: Escuela de Estudios Hispano-Americanos, 1964), 275–84.

[158] Navarro García, *Don José de Gálvez*, 287–303.

[159] *Ibid.*, 292. Unfortunately for de Croix, Viceroy Bucareli opposed the creation of the Comandancia General because it separated that area from the scope of his faculties and, in reality, created a new administrative and territorial entity within the jurisdiction of New Spain. It was no accident that years later a long controversy emerged between the two entities over jurisdiction and autonomy. In fact, it is for this and other reasons that Luis Navarro García speaks of the period as one of a "profound crisis [in the Comandancia General] that would not be fully settled during the years that remained before the end of Spanish domination." Navarro García, *Don José de Gálvez*, 428–29.

authorities commenced a military offensive against rebel Indians along several fronts in northern New Spain in an attempt to exterminate—quite literally— such Indian nations as the Seris, Apaches, and Comanches.[160] As stated by Commander Felipe de Neve in 1784, the strategy aimed "to slay many enemies, take some prisoners, and instill and inculcate in them such terror as they have already experienced, and thus bring nigh the moment of their reduction or extermination."[161]

In the case of Sonora, this campaign required more troops, which led to an increase in the local military from 805 soldiers in 1783 to 906 four years later.[162] As part of this program, in 1784 Commander de Neve set up a company of Ópata Indians in Bacoachi[163] and increased the size of the Indian company at Bavispe, which had been created shortly before in 1781.[164] However, the policy of taking the war into unconquered Indian territories did not pay the dividends that the Crown expected, and in 1786 a new strategy was being

---

[160] Propelled by Charles III and his ministers, New Spain's policy for its northern frontier stressed reinforcing its military strength. At first those defenses served more as a protective measure against incursions by foreign powers than against raids by Indian nations. By the eighteenth century the functions of the presidios had been broadened to include full participation in the open war against rebel Indians. The visitation to the northern presidios by Marquis de Rubí (1766–1768), his recommendations, and the publication of the regulations of 1772 for reforms in the presidios made it clear that the Spanish Crown's policy toward rebel Indians gave precedence to force over diplomacy. Weber, *The Spanish Frontier*, 204–24. In Sonora, one example of the organization of military operations that characterized this period was the 1771 campaign coordinated by Pedro Corbalán, and led in the field by captains from the Terrenate, Tubac, and Fronteras presidios. With the creation of the Comandancia General of the Internal Provinces, punitive campaigns against hostile Indians (called *mariscadas*) continued with the approval of the commander, Teodoro de Croix. AGI, Guadalajara 271.

[161] Felipe de Neve to José de Gálvez, Arizpe, March 8, 1784, AGI, Guadalajara 519.

[162] Both figures include the presidios' officers, priests, and troops. By 1783 Sonora's military consisted of 504 soldiers deployed in six presidios, 168 troopers forming two auxiliary companies, 50 "dragons" (*dragones*), and 83 volunteers from Catalonia. Teodoro de Croix to José de Gálvez, Arizpe, June 30, 1783, AGI, Guadalajara 284. Data for 1787 comes from Jacobo de Ugarte y Loyola, *Plan para el arreglo de la defensa de las Provincias Internas*, Chihuahua, February 1, 1787, AGI, Guadalajara 287.

[163] Felipe de Neve to José de Gálvez, Arizpe, April 5, 1784, AGI, Guadalajara 285. The company of Ópatas at Bacoachi included a lieutenant commander, a second lieutenant, an Ópata captain, two veteran sergeants, and 85 Ópata Indians. This force's functions were to "participate in ongoing campaigns against the enemies' camps, guard the lands immediately around the gold mines at Bacoachi, especially during the seasons when they are worked, provide support to the Fronteras and Santa Cruz presidios . . . and follow to the letter the orders I send it." Felipe de Neve, *Instrucción para el gobierno de la Compañía de Fieles Ópatas. . .*, Arizpe, March 29, 1784, AGI, Guadalajara 285.

[164] Teodoro de Croix to José de Gálvez, Arizpe, August 8, 1782, AGI, Guadalajara 284.

tested in the frontier. This time, trade and gifts would be used as peaceful means to bring Indians into Spanish society.[165]

The new policy coincided with the arrival in the Internal Provinces of a new commander, Jacobo Ugarte y Loyola,[166] who carried orders to authorize the congregation of a large contingent of Apaches in Bacoachi, a group that in that same year had negotiated peace with the company's second lieutenant, Domingo Vergara.[167]

Regarding the increase in Apaches' hostilities during the eighteenth century, some authors have considered the possibility that population movements by other indigenous groups that occupied lands not yet subject to Spanish rule had pushed the Apaches southward, out of their traditional hunting territories on the edges of Spain's dominions, which is one of the classic explanations of the violence characterizing Mexico's northern frontier during the nineteenth century.[168] Although such displacements did occur, the Apaches' most violent response occurred as a result the American westward expansion after 1830[169]

---

[165] This change in policy proved especially productive in New Mexico, where peace treaties with the Comanches spurred a period of demographic and economic recovery after 1785. Factors behind this change include Spanish disinterest in dedicating resources or personnel to the wars, pressures within Indian groups triggered by the effects of epidemics, and their rivalries with other indigenous peoples. John L. Kessell, *Kiva, Cross and Crown: The Pecos Indians and New Mexico, 1540–1840* (Washington, DC: National Park Service, 1979), 401–10; James F. Brooks, *Captives and Cousins: Slavery, Kinship and Community in the Southwest Borderlands* (Chapel Hill and London: University of North Carolina Press, 2002), 164–65; Gutiérrez, *When Jesus Came,* 152–54, 166–75, 300; R. Douglas Hurt, *The Indian Frontier, 1763–1846* (Albuquerque: University of New Mexico Press, 2002), 42–48. According to David Weber, "to some extent, this late eighteenth-century emphasis on trade as the preferred instrument for controlling independent Indians represented a practical response to Spain's declining ability to fight Indians in America as wars in Europe siphoned off Spain's resources. . . . [It] also reflected the Bourbons' larger interest in making their American colonies more profitable." Weber, *Bárbaros,* 181.

[166] Ugarte y Loyola was appointed commander general of the Internal Provinces by royal decree dated October 6, 1785, and took possession on April 20, 1786. Jacobo Ugarte y Loyola to José de Gálvez, Chihuahua, June 1, 1786, AGI, Guadalajara 286.

[167] According to the official version, the Apaches had been asked to come down from "the sierra de Chiricagüi" by Vergara and, having accepted his invitation, appeared in Bacoachi on November 19, 1786. Jacobo Ugarte y Loyola to José de Gálvez, Chihuahua, February 1, 1787, AGI, Guadalajara 286.

[168] Max L. Moorhead, *The Apache Frontier: Jacobo Ugarte and Spanish–Indian Relations in Northern New Spain, 1769–1791* (Norman and London: University of Oklahoma Press, 1968), 9. For a critique of the thesis of the southward displacement of the Apaches, see Cramaussel, "Los apaches," 25. In the case of New Mexico, it has been shown that the cycles of peace and war with the Comanches reflected processes similar to those suggested here. Kessell, *Kiva, Cross and Crown,* 401–10; Brooks, *Captives and Cousins,* 164–65.

[169] Brian DeLay, *War of a Thousand Deserts: Indian Raids and the U.S.–Mexican War* (New Haven, CT, and London: Yale University Press, 2008).

and thus do not suffice to explain the—real or rhetorical—proliferation of Apaches in northern New Spain in the second half of the eighteenth century. For Juliana Barr, the Spaniards' decision to make alliances with the Apaches' foes—such as the Caddos in Texas—"automatically put Spaniards into a hostile position vis-à-vis Apaches." Furthermore, "the spread of Spanish horses and French arms was reorienting native power relations across Texas and the Southern Plains, a development that did not bode well for Spaniards."[170]

However, prolonged periods of open confrontation with Spaniards and other Indian nations eventually exhausted the natural resources of Apache territories and pushed some groups of Apaches into New Spain's northern frontier to "make peace" as a means of securing new sources of subsistence. Pedro Galindo, an officer from the Comandancia General, acknowledged this situation in 1791 and reported to his superiors that "repeated experiences have shown that the lands the Apaches occupy cannot provide for their subsistence needs, and that in their current situation they have no other means of satisfying them than by coming into our territories to steal and harass."[171] In some cases, these circumstances encouraged the Apaches to accept peace agreements with the Spanish authorities, as they did in Bacoachi in 1786. In other cases, some Apache groups between the Gila River and Sonora's northern sierras opted to form alliances with the Navajos in order to keep themselves on the margins of Spain's dominions.[172]

Turning to the motivations that led individuals to join the groups we are analyzing, William Merrill's work on pluriethnic bands in Nueva Vizcaya is of great utility. Upon analyzing the case of a large band that operated in southern Nueva Vizcaya, Merrill discovered that such groups had originally been made up of small bands of Apaches, but later grew "as people dissatisfied with their lot in colonial society abandoned Spanish missions and economic centers."[173] Although these bands had operated along the northern frontier from very early

---

[170] Juliana Barr, *Peace Came in the Form of a Woman: Indians and Spaniards in the Texas Borderlands* (Chapel Hill: University of North Carolina Press, 2007), 160.

[171] Pedro Galindo Navarro to Pedro de Nava, Chihuahua, April 4, 1791, in *Conmutación de la pena de horca impuesta a José Reyes Pozo, soldado de la compañía de indios ópatas de Bacoachi por la de 10 años de arresto por apostasía y sedición de los indios Chiricaguis establecidos en Sonora, 1798*, AGS, Secretaría de Guerra, 7027, exp. 7.

[172] Jacobo Ugarte y Loyola to José de Gálvez, Chihuahua, November 2, 1786, AGI, Guadalajara 286.

[173] William Merrill, "Cultural Creativity and Raiding Bands," in *Violence, Resistance, and Survival in the Americas: Native Americans and the Legacy of Conquest*, eds. William Taylor and Franklin G.Y. Pease (Washington, DC, and London: Smithsonian Institution Press, 1994), 142.

times,[174] it seems that the socioeconomic reorganization which followed on the heels of the expulsion of the Jesuits in 1767 contributed substantially to accentuating this phenomenon.[175] The fact that the most aggressive phase of attacks coincided with the most drastic readjustments of the mission regime seems to be indicative of a connection between these two processes.[176] In this respect, it seems prudent to at least consider the hypothesis that during the second half of the eighteenth century, in a period in which the Franciscans were losing their capacity to organize and distribute both the labor and products of the mission Indians, in which labor relations between those Indians and Spanish settlers were intensifying, and in which the missions were losing more and more of their lands to Spanish colonists, the Indians' living conditions deteriorated. It is highly probable that as the Indians and other increasingly vulnerable sectors of colonial society became more tightly connected to the trade system described elsewhere in this study, they accumulated so much debt that their incorporation into outlaw bands constituted an escape valve to dissipate those tensions.[177]

In his discussion of pluriethnic bands in Nueva Vizcaya, Merrill found that most members of such groups were agricultural workers who had moved between mission towns and Spanish settlements before joining a band. They were not protected by the townsfolk, nor did they have the ability to appear, in one moment, as bandits and, in another, as simple residents of a mission or ranch. Rather, in Merrill's view, members of such bands were men and women, who, due to a variety of pressures (psychological, economic, and social) had abandoned colonial society in order to form "a nomadic raiding version of the *cimarrón* societies." Inasmuch as they constituted concrete forms of socializing

---

[174] Philip W. Powell, *Soldiers, Indians and Silver: North America's First Frontier War* (Berkeley: University of California Press, 1952), 173–74.

[175] William Merrill coincides on this point, though in the case of Nueva Vizcaya he gives priority to other structural factors: "While the adverse effects of the expulsion and secularization undoubtedly contributed to Tarahumara discontent after 1767, the factors motivating their participation in raiding appear to have been linked to the structures of oppression and exploitation intrinsic to Spanish colonial society." Merrill, "Cultural Creativity," 143.

[176] Sara Ortelli analyzed the attacks by Apache bands in Nueva Vizcaya after 1748 and demonstrated that these groups' economic motivations were a product of the strong pressures that the rising prices of foods and other goods exerted upon the most vulnerable sectors of the local population. Ortelli, *Trama de una guerra conveniente: Nueva Vizcaya y la sombra de los apaches (1748–1790)* (Mexico City: El Colegio de México, 2007), 102–12; Ortelli, "¿Apaches hostiles, apóstatas rebeldes o súbditos infidentes?: Estado Borbónico y clasificaciones etnopolíticas en la Nueva Vizcaya de la segunda mitad del siglo XVIII," in *Hegemonías, clasificaciones etnopolíticas y protagonismo indígena, siglos XVII–XX*, eds. Guillaume Boccara and Sara Ortelli (Tandil, Argentina: Instituto de Estudios Histórico Sociales, 2007), 79–94.

[177] On the transfer of the costs of this system to final consumers, see Chapter 4.

individuals from diverse backgrounds, these pluriethnic bands found, in the "cultural creativity" of their members the glue that held them together, thanks to the "modification, elaboration and recontextualization of preexisting beliefs and practices."[178] For Sara Ortelli, these bands' ethnic composition, as well as the threat they represented for the security of frontier societies, were part of exaggerated arguments elaborated by local *hombres fuertes* (leaders) in order to preserve the frontier *status quo*. Soldiers, *hacendados*, missionaries, and merchants overstated the dimensions and characteristics of these pluriethnic bands, and spoke of an open war throughout northern New Spain, in order to justify their privileges and authority over other population groups during the time period when an administrative reform sought to strengthen the Crown's control over these elites.[179]

In Sonora, the search for relative autonomy, the mission regime's heavy burdens, and the dominant trade system imposed upon the Indians and the most impoverished Spanish settlers and castes, contributed to these populations' decision to join such bands. The latter soon came to constitute powerful mechanisms of identification among such a diverse amalgam of people.[180]

Standard narratives on the wars against the Apaches in New Spain's northern frontier argue that these conditions were exacerbated by the idea of the omnipresent threat of Indian raids, which jeopardized Spanish colonization and required the imposition of a permanent state of emergency to govern those territories.[181] In some cases, literature on the Apaches evokes images of death and desolation associated to "the deeds of rapine, torture and murder that were committed by the Apaches in Arizona and the Southwest."[182]

However, as in the abovementioned studies on Nueva Vizcaya, and based on a new reading of official reports on Indian raids in Sonora,[183] this work casts

---

[178] The appropriation of Catholic symbols, rituals, and artifacts in order to inspire and project their activities, the use of peyote to alter the emotional states of captives and thus facilitate their incorporation into the band, and the creation of a network of spies in Spanish settlements, are all discussed by Merrill as samples of the cultural creativity of these bands. "Cultural Creativity," 133–44.

[179] Ortelli, *Trama de una guerra*, 18, 102–12.

[180] De la Torre Curiel, "Enemigos encubiertos," 11–31.

[181] In the case of Sonora, see Louis Lejeune, *La guerra apache en Sonora* (Hermosillo: Gobierno del Estado de Sonora, 1984).

[182] Munk, *Southwest Sketches*, 217.

[183] In this section I use a series of military reports normally entitled *Extractos de noticias sobre las Provincias Internas* ("Extracts of news on the Internal Provinces"). They were written by the acting commander general of the Internal Provinces based on dispatches from military officers stationed in different provinces along the northern frontier, and were sent to the Ministry of the Indies by special courier (*vía reservada*). This correspondence is dispersed in various *legajos* in the Archivo General de Indias (Audiencia de Guadalajara and Audiencia de Mexico).

doubt on both the real degree and the supposedly recurrent nature of violent episodes along the Sonoran frontier. In the case of Nueva Vizcaya, Ortelli demonstrated that those bands never specifically intended to uproot the population of the northern regions, nor should they be interpreted as expressions of interethnic conflicts that sought to subvert Spanish rule there. In response to the economic pressures that colonization imposed on the foundations of the Indians' way of life, the main intention of their attacks was to obtain animals for food and trade.[184] Evidence suggests that this was also the case in Sonora.[185]

According to the reports that Commander Teodoro de Croix sent to Spain, the threat of a widespread revolt in Sonora seemed real to him. In fact, before leaving Mexico City to take up his post he had been informed that Sonora was endangered by an imminent alliance of Seris, Apaches, and Pimas. Some people, the commander reported, openly announced that "the province was doomed."[186] In his correspondence with the Ministry of the Indies, de Croix insisted that the "general uprising that everyone is announcing, with the Apache nation joining the Pimas and Seris" was indeed a possibility.[187] While "everyone" was reporting this imminent, massive rebellion, de Croix himself was one of the main advocates of a frontal war against the Indians, despite the fact that those same indigenous groups had sent petitions asking that they be received in peace at various presidios. Teodoro de Croix's rejection of such

---

[184] Ortelli, *Trama de una guerra*, 98.

[185] The following examples illustrate the variety of scenarios in which those attacks occurred. On April 20, 1777, some "enemy Indians" killed twenty-six men "who were herding their cattle" on the outskirts of Santa Ana. Teodoro de Croix to José de Gálvez, Mexico City, June 25, 1777, AGI, Guadalajara 516. In early 1778, "Apaches" ambushed a group of thirty Ópata Indians "on their way to the presidio of Tucson," took "their clothes," ten burros "loaded with goods for sale, five mules and three horses," wounded six Ópatas and killed three. Teodoro de Croix to José de Gálvez, Valle de Santa Rosa, February 15, 1778, AGI, Guadalajara 276. In 1780, near the presidio of Santa Cruz, five "Apaches" attacked seven *vecinos* who had gone to cut firewood, escorted by two soldiers. One *vecino* was killed by the Indians and another was taken prisoner together with two mules and three horses. Teodoro de Croix to José de Gálvez, Arizpe, December 23, 1780, AGI, Guadalajara 271. On June 6, 1781, "more than thirty enemies surprised the *vecinos* and Indians of the town of Cucurpe who were out working in their fields, [the attackers] killed forty-five people, most of them men, and taking captive forty-four women and children." In addition, they stole cattle and threatened to "return at harvest time and destroy everything." Teodoro de Croix to José de Gálvez, Arizpe, June 30, 1781, AGI, Guadalajara 267. In early August 1785, "a considerable number of Apaches" arrived at the Cieneguilla mines where they killed five people, wounded another and stole the clothes of three more. In that same attack, the Apaches killed 346 head of small livestock and twenty head of cattle, stole over forty cows and an unknown number of horses and mules. Joseph Antonio Rengel to José de Gálvez, Chihuahua, March 2, 1786, AGI, Guadalajara 286.

[186] Navarro García, *Don José de Gálvez*, 291.

[187] Teodoro de Croix to José de Gálvez, Mexico City, March 24, 1777, AGI, Guadalajara 516.

requests was based on the prejudiced opinion he had formed of the Apaches and on his eagerness to instigate an open war against them:

> The Apaches shall never cease to rob because they make their living from this exercise. They prowl around all kinds of people and cannot sustain the good faith they have never known, nor free themselves of the hatred and abhorrence with which they see us, and that fathers have passed on to their sons. . . . [They cannot] adapt to a rational and Christian life as they are lovers of freedom, set in their perverse inclinations, and accustomed to living in the wild.[188]

In addition to the rhetoric on the barbarous and savage nature of the local Indians, the image presented in those reports suggests that the attacking parties enjoyed a numerical superiority that was being "heroically" opposed by a mere handful of Spaniards who, despite being outnumbered, had succeeded in inflicting on their assailants more losses than they suffered:

> More than three hundred scoundrels attacked the house in the ancient presidio at Terrenate, where a party of seven soldiers from the company of volunteers was lodged. Although they did everything in their power to break down the door, the aggressors were forced to retreat, leaving three dead in the field and carrying off, we infer, many wounded. Only two of our group survived. Some 150 Apaches attacked the Cocospera mission, but when they were received valiantly by a sergeant and nine of the aforementioned volunteers, they abandoned their attempt after four hours of battle in which four enemies died.[189]

On another occasion, three hundred Apaches attacked the Fronteras presidio, which was "successfully" defended by the garrison and other residents. The assault ended with the death of four Apaches, while the only casualty on the side of the defenders was one person wounded.[190]

These official reports on the war against rebel Indians' bands in Sonora conveyed at least three explicit arguments. First, the Interior Provinces were under permanent attack by bellicose Indians. The second was that a number of Spanish officers had shown great heroism and courage in the war against the Indian enemies, risking life and limb to defend the local populations, which justified their requests for promotion or official recognition. Third, these displays of efficacy tried to explain that if a few Spaniards were able to hold off hun-

---

[188] Teodoro de Croix to José de Gálvez, Santa Rosa, February 12, 1778, AGI, Mexico 2462.

[189] Teodoro de Croix to José de Gálvez, Chihuahua, September 27, 1779, AGI, Guadalajara 271.

[190] Teodoro de Croix to José de Gálvez, Arizpe, October 30, 1781, AGI, Guadalajara 267.

dreds of Apache raiders, then reinforcing the existing garrisons would ensure the success of a campaign designed to suppress all the Indian rebels.

However, once the Crown decided to offer a general peace to the Indians on New Spain's northern frontier in the early 1780s,[191] the news reports began to present a much less bellicose panorama in those provinces. Apparently, the rhetoric of open war against rebel Indians was not welcomed at a time when trade and defensive measures were the approved policies.[192] Thus, for example, two months after the Chiricagua Apaches had negotiated peace with the Spanish at Bacoachi, in late 1786, Commander Ugarte y Loyola reported that

> the Apaches move from Bacoachi to Arizpe with great trust [and] carry no weapons. They have shown themselves well satisfied with the good treatment that they have seen being offered to the few prisoners we hold there, who are kept in different houses, and they have been seen to escort our people to one or another presidio, which shows that they too are acting in good faith.[193]

This sudden change in tone and emphasis suggests that the war against the Apaches in Sonora was not as virulent as previous military reports depicted it, and that the periods of peace were not characterized by the tranquility that those same documents portray.[194] We might consider that what was presented in Sonora as a permanent state of war with the Indians was in reality a reflection of the mechanisms that Indian bands' members employed in their pursuit

---

[191] Kessell, *Kiva, Cross and Crown*, 401–10. Those arrangements must be understood in the context of the geopolitics of the time, as the indigenous nations along New Spain's northern frontier had begun to see themselves as potential allies of Spain's enemies, among whom England and the United States had begun to play a prominent role. Weber, *Bárbaros*, 214.

[192] This by no means suggests that there is any doubt as to the reality of the threat posed by rebel Indians along the northern frontier. There were, indeed, dramatic moments in which entire settlements were ravaged by cruel attacks that victimized inhabitants with no regard for age or gender. The assault on Teopari—*visita* of Saguaripa, in the highlands of Sonora—in 1781 is a case in point. On February 8, 1781, a group of Apaches attacked Teopari. During that assault, the aggressors "killed fifty people of all sexes and ages, captured twenty-eight, of whom four escaped, burned down the houses, profaned the church, shattered the holy images, carried away the sacred vessels and ornaments, killed all the cattle and animals there, and reduced everything to ashes, leaving the town completely ravaged." Teodoro de Croix to José de Gálvez, Arizpe, March 26, 1781, AGI, Guadalajara 271.

[193] Jacobo Ugarte y Loyola to José de Gálvez, Chihuahua, February 1, 1787, AGI, Guadalajara 286.

[194] This idea echoes María del Carmen Velázquez's skepticism regarding the omnipresence of "Apaches" in documents produced during the late colonial period. In that respect, she suggested not to believe that the many references to the Apaches were proof of their deeds, motivations, and connections with local societies. María del Carmen Velázquez, "Los apaches y su leyenda," *Historia mexicana* 24, no. 2 (1974): 161–76.

of a life outside the colonial order, and as means of securing food and other provisions.[195] Two final examples illustrate this point by demonstrating one Indian band's rapid transition from raiders to negotiators and by documenting the reasons that led a captive Indian to join one of these groups.

On June 6, 1781, a party of "more than 350 Apaches"—actually Pimas, Ópatas, Yaquis, and *gente de razón*, with only a few Seris and Apaches, according to survivors' reports—attacked Cucurpe and "put forty-five people to death, most of them men, and took forty-four women and children prisoner." After causing panic there, this contingent of raiders went to the town of Dolores. However, instead of carrying on their campaign of destruction at this second site, records show a change of objectives and attitudes on the part of that pluriethnic band. Upon arriving at Dolores, the group "treated five residents who were out in their fields peacefully, and then withdrew to a small knoll. They turned over ten women and children in return for blankets, and other household items that those poor folk possessed."[196] Why did the Indians not simply take those items by force, availing themselves of the numerical superiority that this reference leads us to suppose they enjoyed? Having just murdered forty-five people at Cucurpe, why did they spare the lives of those "five residents" of Dolores? While it is clearly difficult to reach a convincing judgment on this point, one may suppose that there existed among the members of those bands personal alliances that led them to discriminate among different population centers.

Finally, the case of José Reyes Pozo shows us how both Indians and Spaniards understood transitions from war to peace, life in the sierra to life in colonial society, foe to friend . . . and a constant vice versa. On the night of

---

[195] Diverse attacks by Seris and Apaches in western Sonora, for instance, seem to have been motivated by such objectives: "The rebel *Tiburones* and Seris have committed several thefts of horses and mules at the Santa Rosalia and San Joseph de Gracia missions. The troops have tracked them but with no favorable outcome. . . , A larger number of Apaches attacked the corral with the horses of the pickets of the Dragons of Spain and Mexico, taking away most of them." Teodoro de Croix to José de Gálvez, Arizpe, April 23, 1780, AGI, Guadalajara 277. Other testimonies point out that the primary objective of the Indians' actions was to steal cows and horses, animals that they captured alive and herded back to their camps in the sierra. Unlike these larger beasts (cows, steers, horses), smaller livestock (sheep, pigs) did not form part of the diet of those indigenous groups and neither, it seems, were they considered merchandise that was useful to them either for purposes of transportation or exchange; so during their attacks the Indians often ignored or slaughtered those animals. Consider, for instance, the report on an Indian raid at Cucurpe (June 6, 1781), which states that the attackers took what they wanted from the residents' farm animals, "spearing all the smaller livestock and stealing their cattle and almost all of the beasts that the residents . . . possessed." Teodoro de Croix to José de Gálvez, Arizpe, June 30, 1781, AGI, Guadalajara 267.

[196] Teodoro de Croix to José de Gálvez, Arizpe, June 30, 1781, AGI, Guadalajara 267.

January 25, 1790, a group of 117 Apaches who had been congregated at Bacoachi left the town, supposedly enticed by José Reyes Pozo. Apparently, Pozo's "seditious speeches" and "perverse ruses" had convinced them that the Spanish were about to slaughter all the Apaches.[197] Pozo's personal background meshes well with this accusation and seems to strengthen the hypothesis of his culpability, which circulated during the early moments of that event. He was an Apache who had been captured at around the age of fourteen and sent to the Huásavas mission to be raised by a couple of Ópata Indians. He had been baptized by a Franciscan named Diego Pozo, from whom he took his surname. On October 8, 1785, when he was about twenty years old, he joined the company of Indian auxiliaries at Bavispe's presidio. He was then transferred to the presidio at Bacoachi,[198] where he deserted on June 20, 1787, heading off to live in the sierra for almost a year. After that, he voluntarily returned to Bavispe and turned himself in to the company commander who took him to Janos to face the commander general. After receiving a pardon, he was admitted once again into military service at Bavispe in 1788. From there, he was transferred to Bacoachi, where he remained until the night of his second desertion. In October 1790, he was captured by a group of Apaches from Bacoachi who had been sent out on a campaign by order of the viceroy and the intendant of Sonora, Enrique Grimarest.

After his arrest, Pozo was taken to Arizpe, where he received a summary trial and was found guilty of the charges of inciting the Apaches to desert and deserting himself for a second time. At first, he was sentenced to die by hanging.[199] However, Pozo's case set off a broad discussion among local authori-

[197] The fugitives included thirty-two men, forty women, twenty-seven boys and eighteen girls. Jacobo Ugarte y Loyola to Viceroy Revillagigedo, Chihuahua, February 5, 1790, in *Conmutación de la pena*, AGS, Secretaría de Guerra, 7027, exp. 7.

[198] His transfer to Bacoachi coincided with the recent congregation of pacified Apaches there. The official reason for Pozo's new assignment was as follows: "it was believed that in order to convince [the Apaches] of their error [in thinking] that all prisoners were killed, [to] reaffirm our friendship, and to settle them in that new establishment, it would be opportune for them to see, meet and have contact with one of their own nation, [who had been] raised and was esteemed by our people, was employed as a soldier [and] would find it easy to change their impressions." Shortly after Pozo's relocation to Bacoachi, nine pacified Apaches came down from the Sierra Pitaicachi, "among them surely many kinsmen and acquaintances. With this new contact and communication it was natural that they would renew and tighten their bonds of kinship and friendship, [though] these events brought effects contrary to those that were rationally and justifiably conceived and expected." Jacobo Ugarte y Loyola to Viceroy Revillagigedo, Chihuahua, February 5, 1790, in *Conmutación de la pena*, AGS, Secretaría de Guerra, 7027, exp. 7.

[199] Roque de Medina, the judge in the indictment brought against Pozo in Arizpe, found the prisoner guilty of the charges of a second desertion, apostasy, and witnessing a death. Thus, he

ties, the viceroy, and the king's Council of War. Even if he were cleared of the charge of inciting the Apaches to flee, there was still the issue of the exemplary nature of the punishment that he should receive for deserting and for the acts of banditry he had committed while in the sierra. This was a difficult case to resolve. The authorities had to consider that applying the death sentence might induce Pozo's relatives and friends to rise up, "and they would surely be followed by all the other [Indian] parties. [This meant] losing in a very short time all the advantages that had been gained at the cost of so many years, [and that] the province would once again be overrun with enemies who harass it." Finally, on September 13, 1798, the king seconded the Council of War's opinion, and dismissed the initial sentence of death by hanging. Instead, Pozo was sentenced to ten years' imprisonment in Sonora and his definitive exile once his sentence had been served.[200]

Leaving aside for the moment the fate that might have awaited Pozo, what interests us here is to discover the motives and concepts that the individuals involved in this episode used to describe their perspectives and to justify or reprove the defendant's misdeeds. The first important point that emerges from the testimonies is that the witnesses and attorneys involved saw Pozo as a soldier who had fulfilled the obligations of military service and received its benefits (wages and food). Second, they saw him as an Apache who had been raised among Ópatas—only two of the witnesses considered him a Christian. Those statements underlined the image of a deserter and stressed the fact that, in the affray that preceded his capture, Pozo had "frequently shot arrows" in an

---

dictated the aforementioned sentence. On January 15, 1791, Commander Pedro de Nava sent the indictment to the viceroy, requesting his opinion. The case was reviewed in Mexico City by the auditor of war, who recommended the death penalty by hanging and that Pozo's head be exhibited "in the most public and frequented place in the capital of Arizpe." On February 23 of that year, Pozo's file was returned to Nava with instructions to carry out Pozo's execution. However, the auditor of war at the comandancia pointed out that the exemplary punishment of an Apache could stir up the province, and suggested imprisonment followed by exile. On July 13, 1791, Nava relayed that message to the viceroy who, upon realizing that the sentences discussed in Mexico City and Sonora might endanger the province, decided to ask the king for his opinion on the matter. *Testimonio de la causa criminal formada contra José Reyes Pozo, soldado de la compañía de ópatas de Bacoachi, desertor de segunda [ocasión] y apóstata a los enemigos apaches las dos ocasiones, y apresado entre los apaches en la última*, in *Conmutación de la pena*, AGS, Secretaría de Guerra, 7027, exp. 7.

[200] On March 5, 1799, Commander de Nava confirmed receipt of the royal order of September 13, 1798 that stipulated Pozo's punishment. After completing his sentence of ten years in prison, Pozo was to be sent to Mexico City and placed at the disposition of the viceroy. During this entire time, the prisoner had been held "at the *obraje* of the Hacienda de Encinillas." *Conmutación de la pena*, AGS, Secretaría de Guerra, 7027, exp. 7.

attempt to elude capture. Protected by other Apache enemies, he and his "compatriots" had been rustling cattle and "doing harm and despoiling the province." Worse yet, he had gone to live with the enemies, "rebelling with them in the sierra" where he stayed "entrenched in the Sierra Blanca."[201]

In his defense, Pozo presented himself as an Apache, "who in the sierra where he [lived] did not do anything [wrong]," stating that he simply lived in the Sierra Pitaicachi and Sierra Batepito. However, he did admit that he had participated in some attacks against the Spanish:

> From Mátape toward the region where the sun sets, he and three other Apaches had taken three horses. . . . [I]n Oposura, bordering the sierra, he had killed a cow in the company of five Apaches, and two more in [that same place]. . . . [N]ear Pívipa they attacked a party of Spaniards who were on a horse drive . . . killing one of them and stealing a cloak. . . . [T]hough he saw the Christian being killed[,] he did not take part as he was with three other young men high up in the sierra. [However, he claimed] that he had never killed anyone, nor had he ever seen the Apaches who were with him kill anyone. . . , that they had stolen twelve or thirteen beasts at Mátape, and that his share [consisted of] . . . the three animals mentioned above, while the rest were taken by the Apaches who were with him, but they were taken by the Spaniards in the Sierra Blanca. . . . [T]hat below Aconchi he and three other Apaches had killed two cows, in Jamaica he and four other Apaches had stolen two more horses. . . , [and] that he had done no more misdeeds than those mentioned.[202]

Pozo himself caused the greatest surprise when he presented his reasons for deserting from the military and life at Bacoachi to return to the sierra. Living in the aforementioned *presidio*, he said, was difficult because of the obligations of military service and because "he could not sleep comfortably." He continued by stating that he and all the other Apaches had fled on their own initiative. There was no need for anyone to incite them as they left Bacoachi simply "because it was their desire to do so." Pozo's arguments showed how easy it was for people to move between the sierra and the Spanish settlements, whether they were involved in military maneuvers with the troops from the presidio, or in the pillaging of Sonora's settlers.

Pozo's defense stressed that his conduct was commonplace among Indians who had only recently been incorporated into Spanish society. Because of

---

201 *Testimonio de la causa*, AGS, Secretaría de Guerra, 7027, exp. 7.
202 *Ibid.*

Pozo's nature and unreliable character, his legal counsel insisted, the defendant could only be deemed a "legitimate Apache" who had lived among his people enough time to

> participate in campaigns against the Spanish and breathe in their sentiments of vengeance and misfeasance that is due to their lack of religion [and] perverse and barbarous customs. And although from the aforementioned age at which he had been taken prisoner and was kept among us until he was twenty-two, that was insufficient for him to abandon the love . . . that he had absorbed from those of his nation, as shown by his repeated flights back to it.[203]

The representative for the Comandancia of the Interior Provinces had arrived at similar conclusions, arguing that friendship and kinship were the primary causes of Pozo's behavior. This official emphasized that Pozo had been captured at an advanced age, when he was already thoroughly identified with Apache customs. Moreover, it was probable that Pozo had responded to "some particular friendship and illicit dealings that, as a young man, he may have had with a young Apache [girl]. And that he would have found it very difficult and sad to leave her [so] his passion pulled him to accompany her, and nothing was able to stop him."[204]

The case of José Reyes Pozo, as understood by this Spanish officer, offers a glimpse into the lives of individuals who decided to develop strategies of socialization and survival on the margins of colonial society (or were forced to do so). Because, as Pozo's attorney argued, it was only natural that people like Pozo—who were only marginally attached to any Spanish settlement, if at all—decided to look for more meaningful companions. Indeed, as this testimony concluded, by joining the Apaches Pozo was persuaded that "he would recover his natural freedom in this way."

THE PROTECTOR OF INDIANS

Living conditions along the frontier imposed severe limitations on various groups that forced them to search for diverse means of cooperation and interdependence to ensure subsistence. In extreme cases, these choices took the form of interethnic alliances in rebel bands and raiding of missions and other Spanish settlements. The search for wealthy patrons and powerful protectors

---

[203] *Ibid.*
[204] Pedro Galindo Navarro to Pedro de Nava, Chihuahua, April 4, 1791, in *Testimonio de la causa*, AGS, Secretaría de Guerra, 7027, exp. 7.

among the elite constituted the antithesis of these violent responses to the colonial system's pressures on local populations.

As the mission regime weakened in the nineteenth century and as the Spanish population progressively strengthened its position in Sonora, it became clear to mission residents that they needed to seek the patronage of persons capable of replacing the model of self-sufficiency and occupational security that the mission regime had provided for so long. This process was especially evident in the mission district administered by the Xaliscan missionaries. As discussed earlier, one constant feature of Franciscan administration in Opatería had been the clergy's limited participation in subsistence activities of those towns. Thus, it is hardly surprising to find that church buildings were crumbling and missionaries were facing problems securing their own sustenance in the late eighteenth century.[205]

For inhabitants of Opatería, as well as for other groups in northern New Spain, the reciprocity that characterized their dealings with Spanish settlers was fundamental to their decision to coexist with, and work within, the mission regime as well as on Spanish-owned ranches and mines. As the Xaliscans' capacity to contribute to the well-being of mission towns in Opatería and Pimería Baja eroded due to the legal limitations imposed on their administration from early times, the residents of those missions found that certain prominent Spaniards could offer their villages some degree of occupational security and access to food supplies. After 1790, and acting on a request by Commander General Jacobo Ugarte y Loyola, Mexico City's audiencia granted the Indians' protectors (*protectores de indios*) the means to intervene in Indian communities' affairs and to represent them in corresponding tribunals. The audiencia declared that the Indians were to turn to the protectors exclusively for legal representation.[206]

---

[205] In an ironic but logical reversal of fortune, there were cases such as that of Fray Francisco Caballero in Bacadehuachi, where the local missionary needed to approach an Indian of the town to offer his annual stipend in exchange for food at some point of the year. In this case from 1794, José Marcial, captain of the Ópata Indians of Bacadehuachi, collected 154 pesos and 7 *reales* at the *caja real* in Arizpe, an amount that represented half of the stipend of Father Caballero. The money was paid to Marcial in July of that year in return for the goods he had given Caballero between January and June 1794. AGI, Guadalajara 451.

[206] Quoted in AGI, Guadalajara 586, f. 500. As a general rule, the various governmental and judicial instances attempted to put this disposition into effect in order to separate the clergy from the affairs of the towns and avoid the problem of having to deal directly with large committees of Indians. One example of this attitude can be seen in the resolution of a suit over land between the Indians of Opodepe and Tuape in 1818, when the attorney of the Intendancy of Sonora insisted that the new distribution of those towns' lands should be carried out with the "attendance of the protectors and not the reverend fathers, doctrinal ministers or Indians themselves." ARAG, Ramo

This identification of mission Indians with their protectors was especially strong in the Opatería district, in contrast to Pimería Alta, perhaps because in the latter area the administration of the Queretarans continued to offer mission residents at least a minimal degree of security, perhaps because the Spanish presence was not so pronounced there, or perhaps because of the importance of the patterns of mobility discussed previously. Whatever the reason may be, the fact is that relations between protectors and Indians in Pimería Alta do not seem to have left any mark in the historical records. In Opatería, in contrast, the Indians' natural animosity seems to have engaged quite well with the practice of relying on protectors. The cases of land conflicts and accusations of rebellion and high treason involving the Indians of Opodepe and Tuape that have survived to the present help us to trace the general configuration of this relationship.[207]

In a suit brought in 1819 by the subdelegate of Sonora, Pedro Ramón Carpena, the Indians from Opodepe were accused of refusing to recognize the authority of the governor's envoy, which had been sent to participate in the elections of new Indian officials. According to Carpena, the residents of Opodepe "recognize no other superior than their protector Don Juan de Gándara."[208] In all probability, their loyalty to Gándara was due to the fact that he was an important *hacendado* and landowner in the valleys between the Sonora and the San Miguel Rivers (mainly in the vicinity of Ures, where his

---

Civil, 424-1-6888, f. 70. The position of protector of Indians dates from 1529 when, in order to prevent the extermination of the Indians of Peru by the abuses of their *encomenderos*, Fernando de Luque was named "protector and attorney [of the Indians of Túmbez and its provinces] to ensure their good treatment, to see what is most convenient in their conversion and to see to their conservation and that no one aggrieves them." This position was later suppressed in 1582, and then reestablished again in the early seventeenth century. Manuel Josef de Ayala, *Diccionario de Gobierno y Legislación de Indias*, vol. XII (Madrid: Agencia Española de Cooperación Internacional-Ediciones de Cultura Hispánica, 1995), 83–89. This position ceased to exist once the Mexican Independence was declared, as this established the equality of all citizens of the new nation. However, in the state of Sonora protectors were re-established in decree 61, dated June 10, 1835. They were to lead the Indians "in all civil matters that occur." BL, M-M 285: 409.

[207] For a more detailed analysis of the role of the protector of Indians in Opatería, see José Refugio de la Torre Curiel, "Un mecenazgo fronterizo: El protector de indios Juan de Gándara y los ópatas de Opodepe (Sonora) a principios del siglo XIX," *Revista de Indias* 248 (2010): 185–212. For a general overview on the evolution of protectors of Indians in other regions, see Constantino Bayle, *El protector de indios* (Seville: Escuela de Estudios Hispanoamericanos, 1945); Charles R. Cutter, *The Protector de Indios in Colonial New Mexico, 1659–1821* (Albuquerque: University of New Mexico Press, 1986); Beatriz Suñe Blanco, "Evolución de la figura del protector de indios en la frontera norte de Nueva España," in *Estudios sobre América: siglos XVI–XX*, eds. Antonio Gutiérrez Escudero and María Luisa Laviana Cuetos (Seville: Asociación Española de Americanistas, 2005), 727–43.

[208] ARAG, Ramo Civil, 147–11–2227, f. 19.

hacienda, Santa Rita, was located). Although, unfortunately, it has not been possible to determine Gándara's importance to the surrounding towns in terms of the number of Indians he employed or the agricultural and livestock output of his properties, several expressions of gratitude reflect the general attitude of the Indians as well as certain local merchants and clergy. One example emerges from the coordinated efforts of the missionary at Opodepe, Fray Luis Romero, a merchant named Ramón Agudo, and Indians from that town, to manufacture bows and lances and take them to the Santa Rita hacienda as gifts for Juan de Gándara in 1818—a gesture made because the Opodepe Indians "wished to offer some service [to Gándara] in his role as protector of that town."[209]

The relationship between Gándara and the Opodepe Indians emerged from a tacit agreement of reciprocity. We are not dealing here with simple submission or subordination to a wealthy neighbor, as on several occasions the Ópata Indians of Opodepe had reminded the Spanish settlers who lived nearby that if they did not show interest in cooperating in communal affairs they would not be allowed to enjoy some of the benefits that, in theory, would become available to all. Thus, for example, in 1818 the Indians from Opodepe informed their Spanish neighbors in El Realito (a nearby village) that if they did not help them to finish the bullfight ring they were building, not only would they be denied access to that facility, but the Indians would not allow the local missionary to visit them nor provide any services. The Indians stated that they had threatened to deny their neighbors the missionary's services because those from El Realito had argued that work on the bullfight ring was voluntary and not obligatory, and that since they had no time to devote to those labors they should be excused from doing so. The people of Opodepe, in contrast, held that if their neighbors were unwilling to cooperate, then they had no reason to allow the minister to visit them, as he pertained to Opodepe and it was no longer their wish that he go anywhere else.[210]

In this context, the Ópatas' participation with Manuel Gándara in armed uprisings against José Urrea in the 1840s and 1850s can be explained by the unwritten agreements of reciprocity and friendship that had existed between the Gándara family and the townspeople of Opatería since colonial times.[211] Once the Gándara family was defeated for the political control of the state of

---

[209] ARAG, Ramo Civil, 427-11-6947.

[210] *Ibid.*, f. 28.

[211] One must keep in mind the importance for the Ópatas of celebrations like the *dagüinemaca* dance, which precisely commemorated the friendship and reciprocity between Indians and Spaniards.

Sonora in 1842, Governor José Urrea soon realized just how difficult it was going to be for him to win the loyalty of the Ópatas. Thus, the most practical solution open to his government consisted of offering Gándara's collaborators a pardon in 1842 and sending them off to combat the Apaches along the eastern frontier of the state as a means of allowing them to "assuage their guilt."[212] However, the Ópatas and Pimas loyal to Juan Tánori, the captain general of those nations, disdained this pardon and continued to wage war for several more years, in effect preventing Urrea's government from imposing control on the towns located in the sierra. Even as late as 1859, Tánori and his followers were still manifesting their opposition to the state government: Their so-called Act of Tepupa refused to recognize Governor Ignacio Pesqueira and supported Manuel María Gándara's bid to lead the state's executive branch. Although Juan Tánori's death in that year dampened resistance among the Ópatas, their identification with local families would continue during the epoch of French intervention under the leadership of members of the Tánori family.[213]

WHEN MISSION RESIDENTS CEASED TO BE "MISSION INDIANS"

The examples of religious interaction, exchange of crops, knowledge of herbal medicine, modifications of town social organization, and the alteration of patterns of Indian mobility analyzed in this chapter are important examples of transculturation processes in northwestern Mexico to which little attention has been paid. What emerges from such analyses is that Indians, missionaries, and Spanish settlers all participated as cultural mediators as they moved between indigenous and Spanish societies, and thus accelerated the reception of cultural, ideological, and material elements of all groups who later modified forms of coexistence and means of subsistence. This analysis of both the processes of transculturation and the participation of these intermediaries during the Franciscan period in Sonora makes it clear that the mission regime introduced important and dramatic changes in the way of life in Indian towns, although it also becomes evident that Spanish civilian settlements generated the strongest links of interdependence.

This work in no way aims to devalue the labor of the Franciscan friars in Sonora. Material vestiges of their work still exist in Pimería Alta. The presence of the Franciscans today in southern Arizona and the preservation of Christian

---

[212] Decree of Governor José Urrea, Hermosillo, August 8, 1842.

[213] Francisco R. Almada, *Diccionario de Historia, Geografía y Biografía Sonorenses* (Hermosillo: Gobierno del Estado de Sonora, 1983), 679–80.

rituals in northern and central Sonora can be explained to a large degree by the active involvement of the missionary friars.[214] However, because of the limitations imposed on the mission regime in the late eighteenth and early nineteenth centuries, the missionaries' models of social organization ceased to respond to the needs of the local indigenous population. Consequently, to maintain or enhance their own subsistence, the Indians found it more convenient to rely on the Spanish settlers who were establishing themselves in the surrounding landscape. This fact had been recognized as early as 1781 by the Franciscan friar Agustín de Morfi during his travels through Opatería, when he observed:

> He who marries a Spanish woman no longer wishes to be treated as an Indian; he disdains the labors and ministries of his relatives; and the same thing happens with women who marry Spaniards. Both of them adopt our dress and forms, and show themselves most anxious to learn the [Spanish] language.[215]

In the long run this was the very reason for the decline of the mission as a viable project of organizing colonized space and Indian lives. The mission as a form of Spanish settlement entailed a combination of economic, political, and socioreligious dimensions. The case of the Pimería Alta region shows that even in the midst of economic constraints, some missionaries could find alternate ways to finance their conversion program. This means that scarcity of funding did not determine the end of the mission institution since it was not an economic enterprise *per se*. In contrast, it was the withdrawal of mission Indians that constituted its decline. Once the mission failed to fulfill the social functions that it originally performed, and as other forms of settlement offered alternatives for the local population, mission residents found it more convenient to withdraw from mission community life, thus ceasing to be "mission Indians" in the sense that they did not have the obligations and prerogatives that living under the tutelage of the friars entailed.

This process was particularly clear in Opatería, where some *vecinos*—like Juan de Gándara—gradually replaced the missionaries as important components of the Indians' negotiation of what Cynthia Radding identified as the colonial pact. In essence, the Indians' search for new forms of security in the face of the gradual collapse of the mission regime during the nineteenth century was, in effect, nothing more than putting old wine into new bottles.

---

[214] This is a good moment to recall that the so-called "route of the Jesuit missions" offered to tourists in Sonora in reality constitutes a tour of the churches built by the residents of Pimería Alta in the final decades of the eighteenth century, during the period of Franciscan administration.

[215] BNFF, 34/733.

CHAPTER 4

Sonora's Frontier Economy in the Late Colonial Period: A Captive Trade Network

How is it possible for a market to exist in a system in which most of the salaries are paid in kind, not in cash, and in which the structural scarcity of currency is so extensively documented? —Ruggiero Romano[1]

During the second half of the eighteenth century in Sonora, as in New Spain more generally, several processes of change under way during the previous decades reached maturity. In the case of Sonora, the transformation of the forms of coexistence between Indians and Spaniards became especially fecund in the socioreligious, demographic, and economic fields, as seen in the ways that the Indian population appropriated Christian ceremonies, in inter-marriage (miscegenation), and in diverse economic relationships.

The Sonoran economies (including that of the missions) were part of a "captive trade network" managed by specific groups of merchants in Mexico City and manipulated at the local level by several intermediaries who passed along the system's operating costs to final consumers through mechanisms such as paying wages in kind and forced indebtedness.[2] Structural analysis of this form of commerce calls into question the relationship that some authors presuppose existed between the market and the transformation of mission towns. Based on new documentary evidence, I argue that the consolidation and expansion of older, coercive forms of work and the extraction of surplus production are features that marked Sonora's transition to the republican period and the destructuring of its mission communities. At the same time, this

---

[1] Ruggiero Romano, *Mecanismo y elementos del sistema económico colonial americano, siglos XVI–XVIII* (Mexico City: Fondo de Cultura Económica, 2004), 339–40.

[2] A first version of this analysis appeared in José Refugio de la Torre Curiel, "Comerciantes, precios y salarios en Sonora en el periodo colonial tardío: Caracterización de un circuito comercial cautivo," *Historia mexicana* 58, no. 2 (2008): 595–656.

study of the economic transformations characteristic of northwestern New Spain is placed in the context of recent discussions concerning the nature and limits of the concepts of local and regional markets in Latin America.

THE ECONOMIC TRANSITION AS A CONCEPTUAL PROBLEM

How did New Spain's commerce networks operate? For decades this question has been central to various economic history studies. Above all, it has been instrumental in the analysis of processes such as silver production and distribution. The scarcity of currency is another subject related to this problem. Likewise, analysis of the links between Indian populations and local trade networks has been framed in this context, revealing the significance of Indian participation in local and regional markets (either as sellers, buyers, brokers, or haulers) as well as its impact on viceregal and imperial trade policies. In a similar vein, studies on free trade and the role played by associations of merchants (*consulados*) have emphasized the impact of diverse trade monopolies on colonial life and have reflected on the multiple ramifications of the dense social, political, and economic networks these groups articulated. Finally, some studies of long-distance commerce have shed new light on the cycles and conditions in which specific market centers supplied foodstuffs and other merchandise to distant lands.[3]

---

[3] On silver and the scarcity of currency, see Ruggiero Romano, *Moneda, seudomonedas y circulación monetaria en las economías de México* (Mexico City: El Colegio de México, Fondo de Cultura Económica, 1998), 27–111; Richard Garner, "Exportaciones de circulante en el siglo XVIII (1750–1810)," *Historia mexicana* 31, no. 4 (1982): 544–98; Pedro Pérez Herrero, *Plata y libranzas: La articulación comercial del México borbónico* (Mexico City: El Colegio de México, 1988), 159–94. With regard to commerce and associations of merchants, see Carmen Yuste López and Matilde Souto, eds., *El comercio exterior de México, 1713–1850: Entre la quiebra del sistema imperial y el surgimiento de una nación* (Mexico City: Instituto Mora, Universidad Nacional Autónoma de México, Universidad Veracruzana, 2000); Bernd Hausberger and Antonio Ibarra, eds., *Comercio y poder en América colonial: Los consulados de comerciantes, siglos XVII-XIX* (Madrid: Iberoamericana, Vervuert, Instituto Mora, 2003); Antonio Ibarra, "El Consulado de Comercio de Guadalajara: Entre la modernidad institucional y la obediencia a la tradición, 1795–1818," in *Mercaderes, comercio y consulados de Nueva España en el siglo XVIII*, ed. Guillermina del Valle Pavón (Mexico City: Instituto Mora, 2003), 310–26; Guillermina del Valle Pavón, "Apertura comercial del imperio y reconstitución de facciones en el Consulado de México: El conflicto electoral de 1787," in Valle Pavón, *Mercaderes*, 259–90. On Indians and local markets, see Juan Carlos Garavaglia and Juan Carlos Grosso, "Indios, campesinos y mercado: La región de Puebla a finales del siglo XVIII," *Historia mexicana* 46, no. 2 (1996): 245–78; Horst Pietschmann, "Agricultura e industria rural indígena en el México de la segunda mitad del siglo XVIII," in *Empresarios, indios y Estado: Perfil de la economía mexicana (siglo XVIII)*, eds. Arij Ouweneel and Cristina Torales Pacheco (Amsterdam: Centro de Estudios y Documentación Latinoamericanos, 1988), 71–85; Jorge Silva Riquer, "La participación indígena en el abasto de la villa de Zamora, 1792," *Secuencia* 29 (1994): 101–25.

Most of these works take for granted two ideas that need to be revised on the basis of new findings. First is the tendency to speak of an integrated colonial market in New Spain. This construction, according to the standard explanations, would have been composed of networks of local and regional markets.[4] On the other hand, the fact that colonial records frequently allude to payments of salaries, credit, sales, and general payments expressed in *pesos*, is normally taken as an indication of the existence of an increasingly monetized economy, which also displayed commercial bonds characteristic of the modern global economy.

In the case of the historiography of northwestern New Spain, the study of local economies coincides with some of these explanations. In her seminal work on agricultural production and the transformation of land tenure systems in Sonora's missions, Cynthia Radding proposed the hypothesis that the transition from a subsistence economy to one in which mission products were destined for the market "weakened the communal structures of the mission pueblos and accelerated the momentum of change toward private landholding and an ethnically mixed population."[5] Building on these considerations, some later studies have insisted that the missions were dependent on regional markets and argued, by the same token, that this dependence involved profound cultural and material changes ranging from the growing demand among Indians for foreign products to a shift from a communal orientation to an emphasis on individual benefits and the insertion of mission settlers into colonial markets as wage workers.[6]

---

[4] On the thesis of integrated regional markets, see Carlos Sempat Assadourian, *El sistema de economía colonial. El mercado interior: Regiones y espacio económico* (Mexico City: Nueva Imagen, 1983); Jorge Silva Riquer, *Mercado regional y mercado urbano en Michoacán y Valladolid, 1778–1809* (Mexico City: El Colegio de México, 2008). We should not forget Ruggiero Romano's criticisms of this idea, especially his argument explaining the circumstances in which merchandise actually circulated throughout Spanish America and how problems of different sorts heavily affected commercial transactions at various levels. Romano, *Mecanismo y elementos*, 273–342. Romano contended that "the traditional and approved hypothesis which posits the existence of multiple and disconnected economies is still more valid than the one which speaks of an internal market." Romano, *Mecanismo y elementos*, 339. Antonio Ibarra discussed this and other ideas by Romano in "Mercado colonial, plata y moneda en el siglo XVIII novohispano: Comentarios para un diálogo con Ruggiero Romano, a propósito de su nuevo libro," *Historia mexicana* 49, no. 2 (1999): 279–308; Romano's rebuttal can be seen in Ruggiero Romano, "Respuesta a los comentarios de Antonio Ibarra," *Historia mexicana* 49, no. 2 (1999): 309–12.

[5] Cynthia Radding, "The Function of the Market in Changing Economic Structures in the Mission Communities of Pimería Alta, 1768–1821," *The Americas* 34, no. 2 (1977): 155.

[6] Ortega Soto, "La colonización española," 188–245; Radding, *Wandering Peoples*, 66–70; Cynthia Radding, *Landscapes of Power and Identity: Comparative Histories in the Sonoran Desert and the Forests of Amazonia from Colony to Republic* (Durham, NC, and London: Duke University

However, in order to gain a better understanding of the incorporation of different population groups into local commercial circuits, it is necessary to inquire about the roles of such groups as producers, consumers, and merchants. Explanations also must incorporate the final destination of these groups' labor products.[7] It is also necessary to explain the conditions in which such incorporation occurred. Jorge Silva and Antonio Escobar have broached this problem clearly by indicating that "the participation [of society in the market] should not be seen just as an exchange of its surplus production, but as a compulsory integration of the inhabitants . . . in the economic organization imposed by the Spanish from the early colonial years."[8] In Ruggiero Romano's view, it is precisely here that the complexity of commercial circuits throughout the Americas is found, and for this reason he suggests analyzing the components of internal trade in Spanish America both individually and collectively, including the scarcity of currency, the lack of price homogeneity, and coercive forms of "selling" goods.[9]

Using the variables identified by Romano, this work analyzes the characteristics of the network of exchanges that linked the province of Sonora to the rest of New Spain in the late colonial period, in order to better comprehend

---

Press, 2005), 55–75; Cynthia Radding, "From the Counting-House to the Field and Loom: Ecologies, Cultures, and Economies in the Missions of Sonora (Mexico) and Chiquitanía (Bolivia)," *Hispanic American Historical Review* 81, no. 1 (2001): 45–88.

[7] Garavaglia and Grosso, "Indios, campesinos," 249–51; Silva, "La participación," 114. Pietschmann shares these same ideas, although I do not agree with him in his attempt to relate these components of Indian economies with a supposed colonial macroeconomy and the apparently growing monetization of Indian communities. Pietschmann, "Agricultura," 72–73.

[8] Jorge Silva and Antonio Escobar, "Introducción," in *Mercados indígenas en México, Chile y Argentina, siglos XVIII–XIX*, eds. Jorge Silva Riquer and Antonio Escobar Ohmstede (Mexico City: Instituto Mora, CIESAS, 2000), 8. Although this idea was originally suggested in order to analyze the "indigenous markets" of Mexico and South America, it is also applicable to the rest of the society.

[9] Romano, *Mecanismo y elementos*, 273–342; see also Romano, *Moneda, seudomonedas*, 241–42. The topic of coercive forms of selling merchandise to captive clienteles is a point that some contemporaneous economic historians consider resolved, but which should be reconsidered. In the 1940s and 1950s this matter was understood as an expression of a feudal system, but forty years later it was found that "the system is sustained by economic exploitation more than by political coercion, and with clearly capitalist motivations." Since that time, coercive forms of work and payment systems "in kind" have been called "credit against wages." María del Pilar Martínez and Guillermina del Valle Pavón, "Los estudios sobre el crédito colonial: Problemas, avances y perspectivas," in *El crédito en Nueva España*, eds. María del Pilar Martínez and Guillermina del Valle Pavón (Mexico City: Instituto Mora, 1998), 23–24. In the present study, I discuss the contrast among coercion, wages, and credit by situating compulsory forms of selling goods in a context of low demographic density to demonstrate that we are not dealing with expressions of a modern capitalist nature but, more precisely, a process characteristic of an *ancien régime* society.

the economic transformations of that frontier society. Two ideas structure this discussion: (1) the exchange of goods in distant areas does not constitute proof of the existence of articulated regional markets, and (2) Sonora's economic system was activated by various forms of coercion.[10]

With no intention of suggesting that the Sonoran case is representative of the totality of commercial circuits in New Spain, what this analysis does call attention to is the need to reflect on the degree of consolidation of distinct regional realities and their aggregation, or lack of same, into broader intellectual or material constructs.[11] The Sonoran case does allow for an understanding of how in one of these regional realities—in this case, a frontier society— links of internal dependence and exploitation were interwoven but without constituting a replica of the forms of economic integration visible in the center of New Spain. Moreover, it sheds new light on consideration of the frontier societies' evolution and the relations that exist between such social orders and their corresponding administrative and economic centers, traditionally expressed in terms of control, subordination, or autonomy, and, more recently, discussed in the language of political negotiation and economic autonomy.[12]

---

[10] Jorge Silva Riquer, Juan Carlos Grosso, and Carmen Yuste, eds., *Circuitos mercantiles y mercados latinoamericanos, siglos XVIII–XIX* (Mexico City: Instituto Mora, Instituto de Investigaciones Históricas, Universidad Nacional Autónoma de México, 1995); Lyman Johnson and Enrique Tandeter, eds., *Economías coloniales: Precios y salarios en América Latina, siglo XVIII* (Buenos Aires: Fondo de Cultura Económica, 1992).

[11] I believe, as does Marcello Carmagnani, that in the context of Spanish America commercial activities are represented by the existence of internal commerce that generates the aggregation of diverse regional markets, but without forming them into a single market. Quoted in Romano, *Mecanismo y elementos*, 342.

[12] According to Sociologist Edward Shils, the concepts of centrality and periphery depended on the degree in which an "order of symbols, of values and beliefs, which govern the society" was accepted by an identifiable group specific to the society; both on the geographic plane and in the terrain of social structure, the periphery existed to the degree in which adhesion to those values and symbols diminished. This binomial was reformulated by Immanuel Wallerstein when he applied it to the study of the nature and functioning of the "colonialist and mercantilist world system that came into being during the early modern era," and identified the center as European states with integrated national cultures and complex economies that subordinated peripheral areas with weak economies that lacked solid state apparatuses. In recent years, Jack P. Greene and Amy Bushnell have reconsidered the theme of the relationship between centers and peripheries, by emphasizing the capacity of peripheries to negotiate their insertion into large American empires with the respective administrative centers, a situation that derives from the control that their inhabitants came to exercise over local authority structures. Amy Turner Bushnell and Jack P. Greene, "Peripheries, Centers, and the Construction of Early Modern American Empires," in *Negotiated Empires: Centers and Peripheries in the Americas, 1500–1820*, eds. Christine Daniels and Michael V. Kennedy (New York and London: Routledge, 2002), 1–13. The relevant aspect of this proposal, and the one that this chapter takes as its point of reflection, is the issue of marginality and its implications, not only with respect to a controlling center, but also as an integral element of regional developments.

THE SONORAN ECONOMY IN THE MID-EIGHTEENTH CENTURY

On the eve of the expulsion of the Jesuits from Sonora, northwestern New Spain was the scene of an ongoing struggle among different societies to negotiate the terms of their coexistence with neighboring groups. On some occasions, a precarious peace was achieved through open or shrouded exclusion; on others, it was attained through the reciprocal inclusion of the mental and material spheres of ancient and recently arrived Sonorans, while the conviction that unresolved tensions between Indians and Spaniards could easily put the frontier in jeopardy due to the imminent incursions of the Apaches loomed over all involved parties. One area of contact between Indians and Spaniards producing more complexity than conflict was the economic domain. Though the wealth of the Jesuit missions or the fabulous bonanzas of local mines are often mentioned, little attention has been given to the complex fabric of the local economy that in reality constituted one of the strongest mechanisms of inclusion in these frontier societies.

By the mid-eighteenth century, Sonora's diverse economies converged in a network of relations between Indians and missionaries, between mines and ranches, and among the missions, presidios, and Spanish villas. Inside the missions, the alms granted by the king to sustain the missionaries were complemented by the products of Indian labor on communal fields and used by the Jesuits to adorn their churches and satisfy certain needs of the Indians and the priests.[13] In her insightful synthesis of the organization of the Jesuit mission economy, Cynthia Radding explains that:

> Sonoran missionaries . . . labored to sustain a system of agrarian communities built on the foundations established by indigenous patterns of subsistence. . . . The Jesuits' disposal of mission surpluses obeyed a "higher purpose" which was essentially non-economic in nature: Christian evangelization and the salvation of heathen souls. . . . The missionaries compelled the Indians to plant

---

[13] In 1744, the Jesuit Carlos de Rojas described this system in the following terms: "[The Indians] work eagerly to maintain their towns and churches; because these churches have no other means of subsistence, nor means of support, than their work. This is the economy that God proposed to the first Jesuit missionaries to maintain these Christians. . . . [Also] the Fathers exploit the cattle that with the help of these same Indians they raise on the fields of their towns, [and] the wheat and corn that these Indians cultivate for their churches, whose product provides subsistence for their churches, the wax, the ornaments . . . [and also for] the priest and his servants, the sacristans, the *fiscales*, the justices of the towns, etc. . . , from the surplus the priest gives them clothes for them and their families: with this same surplus they succor the widows, orphans, etc." *Misión de Nra Sra de la Asunción de Arispe*, BL, M-M 1716: 41.

the *común*, supplying them with seeds and tools, and they disposed of these communal harvests in lieu of the tithes and religious fees collected in secular parishes. During the agricultural cycle of planting, weeding, and harvesting, the missionary fed the Indians assigned to work in the *común* "a brimming plate of *pozole*" three times a day. Communal harvests were distributed among all Indian families who had performed labor services or held political office in the mission, and surpluses were traded for merchandise.[14]

The annual stipend (*sínodo*) that the monarch granted to the clergy, together with the income from the sale of surplus grain and cattle, were used by the missionaries on their periodic trips to Mexico City to stock up on the goods needed to maintain the church, the mission house, and the community. Each year, in late June or early July, the muleteer in charge of transporting this merchandise would leave the capital, follow the route through the Sierra Tarahumara, Parral, and Papigochi, and arrive in Sonora in November; a schedule designed to ensure that the cotton blankets and woolen cloth would arrive in good condition at the onset of winter, precisely when they were most needed.[15]

At the base of the organization of these agrarian communities, there was a principle of reciprocity that fulfilled the expectations of the missionaries and, to a certain degree, sought to satisfy the Indians' needs for food and recreation. The missionaries well understood that showing gratitude and benevolence to the farmers who actually sustained their socioreligious project with their arduous labor was of vital importance in a context in which gift exchange was crucial to ensuring their acceptance among the Indians.[16] Beyond the domains of the Jesuit missions, some observers recognized the importance of coexisting with the Indians under these terms and praised the model of Jesuit administration, which

---

[14] Radding, *Wandering Peoples*, 67–68.

[15] BNFF, 16/301.

[16] Based on the analysis of Jesuit chronicles, official correspondence and the writings of travelers in northeastern North America, Wilbur R. Jacobs showed that the indigenous tradition of gift exchange was taken up by Europeans and marked their relations with the Indians. In his opinion, at the beginning these presents involved a European plea for peace and, later on, an attempt to attract the Indians into a political alliance and then a different pattern of civilization. Wilbur R. Jacobs, *Wilderness Politics and Indian Gifts: The Northern Colonial Frontier, 1748–1763* (Lincoln: University of Nebraska Press, 1966), 13–37. In a similar vein, Francis Paul Prucha emphasizes the importance of this practice in the relations between the early U.S. government and the Indian nations, a situation recognized in the "Intercourse Act" of 1793 as part of a government program destined to "civilize" the Indians. Francis Paul Prucha, *American Indian Policy in the Formative Years: The Indian Trade and Intercourse Acts, 1790–1834* (Lincoln: University of Nebraska Press, 1970), 212–13. For a detailed analysis of the relation between gifts and diplomacy in the Spanish dominions in the Americas, see Weber, *Bárbaros*, 178–220.

[r]ewarded [the Indians] for their labor by giving them and their families [plenty] of food; [by] dressing them and attending them during their illnesses with medicines and other aids that were needed . . . and by granting them wholesome public diversions especially on the days of the patron saints of the missions and their religion, permitting their dances to which they are so inclined, and even bullfights. . .[17]

Around the missions, living conditions were more difficult for those who attempted to survive on the small ranches and mining posts that continuously emerged and disappeared in Sonora. Around 1730, it was estimated that the province of Sonora had sixty-six mission towns and "more than 200 localities of Spaniards, *coyotes* and mulattoes scattered over the land in mines, haciendas, ranches, farms, cattle posts, mining claims, valleys, fields and communities."[18] In the mid-eighteenth century, these small places dispersed throughout the sierras and valleys of Sonora were in pitiable conditions, devastated by Indian uprisings and by Apache and Seri attacks, and inhabited by "a few poor men with their families, [who are] obliged to scrape out an existence by raising cattle or working mines whose [meager] returns do not even compensate their labor."[19] Most of these "mobile populations" depended on the wealth of the surface mines that they discovered, but as soon as the ore was exhausted there, or when its extraction became too difficult or unprofitable, then entire families would move on to a new site, leaving behind only "foundations, vestiges and ruins."[20] Circumstances were no better in the presidios, where the wages assigned to soldiers by the royal treasury (*real hacienda*) were administered by the local captain, who would compensate the troops the equivalent of their wages in merchandise.[21] The consequences of this mechanism were that the captain was able to amass a small fortune, the sol-

---

[17] Enrique Grimarest to Viceroy Revillagigedo, Arizpe, August 16, 1790, BNFF, 35/771.

[18] Cristóbal de Cañas, *Estado de la Provincia de Sonora* (1730), AGN, Historia, vol. 16, f. 159. In New Spain's *casta* system, the term *coyote* was applied to the offspring of mestizo and Indian couples.

[19] Rodríguez Gallardo, *Informe*, AGN, Provincias Internas, vol. 29, exp. 5.

[20] *Ibid.*

[21] A later, but well-documented case, is that of complaints by soldiers at the Terrenate presidio against José Antonio de Vildósola for abuses committed in the payment of wages. In response to the accusations formulated by the soldiers, Vildósola defended his actions by alleging that he had acted in accordance with the conditions in that frontier and following the same conduct as that of other presidios: "However, despite finding that I have not exceeded that which is common in all other presidios and have followed their practices, it seems the stain has fallen only upon me, though I have no fortune as do those captains because of their antiquity." José Antonio de Vildósola, Real Presidio de Terrenate, June 7, 1774, AGI, Guadalajara 272.

diers lived in ever greater misery, and the troops frequently filed complaints against their captains.

In the midst of this precarious existence, however, several forms of economic interdependence can be recognized among the Sonoran populace. The most common was the sale of mission products to the Spanish *vecinos*. However, in addition to their involvement in this trade, several missionaries also served as intermediaries who facilitated the transfer of certain prized goods to the Spanish. In Mátape, for example, for several years the Jesuit Guillermo Borio included among the supplies that he requisitioned from Mexico City varying quantities of silk, Brittany cloth, and textiles that he later sold to the *vecinos* living around his mission. Upon Borio's death, his place in Mátape was taken by Father Miguel Almela, but when this Jesuit refused to enter into such deals with the *vecinos* he soon found himself embroiled in a series of difficulties that led to his removal just a few months later. In another case, around 1764, the missionary at Opodepe, Father Francisco Loaiza, entered into a verbal agreement with one *vecino* to sell mission products at the Saracachi mine.[22]

There were also contractual relations that did not involve the missionaries. For example, every year numerous contingents of Yaquis set out from the missions along the Yaqui River to go to work in the mines at Álamos or El Rosario, despite the protests of the Jesuits.[23] In the sierra towns, contact between Indians and Spaniards became more diversified when the Ópatas proved more willing to work for the Spanish in various tasks, as occurred in the Sahuaripa district where the missions came to be "sorely lacking in people, due to the enticements of the Spanish [that lure] them to the mines, cattle ranches and the production and circulation of alcoholic drinks;"[24] or in Cuquiarachi, where the Ópatas "swarm in great numbers over the land working as escorts for the incoming and outgoing passengers and mule trains."[25]

Another type of contract demonstrates the ancient fabric of exchange networks in which the Spanish discovered how to find a niche for themselves. Thus, for example, some Spaniards arrived in Sonora to reap the benefits of the

---

[22] AGN, Archivo Histórico de Hacienda, leg. 17, exp. 22.

[23] In 1737, the Jesuit Diego González had denounced abuses committed against the Yaquis by the Spanish *vecinos* of those jurisdictions, indicating that they did not respect the laws that stipulated that only 4 percent of the Indians of a town could be employed in mining. He also complained that when the Indians (Yaquis in this case) went to work in the mines they were paid in kind and received advance payments for their labor that put them into debt, thus ensuring their return to the mines. *Informe del padre Diego González sobre misiones de Sonora*, 1737, AGN, Provincias Internas, vol. 87, exp. 7.

[24] Januske, *Breve informe*, n.p., AGN, Archivo Histórico de Hacienda, leg. 278, exp. 2.

[25] *Ibid.*

"kinship links and longstanding friendship" that existed among the Yumas and Pápagos by acquiring "the Nijora prisoners that the Yumas capture and sell . . . through the hands of the Pápagos."[26] The missionaries in Pimería Alta looked on with admiration and satisfaction when the Pápagos visited Caborca every year and in ever greater numbers, where they would remain for two or three months "to go about their business."[27] There was also a trade route between New Mexico and Sonora that allowed Sonorans to acquire animal skins obtained in the Great Plains to the north.[28]

SCARCE CURRENCY AND THE "LABYRINTH OF PRICES"

One of the many problems affecting trade throughout New Spain was the shortage of currency. The silver coined in Mexico City was soon remitted to Spain, Florida, Louisiana, the Caribbean, South America, or the Philippines, either by royal instruction or due to the needs of large-scale merchants and smugglers. In the Sonoran case, the principal means of extracting silver from the province included official remittances, contraband, and the importation of goods by large-scale merchants who operated, at different times, out of San Antonio de la Huerta,[29] Arizpe, and Horcasitas. In northern New Spain, some transactions were made using precious metals (gold, silver) or appreciated textiles (such as Brittany cloth or *bretaña*) as the means of exchange, but this did not constitute a monetization of the economy because these metals and textiles do not have the properties that coins as currency provide in economic systems.[30]

---

[26] Teodoro de Croix to José de Gálvez, Arizpe, January 23, 1781, AGI, Guadalajara 267.

[27] Fray José Mora to the intendant of Sonora, Cieneguilla, June 12, 1793, BNFF, 36/795.

[28] Juan Bautista de Anza to Teodoro de Croix, Santa Fe, May 16, 1780, AGI, Guadalajara 272.

[29] In a description of Sinaloa and Sonora dated 1772, San Antonio de la Huerta is mentioned as "the most distinguished [place] in Sonora because of its commerce. . . . [I]t maintains some twenty-five large stores with clothes and other merchandise, and every year four or five hundred mules arrive there loaded with goods from Europe, Mexico City, Puebla, and Guadalajara.... [M]iners come to exchange their silver and gold for the goods they need and rural folk to sell their grain and other fruits." BL, 99/380 m, 32:7.

[30] As Romano observes, the use of metals does not substitute coins. First, although it can perform some of currency's functions (measure of value, means of storage), it cannot totally replace the most important ones (means of exchange, means of payment), because it is not available to the entire population nor is it practical for small operations. It is not a substitute for money because it does not have the characteristics of money (homogeneity, divisibility, durability, and transportability). Romano, *Moneda, seudomonedas*, 13–14. For this reason, one cannot accept attempts to demonstrate that money circulated frequently by citing transactions paid, not in cash (pesos), but in silver and gold.

Although the royal treasury earmarked significant amounts of money annually to certain representatives of the Spanish Crown in Sonora (local authorities, soldiers, missionaries, and other clergy), this in no way ensured the introduction of currency into the province, at least not in the quantities that might be imagined.[31] Of the factors identified above, the most serious cause of the shortage of currency was identified in 1750 by Diego Ortiz Parrilla, who wrote, "there are no merchants who bring *reales*" into Sonora and Sinaloa,[32] suggesting that the continuous bleeding out of metal and coin from these regions was in no way compensated by the meager amounts of money sent there only to fall into the hands of the main merchants, where most of it remained. As Jesuit missionary Ignaz Pfefferkorn observed, the result of this situation was that in Sonora "there is no currency in circulation."[33]

The accounting books of a trading company established in the city of Arizpe by two merchants named José Luis Fagoaga and Manuel Ximénez del Arenal demonstrate this general phenomenon.[34] Between 1778 and early 1792, Fagoaga and Ximénez received remittances of cash, metals, and documents worth 646,537 pesos from their agent in Arizpe. In order to put this amount into perspective, consider that from 1781 to 1792 the average annual revenue of Arizpe's royal treasury branch (*caja real*) was only 332,507 pesos. This means that the remittances Fagoaga and Ximénez received in Mexico City were equivalent to almost two full years of income for the local *caja real* in Arizpe, a clear indication of the scale of hemorrhaging that the Sonoran economy suffered.[35] Of the remittances that these traders received, 82.2 percent (531,729 pesos) was sent in the form of bills of exchange, 11.6 percent (75,320 pesos) in cash, and 4.3 percent (27,703 pesos) in unminted metals.[36] One might think that the volume of metal and cash that Fagoaga and Ximénez's agent physically sent to Mexico City was of little import within these parameters, as it constituted just 15.9 percent of total remittances. However, to explain the scarcity of currency in Sonora, considering only the

---

[31] Ignacio del Río contends that in 1794 the royal treasuries of Chihuahua and Arizpe received from local merchants 524,192 pesos "in cash," in exchange of remittances to be paid in Mexico City's *caja real*. However, this figure is in fact misleading since these records *only* reflect the nominal amounts surrendered to local authorities by those merchants, and do not speak of the actual means of payment. Del Río, "Comercio, libranzas," 126–28.

[32] AGN, Jesuitas, leg. I-12, exp. 284.

[33] "En Sonora no circula dinero amonedado." Pfefferkorn, *Descripción*, 304.

[34] Further on, I return to the theme of this company to analyze its commercial operations in greater detail. The accounts of this firm are found in AGN, Consulado, vol. 228, exp. 3.

[35] TePaske and Klein, *Ingresos y egresos*, Arispe 1–15.

[36] AGN, Consulado, vol. 228, exp. 3.

amounts that went out does not suffice. The quantities assigned to the province that never actually arrived there must also be taken into account. Regarding this issue, bills of exchange take on great importance. During the 1778–1792 period, Fagoaga and Ximénez received fifty-six such bills from their partner in Arizpe, twenty-seven of which had been written by various officials of the royal treasury and certain functionaries of the Intendancy of Sonora and were thus to be charged against Mexico City's *caja real* in order to pay Fagoaga and Ximénez the handsome amount of 495,226 pesos (76.6 percent of all remittances).[37] The significance of these debits against Mexico City's *caja real* is not hard to understand, as it was obliged to honor these demands right there in the capital city, where Fagoaga and Ximénez maintained their headquarters. Thus, the royal treasury was able to reduce its shipments of money to Sonora because part of the resources that officially corresponded to that province had already been made available to its officials through the merchants. Like the Fagoaga-Ximénez company, several other mercantile societies also took advantage of these channels of circulation of resources. If the effects of this particular case are multiplied by the number and scale of other mercantile societies operating in Sonora, then the reason for scarce currency is clearly demonstrated.

The shortage of currency in Sonora had a cumulative effect that was borne, in the final analysis, by consumers and workers in the moment that they made purchases or received their wages. In the first place, the lack of solvency left local purchasers at the mercy of merchants who arbitrarily established the selling prices of the articles they brought into the provinces. Descending to the level of consumers, the lack of money also operated in favor of those who employed Indian labor on the haciendas or in the mines.[38] By paying their workers' wages in kind and not in cash, employers were free to "tabulate" the goods at a higher price than that which local merchants could ask for the same merchandise. The immediate results of this situation were, on the one hand, "the high price of goods" and the captivity of consumers, who were forced to accept that local merchants, as well as employers, "offer their wares at the price dictated by the urgency of he who seeks them."[39] On the other hand, this system also resulted in high costs and thus low profits affecting most *vecinos*

[37] AGN, Consulado, vol. 228, exp. 3.
[38] This was a common practice in other frontier areas in New Spain and the rest of the Spanish American empire. For instance, "in the pampas near Buenos Aires, [the Guaraní] found work as agricultural laborers or farmers. Most found employment as ranch hands" and received their salaries in kind. Ganson, *The Guaraní*, 65.
[39] Rodríguez Gallardo, *Informe*, f. 30 v.

involved in mining in Sonora, which limited them to searching for minerals only on the surface.[40]

Basing her analysis on the 1750 report drafted by José Rodríguez Gallardo, the *visitador* to Sinaloa and Sonora, Martha Ortega considers this imbalance between the purchasing power of the Sonoran population and the advantages obtained by outsider merchants as due above all to the fact that "in the *gobernación* the peso was *devalued* with respect to the going rate in the center of the viceroyalty." She calculates that the purchasing power of the local people was reduced by 33.32 percent.[41] No doubt Ortega is correct in suggesting that people was in such a disadvantageous position in terms of their purchasing power. However, the reasons for this situation are to be found beyond the devaluation of the peso.[42] Thus, the problem must be placed in the context of the appraisal system used for the wares that were exchanged,[43] as Peter Bakewell has demonstrated for certain transactions involving silver.[44]

What, then, was going on with the appraisal system that ultimately determined prices in Sonora? Here, the words of Rodríguez Gallardo reveal that it was extremely complicated: "[The matter of] prices in this land is a labyrinth. Understanding it requires time, dedication and hard work, and it is an issue that cannot be easily explained." However, he did offer the following scheme: Each kind of merchandise, Rodríguez wrote, had its own "standard price" ("*ley*"); that is, the maximum quantity of *reales* in which each peso used to "pay" for some product was calculated. In addition to this "standard price," there were other tabulators used in the exchange of goods, one of which was called the "*precio de a* peso," while others were based on seven, nine, ten, twelve, and even fourteen reales.

---

[40] *Relación de Sahuaripa* (1778), BL, 99/380 m, 122:12.

[41] Ortega Soto, "La colonización española," 228. Emphasis added.

[42] We must keep in mind that the peso was generally used as a unit of accounting in the region and only to a much lesser degree as a means of physically effectuating payments. Instead of payments in cash, the alternative was to use large nuggets of silver, but even this means of payment was of limited use because in general only miners "or scrapers" had access to this metal. Thus, barter was the mechanism most often used in Sonora.

[43] The figure of 33.32 percent that Ortega presents came from the analysis of an official account presented to the *visitador* Rodríguez, in which he recorded payment for a cow valued at twelve pesos. Upon discussing how the animal might have been acquired, his opinion was that in practice it would have meant an outlay of seven pesos and seven reales, which represented a fraud against the royal treasury for four pesos and one real—during the colonial period, one peso was equivalent to eight reales. As can be seen, no mention is made of devaluations, but of a possible fraud brought about by speculating on the system of appraising goods acquired in Sonora.

[44] Peter Bakewell, *Silver Mining and Society in Colonial Mexico: Zacatecas, 1546–1700* (Cambridge: Cambridge University Press, 1971), 211.

TABLE 4.1. Example "standard price" of traded goods in Sonora

	Rate	Reales paid	Profit rate (%)
Merchandise "at full standard price"	Peso de a 12	12	50.0
	Peso de a 11	11	37.5
	Peso de a 10	10	25.0
	Peso de a 9	9	12.5
Real value of merchandise	Peso	8	
	Peso de a 7	7	12.5

What these tabulators meant in practice was the following: A product such as Brittany cloth had a retail price of, say, one peso—eight reales—per *vara*. However, if a trader found that conditions were favorable to sell a *vara* of such merchandise at its "full standard price"—depending on the purchaser's means of payment, or on his social position—then the seller could argue that the purchaser needed to "pay," or to acknowledge a debt of twelve reales in order to acquire one peso of Brittany cloth rated at "full standard price." Thus, the seller would obtain a profit or, to put it more accurately, would defraud the purchaser of four reales per *vara*. If, on the other hand, he set a price of ten reales then he would realize a profit of two reales on the transaction. However, he might even sell the *vara* at the "*de a peso*" rate, which meant parity between the goods that were being tabulated. In this way, if one wished to "purchase" a *vara* of Brittany cloth by "paying" with corn—which was priced at three pesos per *fanega*—and the cloth were sold at the "standard price," the buyer would have to exchange half a *fanega* of corn for one *vara* of cloth.

Operations such as these did not constitute a devaluation of the peso but, rather, an artificial modification of the price for different kinds of merchandise. The imbalance was generated in the product that was actually exchanged, which the damaged party in such transactions understood as the unavoidable need to pay as much as 50 percent more than an article's real value in order to obtain it or, in the case of those who received their wages in the form of goods, the indignity of being forced to accept perhaps 25 percent less than the fair amount of product.[45]

[45] During his stay in Sonora, José de Gálvez issued various decrees in an attempt to abolish this practice. In a letter dated May 23, 1769, he assured Juan de Pineda that "the principal *hacendados* and miners of these districts" had agreed "with pleasure to eliminate what they call 'standard price' in the payment of wages and workdays, and the resulting unfair reduction of silver to reales that cheated the sweat of the brow of the poor by lowering the value of their labor, and also recognized that it was fair to use this form of regulation to assure that the 'miserable' receive the

TABLE 4.2. Example transaction with merchandise at full "standard price"

Initial value	Seller's account	Buyer's perspective	Final balance
Merchandise valued at 20 reales = 2.5 pesos (1 peso = 8 reales)	Merchandise at full standard price of 2.5 pesos (using peso de a 12) = 30 reales	Payment for merchandise: 30 reales = 3.75 pesos	Buyer surrendered 3.75 pesos in exchange for merchandise worth 2.5 pesos

The trade system that predominated in Sonora functioned to the detriment of both the Indians and *vecinos* of modest, little, or no means. As Rodríguez explains:

> [T]he result is that due to the lack of currency commerce is very prejudicial and damaging to the poor. . . . None more so than the Indians, and for this reason their work is everywhere privileged and attended. . . . [I]n those provinces the entire weight of the standard price falls upon them and has always fallen upon them, because with goods valued "at full standard price" their work has been, and is, paid as if it were the most infamous and despicable currency.[46]

The Franciscans were aware of the disadvantages that this system held for the most innocent party in such exchanges and thus sought to become intermediaries of barter exchanges involving mission products. The opposition of these friars to dealings between Spaniards and mission Indians was justified in 1772 by Fray Esteban de Salazar, who denounced that although the mission Indians

> work and cultivate their fields, and bring in good harvests, they do not [bene-fit] from them, nor enjoy them; because such is the plague of shysters that [in exchange for] four strings of beads, spin tops, rattles and other bagatelles they take their corn and wheat. . . . [The Indians] are left hungry [and] naked [while] the minister is obliged to succor them from the community larder, so that they do not go off to the mountains in search of food.[47]

---

earnings that up to now they have not." BL, M-A 4:3. In a decree of June 2, 1769, José de Gálvez prohibited miners and *hacendados* "from making contracts, adjustments and payments on the basis of 'standard price,' and from reducing silver to reales with a diminishment of one in each peso . . . that . . . has been observed in these provinces in detriment and hindrance of the public good." AGI, Guadalajara 416.

[46] Rodríguez, *Informe*, f. 31 v.

[47] AGN, Provincias Internas, vol. 81, exp. 13, f. 175. Despite José de Gálvez's decrees to this effect, during the Franciscan epoch the "standard price" was still applied in payments of goods and

Given these circumstances, Romano's words can be justified in his discussion of similar people's situation in central New Spain to be applied to the Sonoran context: "[T]he poor are not only poor, but as they are also excluded from the monetary circuit, they are left definitively and irremediably poor."[48]

The Fagoaga-Ximénez Company and Sonora's Captive Clientele

How was the poverty to which Romano refers generated? Or, how did the mechanisms that ensured the merchants this captive local clientele function? The answer encompasses the shortage of currency, as previously discussed, and high transportation costs, an aspect analyzed in the following section. However, there was another series of elements that contributed to forcing the local population to participate in this captive trade network. The inhabitants of Sonora had to accept this participation because, as described below, the systems of payment that existed in the northern provinces (credit sales, advances of goods, wages paid in kind) constituted effective mechanisms to maintain both Indians and Spaniards subject to the interests of merchant and employer groups.[49] The term "captive commerce" is used because in reality the functioning of this exchange system did not depend so much on external factors but, rather, on the mechanisms that both local merchants in the north and merchants in central New Spain adopted to ensure the continued profitability of their activities, and on local consumers' inability to curb those practices.

The case of Luis Fagoaga and Manuel Ximénez del Arenal's company offers the possibility of comprehending just how all these variables came together. In December 1777, Fagoaga and Ximénez del Arenal, merchants in Mexico City, merged parts of their respective fortunes to establish a mercantile company that was to operate in Sonora with an initial capital of 100,000 pesos.[50] They dispatched one Esteban Gach, a small-scale trader from Mexico

---

wages to the Indians that left the missions to work elsewhere. Though the Franciscans also attempted to exploit this system when selling mission products, it is clear that by the 1780s, income to the missions from the sales of their products, their stipends (*sínodos*) and benefits barely sufficed to pay their expenses. Radding, *Wandering Peoples*, 88–91.

[48] Romano, *Moneda, seudomonedas*, 237.

[49] For an example on how this system worked in other regions of northern New Spain, see Gutiérrez, *When Jesus Came*, 321–23.

[50] Focusing on another company based in Mexico City, Clara Elena Suárez speaks of "solid sums of money," or the 47,000 pesos that company's assets were worth. This example could give an idea of the proportions of this Sonoran venture. Clara Elena Suárez Argüello, "Las compañías

City, to Sonora to oversee the company's activities there.[51] As part of his obligations, Ximénez was to send to Sonora the merchandise necessary for operating the store, in addition to keeping detailed accounts of all shipments made. Gach, in turn, was to maintain records of the goods sent to him from Mexico City and to elaborate annual balance sheets showing the financial situation of the company. In faithful fulfillment of his obligation, this clerk transcribed, year after year, the lists of merchandise that arrived at his store right up to the time of his death in 1790.[52]

Ximénez's accounts and Gach's annual balances reveal the commercial dynamics in Sonora by distinguishing two analytical axes: the geographical and economic dimensions of the Fagoaga-Ximénez company's activities.[53] The first question that arises concerns the size of the commercial network that Fagoaga and Ximénez set up (Map 4.1).

Guided by the places of origin of the goods sold in Esteban Gach's store in Arizpe, the first impression is that of a complex internal market in New Spain, capable of taking to Sonora a great variety of goods including cotton cloth from Querétaro; dye from Campeche; razors, sewing supplies, and condiments from Mexico City; blankets from Tlaxcala; hats from Texcoco; ceramics, iron ware, knives, and metal utensils from Puebla; salt, lard, and fish from Álamos and northern Sinaloa; soap and coarse brown sugar from Culiacán; wine from El Paso; figs, dates, and raisins from Alta California; and cattle from New Mexico and California. In addition to these products from within the

comerciales en la Nueva España a fines del siglo XVIII: El caso de la compañía de Juan José de Oteyza y Vicente Garviso (1792–1796)," *Estudios de Historia Novohispana* 28 (2003): 118–22.

[51] José Luis Fagoaga was the majority partner, as he contributed 80,000 pesos of initial capital, while Ximénez del Arenal's share was 20,000. For this reason, the partners had agreed that the latter would take charge of purchases and shipments to Sonora, and would receive Esteban Gach's remittances to Mexico City. The firm's profits were to be split four ways, with two shares (50 percent) going to Fagoaga, and 25 percent each for Ximénez del Arenal and Gach. AGN, Consulado, vol. 228, exp. 3, ff. 121–27.

[52] Unfortunately, it has not been possible to locate the complete series of Gach's annual balances, nor all of the lists of goods that he acquired in Sonora. However, we do have the complete records of Ximénez del Arenal for all the years in which the company operated in Sonora (1778–1792). His lists include the prices at which goods were appraised in Mexico City and offer diverse data on their points of origin, the articles that had higher demand in Sonora, the distribution of materials such as steel, silk, copper, and so on, which make these documents valuable sources for other fields of inquiry beyond economic history.

[53] Once again I take up Ruggiero Romano's analytical model to examine New Spain's internal commerce. In his critique of the concept of the internal market, Romano concentrates on the geographical and economic dimensions of commerce in the Americas by distinguishing, on the one hand, the extension and imperfect nature of trade networks and, on the other, the qualitative variables I have already mentioned. Romano, *Mecanismo y elementos*, 273–342.

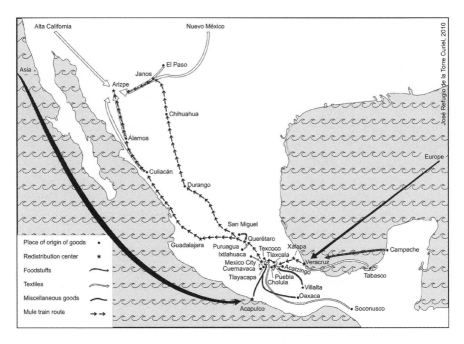

MAP 4.1. Supply routes used by Fagoaga-Ximénez company in Sonora

viceroyalty, imported goods from China (silk, ceramics) and Europe (textiles, wine, and other utensils) make it possible to speak also of an international market that reached such remote places as Sonora. Indeed, on one occasion this type of long-distance exchange was used as the central argument in defining New Spain as "an increasingly integrated market."[54] Nonetheless, as the basis of an argument proposing the existence of a dynamic internal market, it is insufficient simply to cite the diverse origins of the wide variety of goods that found their way to Sonora, because of factors such as supply inconsistency and the high prices that products commanded in the northern provinces.

As Tables 4.3 and 4.4 show, in many cases shipments were sporadic at best, and several years could pass before such goods were required there again, due in part to few buyers. In this context, what the shipments allow us to discern is the composition of the Sonoran clientele, which was characterized by a small number of individuals who had the capacity to acquire luxury goods and a

---

[54] John Kicza, "El crédito mercantil en Nueva España," in Martínez and Del Valle, *El crédito*, 54.

much larger number who acquired goods of lesser value destined for more immediate consumption.

Sonora was undoubtedly linked to the rest of New Spain, as the existence of this extensive supply network clearly indicates. Far from representing a well-integrated market, however, the nature of this trade confirms how effective central New Spain's merchants were in concentrating long-distance trade in the hands of a few.

PRICE INCREASES: TAXES, FREIGHT CHARGES, AND FORMS OF FRAUD

More important even than the geography of this trade network or the irregular frequency with which merchandise arrived in Sonora are the price hikes on goods upon arrival at their destination.[55] Data from the Fagoaga-Ximénez company reflect a period of price stability from 1778 to 1787, followed by a slight increase in the price of European goods between 1787 and 1792, especially for textiles such as *ruan*, *bayeta*, and Brittany cloth. Although Table 4.5 does not reflect the taxes or freight costs paid for merchandise sent to Sonora, showing only the prices at which goods were purchased in Mexico City and Puebla (for products from New Spain) and in the ports of Veracruz and Acapulco (for foreign goods), it still reflects the relative price stability during the period.

An important factor contributing to high prices of goods arriving in Sonora was transportation costs. Extreme cases that have been documented for Sonora indicate that by the late eighteenth century the cost of goods transported by land to that far-off province increased by 20 to 78 percent, depending on such factors as the volume shipped, payment of the *alcabala* (sales tax charged by the Crown), the time of year in which cattle herds were driven to market, and the route. Thus, for example, Manuel Ximénez del Arenal's books on shipments of merchandise to Sonora estimated a price increase of 21 to 25 percent between 1782–1783 and 1792 for goods purchased in central New

---

[55] Recent studies have discussed the possibility that a moderate annual inflation rate of perhaps 0.8 percent occurred during the eighteenth century in New Spain, though some well-grounded criticisms of those calculations suggest, to the contrary, that prices generally tended to move downward in that century. On the inflationary tendency, see Richard L. Garner, "Price Trends in Eighteenth-Century Mexico," *Hispanic American Historical Review* 65, no. 2 (1985): 279–325; and Richard Garner and S. E. Stefanou, *Economic Growth and Change in Bourbon Mexico* (Gainesville: University Press of Florida, 1993). Romano documents the contraction of colonial economies and discusses Garner's posture in "Algunas consideraciones sobre la historia de los precios en América Colonial," in Johnson and Tandeter, *Economías coloniales*, 45–80.

TABLE 4.3. Goods sent by Fagoaga-Ximénez company to Esteban Gach, 1778–1791

Goods and places of origin	Units	1778	1779	1780	1781	1782	1783
New Spain's southeast							
Thread (Campeche)	Arrobas						
Blankets (Villalta, Oaxaca)	Pieces				124.0		
Silk (Oaxaca)	Pounds	23.0		7.0	62.0		45.0
Pepper (Tabasco)	Arrobas						
Northern New Spain							
Wax (Northern New Spain)	Arrobas						
Central Mexico							
Sugar (Mexico)	Pounds			6.0			
White sugar (Mexico)	Arrobas						145.0
Stockings (Toluca)	Dozen	12.0		17.0	24.0		
White pants (Tlayacapa)	Dozen	6.0					
Shirts/tunics (Tlayacapa)	Dozen	6.0					
Ammunition (Mexico)	Pieces			8,000.0			10,000.0
Blankets (Cuernavaca)	Pieces						
Castilian wax	Arrobas			14.0	7.0		7.0
Sweets (Mexico)	Arrobas			14.0			25.5
Soap (Mexico)	Pieces		13,680.0	13,920.0	38,927.0		
Ham	Arrobas			60.0	89.0		
Cotton stockings (Ixtlahuaca)	Dozen						
Woolen stockings (Ixtlahuaca)	Dozen				24.0		
Hats (Texcoco)	Pieces						
Puebla–Tlaxcala							
Blankets (Acatzingo)	Pieces	64.0			46.0		78.0
Blankets (Tlaxcala)	Pieces						
Fine pottery (Puebla)	Dozen	104.0		42.0	76.0		88.0
Ordinary pottery (Puebla)	Dozen						
Hats (Puebla)	Dozen	80.0		140.0	78.0		98.0
Linens (Cholula)	Varas	170.8					
Bajío							
Blankets (San Miguel)	Pieces			6.0	6.0		6.0
"Fresadas" (San Miguel)	Dozen				42.0		131.5

continued on next page

Table 4.3. (continued)

Goods and places of origin	Units	1784	1785	1786	1787	1788	1789	1790
New Spain's southeast								
Thread (Campeche)	Arrobas				7.5			1.0
Blankets (Villalta, Oaxaca)	Pieces	132.0		372.0				
Silk (Oaxaca)	Pounds			157.0	90.0	48.0		105.0
Pepper (Tabasco)	Arrobas				2.0			
Northern New Spain								
Wax (Northern New Spain)	Arrobas	14.0		14.0	14.0	7.0		
Central Mexico								
Sugar (Mexico)	Pounds					0.5		2.0
White sugar (Mexico)	Arrobas	15.5		189.5	137.5	129.0		170.0
Stockings (Toluca)	Dozen	36.0						
White pants (Tlayacapa)	Dozen	0.5						
Shirts/tunics (Tlayacapa)	Dozen	4.0		11.0		2.0		
Ammunition (Mexico)	Pieces	4,000.0						
Blankets (Cuernavaca)	Pieces			34.0				
Castilian wax	Arrobas			14.0				
Sweets (Mexico)	Arrobas	14.0		14.0		19.5		14.0
Soap (Mexico)	Pieces							
Ham	Arrobas				29.0	22.0	30.0	30.0
Cotton stockings (Ixtlahuaca)	Dozen				15.5			
Woolen stockings (Ixtlahuaca)	Dozen	60.0		16.0				
Hats (Texcoco)	Pieces	24.0		106.0		36.0	48.0	
Puebla–Tlaxcala								
Blankets (Acatzingo)	Pieces	115.0		140.0	84.0	18.0	26.0	82.0
Blankets (Tlaxcala)	Pieces			6.0				
Fine pottery (Puebla)	Dozen	198.0		144.0		22.0	42.0	144.0
Ordinary pottery (Puebla)	Dozen	125.0				25.0		
Hats (Puebla)	Dozen			136.6		52.6	24.0	75.0
Linens (Cholula)	Varas							
Bajío								
Blankets (San Miguel)	Pieces	10.0						
"Fresadas" (San Miguel)	Dozen	158.0						

TABLE 4.4. Debtors of Fagoaga-Ximénez company

Name	Occupation	Place of residence	Debt total (in pesos)		
			1782	1783	1785
Victores de Aguilar	Merchant[a]	Horcasitas	52,291	43,400	90,208
Miguel de Arrieta	Merchant[b]	Santa Cruz			55,461
Francisco Luz Núñez	Merchant[c]	Tucson			40,488
Antonio Paz	Muleteer				4,000
Fernando Arredondo	Merchant	Guadalajara	3,000	3,627	
Esteban Gach	Merchant	Arizpe	1,290		1,712
Bartolomé Salido Exudar	Merchant	Álamos			1,032
Juan Manuel Ortiz	Merchant	Álamos	975	555	
Juan Gasiot	Archivist	Arizpe	910	780	676
Pedro Allande	Captain		896		
Pedro de Mata y Viñolas	Lieutenant[d]	Santa Cruz	771	104	
Francisco Velázquez de la Cadena	Royal officer	Cosala			756
Pablo Tries	Carpenter	Arizpe		695	676
Juan Sartorio	Soldier	Pitic		604	294
Manuel Merino y Moreno	Vecino	Arizpe	501	361	361
José Varela	Merchant	Buenavista	491[e]	367	361
Antonio Denojeant	Soldier	Bavispe		398	303
Comandancia General			383		
Toribio Gomez	Shopkeeper				376
Roque Medina	Coronel				432
Manuel Ruiz	Mayor	Álamos		351	351
Antonio Bonilla	Captain		350		319
Manuel de Echegaray	Captain				323
Nicolas De Oz		Arizpe	278	400	176
Salvador Julian Moreno	Vecino	Jamaica		220	408
Jose Antonio Pérez Serrano	Merchant	Arizpe			213
Pedro Corbalan	Intendant	Arizpe	211	261	159
Gerónimo de la Rocha Figueroa	Commander	Fronteras	211		
Miguel Elias González	Priest	Arizpe	208	213	480
Br. Rafael Castro	Priest	Piaxtla			200
Antonio Enríquez de Castro	Merchant	Cieneguita	200		
Juan Ortiz de Rojas	Royal officer	Rosario			196
Roque Garate	Commander	Buenavista	194	596	
Esteban Sola	Lieutenant			189	
Francisco Rodríguez	Landowner	Arizpe	186	185	15
Fr. Cristobal Diaz	Missionary	Mátape		184	
Various individuals			180		932
Cristóbal Arque	Mason				176

continued on next page

TABLE 4.4. (continued)

Name	Occupation	Place of residence	Debt total (in pesos) 1782	1783	1785
Pedro Martín	Merchant	Arizpe	163		
Juan Jose de la Hoz	Accountant	Rosario	161		
Miguel Antonio Cuevas	Priest	Arizpe			152
Fr. Juan Dominguez	Missionary	Aconchi		151	
Manuel de Hugues		Sonora			146
Presidio de Las Nutrias			137		
Tomas Moreno	Vecino	Jamaica	119	896	693
Juan Santini	Royal officer	Cosala	110		
Fernando Antonio de la Torre	Merchant	Chihuahua		100	
Fr. Antonio Jacome	Missionary	Banamichi		100	
Br. Francisco J. Valdez	Priest	Raum		100	
Ignacio Felix Usarraga	Soldier	Tucson		99	76
Br. Jose Ventura Moreno	Priest	Oposura		95	
Juan Manuel Bonilla	Captain		78		
Domingo Vergara	Armorer	Arizpe		75	42
Lic. Manuel Maria y Moreno	Vecino	Oposura		74	501
Sixtos Cervantes	Postman	Arizpe	64	24	
Pedro García	Royal officer	Arizpe	51		
Miguel Martinez	Secretary	Arizpe		47	90
Fr. Salvador Salgado	Missionary	Bacoachi		40	
Santiago Escobosa	Merchant	Horcasitas	39		
Juan Jose Teran	Vecino	Oposura	25	252	
José Joaquín de Arrillaga	Captain	Loreto		19	
Manuel Romualdo Diez Martinez	Merchant	La Ciénega		18	
TOTAL			64,473	55,580	202,784

^a Aguilar was the agent for Fagoaga-Ximénez in San Miguel de Horcasitas. In 1785 he was also the person authorized by the viceregal authorities as the official supplier (*habilitado*) of the presidios located at Altar and Pitic.

^b *Habilitado* of Santa Cruz presidio.

^c *Habilitado* of Tucson presidio.

^d *Habilitado* of Las Nutrias presidio.

^e In 1782 Varela was the *habilitado* of Fronteras presidio.

Sources: AGN, Consulado, vol. 228, exp. 1-2; and vol. 240, exp. 3.

TABLE 4.5. Price range for European textiles sent to Sonora, 1778–1792

	Ruan	Bayeta	Brittany narrow	Brittany wide
1778–1787	3.5–3.8 reales/ vara	4.3–14 reales/ vara	30–54 reales/ piece	35–56 reales/ piece
1788–1792	4.6–5 reales per vara	16–17 reales/ vara	34–60 reales/ piece	32–84 reales/ piece

Note: In some cases these price ranges are too broad because merchants in Mexico City were interested in both lower quality and the finest presentations of the same article.
Source: AGN, Consulado, vol. 240, exp. 2, ff. 188–331.

Spain.[56] For the 1782–1783 period, merchandise bought in Guadalajara for delivery to Sonora was subject to a 75-percent increase due to freight costs, taxes, and the company's costs of representation. In 1792, in contrast, the freight increase for such shipments was "only" 32 percent.[57]

The experience of one Franciscan from the Colegio de Querétaro shows that it did not suffice to distance oneself from local merchants to obtain better prices in Sonora. In 1788, Fray Pedro Arriquibar, a missionary from the town of San Ignacio, received from his colegio's *síndico* (nonreligious who served as buyer)[58] a list of goods totaling 583.39 pesos. However, after celebrating his good fortune in obtaining attractive prices in central New Spain, he was obliged to charge his mission for an additional 456.10 pesos (78 percent of the purchase price) for freight costs.[59] Certain cases related to specific articles will illustrate still more clearly the implications of these costs for daily life in Sonoran settlements.

[56] In 1782, a shipment worth 53,551.7 pesos registered freight costs of 11,254.3 pesos, calculated at "21 pesos 1/8 of a real percent"; that is, 21.0156 percent. AGN, Consulado, vol. 240, exp. 3, f. 478. In 1783, goods sent to Sonora totaled 28,620 pesos, to which a charge of 6,014.6 pesos for freight was added. AGN, Consulado, vol. 282, exp. 1, f. 12. In 1792, goods worth 18,603.5 pesos were sent with a freight charge of 4,665.75 pesos (25 percent). AGN, Consulado, vol. 228, exp. 2, f. 97. Although the source does not specify the route taken by the respective muleteers, it is probable that these goods took the Chihuahua road, as merchandise from Guadalajara is registered with an additional freight cost to the 21 percent increase that was customarily charged.

[57] In 1782, goods purchased in Guadalajara totaled 1,505.3 pesos, to which an outlay for "expenses" of 1,129 pesos was added. AGN, Consulado, vol. 240, exp. 3, f. 480. In 1783, the Fagoaga-Ximénez company had bought, also in Guadalajara, merchandise worth 1,196.3 pesos, which was hit with charges of 897.25 for "costs." AGN, Consulado, vol. 282, exp. 1, f. 13. In the 1792 records, in contrast, only the cost of freight for merchandise sent from Guadalajara to Sonora was noted. On this occasion, for a total of 1,006.75 pesos in merchandise, they paid 322.1 pesos in freight (32 percent). AGN, Consulado, vol. 228, exp. 2, f. 98.

[58] The *síndico* was Don José de los Heros, merchant in Mexico City.

[59] According to the receipt he gave to the muleteer, the goods Arriquibar ordered weighed 101.4 *arrobas*. Freight was charged at a rate of 4.5 pesos per *arroba*. BNFF, 35/761.

Table 4.6. Retail prices for selected goods in Mexico City and Sonora (pesos)

	1777			1788		
	Mexico City	Aconchi	Increase (%)	Mexico City	Cumuripa	Increase (%)
Candle wax from Castile	1.25/pound	2/pound	60			
Fine chocolate	0.33/pound	1/pound	203	0.33/pound	0.75/pound	127
Pottery from Puebla	1/dozen	2.7/dozen	170			
Sugar				2.2/arroba	9.5/arroba	331
Brittany cloth				2.9–9.5/piece	15/piece	58
Bayeta cloth				0.6/vara	1/vara	67

Sources: AMH, *Libro de Cargo y Descarga de la Misión de Aconchi*, 1777; BNFF, 35/764.

Account books from the missions in Aconchi and Cumuripa explain in part the precarious conditions that characterized lives of the Sonorans forced to pay as much as three times more for merchandise than people in central New Spain. Some calculations of price increases on goods in New Spain have estimated that the final purchaser had to pay up to 35 percent more than the real value of a product.[60] However, the data presented here indicate increases that oscillate between 50 and 300 percent of the original cost of products in Mexico City (Table 4.6). As described in the next chapter, in an attempt to avoid this price spiral, the Franciscans (especially those from the Colegio de Querétaro) sought to use the products of the missions collectively to purchase the scarcest goods, or those that arrived in Sonora at the most exorbitant prices, directly in Mexico City. Despite their best efforts and this mechanism, however, the fathers did not succeed in dodging the disadvantages that local commerce in Sonora imposed on consumers. As related in the next chapter, when attempting to collect their stipends, they found themselves once again drawn inexorably into this system of exchange.

This trade circuit was clearly disadvantageous for consumers (soldiers, poorer Spaniards and mestizos, Indians, and missionaries). However, even at this level there were significant variations, as goods were often not available to the entire population under the same conditions. For example, missionaries

---

[60] Clara Elena Suárez Arguello, "El parecer de la élite de comerciantes del Consulado de la ciudad de México ante la operación del libre comercio (1791–1793)," in *Comercio y poder en América colonial: Los consulados de comerciantes, siglos XVII–XIX*, eds. Bernd Hausberger and Antonio Ibarra (Madrid: Iberoamericana, Vervuert, Instituto Mora, 2003), 119.

were often able to strike deals to acquire goods worth more than 500 pesos with local merchants without spending any cash at all, solely "on trust, credit and [their] word," by promising, in exchange, the annual stipend of 350 pesos, "the alms from some masses, and . . . the products of [the] mission."[61] Conditions were very different, however, for the indigenous population, who were often abused by merchants. A 1772 indictment narrates the penury that the Indians of Ures experienced in part due to the "many shysters who arrive in the towns with clothing, that despite normally being of lesser quality, they sell as if they were fine, [and] then pay the minimum price for the [local products]."[62] The accuser affirmed that a vendor approached a woman to offer her a bar of soap (worth half a real) in exchange for an *almud* of wheat[63] (worth 1.7 reales), thus showing his complete disregard for the value of the work of those folk.[64]

As these examples show, the lack of price standardization in the northern provinces of the viceroyalty was due both to structural deficiencies in New Spain (high transportation costs due to poor transport infrastructure) and to inequities in payment and pricing mechanisms, which were often established by vendors and employers when they exchanged or distributed their goods. In these conditions, what has traditionally been called the "internal market" emerges as an interregional trade circuit that in no way responds to global economic fluctuations, but rather, to mechanisms of control and exclusion imposed by the parties who created it.

Having analyzed the role of freight costs in determining the prices of goods sent to Sonora, it is now time to examine in greater detail the mechanisms used by local merchants and employers to ensure their profits. Two mechanisms stand out in the captive nature of this commerce: first, the common practice among sellers of setting the same price for a given product at all levels of quality, and, second, the system of paying wages in kind.

Generally speaking, studies of merchandise prices are based on annual records of production and commercialization of grain, cattle, or other foodstuffs. These records reflect the average price of such products and allow for establishing tendencies over time periods. Results of an analysis of this type applied to goods appearing most often in the books of the Fagoaga-Ximénez company are summarized in Table 4.7.

[61] Fray Salvador del Castillo, *Cuenta de la misión de Cumuripa*, November 21, 1788, BNFF, 35/764.

[62] AGN, Provincias Internas, vol. 81, exp. 7.

[63] The *almud* is a unit of volume equivalent to 4 *cuartillos* or 7.558 liters. It is also one-twelfth of a *fanega*.

[64] AGN, Provincias Internas, vol. 81, exp. 7.

TABLE 4.7. Average prices of selected goods sent to Sonora, 1778–1792

	Chocolate (pesos per pound)	Brittany cloth (pesos per piece)	European *bayeta* (pesos per vara)	Mexican *bayeta* (pesos per vara)
1778	0.32	4.7	0.92	0.52
1779				
1780	0.37		1.18	0.57
1781				0.53
1782	0.41			
1783	0.37		1.75	0.53
1784		11.0		0.59
1785				
1786	0.34	4.3	0.7	0.59
1787	0.31	3.0	2.1	0.56
1788	0.31	4.6		
1789	0.27	4.5		0.55
1790	0.34	5.6	2.0	0.53
1791				
1792	0.34	4.7		0.59

Source: AGN, Consulado, vol. 228.

On the basis of this table, one might assume that product prices in Sonora (or at least of chocolate and Mexican *bayeta*) remained relatively stable during the period of reference, except for lower prices of European textiles up to 1786 and their recovery thereafter. However, upon analyzing the accounts year by year and product by product, the panorama of the price structure of these goods is totally different. The fascinating spectacle of a clever system of price manipulation common in northern New Spain becomes clear. In the late eighteenth century, selling "cats for rabbits" (*gato por liebre*) to people in Sonora was not only a longtime custom but also a well-known one. It was no secret that in Sonora "the same price is affixed to a *vara* of fine Brittany cloth to one that is not [authentic Brittany], or that is poorly made, or that a *vara* of *cotense florete* [another kind of fabric] has the same price as one of crude linen." Taking advantage of this situation, local merchants did not hesitate to "bring the worst goods that because of their poor quality cost them very . . . [little] in Mexico City, and sell them [as if they were of the highest quality], thus making attractive profits and cheating the buyer. . . ."[65] This is precisely the context in which the Fagoaga-Ximénez company operated. The contrast between the selling

[65] Diego Ortiz Parrilla to Viceroy Güemes de Horcasitas, Real presidio de San Miguel de Horcasitas, April 16, 1750, AGN, Jesuitas, leg. I-12, exp. 284.

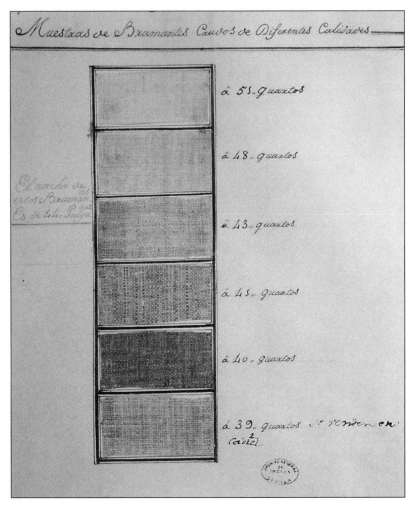

Figure 4.1. Sample of hemp fabrics grouped by quality and price (Source: "Muestras de Bramantes crudos de diferentes cualidades," AGI, Mapas y Planos, Tejidos 012)

prices of *bayeta* and Brittany cloth in Sonora and the cost of those textiles to the merchants provides a key to understanding how this type of commerce was reproduced.

Graph 4.1 shows the quantities of *bayeta* sent by Fagoaga and Ximénez to their partner in Arizpe. This graph reflects the prices of these textiles of varying quality when they were shipped to Sonora. Shipments included both

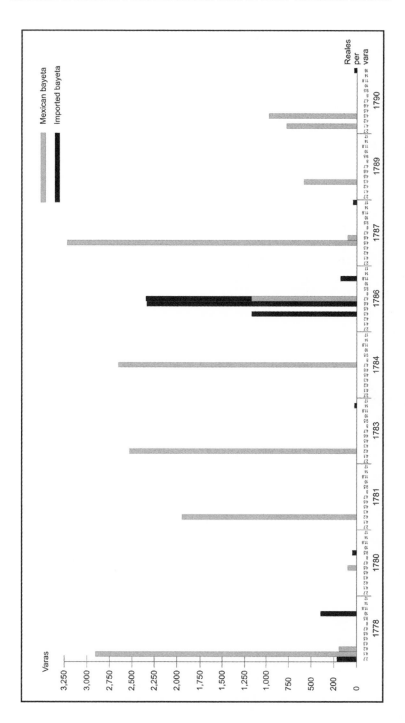

GRAPH 4.1. Mexican and imported bayeta sent to Sonora by Fagoaga-Ximénez, 1778–1790

"Mexican" and European *bayeta*, with the imported fabric having a higher price than that made in New Spain. However, these goods commanded different prices in the market depending on their condition upon delivery to merchants and the quality of their manufacture, even though they were the same kind of fabric. The remittances from 1786 illustrate this point: despite the fact that the shipments consisted of the same imported *bayeta*, the price of the cloth was marked as 4.3, 4.6, 4.7, and 11.8 reales per *vara*. Due to these factors (quality, condition), the statistical mean for the price of *bayeta* in no way reflects the real cost of this product to the merchant. Consider, for example, that the average price for *bayeta* in the same year, 1786, would have been 0.70 pesos (5.6 reales) per vara, a figure that is simply meaningless.

Graph 4.2 shows a similar outcome for Brittany cloth, an imported fabric that once in the hands of merchants was divided by size into three classes: wide, medium, and narrow. These categories were then subdivided into new classes according to quality (superfine, fine, and ordinary). What is interesting about these indices of quality is that when the fabric was distributed in Sonora it was all sold generically as "Brittany cloth."

How onerous was this practice for the final consumer? What was the cost to the people of Sonora of being cheated in this way? To respond to these two queries, another example will be examined. In 1788, the missionary in Cumuripa noted in his account book the purchase of Brittany cloth at a price of 15 pesos per piece.[66] Manuel Ximénez del Arenal's books from late 1787 show no fewer than nine distinct prices for Brittany cloth, ranging from 3 to 6.5 pesos per piece in Mexico City (Graph 4.2).[67]

Table 4.8 shows prices and costs of these textiles in Sonora, and respective profit margins. Of course, merchants in Mexico City had to wait a long time for clients to pay for their purchases, a factor that clearly affected the profit margins the former expected to achieve. Nonetheless, as the analysis demonstrates, this type of exchange implied an inflated price for the final consumers. But this is only half the story. Making payments is the other side of the story, and it was there that merchants found another opportunity to secure handsome profits.

---

[66] BNFF, 35/764.

[67] In that same year, Manuel Ximénez del Arenal recorded the purchase of 3 pieces of superfine, wide Brittany cloth valued at 10.5 pesos per piece and 3 pieces of fine, wide Brittany cloth at 7.5 pesos each. I have not included these pieces in the text because they represent less than 0.1 percent of total remittances and, without doubt, were special orders for a particular client and thus were not for sale in the store in Arizpe. AGN, Consulado, vol. 228, exp. 3.

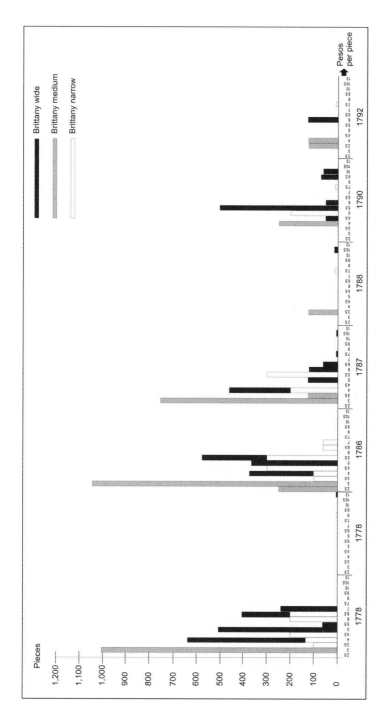

GRAPH 4.2. Brittany cloth sent to Sonora by Fagoaga-Ximénez, 1778–1792

Table 4.8. Example prices per piece of Brittany cloth in Mexico City
and Sonora, 1788

Type of Brittany cloth	Pesos per piece in Mexico City	Plus average freight cost of 35%	Profits (at 15 pesos per piece)	Profit (%)
Medium	3.0	4.05	10.95	270.3
Medium	3.5	4.72	10.28	217.8
Narrow	4.0	5.40	9.60	177.8
Wide	4.0	5.40	9.60	177.8
Wide	5.0	6.75	8.25	122.2
Narrow	5.5	7.42	7.58	102.1
Wide	6.0	8.10	6.90	85.2
Wide	6.5	8.77	6.23	71.0

Source: AGN, Consulado, vol. 228.

Payment Systems for Goods and Wages

The shortage of currency was a distinctive feature of the Sonoran economy and the starting point for a vicious circle that included the exchange of merchandise, the establishment of unique systems of credit, and, finally, payment of wages for labor. Esteban Gach, representative of important commercial interests in the central region of the viceroyalty, recognized this maxim and commented on it with his partner and compadre Manuel Ximénez del Arenal shortly after his arrival in Arizpe. To justify low profits reported during his early years of work in Sonora due to his clients' lack of solvency, he wrote: "[H]ere there is no other means of selling than by credit; otherwise the goods become moth-eaten, because those buyers who show up do not contemplate the idea of spending what they have with them but, rather, of opening an account either here or, if not here, then in some other place."[68] What Gach found in 1782 was a surfeit of merchants, disadvantageous selling conditions, and few buyers, so he was disappointed by his store's performance. After all, during four years of operations in Arizpe his partners had invested 156,267 pesos and he had only been able to send back to Ximénez 29,434 pesos.[69] On the verge of opting to return to Mexico City, Gach informed his partners of his desperation after achieving such meager results: "There is no doubt that the profits shown in this

[68] AGN, Consulado, vol. 228, exp. 1, ff. 40.
[69] Of total remittances, 763 pesos (2.6 percent) was in cash, while 28,671 pesos (97.4 percent) was in bills of exchange. AGN, Consulado, vol. 228, exp. 1.

TABLE 4.9. Examples of price "discounts" offered by merchants in Sonora

	Maximum price	Medium price	Minimum price
Vara of Ruan	2 pesos	1.5 pesos	1.25 pesos
Nominal discount		25%	37.5%

Source: AGN, Jesuitas, leg. I-12, exp. 284.

balance [sheet] are not proportional to the expectations nor to the branch of activity. . . . [T]ime has taught me the impossibility of this commerce, as it would not be easy for myself or any other man . . . to produce results in these conditions."[70] Luckily for the Fagoaga-Ximénez company, precisely in the year in which Gach suggested selling off his stock and returning to Mexico City, the company's fortunes began to recover and the three partners decided to continue their operations in Sonora.

Gach's disappointment was symptomatic of the way that Sonoran commerce functioned, as it was a system in which cash sales rarely occurred but where credit sales, payment in silver, or exchanges of goods were common operating mechanisms in northern New Spain. Given this situation, in order for merchants to recover their initial investment, they had to wait until credit payments became due or devote themselves to the task of searching for the best destination for merchandise exchanged locally. Having recognized the generalized need to sell without immediately receiving cash, from early times traders in the province of Sonora had established what one contemporaneous observer called "the most extraordinary, ridiculous and unusual style of commerce ever carried out in Spain's dominions." This practice consisted of quoting high prices for goods and then offering buyers attractive "discounts" that varied depending on the form of payment that the client guaranteed (credit, mercury silver, smelted silver, goods). This meant that three price levels were established for each product—maximum, medium, and minimum—with the least onerous offered to the best clients (Table 4.9).[71]

The buyers of these goods, on the other hand (Sonoran ranchers, *hacendados*, and miners), also sought ways to make this commerce more tolerable, and they soon found a way to pass on the costs caused by the shortage of currency to other people. The solution was to pay wages in goods (in kind).

---

[70] Esteban Gach to Manuel Ximénez del Arenal, Arizpe, May 28, 1782, AGN, Consulado vol. 240, exp. 3, ff. 485–90.

[71] Diego Ortiz Parrilla to Viceroy Güemes de Horcasitas, Real presidio de San Miguel de Horcasitas, April 16, 1750, AGN, Jesuitas, leg. I-12, exp. 284.

TABLE 4.10. Scheme for paying wages with goods

	Price of goods for employer			Price of goods for employees			Payment of wages		
	Reales	Reales per peso	Price in pesos	Retail price (pesos)	Reales per peso	Price in reales	Wage in pesos	Reales per peso	Reales
	12	8	1.5	1.5	12	18	2.5	7	18
Rates				Employer quotes merchandise worth 1.25 pesos "at full standard price"			Wage tabulated in pesos de a 7 reales"		
Explanation	12 reales = 1.5 pesos			Employer determines that a worker needs 18 reales to pay for merchandise worth 1.5 pesos			Employer pays 2.5 pesos of wages with merchandise worth 1.5 pesos		

Individuals who had people working for them became very interested in obtaining merchandise at the "minimum price." Then, when the time came for them to pay their workers' wages, they would calculate the value of the goods according to the "maximum price," and thus obtain a profit by cheating the workers out of part of their wages (Table 4.10). In 1750, the governor of Sonora, Ortiz Parrilla, had seen this practice and summarized it as follows:

> [T]he miner or buyer of goods who requests and gets these discounts does not do so with an eye to applying them to the payments he makes to the people in his service, especially the Indians; because he always pays them [using] the highest price. Let's say [for example], that a peon earns six pesos per month, which works out to two *reales* per day, discounting festive days, and they are paid with three *varas* of *bayeta* at [a price of] two pesos per *vara*; if we refer to silver at the medium price of twelve *reales*, [then] he has paid his peon with four and a half pesos; and at the meanest price of ten *reales*, [he has paid his peon] with three pesos and six *reales*, leaving the . . . master with a profit of one-quarter or three-eighths of the discount granted him by the trader for the goods purchased. . . . [T]hus by granting credit [to the workers], they are always enslaved; and one who wishes to free himself is condemned to walk about naked for a year in order to achieve it.[72]

---

[72] AGN, Jesuitas, leg. I-12, exp. 284.

Returning to the case of our protagonist, experience taught Gach that if he did not participate in this system of financing goods and paying salaries in kind, the company he represented could not hope for financial success. For this reason, in 1784, when the opportunity presented itself for him to take charge of supplying the presidios in Sonora, he did not hesitate to make an interesting arrangement with the commander general of the Internal Provinces.[73] The contract that Gach and Felipe de Neve signed for supplying the presidios of Santa Cruz, Tucson, Pitic, and Altar is a key to understanding the interaction of elements described thus far.[74]

In broad terms, said agreement (signed on October 8, 1783), established Gach's obligation to supply clothing, tack for horses, and provisions (grain, meat) to the officials and soldiers of the aforementioned presidios during the 1784–1788 period. He was to deliver provisions once a year from his company's stores in Arizpe and Horcasitas. In exchange for his services, Gach would receive from the royal treasury money destined to pay the soldiers' wages. Thus, at year's end he would elaborate individual accounts of the materials consumed by each soldier, and, in theory, distribute to each one the amount that was left over.[75] However, the conditions in which this contract operated turned out to be totally disadvantageous for the presidio residents. Gach had agreed to supply corn and other cereal grains to the four presidios as a complement to his deliveries of clothing and tack for horses, but, as he alleged that he made no profit on grains, he was unwilling to accept responsibility for robbery or "other unavoidable losses that might be occasioned by mice, moisture or other accidents" while the cereal grains were stored in the towns. The agreement between Gach and Neve stipulated that the consumers would have to make up for such losses, as well as pay freight costs and provide military escorts for food deliveries, all of which increased the prices of the goods consumed in the presidios.

---

[73] In fact, the Fagoaga-Ximénez company was involved in supplying merchandise to the presidios in Sonora before this date. However, before 1784 the company's role was limited to sending goods on credit to the merchants and soldiers in charge of the presidios' stores.

[74] Although the accord between Neve and Gach only covered four presidios (Santa Cruz, Tucson, Pitic, and Altar), in the same month of October 1783 the commander general negotiated the same conditions with other merchants for other presidios. In a memo dated October 20, 1783, Felipe de Neve informed José de Gálvez of the conditions in which Gach was to supply the presidios, adding that "under the same clauses, or with differences of little import, don Joseph Antonio Pérez Serrano . . . has been supplying the Fronteras presidio since January of this year. . . . The same conditions having been proposed, I have approved don Manuel Romualdo Diez Martínez, *vecino* [and] trader in Cieneguilla to supply the San Carlos de Buenavista presidio and the company of Pimas Altos located in San Ignacio." AGI, Guadalajara 518.

[75] AGI, Guadalajara 518.

[I]n order to regulate these shrinkages and losses . . . the [signatory] considers it appropriate that one key to the cabin in which they are stored be held by the cashier or clerk who represents him in each presidio, and another by the official, sergeant or corporal that the commandant or troop may appoint, so that witnessing the supplies of grains that arrive, and keeping an exact account of their introduction and distribution in a notebook that is to be enclosed in said cabin, at the end of the year he may deduct the true losses that occur and charge their value to the consumers in proportion to the quantity of grains that each one has received.[76]

This arrangement presupposed other disadvantages for presidio residents, but especially for the soldiers who received their wages annually.[77] For example, in the course of the year, a soldier would never know with certainty the portion of his wages that he had already consumed. Although soldiers received an "account statement" every four months, even this did not inform them of their true situation because prices of their goods and foodstuffs were not calculated until the end of the year, at which time it was possible to tabulate losses sustained by the store. When the moment arrived to calculate final accounts, twenty-five pesos, "or the quota that the authorities might stipulate," were discounted from each soldier as contributions to the presidio's "retention fund."[78] Even after all of this, the *habilitado* (supplier) still had one last opportunity to extract money from the soldiers' pockets, as it was established that if any salary remained, and if the soldier "freely and spontaneously wished to use [same] in the supplier's store, then he would be given goods and effects at the going rate." It seems this final offer of freedom to acquire goods was simply an empty promise, first, because as noted the "going rate" was in fact a creation of the merchants themselves, and, second, because the freedom thus provided was just an elegant metaphor followed by a clause stipulating that if the soldiers did not wish to acquire anything in the store at that time, "no other supplies would be offered in the course of the year without a document or authorization by the captain or commander."

[76] *Ibid.*
[77] Officials and chaplains received their pay on a monthly basis and so had better opportunities to escape the restrictions this system imposed.
[78] The "retention" fund was made up of amounts withheld from the soldiers as a kind of bond, apparently designed to help prevent desertions. Aside from this fund, presidios also had a "gratification" fund that held money destined to pay pensions to invalids, orphans, widow, and retired soldiers. Both funds were kept "separately in a chest with three keys . . . [one for the] captain, [a second for the] lieutenant and [the other for the] first *alférez* or, in his absence, a subaltern official, who would be responsible for any shortages." AGI, Guadalajara 518.

Given these conditions, it is clearly not a coincidence that the years in which Gach was in charge of supplying these presidios were the most fruitful ones for the Fagoaga-Ximénez company. The data in Table 4.3 confirm Gach's stroke of genius by demonstrating the marked increase in shipments of merchandise to Sonora in the late 1780s, which declined once the period stipulated in the contract expired.

As in the presidios, paying wages in kind in mission towns was a fundamental characteristic of the local economy, although a more recent phenomenon.[79] In the missionary sphere, exploiting the personal services of Indians had been common practice until at least 1794, when Commander General Pedro de Nava prohibited the clergy in those provinces from taking advantage of Indian labor without wage compensation.[80] As a result of this prohibition, missionaries were forced to modify their relationship with mission Indians and accept the obligation to pay wages to their cowherds, blacksmiths, overseers, and servants in general. On various occasions, this change in the mission regime has been interpreted as the turning point in the incorporation of Indians into the monetized economy, which allowed them to obtain goods in the market independent of the clergy. In this view, discussions of "wages" and "workdays" make mission laborers emerge as subjects oriented toward the exterior of the community in virtue of their freedom to sell their labor to a mission or a nearby ranch.

However, closer scrutiny of Indian workers in mission communities reveals a distinct reality; unfortunately, data from only one mission in Pimería Alta are available and the period documented is for only five years, 1829 to 1833.

---

[79] Fray Antonio de los Reyes, *Copia del manifiesto estado*, AHMNAH, FF, vol. 66.

[80] This measure was part of a wider program by Pedro de Nava designed to abolish "the method observed in the administration of temporal goods at the missions." As part of this project, the commander general ordered "that the method of community be abolished in those *pueblos de indios* in the provinces under his jurisdiction with more than ten years since their reduction . . . [and] shall continue in new missions only for ten years." With respect to Indian labor, the commander ordered that in the missions and ancient towns "the Indians shall enjoy entirely the same freedom that the law grants them and that the Spanish and other castes—called *gente de razón*— enjoy, to tend their own cattle, cultivate the land, and seed the earth . . . and to be paid on the basis of the working day," entrusting the local justices to see to it that the Indians were paid "in cash on an individual basis…, but that if they voluntarily wish to receive in exchange certain goods, to allow them to do so in their presence." Pedro de Nava, Chihuahua, April 10, 1794, BNFF, 18/377. In compensation for this restriction, the commander had ordered that each Indian head of family, married or widower, who was not yet fifty years old would deliver half a *fanega* of corn per year or twelve *reales* in money as its equivalent. When the Council of the Indies learned of these measures, it passed notice to the King for his approval so that they would carry royal sanction. Royal approval of Pedro de Nava's measures concerning the personal services of the Indians is found in a *real cédula* dated in Aranjuez on June 16, 1797, AGI, Guadalajara 586.

TABLE 4.11. Accounts of workers at Oquitoa Mission, 1829–1833

Name	Occupation	Work period	Monthly wages	Payments in goods (pesos)	Payments in cash (pesos)	Balance (pesos)
Juan J. Hernández	Shepherd	05/11/1830–09/06/1830	6 pesos	19	2	-1.5
Lorenzo	Shepherd	09/06/1830–?	6 pesos	13	5	-10.4
José Orozco	Shepherd	10/22/1830–03/14/1831	7 pesos	37.5	3.3	-14.3
Pío		01/23/1831	7 pesos	2.1	1.2	?
José Agustín		06/11/1830–03/02/1831	6 pesos	54.7	0.75	-9.5
Juan Palomino		10/25/1830–01/27/1831	6 pesos	15.1	1	?
Toribio Caballero	Field laborer	?	6 pesos	27.3	5.2	-12.6
Pedro		32 days	6 pesos	6	2.1	?
Francisco Xavier Monreal	Field laborer	11/8/1830–08/28/1831	6 pesos	37.1	1	-18.0
Pedro Ochoa		07/09/1831–11/13/1831	6 pesos			-4.0
Francisco Caballero		08/01/1831–?	6 pesos	20.5		-17.1
Xavier Caballero	Servant	10/25/1830–11/25/1833	8 pesos	323.75	5	-10.5
José A. Carrillo		11/14/1831–06/14/1832	7 pesos	65.25		-37.0
José Espinoza		12/20/1831–11/24/1832		133		-91.0
Tomás Ortiz	Cowherd	10/9/1829–05/07/1830	10 pesos	81.1	3.6	-15.1
Tomás Ortiz	Cowherd	05/11/1830–08/11/1830	9 pesos	24.6	1	-12.5
Juan Monreal		10/02/1829–04/23/1830	7 pesos	81.25	2.8	-37.0
Juan Monreal		05/18/1830–08/20/1831	7 pesos	128	2.3	-37.3
Juan Monreal		11/12/1831–05/17/1832	7.5 pesos	92		-45.5
Gregorio Serrano	Soap maker	10/15/1829–01/24/1830	12% of product	24	0.5	-6.6
Agustín Serrano	Shepherd	01/22/1830–04/27/1830	7 pesos	20.6		1.5
Ignacio Reyna	Cowherd	09/13/1830–04/28/1833	10 pesos	349	48.1	-76.0
Guillermo Reyna	Cowherd	12/17/1832–04/18/1833	6 pesos	18.1	7.25	-1.25

Source: AFPM, AQ, Letter K, leg. 24, no. 4.

Despite these limitations, it was possible to reconstruct the service schedules of twenty individuals in the Oquitoa mission over the period. These histories, summarized in Table 4.11, help to clarify the transition taking place in Sonoran mission towns in the early nineteenth century.

By comparing the lists of wages paid in goods and money shown in the accounts from Oquitoa, it is clear that the mission economy was based primarily on nonmonetary forms of exchange. Moreover, what is significant for the study of northern New Spain is the high percentage of individuals, who upon completing their work season, were in debt to the missions.[81]

Of these twenty "accounts" or lists of debits and credits, no less than 80 percent (sixteen cases) finished their work owing the mission anywhere from 1.25 to 91 pesos. The story of Francisco Monreal is representative of this situation, as it traces the progressive indebtedness of a worker over time. Monreal was hired on November 8, 1830, to work in one of Oquitoa's agricultural fields. He was promised a monthly wage of 6 pesos and one *almud* of grain.[82]

By August 18, 1831, Monreal had contracted debts with the mission in the amount of eighteen pesos, but continued to work for the mission and by year-end his debt had increased to almost twenty-nine pesos. The missionary continued to give Monreal advances of goods against his wages, and on November 13, 1831 this worker's balance showed a debt of thirty-five pesos, which rose to forty-two by the end of 1832.

It was difficult for most of Oquitoa's cowherds and other employees to avoid becoming indebted to the mission. Only in cases of the few individuals working at the mission for short periods of time (one to three months) was it

---

[81] According to Susan Deeds, this practice was also common during the Jesuit period in northern New Spain. She suggests that the Jesuits "resorted to advancing credit to Indians and castas to keep them from seeking work outside [the missions]." Thus, the use of indebtedness would have served "as a device to prevent mobility," in the context of limited numbers of available laborers. Deeds, *Defiance and Deference*, 138. The effectiveness of debt peonage in helping ranchers, hacendados, and other employers to temporarily retain workers at their service is a matter for further debate, as diverse factors could have contributed to the workers' way out of these constrains—flight, negotiation or rebellion, for instance. What cannot be denied is that advanced payments in kind had an immediate impact on the financial resources and standard of living of workers and employers. However, I acknowledge that both sides of this mechanism accounted for its recurrent practice.

[82] These contracts do not refer to calendar months, but to sets of days worked. Thus, for accounts on the missions and for effects of paying the workers, holidays were discounted as were any days when a worker failed to show up. In the sources available for Oquitoa, it is very difficult to calculate how many working days are represented in the accounts of each of the twenty individuals included in this study. Nonetheless, a prudent estimate would arrive at an average wage of 2 *reales* per day, for cases with a monthly wage of 6 pesos, and of 2.7 *reales* per day for individuals with a monthly wage of 10 pesos.

possible for workers to close out their accounts without debt or with a small balance in their favor, as in the singular case of Agustín Serrano.

How can we explain this high incidence of indebtedness? The answer is the same as that offered in the case of debt peonage on   haciendas during the regime of President Porfirio Díaz (1876–1911, known as the Porfiriato): the existence of a large landless population and manipulation of prices on subsistence goods discussed above.[83] Missions and other employers were able to fix the prices of the goods they gave to workers as compensation. As one Jesuit missionary observed with regard to Indian workers, the practice of paying wages in kind or artificially manipulating payment systems frequently accompanied notorious delays in paying Indians, which caused them in time to be indebted, impoverished, and forced to keep working for their employers "because they are bonded to them for several years as if they were indentured [adscripticios] to the Spaniards or their personal slaves."[84]

As mentioned above, at this stage of goods distribution, price increases were transferred by buyers to final consumers (in this case, cowherds and other mission workers). In Oquitoa's account books we find a classic example of this situation in Tomás Ortiz, the mission's overseer. During his early months of work tending the mission's cattle, Ortiz received a cow valued at 6 pesos as part of his wages. Months went by and in May 1830, the missionary at Oquitoa calculated the balance of the advances "paid" to Ortiz beginning in October 1829, including an adjustment that consisted of adding "two pesos for the increase in the value of the cow originally registered as six [pesos]." According to this logic, the money needed in May 1830 to replace the cow Ortiz and family consumed in 1829 had increased, and thus the two-peso difference was to be taken from his wages.

---

[83] Debt peonage has been defined as "a general term for several categories of coerced or controlled labor resulting from the advancement of money or goods to individuals or groups who find themselves unable or unwilling to repay their debt quickly. As a consequence they are obliged to continue working for the creditor or his assignees until the debt is repaid, and are often further coerced to borrow more or to agree to other obligations or entanglements." David McCreery and Murdo J. MacLeod, "Debt Peonage," in *Encyclopedia of Latin American History and Culture*, ed. Barbara Tenenbaum (New York: Charles Scribner's Sons, 1996), 2:360–62. See also Erick D. Langer, "Debt Peonage and Paternalism in Latin America," *Peasant Studies* 13, no. 2 (1986): 121–27. For Ramón Gutiérrez the key issues are the character of local agriculture and the limited access to land tenure: "[T]he growth of export-oriented agriculture and livestock production on a highly circumscribed land base worked by landless peasants provided the conditions for the development of debt peonage." Gutiérrez, *When Jesus Came*, 323.

[84] Tomás Miranda, *Carta apologética al padre José Utrera*, Cumuripa, February 18, 1755, UAL, Special Collections, MS 184.

COMMERCE AND FORMS OF COERCION

Upon carefully examining the previous references from the early nineteenth century in Sonora, parallels are clear with the large plantations during the Porfiriato that functioned largely thanks to the captive labor at their disposal. It could be justifiably argued that the coercive systems of the two time periods were distinct, the socioeconomic contexts were dissimilar, and the living conditions of the population also diverged. However, what is common to both is that a system tying people to a certain place of residence restricted their personal freedom and used mechanisms based on coercion to ensure their subordination and dependence. These circumstances show clearly that on the eve of the nineteenth century, Sonora's economy reproduced forms of coercion and surplus extraction typical of *ancien régime* societies, in which the flourishing of certain social groups contrasted with the onerous living conditions endured by the rest of the population. To affirm that in the late eighteenth century the indigenous population of Sonora was incorporated in New Spain's market as producers, consumers, and wage workers oversimplifies the socioeconomic relations analyzed in this chapter.

In the Sonoran case, the mechanisms used first by merchants and later by various employers in order to secure substantial profit margins allowed them (as in other areas of northern New Spain) to control the principal government offices in the province or to ensure the complacency of the authorities and thus go on about their business. The primacy enjoyed by the merchants and landowners in Sonora thanks to these two factors is reflected in both their influence in local politics and in the settlement patterns that emerged as the Sonoran population increased. By holding the majority of the population captive through the systems of exchange and wage payments in kind described above, the merchants and landowners definitively altered the face of the Sonoran frontier in the late eighteenth century. Responses by the Sonoran populace to these circumstances included the itinerancy patterns previously discussed (e.g., the pluriethnic bands), as well as patronage networks (e.g., the Gándara family and associates).

The captive trade circuit analyzed here developed in the context of mechanisms transforming New Spain society in the late eighteenth century, but with a particular characteristic. Such trade relations in a frontier society that lived in a constant state of tension because of the (real and imagined) Apache threat and the restrictions imposed on Spanish colonization by the mission regime translated into an evolutionary pattern over time different from the one observed in the central region of the viceroyalty. In northern New Spain, the decline of ecclesiastic institutions would not have to wait until the mid-nineteenth century. Rather, as a result of the economic and political consolidation of groups benefiting from the trade system described in this chapter, it took place several decades earlier than in the core areas of the empire. Together, the economic mechanisms examined here and the social processes examined in the next chapter demonstrate that the periphery of the Spanish empire depended not only on a dialectical relationship with the administrative centers, as Greene and Bushnell have proposed, but that the marginality of the frontiers is expressed in the negotiation with the center, as well as in the search for forms of development that ensure the subsistence of the dominant group.

CHAPTER 5

Local Adaptations of the Franciscan Mission Regime

By the late eighteenth century in Sonora, the trade circuit analyzed in the previous chapter accentuated the economic hardships of the majority of that province's settlers and was fundamental to the political and financial stability of a small group of local merchants and landowners. This captive system of local commerce was complemented by a gradual process of privatization of communally held lands, driven by the growing pressure exerted by Spanish settlers and the internal divisions that plagued Indian communities.[1] In these circumstances, certain processes by then well known in other areas of New Spain were re-created in Sonora. When subjected to a Spanish population eager to occupy their lands, Indian communties in central and western Mexico responded in a variety of ways, including legal action in defense of their lands, open confrontation with their neighbors,[2] and working on surrounding ranches and haciendas with the intent of securing their means of subsistence.[3]

---

[1] Cynthia Radding, *La acumulación originaria de capital agrario en Sonora: La comunidad indígena y la hacienda en Pimería Alta y Opatería, 1768–1868* (Hermosillo: Instituto Nacional de Antropología e Historia, 1981), 13–46; Jerónimo, *De las misiones*; Radding, *Entre el desierto y la sierra: Las naciones o'odham y tegüima de Sonora, 1530–1840* (Mexico City: CIESAS, Instituto Nacional Indigenista, 1995), 119.

[2] William Taylor, *Landlord and Peasant in Colonial Oaxaca* (Stanford, CA: Stanford University Press, 1972); Florencia Mallon, *Peasant and Nation: The Making of Postcolonial Mexico and Peru* (Berkeley: University of California Press, 1995); Peter Guardino, *Peasants, Politics, and the Formation of Mexico's National State: Guerrero, 1800–1857* (Stanford, CA: Stanford University Press, 1996).

[3] Charles Gibson, *The Aztecs under Spanish Rule* (Stanford, CA: Stanford University Press, 1964); John Tutino, *From Insurrection to Revolution in Mexico: Social Bases of Agrarian Violence, 1750–1940* (Princeton, NJ: Princeton University Press, 1986); Bernardo García Martínez, *Los pueblos de la sierra: El poder y el espacio entre los indios del norte de Puebla hasta 1700* (Mexico City: El Colegio de México, 1987); Rosa Alicia de la Torre Ruiz, *Cambios demográficos y de propiedad territorial en la provincia de Ávalos, siglos XVIII–XIX* (Guadalajara, Mexico: Universidad de Guadalajara, 2012).

It was also possible for the Indians of Sonora to mitigate the effects of the contraction of their communal lands by resorting to hunting and gathering activities in the sierra.[4]

In this context, general knowledge of the transition from the colonial
regime to the republican period in Sonora derives mainly from studies of
indigenous labor and land tenure conducted over the last three decades by
Cynthia Radding and Saúl Jerónimo. On the one hand, it has been shown that
in several regions of Sonora various forms of both private land tenure communal property characteristic of Indian peoples coexisted.[5] With respect to the
Indian communities, fundamental changes of the eighteenth century were
related to the distribution of mission lands to the Indians and the increasing
demand for plots located near the missions by the *gente de razón*.[6]

In some cases, these processes have been analyzed from the perspective of a
profound crisis of the mission system.[7] For instance, it has been argued that after
the expulsion of the Jesuits in 1767, when the clergy lost control of the temporalities and Indian labor, the mission system began to collapse.[8] The importance
of the economic hardships that the Sonoran missions suffered in the late eighteenth century cannot be denied, but, as shall become clear in the following, in
the Franciscan period the main problem of financing the missions was not related
only to obtaining sufficient funds, but also to questions of how to administer the
available goods, and to whom the Franciscans could turn in order to satisfy the
needs of both friars and missions. It is at this level that the Franciscan reorganization of the Sonoran missions and the relationships between the mission regime
and the rest of the Sonoran populace take on new meaning and shift the problems of financial resources into a much broader context.

In this section, the focus moves again to the beginnings of Franciscan
administration in Sonora, aiming to highlight structural differences in the plan-

---

[4] Radding, *Wandering Peoples*, 205.

[5] Radding, *Las estructuras*, 13–15; Radding, *Wandering Peoples*, 203–207.

[6] As several authors have demonstrated, both of these processes were marked by much litigation over usurpations and invasions of land by Spanish settlers, Indians, and missionaries. Kessell,
Friars; Jerónimo, *De las misiones*; Radding, "La acumulación originaria."

[7] Ortega Noriega, "Crecimiento y crisis," 185; Vidargas del Moral, "Sonora y Sinaloa," 435.
Jerónimo Romero affirms that "the missions and their property regime blocked the change that
the Bourbons were preparing, so it was decided to eliminate the mission as the axis of regional colonization and advance in the privatization of land tenure." *De las misiones*, 20. From an anachro-
nistic perspective, another author has noted: "One year after the expulsion of the Jesuits, the mission system in Sonora clearly revealed symptoms of what was to be its ultimate disintegration."
Patricia Escandón, "Los problemas," 283.

[8] Jerónimo Romero, *De las misiones*, 105.

ning and execution of the socioreligious projects of the Province of Santiago de Xalisco and the Colegio de Querétaro. On the basis of this initial survey, the narrative proceeds to use the geographical differences outlined in earlier chapters to explain why the mission, understood as a model of social organization, evolved in different ways. The objective here is not to offer a review of individual feats,[9] but to explain the forms of organization, misadventures, and encounters and dis-encounters of the friars entrusted with the administration of the Sonora missions after 1767, as well as their relationships as individuals and as a group with their wider social network.[10] Focusing on the generational changes among the actors involved provides one means of counterbalancing the risk of falling into a rigid institutional analysis.[11] Thus, the analysis centers not only on the generations of missionaries but also on distinct moments in the development of Sonoran society. The following pages, then, deal with the first, second, and third generations of missionaries in Sonora, emphasizing the influence that liberalization of the mission regime and the Indians' transition from "mission children" to Mexican citizens had on the rest of the Sonoran population.

THE MISSION REGIME WHEN THE FRANCISCANS ARRIVED IN SONORA

On February 27, 1767, Charles III implemented one of his most important decisions when he decreed the expulsion of the Society of Jesus from his dominions and the seizure of Jesuit assets.[12] To ensure that the monarch's

---

[9] There is an abundant literature of this kind, especially from the era preceding the 1960s. I refer the reader to the most representative works of this genre: Herbert Eugene Bolton, *Rim of Christendom: A Biography of Eusebio Kino, Pacific Coast Pioneer* (New York: Macmillan Company, 1936); Peter Masten Dunne, *Pioneer Jesuits in Northern Mexico* (Berkeley: University of California Press, 1944); Omer Englebert, *The Last of the Conquistadors: Junípero Serra, 1713–1784* (New York: Harcourt, Brace and Company, 1956).

[10] In this respect I find inspiring Gil Pujol's take on political history. Gil Pujol, *Tiempos de política*. My analysis of the Sonoran missionaries draws on William Taylor's approach to the study of parish priests, which considers them not only as part of an ecclesiastical institution, but also as "individuals and men of their place and time," with distinct personal backgrounds and trajectories, who were involved in parish life in many different ways. Taylor, *Magistrates of the Sacred*, 78–97. Also of great import was my reading of the work on the cathedral governing body (*cabildo catedral*) of Michoacán by Oscar Mazín, who studied that ecclesiastical corporation "as a group and a subject of social relations," on the basis of events in which its individual members participated and the ways in which this group was linked to the wider society in which it was immersed. Oscar Mazín, *El cabildo catedral de Valladolid de Michoacán* (Zamora: El Colegio de Michoacán, 1996).

[11] Luis González y González, *La ronda de las generaciones: Los protagonistas de la Reforma y la Revolución Mexicana* (Mexico City: SEP, 1984).

[12] According to John Elliott, Spanish King Charles III "had his own reasons for disliking the Jesuit order, which he saw as a dangerously powerful international organization unamenable to

wishes were carried out as secretively as possible, the order expelling the Jesuits was sent covertly to Sonora, where it was received by Governor Juan Claudio Pineda, on July 11 of the same year.[13] Meanwhile, the topic of replacing the Jesuit missionaries was already being discussed in Mexico City, and the Franciscan provinces and colegios were chosen to send clergy to take over the missions in the northern reaches of the viceroyalty.

Also in July 1767, the commissary of the Franciscans in New Spain, Fray Manuel de Nájera, and the *visitador*, José de Gálvez, agreed to send fifty-one friars from the colegios of San Fernando de Mexico, Santa Cruz de Querétaro, and Guadalupe de Zacatecas to replace the Jesuits in those missions. The Audiencia de Guadalajara, also in 1767, decided to send a group of friars from the Xalisco province to administer the former Jesuit missions on the Baja California peninsula. This did not come about, though, as disagreements between the newly appointed missionaries and the secular authorities led to assigning the Xaliscans to serve towns in Opatería and certain missions located in Pimería Baja. The missions in Pimería Alta and some of those located in Pimería Baja, meanwhile, had been assigned to the Queretarans. The missions on the Baja California peninsula were finally entrusted to the Fernandinos

---

royal control, and which he suspected, with some reason, of being in collusion with the interest groups involved in the recent overthrow of his reforming minister, Esquilache." J. H. Elliott, *Empires of the Atlantic World: Britain and Spain in America, 1492–1830* (New Haven, CT, and London: Yale University Press, 2006), 309. Stein and Stein have shown that the expulsion of the Jesuits from the Spanish dominions was related to a longstanding conflict between *colegiales*— former students at Spain's *colegios mayores*—and *manteístas* in the Sala de Alcaldes de Casa y Corte (the subsection of the Consejo de Castilla responsible for the security of Madrid). These frictions accounted for the suspicious approval of the unpopular edict dated March 10, 1766, which eventually lead to the riots in Madrid later that month—the *motín* de Esquilache. At some point during the investigations after the *motín*, "Madrid's bureaucratic hierarchy decide[d] to exonerate the most visible of the *motín*'s agents," the president of the Consejo de Castilla—Bishop Diego de Rojas y Contreras, himself a *colegial*—and other *colegiales* from the Sala de Alcaldes. At the same time, investigators blamed the Society of Jesus for the riots in Madrid, arguing that the Jesuits had conspired against Charles III. Stanley J. Stein and Barbara H. Stein, *Apogee of Empire: Spain and New Spain in the age of Charles III, 1759–1789* (Baltimore: Johns Hopkins University Press, 2003), 90–107. In the context of New Spain's missions, the expulsion of the Jesuits brought the Crown at least two benefits. In the short term, it eliminated a corporation that had come to be identified as an important point of concentration of capital and influence in the society. But this policy was apparently also nourished by a desire to reorganize mission communities and bring them more directly under the control of royal officials. This project reached maturity a few years later with the creation of the Comandancia General of the Internal Provinces (1776), and the Diocese of Sonora (1779). McCarty, *A Spanish Frontier*, 5–10; Priestley, *José de Gálvez*, 285–95.

[13] De la Torre Curiel, *Vicarios en entredicho*, 321–22. The February 27 disposition was later confirmed by a decree issued on March 27, 1767 and by the *pragmática sanción* published in Madrid on April 2 of the same year. BPEJ, CM, book 32, vol. IV, ff. 24–37.

TABLE 5.1. Missions assigned to Xaliscans and Queretarans, 1768

Santiago de Xalisco Province		Colegio de Querétaro	
Mission	Missionaries	Mission	Missionaries
Yécora	Bernardo Ponce de León	Tecoripa	Juan Sarobe
Arivechi	José Cabrera	San Ignacio	Diego Martín García
Sahuaripa	Joaquín Ramírez	Saric	Juan José Agorreta
Mátape	Manuel Zuzarregui	Ures	Esteban Salazar
Batuc	José García	Guevavi	Juan Crisóstomo Gil
Huásavas	Antonio Medina	Cucurpe	Antonio María de los Reyes
Bacadéhuachi	José Medina	Onavas	José Antonio Caja
Aconchi	Antonio Oliva	Opodepe	Antonio Canals
Banámichi	Antonio Jácome	Ati	José Soler
Arizpe	Juan Manuel Domínguez	Suamca	Francisco Roch
Baserac	Pedro Cuevas	Cumuripa	Enrique Echasco
Cuquiárachi	José Abalza	Caborca	Juan Díaz
		Bac	Francisco Garcés
		Tubutama	Mariano Buelna y Alcalde and José del Río

Sources: AHMNAH, FF, book 99, f. 87; AFPM, AQ, Letter K, leg. 14, no. 4.

(Franciscans from the Colegio de San Fernando in Mexico City). Once the mission areas assigned to each institution were defined, the friars from Querétaro arrived in May and June 1768 to take up their posts in Sonora, while the Xaliscans did the same in June through September of that year (Table 5.1).[14]

From the moment of their arrival in Sonora, both Queretarans and Xaliscans realized that the trials awaiting them were going to be far more serious than anticipated. Many pueblos whose care and attention had been entrusted to them were practically deserted and mission properties were in a state of ruin after having been left in the hands of a few residents. The dilapidation of mission properties resulted from one or more of the following: negligence, abuse, and demands by military authorities to supply food for troops on the hunt for Seri and Apache rebels.[15]

In order to support the missionaries and ensure their sustenance, Viceroy de Croix promised an annual stipend (*sínodo*) of 300 to 350 pesos for each

[14] McCarty, *A Spanish Frontier*, 43–51. According to Lino Gómez Canedo, Governor Pineda turned over the fourteen missions that had been assigned to the Queretarans on June 9, 1768. Gómez Canedo, *Sonora hacia fines*, 29.

[15] McCarty, *A Spanish Frontier*, 39–40.

friar, depending on the mission zone, direct from the royal treasury.[16] For the same purposes, the governor of Sonora ordered the royal administrators who managed mission properties to hand over to the Franciscans "the churches, holy vessels, priests' clothing, and also residences and . . . necessary furnishings . . . and other effects pertaining to the service [of the mission] . . . and also the books . . . except those of the mission accounts."[17]

In certain towns, such as Tubutama, Ati, Tecoripa, Cumuripa, and Ónavas, the missionaries were fortunate, as they received houses and churches that were in good condition, as well as sufficient vestments and other materials to celebrate the divine offices. In other cases, such as Caborca, the friars arrived to find the church buildings on the brink of collapse.[18]

With the formal installation of the Franciscans in the missions, two distinct administrative models would emerge. In the late eighteenth century, Franciscans associated with the Xalisco province were devoted primarily to administering parishes and Indian *doctrinas* in older regions of Spanish settlement. Although missionary work was by no means foreign to them, by that time the latter did not constitute the main objective of their ministry.[19]

The Colegio de Querétaro, in contrast, was devoted from its beginnings to propagating the faith (*propaganda fide*). Thus, planning for and establishment of missions among both Catholics and neophytes comprised its essential objective. These antecedents marked an enormous difference when, in 1767, these two institutions agreed to send friars to Sonora. While the Franciscan Province of Xalisco limited itself to appointing Father Manuel Zuzarregui as its commissary of missions in Sonora, entrusting him with the government of his eleven colleagues, the Colegio de Querétaro sent its "president of missions" with detailed instructions on how the missionaries were to be governed and carry out their ministry. In addition to recommending that missionaries treat their catechumens kindly, strive to teach the Castilian language and Christian doctrine, treat the Spaniards cordially, and procure the largest number of Indians possible for their missions, the guardian and the governing body of the colegio also required the president of their missions to reconnoiter the territory where those towns were located in order to become familiar with their

---

[16] In Ures and Cucurpe, a stipend of 300 pesos was initially assigned, but it was later adjusted in line with the rest of the missions in Pimería Baja and Opatería at 309 pesos 6 *reales* 6 *granos*, while in Pimería Alta the figure was 350 pesos. AGN, Archivo Histórico de Hacienda, leg. 318, exp. 2.

[17] AFPM, AQ, Letter K, leg. 14, no. 35.

[18] AFPM, AQ, Letter K, leg. 14, no. 8.

[19] De la Torre Curiel, *Vicarios en entredicho*, 247–350.

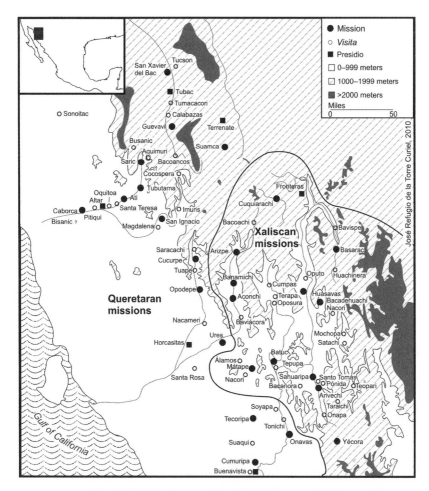

MAP 5.1. Missionary districts in Sonora, 1768

resources and "the [Indian] nations that wander around dispersed and could be added to the missions."[20]

[20] The father president received special instructions to ensure that none of the missionaries would become entangled in problems with the settlers in Sonora. He was recommended to keep the Queretarans from making reports or comments "on [such] matters or persons." With respect to their dealings with the Indians, the Queretarans were warned that it was not convenient to deprive the Indians of "civil treatment, communication, commerce, and proximity to Spaniards"; but, above all, the friars were entrusted with ensuring that the Indians earned their own subsistence through hard work and "the possession of their properties, fruits, and effects in particular and private domain." *Instrucción dada al presidente de las misiones de Sonora*, Santa Cruz de Querétaro,

In fulfillment of those instructions, the missionaries from Querétaro drafted a long series of reports in 1768 describing the material and spiritual conditions they encountered in the fourteen missions assigned to them. A recurring theme in these reports was denunciation of poor conditions. Churches and residential buildings were so badly neglected that they were about to collapse. The Indians had "little instruction, great liberty, no subordination [to authority], too much idleness and an excess of defiance," according to one friar who lamented the policy adopted by the governor of Sonora prohibiting the missionaries from using Indian labor.[21]

The enterprises of these two religious institutions were launched from distinct frameworks of internal government, although both lacked financial support. The stipend promised them was insufficient to cover the missions' expenses, including maintenance of the missionaries' homes, the churches, and the friars themselves. Although the missionaries could turn to the administrators of the missions' temporalities to obtain certain goods that were then charged against their stipend, such effects were sold at prices so high that, as one missionary said, "600 pesos do not suffice for each individual per year, even though one lives in great discomfort and poverty."[22]

In an attempt to remedy these problems, in 1769 José de Gálvez ordered the commissaries administering mission properties to hand over to the friars all of the goods, cattle, and other effects that had been entrusted exclusively to their care. Traditionally, it has been thought that Gálvez's decree worked to the exclusive benefit of the Queretarans, as the Xaliscans did not recover administration of the temporalities at the same time.[23] This idea is based on an interview between Father Buena and José de Gálvez in Álamos on June 3, 1769, in which the *visitador* agreed that the Queretarans should administer the temporalities of their missions.[24] Because this order mentioned only the missionaries from Querétaro and no similar decree has been found concerning the Xaliscan missions, historians have assumed that the royal commissaries of Opatería and

---

August 4, 1767, AFPM, AQ, Letter K, leg. 14, no. 3. This *Instrucción* phrases almost literally the tasks assigned to the Queretarans by Viceroy de Croix in his petition to that institute to send missionaries to Sonora. Marqués de Croix to the guardian of the Colegio de Querétaro, Mexico City, July 8, 1767, AFPM, AQ, Letter K, leg. 14, no. 1.

[21] Fr. MCC, 201, exp. 3–49, and *ibid.*, 202, exp. 9–16.

[22] Fray Juan Díaz to the discretory of the Colegio de Querétaro, Caborca, August 8, 1768, Fr. MCC, 201, exp. 3.

[23] McCarty, *A Spanish Frontier*, 66, 101; Radding, *Las estructuras*, 15; Escandón, "Los problemas de la administración," 288.

[24] José de Gálvez, Álamos, June 3, 1769, AFPM, AQ, Letter K, leg. 14, no. 10.

certain areas of Pimería Baja continued to administer their temporalities. However, indirect testimonies suggest the Xaliscans also received authorization to administer the properties of their missions, although at a somewhat later date and for a shorter period.[25]

Despite these dispositions, in the early years the mission economy did not improve to the degree that the Franciscan fathers had hoped. Many structural problems affecting the missions in the early years derived from changes in Spanish policy regarding the governance of this institution. The Crown was looking for ways to restrict the missionaries' role to that of spiritual guides for the communities by excluding them from the election of local authorities, prohibiting them from exploiting unpaid Indian labor, and reserving for local justices only the use of force to control the Indians' behavior.[26] Some authors find in these measures an attack on the privileges of the religious corporations, or another example of the secularization and centralization of power in late colonial society. A variety of evidence suggests that the missions' social functions had changed by the last third of the eighteenth century. As a result, their economies were also in need of adjustment. Throughout New Spain, missionary districts were established to fulfill specific social functions. For instance, in Durango and Nueva Vizcaya's Santa Bárbara province, mission districts were expected to congregate dispersed Indian groups as a means of securing the Indian labor that the nearby mining towns and ranches required. In Nayarit and Yaquimi, the acceptance of missionaries by local Indians was symbolic of an armistice between the Spanish authorities and peoples only tenuously subject to Spanish dominion. There, the missions offered the best alternative for negotiating peace.[27] In Sonora, in contrast, the missions had been founded as

---

[25] On October 7, 1770, Viceroy Marqués de Croix ordered that "the temporalities of the missions which they are administrating at present" be turned over to the Sonoran missionaries. AGN, Jesuitas, leg. I-6, exp. 6. Given that the Queretarans had received the temporalities in 1769, we can infer that this order alluded to the Xaliscans. In mid-1771, the latter complained that they were still dependent on the *comisarios reales* for the disposition of mission properties, which suggests a marked delay in the implementation of the order cited above. AGN, Jesuitas, leg. I-6, exp. 4. A suit in 1777 over the use of temporalities brought by the inhabitants of Nacameri against the Xaliscan missionary in Opodepe shows that the friars from the province of Xalisco had taken control of mission properties there. BNFF, 34/735. However, by 1780, the litany of complaints by the local population over this prerogative had led the Xaliscans to try to refrain from handling the missions' assets. BPEJ, CM, book 44, ff. 310–12.

[26] McCarty, *A Spanish Frontier*, 53, 65; Fray Antonio Barbastro to Fray Diego Ximénez, Tubutama, June 17, 1783, AFPM, AQ, Letter K, leg. 16, 2nd portion, no. 19.

[27] Cramaussel, *La provincia*; Spicer, *Los yaquis*; Jean Meyer, "Las misiones jesuitas del Gran Nayar, 1722–1767: Aculturación y predicación del Evangelio," *Trace* 22 (1992): 86–101; José Ortega, "Maravillosa reducción y conquista de la provincia de San Joseph del Gran Nayar, Nuevo

outposts marking the advance of Spanish colonization, while at the same time they provided alternative forms of social organization to the Indians in the aftermath of the dissolution or alteration of their ancient forms of subsistence.[28] By the late eighteenth century, these two functions were being disputed by Spanish settlers, and for this reason the series of decrees mentioned above must be situated in the context of supporting secular Spanish settlement.

As far as the missionaries were concerned, the complexity of these transformations could be expressed quite simply: the pressures weighing on the mission regime did not allow them to achieve the results expected of them. Something was not functioning correctly and when plans fail, dissent soon arises. From within the ranks of the missionaries, Fray Antonio de los Reyes began to suggest a profound reform in the method of governance. In 1772, de los Reyes described a series of localities that contained "a small number of souls" barely civilized and only poorly instructed in Christian doctrine. This Franciscan stated that the dispersion of mission Indians was notorious, as they preferred to roam around the mining towns and not settle down in their poorly constructed quarters. This dark image was further complicated by the so-called *rescatadores* who came to the missions to purchase the products of Indian labor at low prices.[29]

To a great extent, de los Reyes's criticisms identified the missionaries themselves as responsible for the material ruin of the missions. In his view, the friars were poor managers of temporalities, and lacked zeal in facilitating Indian labor and diligence in teaching religious doctrine and the Castilian language. In response, the Colegio de Querétaro appointed Fray Diego Ximénez to analyze de los Reyes's criticisms and proposals. In his reply, Ximénez tried to show that the Franciscans were not responsible for the difficulties affecting the Sonoran missions. Moreover, citing extracts from one of de los Reyes's own writings, he pointed out that his fellow friar recognized the causes of the difficult living conditions in Sonoran as the hostility of Indian enemies, poor town planning, and avarice of the *gente de razón*, the poor example they set, and the abuses they committed against the Indians.[30] However, the Franciscans at Querétaro disagreed with this conclusion that its missionaries were not responsible for the

---

Reino de Toledo" in *Apostólicos Afanes de la Compañía de Jesús, escritos por un padre de la misma sagrada religión de su provincia de México*, ed. Francisco Javier Fluvia (Barcelona: Pablo Nadal Impresor, 1754), 1–223.

[28] Radding, *Entre el desierto y la sierra*, 61–62.

[29] Fray Antonio de los Reyes, Mexico City, April 20, 1772, AHMNAH, FF, vol. 66, ff. 52–61; and de los Reyes, *Estado de la Provincia de Sonora*, Mexico City, July 6, 1772, AHMNAH, FF, vol. 65, ff. 1–22.

[30] AFPM, AQ, Letter K, leg. 16, no. 13 (commenting on the report of April 1772).

problems of the pueblos under their administration because de los Reyes had already brought his reports to the attention of the viceroy and the court of Madrid as part of his efforts to promote "a new establishment" or form of government in Sonora that would do away with the existing "political, civil, economic and ecclesiastical disorders."[31]

The Queretarans did not share de los Reyes's opinions concerning the need for radical reorganization of Sonora in general, and of the missionary administration in particular. Thus, it was necessary to present an alternative plan for reforms allowing the missions to confront the problems that de los Reyes had pointed out and Ximénez had seconded. With this idea in mind, on March 30, 1773, the latter presented an appeal containing his institution's counterproposal to the viceroy of New Spain. The first item that the missions needed was a military escort to be selected by each priest from among the soldiers at the nearby presidios. The escort would defend the mission residents, protect the missionaries in their travels, pursue fugitive Indians, and force the natives to attend religious instruction and "incline them to work." Moreover, Father Ximénez asked that the missionaries be granted judicial faculties in their districts so that they could correct the Indians, when necessary, arguing that the clergy were not only the natives' spiritual fathers but also their temporal ones. The third point of Father Ximénez's appeal explained the need to prohibit the Indians from leaving the missions to work for Spanish settlers, "as they should be under the sole discretion and control of the missionary fathers." Father Ximénez then asked that the practice of Indians and Spaniards living in close proximity be banned, as well as all commerce between them, because both of these practices had, from the very beginning, worked to the detriment of the natives. Finally, the document reaffirms the need to assign two missionaries to each mission located in those towns.[32]

Accepting Ximénez's proposals presented three challenges for the secular authorities: (1) weakening the line of defense formed by the presidios along the northern frontier, (2) making additional outlays of resources to sustain the new missionaries, and (3) consolidating an extensive geographic domain in which the Franciscans would exercise ecclesiastical, civil, and military authority. Such matters as modifying the defensive scheme of the presidios and obliging the royal treasury to make greater outlays were extremely delicate at the time, and were often simply passed over by the authorities. Thus, Viceroy Bucareli rejected the petitions of the Queretarans, although he did authorize the mis-

[31] AHMNAH, FF, vol. 66, f. 58.
[32] AGN, Californias, vol. 39, exp. 2.

sionaries from that colegio to oversee the relations between Indians and Spaniards, as he considered it "quite proper to the good Christian and political government of the Indians that they live in subordination."[33]

Once informed of the viceroy's response, the Queretarans insisted that at the very least he accept the proposal of assigning two friars to each mission. Once again, the reply from the authorities was a resounding "no," although on this occasion it was accompanied by a counterproposal that the colegio reduce the number of missionary districts it was administering in Sonora by combining ("congregating") some mission towns. In this way, two friars would be made available to attend to the needs of each mission. The Queretarans considered this an attractive option in their attempts to reform the Sonoran missions, and in 1774 they commissioned Fathers Antonio Ramos and Juan Díaz to visit the missions in Pimería Alta and Pimería Baja. The reports of Ramos and Díaz convinced their superiors in Querétaro of the impossibility of moving the missions from their existing sites, thus running the risk of leaving some regions of Sonora virtually unpopulated. Moreover, residents' objections to being relocated suggested that such a move would imply other serious inconveniences. In addition to these observations, Díaz, who was commissioned to visit Pimería Baja, reported a considerable number of Spaniards and *castas* already living in those missions.[34] On the basis of these testimonies, Father Ximénez, the recently elected guardian of the Colegio de Querétaro, proposed to Viceroy Bucareli that the Queretarans abandon their eight missions in Pimería Baja and concentrate their efforts solely in Pimería Alta.[35]

The viceroy accepted this petition in a decree dated May 24, 1775, and his first thought afterward was to consult with the bishop of Durango, Antonio de Macarulla, to see if he would be willing to secularize the missions in Pimería Baja. When the bishop refused to accept responsibility for those poverty-stricken missions populated by Indians whose complete subordination to Spanish rule was far from certain, Bucareli decided to offer the Cucurpe, Opodepe, Ures, Onavas, San José de Pimas, Cumuripa, Tecoripa, and Pitic missions to the Xalisco province. The Xaliscans readily accepted the viceroy's invitation and in August 1775 arrived at their new destinations. Thus, by the end of that year, their missionary district had grown to a total of nineteen missions (Map 5.2).[36]

[33] *Ibid.*

[34] See Chapter 2.

[35] Fray Diego Ximénez to Viceroy Bucareli, Mexico City, December 6, 1774, Fr. MCC, 201, exp. 3.

[36] Fray Diego Ximénez to Fray Juan Díaz, Querétaro, June 17, 1775, AFPM, AQ, Letter K, leg. 17, no. 9; De la Torre Curiel, *Vicarios en entredicho*, 323–24.

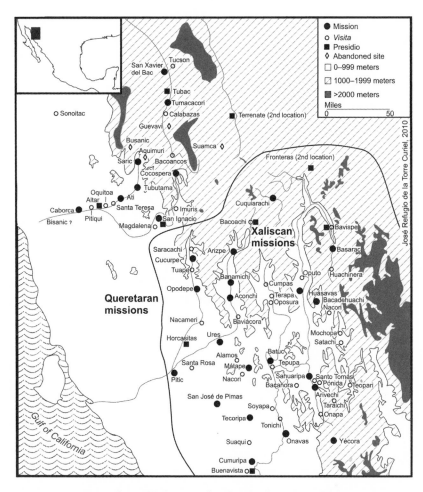

MAP 5.2. Missionary districts in Sonora, 1776

The differences of opinion between de los Reyes and Ximénez, together
with the transfer of the missions to the Xaliscans, confirm the transformation
of the social network containing the Sonoran missions. Both men had firsthand
familiarity with the problems of the missionary administration in Sonora, and
their proposals reveal prevailing ambivalent attitudes about the mission regime.
De los Reyes was convinced that the missions should advance toward an intermediate status between mission and parish, although he did not yet propose
secularization. To ensure the Hispanization of the Indians, he argued, it was
necessary to stimulate their productivity, grant them new freedoms, and place

the missions under diocesan jurisdiction. Ximénez, in contrast, favored taking a step backward in the transformation of the mission towns and treating them as the beachheads of Spanish settlement, thus keeping missionary prerogatives intact. When the authorities adamantly refused to take this backward step, the Queretarans opted to move to Pimería Alta, the area in which the missions were still fulfilling that social function.

Now focused exclusively on Pimería Alta, the Queretarans began to define the approach they would employ in these new circumstances. At that time, Fray Francisco Antonio Barbastro headed the Queretarans in Sonora, so it was his responsibility to propose the governing regime to be implemented by his fellows. The most delicate aspect of the mission economy was managing the temporalities. It was necessary for all concerned to be prudent in this matter because, unlike their Jesuit predecessors, numerous restrictions were imposed on Franciscans in the administration of worldly goods. Accordingly, Barbastro recommended that the Queretarans strive to reconcile this responsibility with the institution's vows of poverty. "We are to be poor and to appear as such," he affirmed in a letter to his fellow missionaries dated in 1780. Appearing to be poor was not a complicated task, as it entailed only that the friars be moderate in their use of mission assets. In reality, however, poverty was more complex, as it obliged them to detach their hearts from material goods, even though at the same time their ministry required them to administer mission temporalities. In his lengthy missive, Barbastro explained that it was entirely legitimate for the missionaries to accept alms, "as long as it is not the missionary [himself] who receives the money," and as long as they were applied to the needs of the Indians. In administering a mission's communal properties, the Franciscans were to ensure that the Indians worked regularly and did not sell their products cheaply, although popular opinion held that those activities converted them into virtual "estate administrators" who were in violation of both canon and common law. Barbastro did not share this view, reasoning that what the Queretarans were doing in Pimería Alta was "nothing more than counseling the [Indian] governor as to what is best, . . . out of charity. . . ." In his approach to the issues of managing money and purchasing and selling goods, Barbastro distinguished between two types of commerce. If it became necessary for a friar to actually handle money in the execution of such transactions, then the act of making payment would have to be carried out by a third party representing the missionary. On the other hand, if agreements were based on the exchange of goods (as occurred in most cases), then there was no obstacle to the missionaries themselves intervening as often as was deemed necessary. Barbastro explained that barter (*trueque*) allowed them "to purchase in the same way as we may sell; and thus we can establish a price for an article, sell it, and even look for a buyer." Finally, he made it clear that the prime beneficiary of Indian labor was to be the mission church,

> because the personal services that the Indians provide for the growth and conservation [of the churches] . . . [are] admitted in place of the tithes, first fruits, [and] ecclesiastic fees . . . [that] they are obliged to pay, like all other Christians, for the sustenance of the mission church and its missionary, and in conformity with this, if the church has needs then such goods may not be invested in any other thing.

If there were a surplus once the needs of the church and the minister had been taken care of, then it could be used to succor the Indians, beginning with widows, orphans, and the ill, and then including the entire community.[37] In this lengthy exposition, Barbastro established the moral foundations of the exploitation of Indian labor and authorized the commercial relations in which the missionaries were implicated. This brought tremendous relief to such economically important missions as that of Caborca where, according to one Franciscan, as soon as the Spanish settlers found out that the Indians were planting, "they would implore [the missionary] to receive money in advance," in order to ensure that they would receive the product.[38] By the same token, Barbastro's missive authorized the friars to barter with the goods they indicated in their annual requisitions (*memorias de géneros*), and this became perhaps the most common mercantile practice among them, though one that the Jesuits had prohibited on various occasions. A letter from the missionary at Saric to the guardian of the Colegio de Querétaro clarifies this trade's importance for those establishments. In his missive, he requests that his *memoria* include neither foodstuffs nor perishable products, as they were of no use to him in the trade. He preferred instead products in great demand in Sonora:

> The *memoria* that I include has been thoroughly contemplated, so that only those things I request be sent, and nothing else, as I do not consider confections [*chomite*] to be necessary here, nor wax, nor wine, nor oil, nor spices, as all of these things just accumulate and become burdensome; what is very

---

[37] Fray Francisco Antonio Barbastro to the missionaries of Pimería Alta, Tubutama, April 30, 1780, AFPM, AQ, Letter K, leg. 16, 2nd portion, no. 3.

[38] Fray Florencio Ibáñez to the guardian of the Colegio de Querétaro, Fray Esteban Salazar, Saric, May 29, 1783, AFPM, AQ, Letter K, leg. 16, no. 12.

important is many pieces of cotton cloth, coarse woolen cloth, *paño* and *bayeta*, but not that of Mexico City, as it does not stand up to hard work.[39]

Thanks to this operating system and the benefits previously noted,[40] by 1783 the Queretarans had been able to construct—right from their foundations—churches at Buenavista, Ures, Pitiquí, San Ignacio, and Tubutama. The latter three were built with thick walls of brick and cement. Furthermore, over the course of seven years, the Queretarans had also restored the churches at Tonichi, Opodepe, Cocospera, Calabazas, Oquitoa, and Caborca, and undertaken the construction of San Xavier del Bac's church, the most important building project ever undertaken by the Franciscans in Pimería Alta.[41]

New Mode of Governance: Custody of San Carlos de Sonora

While in New Spain the Franciscans from the Province of Xalisco and the Colegio de Querétaro thought that the administrative reorganization of 1775 would bring about the missions' material and spiritual improvement, de los Reyes's initiative had been well received in Madrid, and a reform of much larger proportions was being developed. The Spanish court was well aware that despite recent changes in Sonora, the missions there were still immersed in turbulent waters, especially those in Pimería Baja.[42] Creation of the Diocese of Sonora in 1779 and the appointment of de los Reyes as its first prelate, together with the founding of the missionary San Carlos de Sonora Custody in 1783, constituted the clearest evidence of the monarch's support (and, above all, that of José de Gálvez, head of Spain's Ministry of the Indies) for the reform proposals presented years before by the recently appointed bishop. The fact that parts of the pontifical brief authorizing the creation of the custody are exact transcriptions of one of de los Reyes's earlier reports confirms the growing importance that this Franciscan had attained in the court of Madrid.[43] More

---

[39] *Ibid.* On the prohibition of the Jesuits to commercialize goods sent from Mexico, see AGN, Archivo Histórico de Hacienda, leg. 17, exp. 22.

[40] See Chapter 4.

[41] Fray Francisco Antonio Barbastro to Fray Diego Ximénez, Tubutama, June 17, 1783, AFPM, AQ, Letter K, leg. 16, 2nd portion, no. 19.

[42] Testimonies on these problems are found in the correspondence between Viceroy Martín de Mayorga, the minister provincial of Xalisco (Fray Juan Prestamero), and the commissary of the Xaliscan missions in Sonora (Fray Antonio López Murto), BPEJ, CM, book 44.

[43] On November 17, 1779, Pope Pius VI approved the creation of the custody of Sonora in his brief entitled *Exposuit Nobis*, the text of which coincides almost entirely with one of the

importantly, it testifies to the coincidence of two complementary projects. First was de los Reyes's interest in creating a diocese that would replicate the governance of Sonora and Sinaloa's boundaries in ecclesiastical terms. He would be at the helm directing the transformation of the missions into more industrious population centers complete with schools and organized according to the principles of European civility. The second project related to the Crown's desire to effectively incorporate New Spain's northern frontier into its dominions, in this case under the watchful eye of a prelate who seemed willing to serve as precisely the kind of royal functionary that the monarch was seeking among his ecclesiastics.

The creation of the custody of Sonora presupposed unification of the Queretaran and Xaliscan missions into a single Franciscan jurisdiction and installation there of de los Reyes's "new mode of governance" for the missions. This was the context in which, after spending almost seven years at the court of Madrid, de los Reyes returned to New Spain (August 1782), as the bishop-elect of Sonora and "Apostolic and Royal Delegate for the reorganization of the missions." On the basis of de los Reyes's reports, the king had become convinced that the Indians in Sonora were living as slaves, exploited by the missionaries in an oppressive regime that in no way ensured their incorporation as vassals of the sovereign. The monarch believed that the custody's creation seemed to offer the panacea needed to free Sonora's population from the weighty burden of the missions. In contrast, Barbastro believed that the establishment of this new jurisdiction for the missions administered by Queretarans and Xaliscans was nothing more than a product of the venom that de los Reyes spread at the court of Madrid against him and his companions.[44]

The new custody's objective was to unite the two missionary districts of Sonora into a single entity, independent of Xaliscan and Queretaran superiors. This new administrative scheme sought to bring the missionary enterprise under the direct supervision of the bishop or, as Barbastro put it, "to ensure that the missions have only one prelate and that he be close to the govern-

---

proposals de los Reyes presented to José de Gálvez. See Pius VI, *Breve Apostólico*; and Fray Antonio de los Reyes, *Plan para arreglar el gobierno espiritual de los pueblos y misiones en las provincias septentrionales de Nueva España. . .*, San Ildefonso, September 16, 1776, AGI, Guadalajara 586.

[44] In a letter to the commander general of the Internal Provinces, the king had touched on these points by announcing the imminent reform of the Sonoran missions: "I am well informed that the Indians of these frontiers are enslaved, and so you shall procure that they be placed in liberty as my loyal vassals, as I shall later send a new government to the missions." Cited in a letter from Fray Francisco Antonio Barbastro to Fray Diego Ximénez, Tubutama, June 17, 1783, AFPM, AQ, Letter K, leg. 16, 2nd portion, no. 19.

ment."[45] De los Reyes's project coincided to a large degree with the Bourbon ideals of centralized administration, urbanism, and civility. By setting up the custody, the authorities sought to congregate the Indians in "true towns" to replace the irregular collections of isolated dwellings that had characterized the missions. Those towns would then form nine mission districts, each of which would have an administrative center (*cabecera*) where a large convent (*hospicio*) would be constructed and put under the administration of a friar elected as *vicario*. This friar would then meet regularly with the head of the custody (the *custos*) to discuss matters of concern, while the latter would keep the bishop informed as to mission business.[^46]

The custody's government also envisioned important changes for mission Indians. Once organized under this new scheme, the indigenous population of each mission was to be divided into three sections, each of which would be obliged to devote two days of labor per week to community tasks. No male member of the town would be exempt from this obligation, even if he also worked for the Spanish settlers beyond the mission's boundaries. Once they had fulfilled this obligation, the Indians could be granted permission to work in nearby mines and ranches at their own convenience. The most onerous aspect of this system, then, was that the Indians were also assigned to construct the convents needed for the nine *hospicios* that were to be established in the custody, and to sustain the friars that would take up residence there.[47]

Despite the internal divisions that this project generated among the Sonoran missionaries, and notwithstanding the financial difficulties that the arrival of more friars and the construction of the new convents entailed, on October 23, 1783, Fray Antonio de los Reyes presided over the inauguration ceremony for the San Carlos de Sonora custody (Map 5.3).

Assembled in the bishop's residency in Ures, some of the Queretaran and Xaliscan missionaries learned about the contents of the royal decree and statutes authorizing and regulating the custody's creation. After informing the friars about his commission, de los Reyes made use of the powers received from the Franciscan commissary general of the Indies to elect the first *custos* and governing body of the recently created institution; the elected friars were Fray Sebastián Flores, as *custos*, and Fathers Roque Monares, Francisco Jurado, Antonio Barbastro, and Antonio Ahumada as members of the custody's definitory (council).

---

[45] Fray Francisco Antonio Barbastro to Fray Diego Ximénez, Tubutama, November 23, 1783, AFPM, AQ, Letter K, leg. 16, 2nd portion, no. 30.

[46] Fray Manuel de la Vega, *Estatutos Generales*, AHNM, Diversos, 29, no. 10.

[47] AFPM, AQ, Letter K, leg. 16, 2nd portion, no. 26.

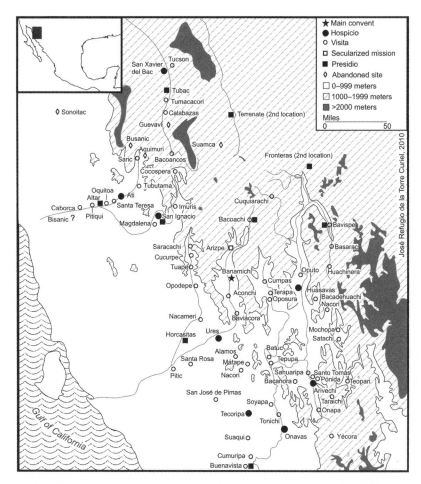

MAP 5.3. Missionary custody of San Carlos de Sonora, 1783–1790

Two days later, on October 25, the bishop and the custody's definitory met to select the location of the nine convents (*hospicios*) that should serve as administrative centers for the equal number of new missionary districts.[48] Banamichi was elected as the residence of the *custos*, while the other eight *hospicios* were to be located at Ures, San Ignacio, San Francisco de Ati, San Xavier

[48] Arricivita, *Crónica seráfica*, 566–67; Fray Sebastián Flores to Guardian Fray Esteban de Salazar, Ures, November 30, 1783, AFPM, AQ, Letter K, leg. 16, no. 12. The proceedings of the foundation of the custody can be found in *Copia de lo actuado por el Sr Obispo en el Pueblo de Ures*, Ures, October 28, 1783, AFPM, AQ, Letter K, leg. 16, 2nd portion, no. 26.

del Bac, Huásavas, Arivechi, Tecoripa, and Onavas.[49] Thus, by the end of 1783 de los Reyes's dream seemed to have materialized. Thirty-four friars and twenty-five missions grouped in nine missionary districts and one governing body seemed to be a promising start. However, the roots of discord had been expanding long before the bishop won this battle.

REACTION AGAINST THE CUSTODY

On January 21, 1782, while still in Spain, Fray Antonio de los Reyes sent a letter to the recently elected guardian of the Colegio de Querétaro, Fray Esteban de Salazar, congratulating him on his election. De los Reyes had spent several years in Spain recruiting new friars for the Queretaran missions in Sonora; thus, he took this opportunity to inform the Colegio de Querétaro's guardian that thus far he had recruited twenty Franciscans and that he was about to return to New Spain. However, the most important part of the letter was his warning that the new friars would join the Colegio de Querétaro and eventually help in the missionary activities in Sonora *if*, emphasized the correspondent, "you and that Apostolic college favor the reform of the missions and the creation of the custodies that the king . . . has ordered to be erected in the Internal Provinces. . . , which I will oversee given the faculties that His Holiness and the king have granted me."[50]

It did not take too long before the Colegio de Querétaro realized that a serious threat was around the corner. The tone of de los Reyes's letter was self-explanatory and was sufficient to announce that the Queretarans were supposed to yield to the bishop their jurisdiction over their friars and missions in Sonora. A royal decree issued on May 20, 1782, confirmed this impression and put the Queretarans on the alert anticipating the arrival of de los Reyes that same year.[51]

In August 1782, de los Reyes reached Veracruz and immediately informed the guardian of Querétaro that after a stay in Mexico City for his consecration as bishop of Sonora he would continue his journey to the north.[52] In November, de los Reyes arrived in Querétaro, immediately displaying the royal

---

[49] AFPM, AQ, Letter K, leg. 16, no. 12.

[50] Fray Antonio de los Reyes to Fray Esteban Salazar, Port of Santa María (Spain), January 21, 1782, AFPM, AQ, Letter K, leg. 16, no. 11.

[51] Arricivita, *Crónica seráfica*, 565. The royal decree informed the guardian of the Colegio de Querétaro about the king's decision to establish four custodies in New Spain.

[52] Fray Antonio de los Reyes to Fray Esteban Salazar, Veracruz, August 5, 1782, AFPM, AQ, Letter K, leg. 16, no. 11.

decree, statutes, and papal brief that established his authority, functions, and jurisdiction as bishop of Sonora and reformer of New Spain's missions. The Queretarans agreed to acknowledge de los Reyes as reformer of the missions, but as for the ample faculties that such appointment entailed they decided not to take any official position before consulting with the other two apostolic colegios in New Spain. This strategy allowed the Queretarans to discuss the situation with colleagues in Zacatecas and San Fernando de Mexico; under the initiative of San Fernando's guardian, the three colegios requested the counsel of four lawyers, who confirmed the Franciscans' feeling that the documents carried by de los Reyes did not comply with the formal requisites of an official order to be obeyed in New Spain.[53] Thanks to this legal snag, in December 1782 the three seminaries officially announced that they would not support creation of the custodies; moreover, they decided to appeal to the viceroy and the king while informing them about the impossibility of erecting the custody under de los Reyes's terms. In the case of the Queretarans, the guardian instructed the head of their missions, Fray Antonio Barbastro, not to give up those missions to the bishop.[54] Barbastro's answer was comforting for the guardian. He asserted that at least in Pimería Alta no missionaries were willing to embrace the custody.[55] Following the instructions of his seminary, Barbastro informed the Queretarans stationed in Pimería Alta about their institution's official position. In response, evidence of the missionaries' loyalty to their colegio started to arrive in Querétaro. The missionary at Oquitoa, for instance, did not hesitate to express his resolution to side with his seminary in this conflict: "With regard to these missions, I will persevere working [in Sonora] as long as that blessed colegio be in charge of [the missions]; but if they are segregated [from the colegio] and incorporated into the custody, there is no way for me to continue working here."[56]

---

[53] The royal decree exhibited by de los Reyes did not have the approval of the Council of the Indies, nor did it bear the endorsement of the viceroy. As for the statutes and papal brief, the copy presented by de los Reyes did not bear any stamp or signature that demonstrated its authenticity. Under these circumstances, one of the lawyers stated, such documents should not be obeyed, since de los Reyes could not "carry on his commission before proving it actually exists, for his jurisdiction should not be assumed but demonstrated." AFPM, AQ, Letter K, leg. 16, no. 10.

[54] Proceedings of the meeting of the discretory of the Colegio de Querétaro, December 20, 1782, AFPM, AQ, Letter K, leg. 16, no. 9. Unfortunately, no similar response from the Xaliscans has been found for the years before 1791.

[55] Fray Francisco Antonio Barbastro to Fray Esteban de Salazar, Tubutama, January 16, 1783, AFPM, AQ, Letter K, leg. 16, 2nd portion, no. 14.

[56] Fray Juan Gorgoll to Guardian Fray Esteban de Salazar, San Antonio de Oquitoa, April 12, 1783, AFPM, AQ, Letter K, leg. 16, no. 12.

De los Reyes was aware of this general opposition, but he was unshakably committed to his objectives. According to the Queretarans, when de los Reyes first learned about their opposition to the custody of Sonora, he cried out that he "did not need the assistance of the [Franciscan] provinces or the [apostolic] colleges" to set up the custody, "for he would carry out his plans in association with [Commander] Croix only."[57] De los Reyes left Querétaro toward the end of 1782, lamenting the lack of cooperation from his brethren. In July 1783, the bishop reached Sonora, spending several weeks in Álamos and its vicinity, finally arriving in Arizpe on September 22, 1783.[58] De los Reyes hoped to meet Teodoro de Croix, his would-be ally, in that city; however, that was not possible as Croix had left Arizpe days before after being replaced by Felipe de Neve as commander general of the Internal Provinces. The bishop did not wish to remain in Arizpe, the episcopal see of his diocese, and decided to move to Ures. As noted previously, the bishop brought the Queretaran and Xaliscan missionaries there in October 1783 for the inauguration ceremony of the Sonoran custody.

In January 1784, the *custos* Fray Sebastián Flores died. Immediately after Flores's funeral, a vice-*custos* was elected. To the dismay of Bishop de los Reyes, the election favored Barbastro, unconditional ally of the Colegio de Querétaro and the most recalcitrant critic of the bishop and his custody. In Barbastro's view, the custody lacked legitimacy—the Laws of the Indies and the precepts of the Franciscan order established that the missionaries were not under the jurisdiction of any bishop, but were subject to their immediate superior, that is, Barbastro himself, as former head of the missions and now vice-*custos* of San Carlos de Sonora. As a matter of fact, shortly after his election as the custody's superior, Barbastro had already sent a report to Commander General Felipe de Neve, synthesizing his objections to creating the custody as follows: (1) The reports that documented the need to create a custody were based on inaccurate remarks by de los Reyes, who had exaggerated what he saw and faked what he did not know. (2) It was impossible to establish the custody due to the lack of missionaries, funds, and material conditions necessary to comply with the custody's statutes. (3) Even accepting that the missions needed to be reformed, the custody was not the most viable solution. (4) The custody would cause a tremendous setback to the mission enterprise if the friars remained in *hospicios* rather than among the Indians.[59]

---

[57] *Ibid.*

[58] Stagg, *The First Bishop*, 74–80; Navarro García, *Don José de Gálvez*, 434.

[59] Fray Francisco Antonio Barbastro, Tubutama, December 24, 1783, AFPM, AQ, Letter K, leg. 16, 2nd portion, no. 32.

In addition to these formal reasons, Barbastro's opposition to the custody and the bishop arose from personal differences. On several occasions Barbastro had shown anger regarding de los Reyes's negative comments about the missions and the missionaries' work. Barbastro was a particularly zealous missionary, committed to his ministry as head of the Pimería Alta missions and extremely proud of the good name and reputation of his seminary. For those reasons, the idea of "reforming" the missions was an affront to his work as missionary leader and to the reputation of the Colegio de Querétaro. This matter was also a personal issue, declared Barbastro: "I consider myself obliged as a matter of conscience to keep the good name [of the Colegio de Querétaro] and to regain the fame that has been taken from me by he who has told the king that these missions are ruined."[60] The phrasing of de los Reyes's criticisms was particularly insulting, said Barbastro, because the bishop always referred to him as the "president of those ruined missions," thus implying that the spiritual and material ruin of the missions was the fault of a group of friars who were not only useless but "pernicious."[61]

Given the above institutional and personal differences, Barbastro ordered the Sonoran missionaries not to acknowledge de los Reyes's jurisdiction and not to obey the bishop's mandates "under penalty of excommunication."[62] Barbastro's position increased tensions throughout the custody and put the Sonoran missionaries between a rock and a hard place. As the bishop made clear in one of his descriptions of Sonora, the projected reform of the missions was not working because of the lack of cooperation of Barbastro and his brethren. Only in those missions under the care of the Spanish friars that had arrived in Sonora with the bishop could one find orderly populations. That was the case, said de los Reyes, of Ures, Cucurpe, Huásavas, and Bacadehuachi, missions in which ten Spanish missionaries had reorganized the local population according to the statutes of the custody. In contrast, Pimería Alta, the Xaliscan-administered missions of Tecoripa, Opodepe, Mátape, Banamichi, Basarac, and Bacoachi, as well as Aconchi (Barbastro's residence) were strongholds of opposition to the bishop.[63]

---

[60] Fray Francisco Antonio Barbastro to Fray Esteban de Salazar, Tubutama, January 16, 1783, AFPM, AQ, Letter K, leg. 16, 2nd portion, no. 14.

[61] Fray Francisco Antonio Barbastro to Fray Esteban de Salazar, Tubutama, March 1, 1783, AFPM, AQ, Letter K, leg. 16, 2nd portion, no. 16.

[62] Fray Antonio de los Reyes to Guardian Fray Juan Sáenz Gumiel, Sonora, April 28, 1785, AFPM, AQ, Letter K, leg. 16, no. 11.

[63] Fray Antonio de los Reyes, *Relación clara y metódica de todas las misiones establecidas en la diócesis de Sonora*, Sonora, September 15, 1784, BNFF, 34/759.

Despite this opposition, the bishop won the first battle in 1783 by formally establishing the custody and he would score again on January 14, 1784, when the king issued a royal decree ordering the viceroy of New Spain to dismiss any appeal or legal recourse submitted by the Franciscans asking for dissolution of the custody. Moreover, the king instructed his representative in New Spain to assist Bishop de los Reyes in the creation of additional Franciscan custodies in the viceroyalty.[64]

Encouraged by this turn of events, the bishop took a decisive step toward the effective reorganization of the missions. Early in 1785, de los Reyes called Barbastro to a meeting in Álamos, stating that they needed to discuss the way that the custody should be governed. Barbastro believed that the purpose of the bishop was to remove him from his office and, if possible, to send him back to Querétaro. En route to Álamos, the vice-*custos* stopped at Onavas, near the custody boundary. As he would explain later, he could not leave the custody without his "legitimate prelate's" permission. Barbastro informed de los Reyes about his reasoning, to which the bishop replied that he was Barbastro's "legitimate prelate" and as such authorized him to visit Álamos. Barbastro argued that he would not obey the bishop since his superior was the Franciscan commissary general according to the statutes of the custody, and thus he decided to stay in Onavas. Although Barbastro's decision was well grounded, de los Reyes would not accept such an act of defiance. Outraged by this excuse, the bishop asked for the help of the civil authorities, and on March 13, 1785, the vice-*custos* finally arrived in Álamos, escorted by the local justices, as the bishop's prisoner.[65] While jailed in Álamos, Barbastro was interrogated by de los Reyes on matters concerning the custody's poor organization. Barbastro refused to answer the bishop, who insisted on blaming him for the internal divisions among the Sonoran missionaries.

Once the interrogatories were concluded, Barbastro was set free and returned to Banamichi. In that town he learned that the missionaries were about to leave Sonora, as they had been told that Barbastro would be sent back to Querétaro and the bishop would appoint a new *custos*. Barbastro's imprisonment was the turning point in the turbulent history of the custody. News of this incident soon circulated throughout Sonora. It also reached the commander general—now residing in Chihuahua—who openly repudiated de los

---

[64] *Informe de los procuradores de los tres colegios sobre la fundación de la Custodia de Sonora*, January 14, 1784, AFPM, AQ, Letter K, leg. 16, no. 15.

[65] Fray Antonio Barbastro to Guardian Fray Juan José Sáenz Gumiel, Álamos, April 15, 1785, AFPM, AQ, Letter K, leg. 16, 2nd portion, no. 57.

Reyes's conduct. Barbastro then decided to change his strategy, replacing reports and appeals with direct action and litigation. In an angry letter addressed to the guardian of his colegio in May 1785, the vice-*custos* announced that he would no longer tolerate abuses whether from the bishop or the friars supporting de los Reyes's project. He decided to punish all the assaults upon his person and jurisdiction as well as all the wrongdoings of the bishop's allies. To achieve this, he acknowledged that "it will be indispensable to incarcerate [some] friars and to ask for the aid of the soldiers." Whatever the costs, Barbastro wanted to set an example and to show who the head of the mission enterprise was:

> It is now time for all those "little Fathers" who think that Father Barbastro should please the bishop, to see . . . who the real Father Barbastro is. . . . I foresee now the biggest scandals ever seen in this kingdom. . . . [T]here is no peace and there will be none, and I would add that we cannot have peace until all the recent innovations be destroyed and things return to their primitive state. . . . No matter what the bishop's friends want [me] to be, Father Barbastro has proved his orderly conduct in the court of Chihuahua and he will do so in the courts of Guadalajara, Mexico City and Madrid. There was a time for religious harmony and fraternity; there was a time for pacific and prudent measures; it is now time for changing the means to prove one's argument. . .[66]

In fulfillment of his promises, Barbastro filed a complaint in the Comandancia General in Chihuahua against the bishop's interference in custody governance. The bishop responded by issuing an injunction against Barbastro from performing any religious activity in the Diocese of Sonora. Barbastro did not observe the prohibition in the missions of the custody, he explained, for they were not under episcopal jurisdiction.[67] During the following months, the conflicts between de los Reyes and Barbastro continued, and the mutual denigration and belittlement fueled the accusations that each party filed before diverse secular and ecclesiastic authorities.[68] This climate of conflict made it impossible for the custody to progress in any area, as the *custos* "was incapable of establishing anything at all and his subjects obeyed nothing."[69]

---

[66] Fray Francisco Antonio Barbastro to the guardian of the Colegio de Querétaro, Banámichi, May 3, 1785, AFPM, AQ, Letter K, leg. 16, 2nd portion, no. 58.

[67] Fray Antonio Barbastro to Guardian Fray Juan José Sáenz y Gumiel, Banámichi, July 6, 1785, AFPM, AQ, Letter K, leg. 16, 2nd portion, no. 60.

[68] Examples of these accusations can be found in AFPM, AQ, Letter K, leg. 16, 2nd portion, no. 65–68.

[69] Arricivita, *Crónica seráfica*, 568.

DISSOLUTION OF THE CUSTODY

In 1787, Bishop de los Reyes's death brought hope that his successor, Fray Joaquín Granados, would aid the missionaries in their desire to return to the previous regime. At this time, the Xaliscans began to prepare an official position with regard to the custody. Although some Xaliscans had decided to side with Barbastro during the most difficult times, the Province of Santiago de Xalisco was conspicuous for its silence.[70] At the request of the bishop of Guadalajara, in 1791 these friars officially added their official opinion supporting the dissolution of the custody. In response to the bishop's inquiry, the guardian of the Xaliscan convent in Guadalajara, Fray Tomás Eyxarch, presented a report supporting Barbastro's opinions about the custody. In general terms, Eyxarch's asserted that the custody statutes required "many impractical things." As an example he cited the clause calling for ten to twelve missionaries living in the custody's main convent on a permanent basis.[71]

Recognizing the problems that the experiment had created in Sonora, the king dissolved the custody by royal decrees dated July 16, 1790 and August 17, 1791, in which he ordered the missions returned to the form of governance existing prior to the custody's establishment.[72]

Although de los Reyes's plans never achieved the success that he dreamed of, they did have an impact in the short and long term. The discord among the friars in the custody and the disorganization of mission work stand out as the two immediate consequences. Not all proposals included in de los Reyes's project, however, were wrongheaded. He was correct in asserting that it was possible to modify the lifestyle of Sonoran settlers. Most missionaries had traditionally thought it necessary that Spaniards and mission Indians live separately, and de los Reyes had shared this view. However, the occupational structure that developed in the midst of the Franciscans' disputes provided the Indians with a certain freedom to leave the missions for occasional short periods that later became rather frequent. Once this pattern had been established within the mis-

---

[70] Perhaps this silence should be attributed to the lack of documentary evidence that might reveal a more active involvement of the governing bodies of the province of Xalisco in the discussions over the creation of the Sonora custody.

[71] Fray Tomás Eyxarch to the bishop of Guadalajara, San Francisco de Guadalajara, December 6, 1790, AFPM, AQ, Letter K, leg. 16, no. 37.

[72] BPEJ, CM, book 44. On July 9, 1788, Fray Antonio Barbastro petitioned the king to eliminate the custody, demonstrating that he had the support of the commissary general of the Indies. In response to this missive, the king sent a royal order to the bishop of Durango, dated July 16, 1790, asking for his opinion on the case. BNFF, 17/360. The bishop of Guadalajara's request to Father Eyxarch is related to this call for reports.

sion regime, it proved difficult for the missionaries to control once the custody was dismantled.

CHANGES IN MISSION ADMINISTRATION AND GENERATIONAL CRISIS

When the custody experiment ended the civil and ecclesiastical authorities of Sonora and New Spain tried an alternative approach, which was designed to relieve the growing tensions between the populace and the missionaries. In certain areas of Pimería Baja and Opatería, the Xaliscans had been involved in ongoing conflicts with both the local authorities and their Indian charges for reasons that ran the gamut from changes in personnel ordered by the Xaliscan authorities to oft-cited land disputes.[73] In this conflict-ridden context, the secularization of the missions began to be seen as the solution that would ultimately free the local Indian population from the missions. In addition, sending additional priests to Sonora would no longer be necessary at a time when the Franciscan Province of Xalisco was suffering a severe shortage of personnel.[74]

It was becoming clear to both the Franciscans and the authorities—civil and ecclesiastical—that the towns in Pimería Baja and Opatería were demanding a change of spiritual governance. However, the scarcity of priests in Sonora obliged the authorities to maintain the missionaries in those towns.[75] It was for this reason that, although both types of authority deemed the secularization of the Sonoran missions necessary, the process was rather long and tortuous. As the cases of the missions secularized in 1791—Banamichi, Aconchi, Mátape, Ónavas, and Ures—demonstrated, bringing the mission regime to an end temporarily eased the pressures that had accumulated between the faithful and the friars over the disposition of those communities' resources. However, it presupposed another problem: the new priests assigned to them would be looking after parishes that could not guarantee the income deemed necessary to sustain an acceptable standard of living.[76]

---

[73] Fray Antonio Barbastro to Guardian Fray Esteban Salazar, Saric, November 4, 1781, AFPM, AQ, Letter K, leg. 16, 2nd portion, no. 7.

[74] De la Torre Curiel, *Vicarios en entredicho*, 158–75.

[75] Fray Antonio Barbastro to Guardian Sáenz de Gumiel, Aconchi, November 22, 1790, AFPM, AQ, Letter K, leg. 16, 2nd portion, no. 70.

[76] Fray Antonio Barbastro to Guardian Sáenz de Gumiel, Ures, September 11, 1791, AFPM, AQ, Letter K, leg. 16, 2nd portion, no. 76; Barbastro to Sáenz de Gumiel, Aconchi, November 16, 1791, AFPM, AQ, Letter K, leg. 16, 2nd portion, no. 77. Ana Luz Ramírez Zavala and Abby Valenzuela Rivera, "De misiones a parroquias: La empresa de secularización en Sonora," in *Misiones del Noroeste de México: Origen y destino 2005*, eds. José Rómulo Félix Gastelum and Raquel Padilla Ramos (Hermosillo, Sonora: Fondo Regional para la Cultura y las Artes, Consejo Nacional para la Cultura y las Artes, 2007), 41–51.

One of the main problems that the missionary administrations faced after the dissolution of the San Carlos de Sonora custody was how to manage communal property. For the Xaliscans, this new order of things (or the old system now revived) presented them with the challenge of continuing to administer those towns while receiving only the annual stipend. As described earlier, they had removed themselves from handling mission properties and resources in the early 1780s.

In contrast, the Queretarans had sustained their management of the temporalities in Pimería Alta, despite growing criticisms by mission residents (both Indian and Spanish), who accused them of being usurers and usurpers of communal property, in addition to denouncing them for establishing monopolies on the sale of grain and remitting thousands of pesos back to their seminary in Querétaro.[77] Thanks to their handling of the temporalities in the Pimería Alta missions, major improvements had been made in church construction and maintenance: the solidity of the temples at Caborca, Tubutama, Cocóspera, and Saric, the adornment of the recently concluded building at Pitic, and the magnificence of the church at San Xavier del Bac bore no comparison with the mission towns in Pimería Baja and Opatería.[78]

However, handling those financial resources had led the Franciscans to develop links—disadvantageous in many respects—with merchants who had gained prominence in Sonoran society. Around 1790, on the eve of the formal dissolution of the custody of San Carlos, severe forms of dependency came to light.[79] Although arrangements with merchants had clearly contributed to the apparent flourishing of those mission towns, in reality they had compromised the missions' survival in the medium term.

The relationship between merchants and missionaries took three forms that were almost always interconnected: cashing stipends, purchasing mission products, and financing projects in the missions. A suitable starting point for explaining this interrelationship is the practice, first suggested by the missionaries but later made obligatory by the government, of the missionaries appointing one

[77] Fray Antonio Barbastro to Commander General Felipe de Neve, Tubutama, May 4, 1784, AFPM, AQ, Letter K, leg. 16, 2nd portion, no. 43.

[78] The church at San Xavier del Bac was the most important construction project in Pimería Alta in the early decades of the Franciscan presence. Father Velderrain had begun building in the 1780s, and by 1792 the expectation was that Father Llorens would complete the project that year. Barbastro to Fray Juan José Sáenz de Gumiel, Aconchi, May 28, 1792, AFPM, AQ, Letter K, leg. 16, 2nd portion, no. 82. It was said that the church at San Xavier del Bac was being built "with such pomp, beauty and adornment that it is generally [felt] that it will stand out among the churches of Guadalajara and Mexico City." Barbastro to Commander Pedro de Nava, Aconchi, December 20, 1793, AFPM, AQ, Letter K, leg. 16, 2nd portion, no. 89.

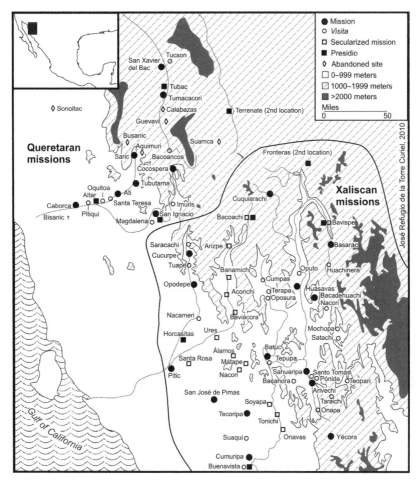

MAP 5.4. Missionary districts in Sonora, 1791

person to travel to the payment office (*pagaduría*) located in Arizpe with the corresponding powers of attorney required to collect each missionary's annual stipend. As these funds were sent at the end of the missionary's year of service, the agents (*apoderados*) took upon themselves a second task, namely supplying all the products the friars required for the entire year. They would then adjust their accounts at the end of each period when the new stipends were about to arrive at the office in Arizpe. In the interim, it was not unusual for these *apoderados* to obtain benefits by commercializing mission products, the outcomes of which they would include in each priest's annual account.

Judging by the data in Table 5.2, this type of contract rarely turned out to be satisfactory for both parties: Of the 122 cases recorded in this five-year period, the missionaries used the same agent to manage their stipends in consecutive years on only twenty-one occasions. Table 5.2 thus illustrates the importance of the role that these "merchants-as-agents" of the Franciscans in Sonora played in financing the missions throughout the year. The mechanisms of speculation and the manipulation of prices and payment systems, analyzed in the previous chapter, make clear the disadvantages imposed by this system on the mission economy. The onerous credit system in the long run became one of the main factors that led to the ever increasing and irreversible indebtedness of several missionaries.

The information available for the 1790–1794 period demonstrates the strategies adopted by both Xaliscans and Queretarans. While the former showed a greater inclination to name their agents separately, the Queretarans in Pimería Alta attempted to negotiate their arrangements with a single merchant, in the hope that this would allow them to achieve better terms in obtaining the annual supplies their missions required.

The fact that the Queretarans negotiated collectively with only four merchants in this period (Manuel Fernández de la Carrera, Ignacio Bustamante, Roque Guizarnotegui, and Martín de Zubiria), provides proof of their greater efforts in planning the mission economy. The missionaries turned to these local merchants hoping to satisfy their basic necessities by entrusting them with the total amount of their stipends, with which the traders were to obtain goods not easily obtained in the local economy (e.g., foodstuffs not produced on the missions, tools, and cattle). In contrast, the more expensive and scarce products they needed (cocoa, sugar, textiles) were acquired through the Colegio de Querétaro and paid for with a portion of the product of the temporalities that the missionaries negotiated with merchants in Mexico City, and then shipped under less onerous conditions.[80]

[79] This does not mean that prior to this date such connections did not exist, only that it is somewhat easier to document them afterward, because of the scarcity of sources for the 1783–1790 period, and the fact that toward the latter date the records of the *caja real* in Arizpe began to register important links between the two groups.

[80] Fray Francisco Iturralde to the missionaries in Pimería Alta, Santa Teresa, October 25, 1792, Fr. MCC, 203, exp. 22. During the 1790s, the merchant who assisted the Colegio de Querétaro with these operations was Don José de los Heros. All the missions in Pimería Alta received goods sent by this trader. According to one friar, the amount of such remittances totaled "large quantities" (*gruesas cantidades*), a fact confirmed when we learn that in March 1798 the San Ignacio mission alone owed him 2,875 pesos. Barbastro to the discretory of the Colegio de Querétaro, Aconchi, July 30, 1793, AFPM, AQ, Letter K, leg. 16, 2nd portion, no. 93; Fray Francisco Iturralde to Guardian Fray Francisco Miralles, Tubutama, March 3, 1798, Fr. MCC, 203, exp. 24.

TABLE 5.2. Agents appointed by missionaries to collect respective
stipends, 1790–1794

	1790		1791	
Agent	Stipend	Missions	Stipend	Missions
Manuel F. Carrera	350	Ati, Caborca, Saric, Tumacácori, San Ignacio, Tubutama, Cocóspera		
Manuel F. Carrera	309	Ures, Bacadehuachi, Guásavas, Aconchi, Arivechi, Cucurpe	309	Bacadehuachi, Guásavas
José Pérez	350	San José de Pimas, Opodepe	350	Opodepe, San Ignacio
José Pérez				
Juan Franco	309	Basarac		
Martín Zubiria	309	Mátape		
Martín Zubiria	350	Cumuripai		
Rafael Morales	400	Bacoachi	350	Cumuripa
Agustín Cano	350	Tecoripa, Ónavas	350	Tecoripa, Ónavas
Agustín Cano	309	Sahuaripa, Yécora	309	Sahuaripa, Taraichi
José Rivero			309	Pitic
José Rivero			350	S.J. de Pimas
Ignacio Bustamante			309	Mátape, Aconchi, Banámichi, Ures, Cucurpe, Arivechi
Ignacio Bustamante			350	Caborca, Saric, Oquitoa, Bac, Tumacácori, Ati, Cocóspera, Tubutama
Ignacio Bustamante			400	Bacoachi
J. Fernández			309	Basarac
Fray Madueño			309	Banámichi
Pedro García			309	Ures, Arivechi
Roque Guizarnotegui			309	Aconchi
Fray Lorenzo Simó				
Francisco Fernández				
Roberto García				
Roberto García				
Miguel Morales				
Miguel Palacios				
M. Bustamante				
José Vélez				
F. Carrera				
José Marcial				

(continued on next page)

TABLE 5.2. (continued)

Agent	1792		1793	
	Stipend	Missions	Stipend	Missions
Manuel F. Carrera				
Manuel F. Carrera	309	Bacadehuachi	309	Guásavas, Oputo
José Pérez	350	Bac, Opodepe, San José de Pimas	350	Bac, Opodepe
José Pérez			309	Basarac, Ures
Juan Franco				
Martín Zubiria			309	Sahuaripa
Martín Zubiria			350	Cocóspera
Rafael Morales	350	Cumuripa, Mátape	350	Cumuripa
Agustín Cano	350	Tecoripa		
Agustín Cano	309	Sahuaripa, Taraichi		
José Rivero				
José Rivero				
Ignacio Bustamante			309	Bacadehuachi, Pitic Cucurpe, Aconchi
Ignacio Bustamante			350	Caborca, San Ignacio, Tubutama, Tumacácori, Ati, Saric, Cocóspera
Ignacio Bustamante			400	Bacoachi, Aconchi
J. Fernández				
Fray Madueño			400	Banámichi
Pedro García	309	Pitic, Guásavas, Cucurpe		
Roque Guizarnotegui	350	Cocóspera, Ati, Saric Tumacácori, Caborca, San Ignacio, Tubutama		
Fray Lorenzo Simó	400	Bacoachi		
Francisco Fernández	309	Basarac		
Roberto García			309	Arivechi, Taraichi
Roberto García			350	Tecoripa
Miguel Morales			350	S.J. de Pimas
Miguel Palacios			309	Pitic
M. Bustamante				
José Vélez				
F. Carrera				
José Marcial				

(continued on next page)

Table 5.2. (continued)

	1794	
Agent	Stipend	Missions
Manuel F. Carrera		
Manuel F. Carrera	309	Guásavas, Cucurpe
José Pérez	350	Opodepe, Nacameri, S. Ignacio, Tecoripa
José Pérez	309	Bacadehuachi, Ures
Martín Zubiria	309	Sahuaripa, Taraichi, Arivechi
Martín Zubiria	350	Caborca, Bac, Ati Tubutama, Tumacácori
Rafael Morales		
Agustín Cano		
Agustín Cano		
José Rivero		
José Rivero		
Ignacio Bustamante	309	Banámichi
Ignacio Bustamante		
Ignacio Bustamante		
J. Fernández		
Fray Madueño		
Pedro García		
Roque Guizarnotegui	309	Aconchi
Fray Lorenzo Simó	400	Bacoachi
Francisco Fernández		
Roberto García		
Roberto García		
Miguel Morales		
Miguel Palacios		
M. Bustamante	350	San José de Pimas
José Vélez	309	Basarac
F. Carrera	350	Cumuripa
José Marcial	309	Bacadehuachi

Source: AGI, Guadalajara, 451.

The third aspect of this interrelationship consisted of the merchants providing resources to equip the churches or to initiate the construction projects that were so common during the Franciscan period in Sonora. Together with the direct use of mission products and the occasional alms obtained in the province, this was a primary mechanism that made it possible to remodel and erect several churches in Sonora, especially in Pimería Alta, in the final years of the colonial period.[81] However, problems for the mission regime also emerged here, first because they had to find a person who was not only sufficiently wealthy but also willing to advance the large sums required for such works; and, second, those loans had to be paid back. In some situations, the missionaries had to search diligently for such a benefactor,[82] while in others the prospect of profiting from mission products attracted just such a person at the opportune moment. In either case, the second problem—meeting the payment schedule—was equally challenging. The debt accumulated by the Pitiquí mission after 1780, in the times of Fray Pedro de Font, illustrates both situations:

[A]t that time the church in this town was being built, and the project had progressed greatly. The town was also in a good state, and its harvests were sufficient to carry on and finish the work. [Then] Father Font came [to the mission] and as he got off on the wrong foot there were no harvests with which to continue the work or to sustain the missionary. The project was suspended for this reason. Then a merchant from La Ciénega, located some fourteen leagues from the town and who now lives in Puebla . . . in his own interest lent [money to Font] not only to proceed with the work, but also to build a substantial house of cement and brick. The two of them then calculated what the town would have to pay with its products. Father [Font] did not put one brick in the church; [but] initiated other works and the house. A year later, the Father died [and] the house remained [unfinished]. The debt was considerable. The Father who came to the mission at Caborca . . . finished the church's

---

[81] One matter that stands out in a succinct list of the dates of church building and remodeling in Sonora is the construction activity during the Franciscan period in Pimería Alta. George Eckhart, *A Guide to the History of the Missions of Sonora, 1614–1826* (Tucson: Eckhart, 1961); Pickens, *The Missions of Northern Sonora.*

[82] Made desperate by the lack of support from the Colegio de Querétaro, on one occasion during his search for financial aid Father Barbastro wrote to the guardian of that convent: "I understand quite well that the colegio is not financed by [Count] Terreros who might supply great quantities, and that there [in Querétaro] as here, each one needs what he has, but seeing that what has been requested has been so well used in Cocospera, San Xavier and other missions, [where] they are building very fine churches, I interceded for them to solicit the colegio's support. . . ." Barbastro to the guardian of the Colegio de Querétaro, Aconchi, September 20, 1793, AFPM, AQ, Letter K, leg. 16, 2nd portion, no. 95.

dome, paid off as much of the debt contracted by Father Font as he could until the town's [agricultural] resources ran out due to the scarcity of water that had once flowed abundantly there. . . . [A]fter that nothing was paid, though the merchant, who is don Francisco Guizarnotegui, has requested payment. But as the agreement was to pay him with the [communal] products of the town, and it has produced nothing, he has been paid nothing since it was ruined.[83]

Using mission resources and Indian labor, even for the purposes noted above, had a high cost for the community, and in a sense it also impacted the missionaries themselves. For the Indians who resided on the missions, unpaid labor was the bone of contention that triggered discord with the missionaries, and that also stiffened residents' complaints about the excesses of the Franciscans. For the missionaries, managing the temporalities was a task that went against their main objective, which was to convert the Indians. As the missionary at Oquitoa observed in 1793, all friars' energies had to focus on finding ways to obtain the funds needed to pay for the goods they ordered from Mexico City; and that, Fray Francisco Moyano continued, was a never-ending task:

> [E]ach one is like an owner . . . dealing and contracting, receiving and spend-ing as he sees fit. . . . How low is the respect for . . . the minister, [and] how little the respect for the word of God that he utters, can be inferred from the constant friction that results from this way of life with the laity. . . . I have always found this repugnant and though force of habit has led me to follow the way common to all, still I [recognize that] . . . this [way] is totally opposed to our state and ministry.[84]

Just twenty years after requesting that the *visitador*, José de Gálvez, confer the administration of communal properties to the missionaries, the Queretarans were about to renounce this concession. After searching diligently for complex theological arguments to justify their handling of monies, they now decided this responsibility generated numerous problems. For this reason, in 1793, when Commander General Pedro de Nava ordered that instead of personal services, all male Indians under fifty years of age would cooperate in providing the missionary's sustenance by donating half a *fanega* of corn or twelve *reales*, the Queretarans rejected the measure "as it is contrary to our

---

[83] Fray Francisco Iturralde to Fray Francisco Miralles, Tubutama, March 3, 1798, Fr. MCC, 203, exp. 24.

[84] Fray Francisco Moyano to Guardian Fray Juan José Sáenz de Gumiel, Oquitoa, May 3, 1793, AFPM, AQ, Letter K, leg. 16, no. 12.

poor institute which is content with the alms that the king, Our Lord, gives us in the *cajas reales.*"[85]

This change in the missionaries' attitude toward communal properties occurred at a time when political leaders in New Spain attempted to reform the general situation of the mission towns in order to equalize Indians' property rights with those of Spaniards and other castes. As in other regions of the viceroyalty, the aim of local authorities was to eliminate the personal services that the Indians had long been providing and thus force the missionaries to pay them for their work.[86] It must be made clear that these measures were not designed for the express purpose of "destroying the missions," or of fostering capitalism by privatizing land, as has often been argued.[87] What the Crown sought was a society that would, in general, devote itself more efficiently to productive activities (mainly agriculture and ranching). Thus, in both Spain itself and its overseas dominions, the Crown was trying to break up corporate territorial properties and encourage private property in land. During the eighteenth century, this process was accelerated by increasing tensions within indigenous communities related to population growth, conflicts between *cabeceras* and subordinate villages (*pueblos sujetos*), and the rise of new groups of *macegual* and mestizo rulers who controlled local governments replacing old caciques and members of the indigenous nobility.[88]

One of the best examples of this policy in New Spain's northern provinces was the reform of temporalities administration decreed by Commander General de Nava in 1794.[89] In essence, this decree sought to abolish "the

[85] AFPM, AQ, Letter K, leg. 16, 2nd portion, nos. 97, 99.

[86] An example of this policy is found in the *Nuevo plan de administración* for the Nayarit missions, approved by Viceroy Marqués de Branciforte in 1794, after three years of conflicts over these issues between the Xaliscans and the Audiencia de Guadalajara. De la Torre Curiel, *Vicarios en entredicho*, 283–85. It is highly probable that these reform projects along the frontier of New Spain echoed ideas on redistributing land to the Indians and generally modifying the colonial administrative apparatus that José del Campillo y Cossío had expressed in Spain in the mid-eighteenth century. Compiled and published in 1789 in his *Nuevo sistema de gobierno económico para la América*, those ideas were widely accepted both on the peninsula and in New Spain. Enrique Florescano and Isabel Gil Sánchez, "La época de las reformas borbónicas y el crecimiento económico, 1750–1808," in *Historia General de México*, vol. 1, ed. Daniel Cosío Villegas (Mexico City: El Colegio de México, 1976), 488.

[87] Jerónimo Romero, *De las misiones*, 91–105.

[88] De la Torre Ruiz, "Mojoneras," 167–75; Margarita Menegus, *Los indios en la historia de México. Siglos XVI al XIX: Balance y perspectivas* (Mexico City: Fondo de Cultura Económica, Centro de Investigaciones y Docencia Económicas, 2006), 49–51.

[89] Pedro de Nava, Chihuahua, April 10, 1794, transcribed in AFPM, AQ, Letter K, leg. 16, 2nd portion, no. 103.

ancient method of community" in Indian towns that had been "reduced" ten or more years ago. This meant that only recently converted populations would retain the existing form of governance, and those only for a period no longer than ten years. Moreover, the goal was to treat Indians as owners of their cattle, land, and products of their labor, thereby putting them on the same footing as the rest of the local population. The Indians would be free to accept work in any activity they wished (including service to the missionaries), but their employers would be obliged to pay them for their labor. Finally, the commander general decreed the division of communal lands, leaving one part to be worked for the common benefit, while the other fields were to be distributed among the individual Indians of each locality.

Pedro de Nava's reform plans presupposed, on the one hand, granting mission Indians the freedom to dispose of their lands and products as they saw fit and, on the other, limiting the missionaries' influence in matters beyond the sphere of their spiritual tasks. The varied impact of these reforms was matched only by differences in the settings in which they were applied and the opinions of missionaries with respect to their implementation.[90] In contrast, one of the few constants at the time was that the reforms decreed by de Nava came in response to the growing non-Indian population along New Spain's northern frontier in the late eighteenth century, and their growing demand for agricultural land and workers.[91] Against this backdrop, it is hardly surprising that the Sonoran areas where the reforms were implemented most rapidly (the central valleys and the piedmont, seat of the Xaliscan missionary district), were also those that registered the highest number of claims to land by private individuals in the early nineteenth century.[92]

[90] In Texas, pressures exercised by the civilian population hastened the enactment of these reforms. In 1793, the Franciscans were separated from handling temporalities in San Antonio de Valero, and by the following year this measure had been extended to the rest of the Texas missions. Some analyses of this process have suggested that it constituted a "partial secularization" of the Texas missions, and that the measure left them at the mercy of "secular avarice," "unscrupulous townspeople," and "land speculators." Félix D. Almaraz, "San Antonio's Old Franciscan Missions: Material Decline and Secular Avarice in the Transition from Hispanic to Mexican Control," *The Americas* 44, no.1 (1987): 1–4; Almaraz, *The San Antonio Missions*, 6, 8–19.

[91] In New Mexico between 1779 and 1784, the *vecino* population increased by more than 16 percent per year. After 1790, *vecinos* began a process of applying for grants to unsettled lands upon which to found new villages. Frank, *From Settler*, 47, 119.

[92] According to Jerónimo's figures, 46 percent of all land claims registered in the entire territory of Sonora from 1770 to 1829 involved towns from the Xaliscan missionary district. Jerónimo Romero, *De las misiones*, 123–35.

The Communal Properties of Franciscan Missions in Sonora

For the missionaries of the Xalisco province stationed in Pimería Baja and Opatería, Pedro de Nava's decree simply reflected their everyday experience since the late 1770s. Having lost control of Indian labor and denied larger annual stipends, those missionaries seemed to be "so poor that if [they] managed to have lunch, they had nothing left for dinner."[93]

Many years had passed since the friars had participated in managing temporalities, as their activities revolved around preaching to Indians who wished to attend the missions' religious activities. The exception to this rule was the mission at Ures, where the intendant of Sonora had allowed Fray Martín Pérez to continue handling mission properties. When the reform projects of 1794 were announced, Father Pérez implored the intendant to ignore de Nava's orders.[94] For the other Xaliscans—concerned about the deplorable state of mission churches and their own inability to control the indigenous population—de Nava's reforms were yet another step toward the material ruin of those towns. The Xaliscans had been expecting a reform plan to restore the missions in Pimería Baja and Opatería to their ancient splendor, but de Nava's orders were oriented toward consolidating the forms of socioeconomic interdependence sanctioned by Spanish colonization, and thus precipitated events in quite the opposite direction from what the missionaries had hoped. In an effort to appropriately document their sentiments, in 1797 the Franciscan Province of Xalisco commissioned Fray Juan Felipe Martínez to report on the state of those missions.[95] At the end of his visit, Martínez sent a report to the commander general showing that almost all churches and missionary houses on those missions were on the verge of collapse, with the exception of Huachinera, Huásavas, and Nácori, where they had been better preserved. Fray Martínez asserted that the clergy's hands were tied. Almost no Indian families gave individual missionaries a half-*fanega* of corn, and as a result, the friars suffered many hardships. Martínez wrote to the commander in his report that he was "not to understand by this . . . that I am

---

[93] Proceedings of the meeting of the Definitory of the Province of Xalisco dated May 17, 1796, BPEJ, CM, book 50, vol. V, f. 21.

[94] AGES, Fondo Ejecutivo, vol. 43, exp. 5.

[95] This *visita* is important not only because of the objectives alluded to, but also because it was contemporaneous with the *visita* that Fray Diego de Bringas began in 1795 to the Queretaran missions in Sonora, as it clearly portrays the differences between those two missionary districts, as well as the problems that the two models of mission administration confronted around the same time. Bringas's *visita* is analyzed below.

asking that my fellow friars be entrusted with the temporalities of the mission, but I do state categorically and truthfully that they cannot [continue to] subsist in this way."[96]

It was clear that the Xaliscans had left the task of finding a remedy for their ills in the hands of the government. Commander de Nava, the bishop of Sonora, and Intendant Alejo García Conde accepted the challenge and, in 1797, began to discuss the viability of forcing the Indians and other mission residents to collaborate in church reconstruction and the possibility of using mission assets for that purpose. The intendant of Sonora was convinced that the only way to help those missions was to make use of their communal goods. He expressed this view in April 1799 when he presented the commander general with a project for managing those properties that cited the precedent of the mission administrators appointed in 1767, but included the novel idea of assigning them a salary equivalent to 10 percent of the annual product of those goods.[97] It was thought that this system would make it possible, in a period of perhaps ten years, to garner sufficient resources to remodel all the churches, with the Indians and other residents, of course, obliged to provide the required labor for those projects. However, García Conde's idea did not prosper because mission enterprises in Pimería Baja and Opatería did not "increase and multiply" as he had expected and the churches there continued to crumble.

By the time that Fray Juan Felipe Martínez petitioned for the intervention of the intendant in support of the Xaliscans, the missions in Pimería Baja and Opatería had entered a cycle of visible physical deterioration complicated by the continuing erosion of communal holdings. The analysis of the inventories of communal holdings from various missions allows for an explanation of the differences between the downward spiral of Xaliscan missions' temporalities and the ups and downs of mission assets in the Queretaran district.[98]

---

[96] Fray Juan Felipe Martínez to Commander General Pedro de Nava, Ures, June 8, 1797, BNFF, 36/806.

[97] Alexo García Conde to Commander General Pedro de Nava, Arizpe, April 24, 1799, BNFF, 36/806.

[98] As their name indicates, these were lists in which stocks of grain, cattle, "money," furnishings, church clothing and adornments, buildings, and, occasionally, the debts in favor and against the missions were written down. These inventories were prepared when a mission was transferred (from one missionary to another, from the clergy to a representative of the Crown, or *vice versa*), or during the *visita* of an ecclesiastical authority. In and of themselves, the inventories of temporalities do not allow us to reconstruct the evolution of the mission economies, as they give no idea of the circulation of mission products, nor of the volume of goods produced from one year to another, nor of the quantities of goods that were sold, consumed, or stolen during the year. Interpretation of volume measures used in these sources is also problematic, since they indistinctly use vague categories as *"trigo en greña"* [bulk wheat], *"carretas de trigo"* [wagons of wheat], or

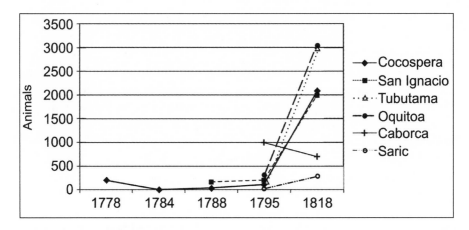

GRAPH 5.1. Cattle in Queretaran missions, 1778–1818 (Sources: 1778 in BNFF, 34/736; 1784 in AFPM, AQ, Letter K, leg. 16, no. 23; 1788 in BNFF, 35/761 and 35/762; 1795 in AFPM, AQ, Letter K, leg. 18, no. 17; 1818 in AGN, Misiones, vol. 3, exp. 3)

With respect to the towns located in Pimería Baja and Opatería, there are inventories from the 1771–1796 period, while for Pimería Alta, inventories of holdings have been found for the years 1778 to 1830. The most important data contained in these documents are figures related to cattle (*ganado mayor*); goats, sheep, and occasionally pigs (*ganado menor*); and to stores of wheat, corn, and other grains and legumes (beans, chickpeas, lentils). When we compare the records of cattle, goats, and sheep from the Queretaran and Xaliscan missions, respectively, two opposite tendencies emerge. The missions in Pimería Alta experienced a consistent increase in livestock numbers in the late eighteenth century and into the nineteenth century. By 1818, for example, Tumacácori and San Xavier del Bac had gathered herds of 5,000 to 7,000 animals respectively. Except for Caborca the rest of Pimería Alta mission districts showed the same pattern (Graph 5.1). In contrast, in the late eighteenth century, towns in Pimería Baja and Opatería in general suffered a decrease in their holdings of all kinds of livestock, although there were notable exceptions, such

---

"*sacos de mazorcas*" and "*sacos de maíz*" [sacks of cobs and corn], and specific volume measures such as *fanegas* of wheat and corn. From Radding's perspective, this problem could be solved by equating those fuzzy categories with standard ones. *Wandering Peoples*, 89–95. Since I could not assign a reliable standard to these imprecise volume measures, my analysis of the evolution of missions' temporalities focuses on lists of produce that consistently used *arrobas* or *fanegas*.

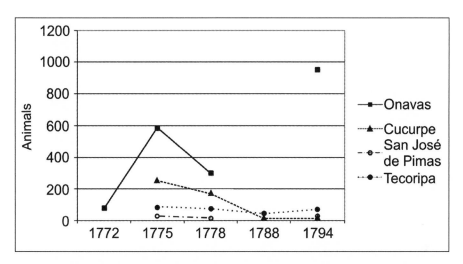

GRAPH 5.2. Cattle in some Xaliscan missions, 1772–1794 (Sources: 1772 in AGN, Provincias Internas, vol. 81, exp. 6; 1775 in AFPM, AQ, Letter K, leg. 17, nos. 1–8; 1778 in BNFF, 34/736; 1788 in BNFF, 35/763 and 35/764; 1794 in AGN, Misiones, vol. 2, exp. 2)

as Opodepe, where 3,215 animals (*ganado mayor*) were registered in 1778, and Onavas, which appears to have maintained herds consisting of perhaps one thousand animals (Graph 5.2). The data available for small animals indicate variation for the missions in Pimería Alta: While towns such as Cocospera, Tumacácori, San Xavier del Bac, and Caborca show slight downward movement, San Ignacio, Oquitoa, and Saric managed to maintain or increase their herds between 1795 and 1818. In contrast, a markedly negative tendency characterized the mission settlements in Pimería Baja and Opatería in the 1775–1794 period, where San José de Pimas was the only exception (Graphs 5.3 and 5.4). Finally, grain production in Pimería Alta suffered a gradual decline in all the missions (Graphs 5.5 and 5.6).

What is the significance of these tendencies? The first conventional conclusion derived from data on reduced temporalities of some missions is that in the aftermath of the Jesuits' expulsion, the Franciscans received missions already so debilitated that it proved impossible to restore them to their earlier splendor. Hence, the idea took hold that the mission system was in crisis throughout the Franciscan period. However, the general context of the evolution of the Franciscan mission regime and the consolidation of Spanish colonization suggests that these tendencies should be understood in another way.

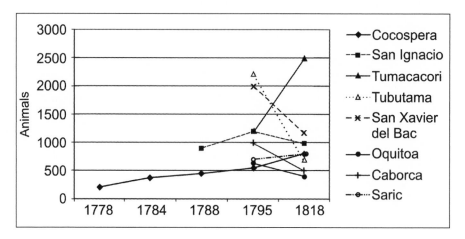

GRAPH 5.3. Sheep, goats, and pigs in Queretaran missions, 1778–1818 (Source: Graph 5.1)

Beginning with Pimería Baja and Opatería, mission temporalities shrank markedly under royal administrators,[99] but beyond the negligence of the latter and/or the friars' own deficiencies, the main obstacle to increasing communal goods in those areas was the lack of interest among the Indians in working for the missions. The legal restrictions imposed on the Xaliscans upon their arrival in Sonora[100] prevented them from forcing the Indians to fulfill their obligation to provide communal labor, while at the same time prohibiting them from employing livestock handlers without paying them for their services. Thus,

---

[99] Traditionally, the negligence and greed of those administrators (*comisarios reales*) have been seen as the reasons for the decline of mission properties. However, one element that has not been considered in depth, and that has proven impossible to quantify, is the use that the local authorities made of such goods at different times. It is known, for example, that during his *visita* to Sonora, José de Gálvez used mission cattle to supply his troops and it is certainly possible that part of the remittances he sent back to Mexico City came from the missions' temporalities. Juan Manuel de Viniegra, *Varios papeles escritos despues de praticado el viaxe a Californias, Sonora, y Nueva Vizcaia por el visitador general del reino de Mexico, Don José de Gálvez*, BL, MSS 86/87 cm.

[100] In terms of economics, the restrictions placed on the Xaliscans began when they arrived in Sonora. Upon assigning them their missions in 1768, Governor Juan de Pineda stipulated that the missionaries were to look to the royal administrators for sustenance, and that the latter would give them all they needed against their stipend, originally fixed at 250 pesos. AGN, Jesuitas, leg. I-6, exp. 4. With respect to their functions in the missions, it was established at the time that the missionaries would only intervene in spiritual matters, and were prohibited from forcing the Indians to perform unpaid labor.

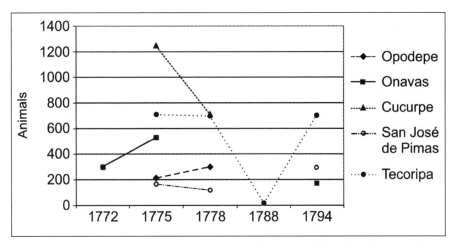

GRAPH 5.4. Sheep, goats, and pigs in Xaliscan missions, 1772–1794 (Source: Graph 5.2)

while the herds of cattle on the missions were shrinking and the missionaries were facing problems in organizing Indian labor, the Spanish settlements in Pimería Baja and Opatería were slowly being consolidated and were producing their own resources. According to a 1778 report, in the fourteen haciendas and ranches mentioned in those regions there was a total of 1,515 head of cattle and 3,572 goats and sheep. Add to these figures the 1,989 head of cattle and 1,903 sheep and goats located at two mining sites and in neighboring villages, as well as the 6,334 head of cattle and 6,880 sheep and goats in the jurisdiction of Arizpe.[101] The data show that in 1778 the average number of animals on each ranch or hacienda was approximately equal to the holdings of the mission settlements (100 to 200 head), the same data also indicate an alternative mode of organization emerging surrounding the missions and that depended on the mission Indians' labor. The material ruin of the churches and the missionaries' difficulties in securing their subsistence in Pimería Baja and Opatería by no means constituted a crisis for the residents of mission towns, as they were increasingly able to ensure their subsistence outside the mission complex.

As stated above, in 1794 de Nava decreed that missionaries would no longer control material assets. The Xaliscans were hardly affected by this meas-

[101] Pedro Corbalán, *Estado que manifiesta el no. de poblaciones correspondientes a esta jurisdicción, distancias y rumbos de la capital. Bienes que poseen sus habitantes, y lo demás que se expresa en las casillas*, Álamos, September 30, 1778, BNFF, 34/736.

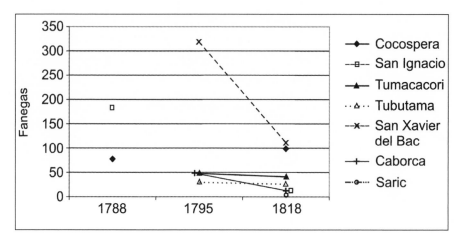

GRAPH 5.5. Production of corn, other grains, and legumes in Queretaran missions, 1788–1818 (Source: Graph 5.1)

ure, because their handling of such property had turned out to be more a source of conflict than a means of satisfying their subsistence needs. The Quereterans' circumstances in the Pimería Alta were different than those of the Xaliscans, and so too were their subsequent experiences and outcomes in the late eighteenth and early nineteenth centuries. Similar to the Xaliscans' missions, upon their arrival the Queretarans had received churches "made of adobe with roofs of grass and dirt," most of which were "destroyed [while] others [were] on the verge of ruin."[102] Like the Xaliscan missionaries, in the beginning the Quereterans depended on the royal commissaries to provide for their needs and sustenance. Timely requests to the Colegio de Querétaro, that seminary's rapid response, and José de Gálvez's 1769 disposition to permit the Quereterans to administer temporalities resulted in a situation quite different from that of their Xaliscan brethren. Due to the precarious conditions of that frontier region, the Queretarans managed not only to gain control of the administration of temporalities but were also allowed to intervene in the social organization of the towns under their care, to monitor dealings between Indians and Spaniards, and to ensure that the Indians farmed individually and fulfilled their obligation to work three days per week on communal lands.[103]

---

[102] Fray Juan Díaz to the discretory of the Colegio de Querétaro, Caborca, August 8, 1768, Fr. MCC, 201, exp. 3.
[103] Fr. MCC, 201, exp. 11.

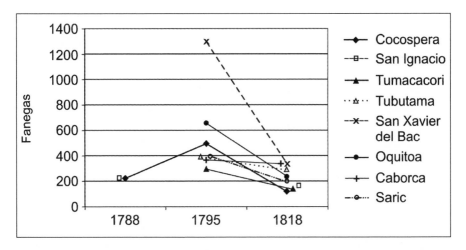

GRAPH 5.6. Production of wheat in Queretaran missions, 1788–1818 (Source: Graph 5.1)

Consequently, in just two years the Queretarans had resupplied their missions with the cattle and grain needed to ensure the survival of the mission communities. For example, in early 1771 Fray Francisco Garcés reported that he had purchased some 400 head of cattle for the mission at San Xavier del Bac.[104] At the Ati mission, meanwhile, Fray José Soler wrote in 1772 that the mission had almost 3,000 pesos in gold, silver, and *reales*, generated through dealings with the mining town of La Ciénega.[105] In Santa Rosalía, *visita* of Ures, Father Barbastro finished a new church before 1775—when the mission was transferred to the Xaliscans—by investing 5,000 pesos in construction; and new churches were erected in Nacameri (*visita* of Opodepe), Buenavista, and Tonichi. All of these projects were characterized as "quite costly."[106]

Although records are lacking to document the production, consumption, and circulation of mission goods in Pimería Alta, reports on various construction projects and the equipping of churches in the late eighteenth century sug-

---

[104] Unfortunately, the missionary said, on February 10 of that year the Apaches had raided the mission, carried away much of its cattle and slaughtered some 350 sheep and goats. Fray Francisco Garcés to Fray Mariano Buena y Alcalde, San Xavier del Bac, February 20, 1771, AFPM, AQ, Letter K, leg. 14, no. 6.

[105] Fray Joseph Soler to Fray Juan Crisóstomo Gil de Bernabé, Ati, May 26, 1772, Fr. MCC 202, exp. 10.

[106] *Copia de la visita hecha este año de 1775 por el P fr. Juan Díaz, presidente de las misiones de la Pimería baja, por mandado de el MRP fr. Antonio Fernández,* Fr. MCC, 201, exp. 5.

gest a gradual recovery of local economies in that period. This recovery may explain the initiatives taken by the Diocese of Sonora and local civil authorities to try and persuade the Indians on those missions to pay tithes.[107]

Inventories of temporalities from 1795 suggest that the missions in Pimería Alta survived thanks to a combination of product sales (on credit and by receiving payments for future harvests) and loans from private individuals and subsidies from the Crown (missionaries' stipends). In that year, the eight missions in Pimería Alta recorded credits (outstanding accounts owed the missions) totaling 7,881 pesos, while they owed 11,292 pesos.[108] As explained in these and other inventories, these debts arose in part from purchases made "on credit" of items acquired through the Queretarans' agent in Mexico City, but the lion's share derived from purchases of materials for church construction. Let us consider, for example, the case of San Xavier del Bac, where by 1790 successive stages of construction had resulted in a cumulative debt of 7,000 pesos. By 1795 this debt had been reduced to 3,944 pesos, and the project was close to conclusion, as construction had begun on the first stage of the steeples, and the interior had been equipped with "five collaterals made of golden stucco and colors [and] forty statues."[109]

For mission residents, the Queretarans' management of the mission economy was a burden that proved difficult to bear, especially given the gradual decline of the indigenous population in the missions during the late eighteenth century, when increasing demands for labor fell upon a constantly shrinking base of Indian workers.[110] It might be said, then, that although the Pimería Alta missions may not have experienced financial crisis, mission residents were indeed mired in a crisis of excessive demands on their labor.

As the president of the Queretarans, Fray Faustino González, would reveal in 1820, by the end of the eighteenth century, the missions' emerging financial problems derived less from declining agricultural and livestock production than from the fact that the missions "no longer had outlets for their products."[111] This contraction of the market for mission products was further complicated by the wars of independence and the early years of the Mexican Republic, when payment of the missionaries' stipends was suspended (after 1814), and by the inability (or disinterest?) of mission debtors to fulfill their

---

[107] Fr. MCC, 202, exp. 4.
[108] AFPM, AQ, Letter K, leg. 18, no. 17.
[109] *Ibid.*
[110] See Chapter 2.
[111] AGN, Misiones, vol. 3, exp. 36.

commitments. In 1829 various debtors owed the Pimería Alta missions a total of 61,500 pesos.[112]

In 1828, the state government expelled the Spanish missionaries and confiscated their effects. Kieran McCarty identifies that moment as the one that marked the beginning of the end of the mission economic system in Pimería Alta,[113] because in addition to disrupting the model of exploiting communal labor originally designed by the Jesuits and maintained by the Franciscans, these events resulted in the virtual exhaustion of the reserves of communal goods (Graphs 5.1, 5.3, and 5.5). By the same token, they allowed the Indians who resided on the missions to escape from the clergy's control by taking advantage of the legal alternatives that the Mexican government had put within their reach and that allowed them to be treated as *citizens* and to seek the support of local authorities to avoid being subjected to communal obligations.

Generational Crisis in the Pimería Alta Missionary District

In Pimería Alta, de Nava's reforms meant not only taking administrative functions out of the clergy's hands but also, and above all, standardizing the missions along the frontier with other population centers in Sonora (all of which had been founded at least ten years earlier). This new policy jeopardized plans by the Queretarans to establish missions between California and New Mexico, and their reactions, of course, were not long in coming. Nava's 1794 decree was soon answered by a series of reports designed to demonstrate the deleterious effects that this policy would have for the advance of Spanish colonization and settlement into the Gila and Colorado River valleys.

---

[112] The *memoria* that the secretary of government of the Estado de Occidente read to the state congress in 1829 indicated that the presidios of Sonora owed the missions 4,456 pesos, while private debts owed the missions totaled 27,097 pesos. José Francisco Velasco, *Noticias estadísticas*, 133. To these sums we must add thirty thousand pesos that the government owed for unpaid stipends.

[113] McCarty, *A Frontier Documentary*, 19. When considering the place of the missions in Pimería Alta in terms of supplying merchandise to the towns in northern Sonora, and keeping in mind the amount of debt that certain corporations and individuals owed those establishments, Kieran McCarty's opinion on the relationship between these elements and the expulsion of the Spanish missionaries from the region cannot be ignored. It is probable, as McCarty suggests, that the Sonoran government together with merchants from Sinaloa perceived several advantages in doing away with this model of socioeconomic organization. McCarty's view is based on a letter from Fernando María Grande, dated in Magdalena on November 1, 1828, in which this commissioner in charge of securing the temporalities suggests selling mission properties as a means of resolving the local government's urgent need for resources. McCarty, *A Frontier Documentary*, 17–18.

The Franciscans' response to the reform soon revealed that the missionary enterprise in Pimería Alta was seriously compromised by differences among the Queretaran missionaries themselves.[114] The differences can be summarized as whether to directly administer mission properties (as the Jesuits did), or adjust the Sonoran reality to the spirit of Franciscan principles. The division was expressed in terms of familiarity with frontier societies through allusions to their experience in mission activities and, in a broader sense, to distinctions between "older" and "younger" missionaries as part of broader processes of identity formation, or social identity in this case.[115]

By the mid-1790s, Fray Francisco Antonio Barbastro had emerged as the spokesperson for the second generation of Queretarans in Pimería Alta,[116] that is, those who had arrived on the eve of the creation of the custody of Sonora and had survived the period during which the first bishop of Sonora attempted to reform the mission regime in northern New Spain.[117] In addition to

[114] For an analysis of a similar process taking place in the context of California missions, see Rose Marie Beebe and Robert M. Senkewicz, "Uncertainty on the Mission Frontier: Missionary Recruitment and Institutional Stability in Alta California in the 1790s," in *Francis in the Americas: Essays on the Franciscan Family in North and South America*, ed. John F. Schwaller (Berkeley, CA: Academy of American Franciscan History, 2005), 295–322.

[115] For a more detailed analysis of these disputes among Queretaran missionaries in Sonora as expression of group identity formation, see José Refugio de la Torre, "Franciscan Missionaries in Late-Colonial Sonora: Five Decades of Change and Conflict," in *Alta California: Peoples in Motion, Identities in Formation, 1769–1850*, ed. Steven W. Hackel (Berkeley and Los Angeles: University of California Press, The Huntington Library, 2010), 47–75. When discussing the concept of social identity, Tajfel and Turner explain that individuals identify with and behave as part of social groups by means of internal and external processes of categorization, identification and comparison. Richard Jenkins' discussion on *vis-à-vis* relations and people's understandings of themselves and of others have been applied to the Queretaran missionaries in my own work. Henri Tajfel, ed., *Social Identity and Intergroup Relations* (Cambridge: Cambridge University Press, 1982); John C. Turner, *Rediscovering the Social Group: A Self-Categorization Theory* (Oxford: Basil Blackweel Ltd., 1987); Richard Jenkins, *Social Identity* (London and New York: Routledge, 1996).

[116] A Spaniard probably born around 1734 in the villa of Cariñena (Aragon), Barbastro arrived in New Spain in 1770, stayed at the Colegio de Querétaro for a couple of years, and then went to the missions in Sonora around 1773. Gómez Canedo, *Sonora hacia fines*, 9–10.

[117] A first generation of missionaries can be identified between 1767 and the end of the 1770s, consisting of the first Queretarans in charge of the former Jesuit missions. From the late 1770s to the creation of the San Carlos custody in 1783, a new generation of Franciscans appeared in Sonora, including Father Barbastro. By the decade of 1790, the second generation of Franciscans in Sonora had nearly died out, due to the deaths of several priests and the return of several friars that Bishop de los Reyes had brought from Spain to found his custody. The transition from this generation to that of the newly arrived missionaries of the third generation, would be characterized by a long series of personal attacks and differences of criteria concerning evangelization and mission administration. It must be understood that among the members of the third generation of missionaries there were some notable cases of individuals who immediately identified

Barbastro, Fathers Baltasar Carrillo, Francisco Iturralde, Francisco Moyano, Juan Bautista Llorens, Lorenzo Simó, and Juan Santiesteban were the "old school" missionaries who, upon receiving news of the recent reform of mission government, simply acknowledged reception of the commander's dispositions and assured de Nava that they would suspend their administration of mission properties as soon as they had completed the last construction projects they had undertaken.[118] Whether because of the experience they had acquired during many years of work in those provinces, or for other reasons, the fact is that the "older" missionaries had learned that they could survive the policy changes of the civil authorities simply by feigning fulfillment.[119] Their advanced age had led those priests to reconsider their posture regarding mission government. They supported in principle managing communal properties through agents and depositaries (*procuradores* and *depositarios*) as their constitution mandated, but experience had taught them that only the personal handling of accounts and holdings could guarantee the missions' material and spiritual progress. Nonetheless, the natural fatigue they felt after so many years of rumors and criticism from residents over this system of management had also convinced them that it would perhaps be better in the long run to abandon this type of administration if it seemed that improvements would not occur.

This posture contrasted sharply with the ideas of the new missionaries who arrived in Pimería Alta in the early 1790s. While they shared the older friars' ideal of expanding the missions toward the Gila and the Colorado Rivers, they

---

themselves with the "older missionaries" and even became their close collaborators. Those who stood out in this sense were Fathers Narciso Gutiérrez and Antonio Diez, protagonists, in the early nineteenth century, of serious confrontations with members of the younger generation of Queretaran missionaries.

[118] This was the case of the missions at San Xavier, Cocospera, Santa Magdalena, Saric, and Santa Teresa. In his petition to the commander general, the Queretaran president indicated that the required permission would be effective for only one year—sufficient time, in his estimation, to conclude the construction of those churches. Barbastro to Commander General Pedro de Nava, Aconchi, April 29, 1794, AFPM, AQ, Letter K, leg. 16, 2nd portion, no. 103. Despite these proposals, by 1798 the missionaries in Pimería Alta were still managing the missions' assets, though they had received notice that they would soon have to turn them over. Fray Francisco Iturralde to Guardian Fray Francisco Miralles, Tubutama, March 3, 1798, Fr. MCC, 203, exp. 24.

[119] Father Barbastro had commented on this matter on one occasion: "Since the comandancia was established there has been a flood of providences that still fall by the bucketful, with order being scarcely observable. . . . Last year, I clearly told the commander general face-to-face: Sir, it is well that [you] grant this and that providence, but I am not asking for [new] providences . . . [but] the fulfillment of those already given. Your Lordship can be sure that [your providences] will not be fulfilled, because those of your antecessors have not been fulfilled either." Barbastro to Guardian Fray Juan Francisco Rivera, Aconchi, December 3, 1793, AFPM, AQ, Letter K, leg. 16, 2nd portion, no. 102.

insisted that the missions retain only indirect control of temporalities through agents. They also insisted upon exercising the principles of authority consecrated in the old method of government in the mission communities. In this new generation of missionaries, Fray Diego Miguel Bringas would play a fundamental role in articulating what they considered to be the most appropriate method of moving their socioreligious project forward. Moreover, it was Father Bringas who went to the missions in Pimería Alta as *visitador* to evaluate the work of the older missionaries, to become familiar with the problems those missions were confronting, and to discover the roots of the accusations that some new missionaries had made to the Colegio de Querétaro's discretorium against their older colleagues.

An examination of various documents from the period reveals how this generational rupture developed. After dissolving the custody of San Carlos de Sonora in 1791, Barbastro initiated negotiations with his colegio, the bishop of Sonora, the commander general and the intendant of Sonora to allow his college to take possession of the old missions and attempt, once again, to penetrate the Papaguería. Barbastro suggested that the Queretarans' arrival should reflect great poverty by bringing only a few agricultural implements. He proposed that the friars leave the cattle at the missions in Pimería Alta to avoid possible raids by hostile Indians. Efforts should be made to attract a few Spanish families to settle around the missions, though they would be prohibited from living inside the Indian towns. Above all, however, he argued that the Franciscans should exercise universal jurisdiction (*omnímoda jurisdicción*) over the missions of those new establishments.[120] A military escort would not be necessary, he said, because in those lands it was actually more dangerous to be accompanied by soldiers than to travel alone. Furthermore, he argued, if the local authorities did not support the venture because they did not wish to deal with the coexistence of Indians and Spaniards, then that was even better for the friars, as they would be able to enter those new territories on their own, as their forebears had done in "the olden days."[121]

Barbastro's proposal consisted of placing the new mission district entirely under the authority of the missionaries and extending into that region the same mode of governance that he had sanctioned for Pimería Alta. The problems with this plan were, on the one hand, that the Colegio de Querétaro's discretorium

[120] Barbastro to Guardian Juan José Sáenz y Gumiel, Aconchi, January 31, 1791, AFPM, AQ, Letter K, leg. 16, 2nd portion, no. 71.

[121] Fray Antonio Barbastro to Guardian Sáenz y Gumiel, Aconchi, August 29, 1792, AFPM, AQ, Letter K, leg. 16, 2nd portion, no. 86; Fray Antonio Barbastro to Guardian Sáenz y Gumiel, Aconchi, January 25, 1793, AFPM, AQ, Letter K, leg. 16, 2nd portion, no. 90.

had begun to question the rectitude of the mode of government over which Barbastro presided, while, on the other, the friars at the colegio considered it "inconvenient" to throw themselves into the Papaguería venture without the Crown's approval. Influenced by these two arguments, the Queretaran discretorium opted to draw out the process, promising only to study Barbastro's proposals "in due time." Barbastro knew this meant his project had been subtly rejected by the discretorium. He realized that times had changed and it was difficult for the younger priests who had no direct experience of missionary work in those far-off provinces to understand the needs of frontier missions.[122]

While the discretorium continued to fan Father Barbastro's slender hopes, the Colegio de Querétaro received reports from certain missionaries in Sonora containing accusations of the improper handling of properties and monies by Barbastro and his fellows, and citing other abuses that put "the souls of those older missionaries in peril." Intrigued by these reports, and made uneasy by Barbastro's form of government, in March 1795 the discretorium of the Colegio de Querétaro appointed Fray Diego Miguel Bringas—up to then the colegio's chronicler—to visit the missions in Pimería Alta. The objectives of his visit, Bringas was instructed, were twofold. First, he was to pull the missions out of their temporal and spiritual ruin by convincing the local authorities to allow the missionaries to continue managing the temporalities and by correcting the excesses he encountered through whatever means he deemed necessary. Second, he was specifically entrusted with the task of finding a way to expand the missions into the Papaguería region.[123]

Historians have traditionally considered this second task as the most important aspect of Bringas's visit to Pimería Alta, partly because nine missionaries accompanied him to this specific end.[124] Above all, the memorial that the *visitador* sent to the king in 1796 to request his support for the establishment of new missions there underscores the visit's importance.[125] Beyond the rich narrative of

---

[122] On one occasion he reflected, "To the misfortune of the poor missions and missionaries, very few of the friars who make up the discretory have been at the missions." Fray Antonio Barbastro to the discretory of the Colegio de Querétaro, Aconchi, July 30, 1793, AFPM, AQ, Letter K, leg. 16, 2nd portion, no. 93.

[123] *Poder, instrucciones, comisión para visitar las misiones de la Pimería Alta y facultad para desfiliar en caso necesario que dio el V Discretorio al visitador que envió a Sonora, 1795*, March 30 and 31, 1795, AFPM, AQ, Letter K, leg. 18, no. 10.

[124] The missionaries who accompanied Bringas were Fathers Pascual Rodríguez, Mariano Bordoi, Pedro Amorós, Francisco Cobas, Angel Alonso de Prado, Andrés Sánchez, Pablo Mata, Andrés Garaigorta, and Ramón López. AFPM, AQ, Letter K, leg. 18, no. 11.

[125] The translation and publication of Bringas's report have played an important role here. Matson and Fontana, *Friar Bringas Reports to the King*.

Bringas's report, it should be noted that his expansion project did not materialize and that the primary motive behind this visit was to attempt to resolve serious problems in the internal organization of the Pimería Alta mission district.

The excesses that Bringas had been sent to correct were linked to the theme
of the generational rupture mentioned above. The discretorium had invested
Bringas with full powers to disaffiliate missionaries (*desfiliar*, that is, separate
from the colegio), to order their return to Querétaro, and to take whatever measures he felt were appropriate to remedy those missions' decadent condition. In
other words, the discretorium had sent Bringas not only to verify the status of the
situation in Sonora, but also to remove the older friars from their missions.[126]

As a matter of fact, Bringas had been sent to Pimería Alta just a few weeks
after the discretorium had demanded that Barbastro explain the accusations
leveled against him by Francisco Villaseca, a recently arrived missionary in
Sonora. Villaseca had declared to the discretorium that it was probable the
friars assigned to those missions were headed straight to hell because they did
not obey the Franciscan rules related to poverty, and because they possessed
herds of animals and openly bought and sold merchandise. Moreover, the president of those missions—Barbastro—was aware of everything, consented to it,
and even set an example for others. Finally, he accused the head of the missions
of constructing a house in Aconchi at immense expense. As far as Barbastro was
concerned, the accusations against him reflected the enormous abyss that
existed between missionaries accustomed to life on the frontier and those who
had but recently arrived:

> When a European priest comes to [the New World], he sees and hears many
> things that cause him grave dissonance . . . [such as] naked Indians, women
> showing their breasts, indolent, filthy people, a language they do not under-
> stand; he sees the minister at the altar but also in the corral, feeding the chick-
> ens; selling lard, candles, soap, rags, etc. He sees him receiving everything he
> is given . . . [and] judges everything as illicit, at times verging on sin. . . . As
> he sees the minister doing all these things with no remorse, he judges him
> obstinate and incapable of repair; and finds no other solution than to return to
> the convent. It does not occur to him to inquire conscientiously but only to
> report to the prelate.[127]

---

[126] The discretory acknowledged this purpose in the following terms: "There is no other
remedy than to recall those priests who have grown old . . . amid these faults of observance." The
discretory of the Colegio de Querétaro to Fray Diego Bringas, Querétaro, March 7, 1796, AFPM,
AQ, Letter K, leg. 18, no. 21.

[127] Fray Antonio Barbastro to Fray Juan Alias, Aconchi, February 22, 1795, AFPM, AQ,
Letter K, leg. 16, 2nd portion, no. 109.

The defense Barbastro presented to Fray Juan Alias—who was appointed by the discretorium of Querétaro to resolve this case—was quite simple: The oldest argument elaborated to criticize the labors of the missionaries assigned to Sonora, he asserted, was that it was impossible for them to observe the rules of the Franciscan order. It had been used, he said, by Fray Antonio de los Reyes in his attempts to promote reform, and several priests continued to use it as an excuse, "some in order to get away, others to avoid coming." The problem was that in order to survive on those missions it was necessary for the missionaries to administer mission properties and make business transactions in the name of those establishments, even though many of them found such activities repugnant. With respect to the house in Aconchi, Barbastro clarified that as the discretorium was well aware, efforts had been going on for several years to promote the establishment of the Third Order of Penitence in that town, and it was for this purpose that he had built the house and chapel. In conclusion, Barbastro emphasized, he was sure that he had proven the error of all the accusations made against him, and that the entire episode had in fact been nothing more than a ploy devised by Villaseca to obtain his return to the college. In closing his defense, Barbastro put the following words into Villaseca's mouth: "This life is not fit for me, there is no stipend. . . . So, how shall I get out [of Sonora]? Though I return to the college without permission, I shall say that I have come in order to avoid condemnation." Barbastro concluded by reaffirming the disposition required of those priests who went to work in Sonora, implicitly praising the quality of the older missionaries and criticizing the prejudices of the younger friars: "One must arrive prepared to suffer labor and hardships, for if one recalls [life at] the colegio then all is lost. . . . [I]t is here, here where even the most valiant lion must bow his head."[128]

Although Barbastro was successful in his defense, his presence in Pimería Alta was no longer deemed necessary.[129] Barbastro never returned to Querétaro, but his resignation from the post of *padre presidente* in Pimería Alta was accepted. In 1795, Bringas named Fray Francisco Iturralde to replace Barbastro, in recognition of Iturralde's long-term experience.[130]

---

[128] *Ibid.*

[129] It was clear to Barbastro that he had lost favor with the discretorium of the colegio, and the incident with Brother Villaseca confirmed this impression. In his correspondence with a friar at Querétaro, he wrote: "I know clearly, Father guardian, that I lost [favor with] the discretorium, and therefore everything I propose and say will always be seen as suspicious." Barbastro to the guardian of the Colegio de Querétaro, Aconchi, July 24, 1795, AFPM, AQ, Letter K, leg. 16, 2nd portion, no. 118.

[130] For the same reason, the discretory opposed this appointment, as it placed another of the old missionaries in the presidency, and this time, one who had always been very close to Father

The trouble between Villaseca and Barbastro was not an isolated incident in Pimería Alta, as the frictions that emerged between older missionaries and newer ones led to similar accusations elsewhere. For example, Fray Lorenzo Simó was accused by a recently arrived missionary, Fray Ángel Collazo, of living with a woman in Cucurpe, Bacoachi, and Caborca.[131] Upon his arrival in Sonora, Bringas immediately insisted that two of Barbastro's allies, Fathers Narciso Gutiérrez and Antonio Díez, return to Querétaro, though his plan was frustrated when Iturralde and Barbastro interceded on their behalf and took them in as auxiliaries on their respective missions.[132]

Despite these differences, which were quickly resolved through diplomatic means, Father Bringas's visitation transpired in relative tranquility from July to December 1795.[133] Once it concluded, he drafted a report in which he attempted to curry the favor of the king and conserve the administration of temporalities in Pimería Alta. In his report he argued that the residents of those missions were still early conversions (*conversiones vivas*), even though they had been founded more than 100 years earlier, and that the missions constituted a veritable "frontier with heathenism." Bringas also requested support for financing the establishment of new missions in the Papaguería, and requested that the missionaries be responsible for that venture rather than local civil authorities, as had occurred in 1781 when several missionaries and settlers were killed by Yuma Indians.[134] Papaguería missions should be established, he asserted, by following the proven method of entrusting such tasks to missionaries while providing them with adequate military escorts and authorizing two friars for each mission.[135]

Upon Bringas's return to Querétaro, establishing new missions became a priority for the discretorium. In subsequent years the responsibility for promoting this matter among the viceroyalty's civil and ecclesiastical authorities

Barbastro. The discretory of the Colegio de Querétaro to Fray Diego Bringas, Querétaro, March 7, 1796, AFPM, AQ, Letter K, leg. 18, no. 21. Iturralde was informed about his appointment in September 1795. Fray Diego Bringas to Fray Francisco Iturralde, Aconchi, September 13, 1795, Fr. MCC, 202, exp. 52.

[131] Fray Antonio Barbastro to the discretory of the Colegio de Querétaro, Aconchi, May 19, 1795, AFPM, AQ, Letter K, leg. 16, 2nd portion, no. 112.

[132] Discretory of the Colegio de Querétaro to Fray Diego Bringas, Querétaro, March 7, 1796, AFPM, AQ, Letter K, leg. 18, no. 21. Fray Francisco Iturralde to Guardian Fray Sebastián Ramos, Tubutama, May 31, 1797, AFPM, AQ, Letter K, leg. 18, no. 23.

[133] *Testimonio de la visita efectuada por el Pe Bringas a los catorce pueblos que componen las ocho misiones de la Pimería alta*, AFPM, AQ, Letter K, leg. 18, no. 17.

[134] AFPM, AQ, Letter K, leg. 18, no. 25.

[135] *Testimonio de la visita*, AFPM, AQ, Letter K, leg. 18, no. 17.

fell squarely on his shoulders, as did the task of securing various sources of financing for that enterprise.[136]

With the *visitador* back in Querétaro, the differences among the Franciscans in Pimería Alta intensified once again and a storm of opposing arguments raged across the land. Iturralde, the new *padre presidente*, faced increasing difficulties as the missionaries' initiatives often ran counter to his directives. In 1797, this circumstance caused a confrontation between Fray Florencio Ibáñez and Iturralde, which led to the former receiving permission to return to the colegio a year later.[137] In another case, this one from 1798, Fray Pascual Rodríguez became disenchanted with the situation in Sonora and "bowed his head" just three years after accompanying Father Bringas to Sonora. He asked for and received approval to leave Pimería Alta and return to Querétaro.[138]

Barbastro died in Aconchi in June 1800,[139] effectively taking the backbone of the Queretaran missions in Sonora with him, as it was he who had brought cohesion to the second generation of missionaries. Although Barbastro was survived by a few members of his generation, by the early nineteenth century some of them had returned to Querétaro and others had broken their affiliation with the colegio. A few remained in Pimería Alta, but only to be cared for during illness and old age by younger missionaries.[140] Thus came the turn of the third generation of Franciscans to work in the region. They arrived in the late eighteenth century and comprised the final contingents of missionaries who came from Spain to take charge of the missions.[141] At this point in time, the available sources include reports on the missionaries from the Xalisco province, thus allowing comparison of the different regions of Sonora.

---

[136] Fray Diego Bringas to Commander Pedro de Nava, Chihuahua, March 15, 1796, AFPM, AQ, Letter K, leg. 18, no. 28; *Diligencias que hizo el Venerable Discretorio para conseguir que se consignasen a beneficio de las misiones del colegio las limosnas que dejó el difunto capitán don Francisco de Zúñiga, 1800–1804*, AFPM, AQ, Letter K, leg. 18, no. 37.

[137] Fr. MCC, 203, exp. 21. After fifteen years of work on those missions, Father Ibáñez was expelled from Sonora by Iturralde because, as he told the colegio, "in truth [Ibáñez] is not fit for the missions." Fray Francisco Iturralde to Guardian Fray Francisco Miralles, Tubutama, May 4, 1798, Fr. MCC, 203, exp. 26.

[138] Fr. MCC, 203, exp. 26.

[139] Gómez Canedo, *Sonora hacia fines*, 9.

[140] For example, Father Iturralde returned to Querétaro at some point after Barbastro's death, and around 1813 was *interim* president of his colegio. BL, M-A 25:3, document 1. Fathers Juan Bautista Llorens and Lorenzo Simó were accepted in the province of Santiago de Xalisco in 1797, and both continued to work in the Sonoran missions until their deaths, though assigned to Basarac and Bacedhuachi, respectively. BPEJ, CM, book 50-V, ff. 59, 80.

[141] De la Torre Curiel, *Vicarios*, 339.

CHAPTER 6
Leaving Sonora

In the early years of the nineteenth century, the Colegio de Querétaro's discretorium came to the decision that revitalizing missionary activities in Sonora was once again necessary. The topics of mission reform and the expansion into Papaguería would hardly have seemed novel by then, but they still fired the imagination of discretorium participants, who considered them to be longstanding tasks. At the beginning of the nineteenth century, this new reform movement was led by Fray Juan Bautista Ceballos who, curiously, had remained aloof from the missionary experience in Sonora, but was convinced of the need to "reform the customs" of his confreres stationed in those far-off lands. Ceballos had been a member of the Colegio de Querétaro's discretorium until he was named *comisario prefecto* and sent to visit the Queretaran missions in 1809.[1] After drawn-out negotiations in Querétaro and Mexico City to obtain the necessary funds and to convince other Franciscans to accompany him to Pimería Alta, Ceballos and his entourage finally began their journey in December 1812, arriving in Sonora in mid-1814.[2] Ceballos's traveling companions were Friars Pedro Ruiz, Francisco Fontbona, Miguel Montes, and Matías Creo, the "young blood" who quickly encountered great difficulty in working with older priests in Sonoran mission districts.

The importance of Ceballos's *visita* lies in the changes that he introduced in the Pimería Alta mission towns. Given the historical moment of his visit, it fell to Ceballos to organize the missions in Pimería in accordance with the constitutional regime promulgated in 1812 in Spain. Upon his arrival in Sonora, Ceballos found that according to the Constitution of Cadiz (1812), "national *alcaldes*" had been elected to replace the old local authorities (Indian governor and other justices). A fervent supporter of this system of government and of

---

[1] BL, M-A 25:3, document 16.
[2] BL, M-A 25:3, document 9.

putting the Indians on an equal footing with other settlers, Ceballos promoted the idea that the missions should pay the Indians for their labor, "as they do . . . non-Indian workers" and, moreover, that they should carry out their obligation of distributing individual plots of land to them.[3]

Ceballos's dispositions received a warm welcome in such towns as San Ignacio, Cocóspera, Tumacácori, and Tubutama, which were administered by newly arrived missionaries. However, it was quite a different story to try to convince the older missionaries to accept this new order. Friction between the *visitador* and the new head of the Pimería Alta missions, Fray Francisco Moyano, over these matters did not take long to surface. In Ceballos's view Moyano would never accept these novelties in Oquitoa and San Xavier del Bac because he was "stuck on the idea that the Indians should work for him receiving nothing in return," and because his accustomed way of fulfilling his obligation to aid the Indians was to give them thin blankets for which he charged a *fanega* of wheat.[4]

Upon concluding his visitation in Pimería Alta, Ceballos went to the town of Ures, where he intended to establish a seminary-like convent (*hospicio*) for the missionaries of Sonora.[5] By early 1815, the Crown had minimized reforms of the governance system for mission towns, and, as on previous occasions, had simply returned to the "old system of governance" and the practice of electing indigenous governors and *alcaldes*.[6] Despite this, the 1814 reform had left a noticeable mark on Pimería Alta. On the one hand, Indians from several missions had taken advantage of the freedoms guaranteed in the Cadiz Constitution and abandoned the mission settlements, while those who opted to remain refused to be treated as neophytes subject to the missionary. Meanwhile, Ceballos's visit had polarized the missionaries in Pimería Alta to such a degree that personal relationships were strained.

As had occurred previously, this division between older and younger missionaries stationed in Pimería Alta soon became evident in bitter disputes, mutual accusations, and even desertions by a few missionaries in rather unsavory circumstances. One of the first signals of disquiet among older missionaries came from Fray Juan Bautista Llorens just a few months after the conclusion of Ceballos's visitation. For Llorens, it was clear the visit had completely

---

[3] BL, M-A 25:3, document 13.

[4] *Ibid.*

[5] BL, M-A 25:3, document 15.

[6] Fray Francisco Moyano to Guardian Fray Diego Miguel Bringas de Manzaneda, Oquitoa, June 4, 1815, BL, M-A 25:3, document 8.

[7] Fray Juan Bautista Llorens to Guardian Fray Diego Miguel Bringas, San Xavier del Bac, April 4, 1814, BL, M-A 25:4, document 6.

upset the Pimería Alta friars because arguments in favor of freedom for the Indians had tied the missionaries' hands in terms of carrying out their ministry in those towns.[7] After Ceballos's departure, it became virtually impossible to convince the Indians to attend mass or religious instruction and even more difficult to convince them to remain in the mission settlements. Even the Pápagos who frequented those towns no longer stayed with the missionaries for the same reasons. "There is no one among the older Fathers who does not regret these events," lamented Llorens in early 1815, as everything on the missions had been reduced "to liberty [and] land distribution."[8] Llorens then informed his superiors that he had been accepted into the Xalisco province and planned to serve on one of the Xaliscan missions in Sonora.

Other missionaries who expressed disillusionment included Francisco Moyano, Narciso Gutiérrez, and Diego Gil. They knew the visit had been a stratagem that Ceballos wielded "against the old missionaries," and thus used all available means to prevent the dispositions dictated by Ceballos during his visitation from taking effect.[9] Regarding Fray Gil, upon arriving in Sonora, Ceballos explained to the guardian of the Colegio de Querétaro that Gil was the missionary most responsible for the abuses he was trying to correct. Gil returned to Querétaro shortly afterward.[10]

Discord among the Franciscans in Pimería Alta reached its apex when two of the younger Queretarans defied their superiors' authority in public. The first case involved Fray Francisco Fontbona, who in 1815 traversed several of the Sonoran missions dressed as a layman, mounted on horseback, attending fiestas here and there, ignoring his father president, and resorting to fisticuffs with anyone who got in his way.[11] Also in 1815 and equally alarming, at least among the older missionaries, was Fray Matías Creo's threats against a fellow Franciscan and holding local authorities at gunpoint in an attempt to move of his own free will to a town other than the one to which he had been assigned. To the utter consternation of the older missionaries, for several days Creo hurled insults in public at the Franciscan chief of the Queretaran missions (then

[8] Fray Juan Bautista Llorens to Guardian Fray Diego Miguel Bringas, San Agustín del Tucson, January 4, 1815, BL, M-A 25:3, document 5.

[9] Fray Narciso Gutiérrez to Fray Diego Gil, May 28, 1815, BL, M-A 25:4, document 7.

[10] Fray Juan Bautista Ceballos to Guardian Fray Diego Miguel Bringas, San Francisco Xavier del Bac, July 7, 1814, BL, M-A 25:3, document 13.

[11] BL, M-A 25:4, document 6. Due to scandals surrounding him and his refusal to allow Fray Francisco Madueño to carry out a juridical inquiry into his conduct in Pimería Alta, Fontbona was recalled from the missions by the Colegio de Querétaro in 1817 and taken prisoner to be returned to Spain. ARAG, Ramo Criminal, 131-2-1979, 1817.

Fray Francisco Moyano).[12] As Moyano would contend later, Ceballos (the *prefecto comisario*, sent to Sonora to "reform the customs" of the missionaries) devoted his labors to returning the older friars to Querétaro because they failed to support his dispositions, rather than dealing with the outrageous behavior of certain younger missionaries. In his defense several months after those incidents, Ceballos alleged that "the missionaries who have been accused are not as bad as they seem to have been portrayed to the discretorium."[13] In his opinion, a week of spiritual exercises would suffice to correct the path of the new friars, while the older missionaries—including the *padre presidente*—should be sent back to Querétaro because they handled mission assets, "although this was not to be taken as punishment."[14]

Aside from the discord among the missionaries triggered by Ceballos's visit, the most significant effect that this episode had on the missions in Pimería Alta was the Indians' enthusiasm for the same civil rights that Spanish settlers enjoyed. Although the real meaning of equality and liberty for the citizenry had been long debated in Spanish courts, for mission town residents it was clear these concepts were to be understood as the right to own property and freedom of movement in Sonora. By supporting these constitutional principles, Ceballos unknowingly set in motion a process that contributed to ending the mission regime in the nineteenth century. Once these freedoms had been granted to mission residents, it proved impossible to rescind them and subject the Indians once again to the missionaries' authority.[15]

---

[12] Fray Narciso Gutiérrez to Fray Diego Gil, place not specified, April 26, 1815, BL, M-A 25:4, document 8; Fray Matías Creo to Fray Diego Miguel Bringas, Saric, January 23, 1815, BL, M-A 25:3, document 7.

[13] Fray Juan Bautista Ceballos to Fray Diego Miguel Bringas, Ures, June 14, 1815, BL, M-A 25:3, document 15.

[14] *Ibid.*

[15] Years later, the indigenous captain of Caborca, Enrique Tejeda, together with the *alcalde* of that town and an Indian named Juan Antonio Valenzuela, the *alcalde* of Pitiquito, wrote to the president of the missions that from 1814, when "freedom was granted so that as *vecinos* we would be equal in lands and fruits of the fields with the *vecinos* [of Spanish origin], the Christian subjection that we had enjoyed from our Father ministers for our spiritual and temporal good began to be lost. . . ." One of the problems with these freedoms, the three men avowed, was that every time a minister attempted to defend the Indians from abuses at the hands of the Spanish settlers, the latter invoked the argument of equality among *vecinos* and Indians, which made the intervention of third parties in favor of the latter quite useless. Enrique Tejeda to Fray José María Pérez Llera, Caborca, February 28, 1835, AGES, Fondo Ejecutivo, vol. 62, exp. 10.

THE EXPULSION OF SPANIARDS AND ITS AFTERMATH IN PIMERÍA ALTA

Just when it seemed that things could not get any worse for missionaries in Sonora due to their internal problems, the growing land acquisition by Spanish settlers, and the missionaries' loss of control of the indigenous population, the state government struck the final blow to the mission regime. On February 12, 1828, the government of the Estado de Occidente (present-day Sonora and Sinaloa)[16] decreed the expulsion of Spaniards in accordance to the widespread belief that they posed a major threat to Mexico's political stability.[17] For the missions, this measure meant not only that all missionaries of Spanish origin would be expelled, but also that the mission properties heretofore administered by those friars would pass "into the hands of individuals appointed by the government."[18]

In the early months of 1828, a rumor began to circulate among the Queretarans that in addition to expelling Spanish priests, the Mexican government might also order them, in effect, to dissolve the missions. On the other hand, it was understood that discussions continued in Mexico City on certain aspects of the expulsion policy, which fueled hopes among the Franciscans. In an attempt to calm his fellows, the guardian of the Colegio de Querétaro, Fray Miguel Molina, stated that they should not anticipate events by abandoning the missions, "as it is not an expulsion of Creoles but of *gachupines*." Moreover, he affirmed that he had well-founded hopes that the Franciscans would receive special consideration, and requested that Spanish priests Rafael Díaz and Faustino González remain calm and "stay quiet."[19]

The 1828 expulsion decree by the Estado de Occidente stipulated that certain individuals might be exempted, including those who possessed a Mexican citizenship document issued by the state legislature, those over sixty years of

---

[16] Under the Mexican Constitution of 1824, the provinces of Sonora and Sinaloa were grouped together in one entity called the Estado Interno de Occidente, which had its capital in El Fuerte. Vidargas, "Sonora y Sinaloa," 430–31.

[17] Decree 43 of the Congress of the Estado de Occidente, issued in Concepción de Álamos, BL, M-M 285:72. On December 20, 1827, the Mexican government issued the first law of expulsion of Spaniards. For an analysis of the context and effects of this and subsequent expulsion laws, see Harold D. Sims, *The Expulsion of Mexico's Spaniards, 1821–1836* (Pittsburgh, PA: University of Pittsburgh Press, 1990).

[18] Arizpe, January 22, 1828, AGES, Fondo Ejecutivo, vol. 37, exp. 3.

[19] Fray Miguel Molina to Fray José María Pérez Llera, Querétaro, January 23, 1828, BL, M-A 25:4, document 17; and Molina to Pérez Llera, Querétaro, August 29, 1828, BL, M-A 25:4, document 16.

age who held real estate worth a minimum of 30,000 pesos, and those who were unable to abandon the territory due to illness. Several clergymen sent the legislature certificates documenting their age and precarious health conditions. Franciscans Diego García and Francisco Robles were the first missionaries to be granted this exemption in late 1828.[20] In subsequent months, Spanish Franciscans Juan María Torres, Faustino González, Luis Temblet, and Miguel Gallo also received permission to remain in Sonora.[21]

The expulsion decree had a drastic effect on the Pimería Alta missions because most Queretarans on site were born and educated in Spain. Of the seven Queretarans registered in Pimería Alta in late 1827, only two, José María Pérez Llera (the *padre presidente*) and Rafael Díaz, were allowed to remain at the helm of their respective missions the following year.[22] At some time in

[20] García was exempted as he had proven on September 29, 1828, that he was sixty-two years old, had been "in the [Mexican] Republic for 39 years and had a permanent physical impediment." Robles, the retired chaplain of the Fronteras presidio, was also exempted for these reasons, as he was born on October 21, 1767. AGES, Fondo Ejecutivo, vol. 37, exp. 3. It is not clear whether these two priests did in fact remain in Sonora, as a list of expelled Spaniards from 1829 includes their names. AGES, Fondo Ejecutivo, vol. 37, exp. 6. On November 25, 1830, Fray Francisco Robles presented the *alcalde* of Arizpe with a "passport from the Senate" allowing him to reside in Mexico. On January 11, 1831, he was still living in Arizpe, as it appears that there were doubts as to whether the state government's order of November 20, 1830—which stipulated Robles's expulsion—was to be enforced. In the meantime, Robles won some time by alleging his advanced age and illness. This case reached the vice-president of Mexico, but there is no known evidence of his response. AGES, Fondo Ejecutivo, vol. 37, exp. 8.

[21] Fray Juan María Torres obtained his license "due to a permanent physical impediment" and was allowed to remain in Altar, while Fray Faustino González stayed on at Caborca. By a "resolution of the High Government," Fray Diego García was also exempted; he stayed in Oputo, while Fray Luis Temblet remained at the Bavispe presidio. Manuel Escalante, *Lista Nominal de los Españoles Expulsos del Departamento de Arispe*, Arizpe, January 6, 1830, AGES, Fondo Ejecutivo, vol. 37, exp. 6.

Due to "reasons of great import," the state governor permitted Fray Miguel Gallo to stay at the mining town of San Antonio de la Huerta. José Manuel de Huguez, head of the department of Horcasitas to the state governor, Ures, January 19, 1830, AGES, Fondo Ejecutivo, vol. 37, exp. 6. However, by mid-1831, Gallo had been taken to Guaymas to await eviction from the province. The Xaliscans petitioned the governor to recognize the bishop of Sonora's intention to send Gallo to Onavas, but it seems that the governor did not accept their request, because in July 1831 Gallo was still in Guaymas, and no decision had been taken with respect to his case. AGES, Fondo Ejecutivo, vol. 37, exp. 8. Three years later, Gallo appears in the records of the province of Santiago de Xalisco as a missionary in the sierra Tarahumara. De la Torre Curiel, *Vicarios en entredicho*, 348.

[22] Left alone in Pimería Alta, Pérez Llera and Díaz divided the district up in the following way: "the towns to the west"—Magdalena, Santa Ana, Tubutama, Santa Teresa, Ati, Oquitoa, Pitiquito, Caborca, and Bisani—were placed under the administration of the former; "the towns to the north"—Terrenate, Imuris, San Ignacio Caborica, presidio de Santa Cruz, Tumacácori, Presidio de Tubac, San Xavier del Bac, and the town and presidio of Tucson—were entrusted to Díaz. Fray José María Pérez Llera, *Apuntes sobre los acontecimientos de las misiones que mantuvo este*

1828, they were joined by former Xaliscan missionary Juan Maldonado, who was assigned to Tubutama and Oquitoa, bringing the number of Franciscan clergy in Pimería Alta to three.[23]

Meanwhile, the effects of the expulsion decree on the Xaliscan missions were relatively minor. Only two missions, San José de Pimas and Opodepe, were abandoned as a result of the laws of expulsion. Of the eleven friars stationed in Pimería Baja and Opatería in 1827, only Fray Dionisio Oñederra was absent for a time from the missions. Of the remaining ten missionaries, Maldonado joined the Queretarans in Pimería Alta in 1828. Soon thereafter, Fathers Mariano Nieto, Miguel Tellechea, and Agustín Zaldúa arrived to work in the missions. In 1830 the Xalisco province maintained twelve friars on its missions in Sonora.[24]

To enforce the expulsion decree, the Estado de Occidente government commissioned Santiago Redondo and Fernando Grande, a top government official in Arizpe, to visit Pimería Alta and determine the condition of mission properties there.[25] Just a few months later, Redondo resigned and submitted to Grande inventories of four missions located along the Concepción River. On July 25, 1828, Grande was appointed general administrator of mission temporalities in Pimería Alta; in this new capacity, he moved to secure those properties by naming several civil administrators in an attempt to avoid their ruin "due to the [state of] abandonment in which they were left."[26] In exchange for these services, Grande reached an agreement with the new administrators authorizing them to take a monthly salary of twenty to twenty-five pesos from the mission fund and use whatever amounts were necessary to pay the cattle handlers and other workers. Grande and his group prepared various inventories, which

---

Colegio de la Sma Cruz de Querétaro en la alta pimería, Departamento de Sonora desde el año de 1821 hasta el de 1841, AFPM, AQ, Letter Q, no. 20.

[23] Fray José María Pérez Llera to the governor of the Diocese of Sonora, San Ignacio, October 22, 1828, BL, M-A 25:4, document 20. Vidargas, "Sonora y Sinaloa," 438. Pérez Llera, *Apuntes*, AFPM, AQ, Letter Q, no. 20. For a few months between 1828 and 1829, Fray Agustín Zaldúa from the Tarahumara missions, made attempts to join the Queretarans in Pimería Alta, and was even named president of those missions, though by 1830 he joined the Xaliscans in Sonora instead, without taking possession of his post in Pimería Alta. Pérez Llera, *Apuntes*; Fray Miguel Molina to Fray José María Pérez Llera, Querétaro, January 9, 1829, BL, M-A 25:4, document 23.

[24] De la Torre Curiel, *Vicarios en entredicho*, 341.

[25] AGES, Fondo Ejecutivo, vol. 62, exp. 9.

[26] In San Ignacio, Mariano Romo was appointed administrator; in Cocospera, José Blas de León; in Tumacácori, Tomás Ortiz, who was later replaced by Ramón Pamplona and Buenaventura López; in San Xavier del Bac, Juan Ignacio Zapata; in Tubutama and Oquitoa, José María Leiva, Francisco Redondo, and Francisco Mendoza; in Caborca, Lorenzo Varela. AGES, Fondo Ejecutivo, vol. 62, exp. 9; BL, M-A 25:4, document 36.

showed that by 1829 the missions in Pimería Alta were well endowed with cattle and grain. Just a year and a half later, however, mission goods had been significantly reduced.

In Tubutama, for example, the civil administrator, Francisco Redondo (son of the *alcalde* of Altar, Santiago Redondo), registered sales of 400 sheep and almost 40 head of cattle in only eight months, in addition to charging the mission a total of 243 pesos for "provisions supplied to cattle handlers" and 174 pesos for partial payment of his salary.[27] Redondo also obtained salary income for "administering" the assets of Oquitoa and two other unidentified missions that he neither visited nor administered in practice. Despite subsequent legal action, the political influence of Redondo's father saved him from having to repay the money he had received as salary.[28] In another case, the administrator of Saric's temporalities, Ignacio Pérez, sold sixteen donkeys and one horse, a transaction that earned him 122 pesos that he never turned over to the mission fund.[29] The mission at San Xavier del Bac, meanwhile, had simply been abandoned to its fate by its administrators: "[B]ecause its fruits did not compensate the expenditures made, the mission house was closed. . . , thus paralyzing its operations."[30]

With the properties of the missions being managed in this way, it is hardly surprising that the administrators' final accounts showed the missions as virtually depopulated, in ruins, and even owing several hundred pesos to their erstwhile managers. Mission residents fled not only because of the missions' impoverishment, but also to avoid problems related to the new administrators' abuses. Consequently, argued Manuel Arvizu in early 1830, the state government would be well advised to return the administration of temporalities to the missionaries. After a personal visit to Pimería Alta, Arvizu asserted that the only way to keep the Pimería Alta settlers in place was to guarantee the subsistence of the Franciscan missionaries there, though this would mean allowing them access to temporalities.[31]

[27] BL, M-A 25:4, document 36.

[28] *Ibid.*, documents 42–43.

[29] *Ibid.*, document 40.

[30] Fernando Grande to the state governor, Cucurpe, May 25, 1830, AGES, Fondo Ejecutivo, vol. 62, exp. 9.

[31] Fray José María Pérez Llera resided in San Ignacio, whence he administered Imuris, La Mesa, Terrenate, Santa Ana, San Lorenzo, the mission at Magdalena, and other ranches. Fray Rafael Díaz was in charge of Cocospera and the presidios of Santa Cruz, Tubac, and Tucson, the missions of Tumacácori and San Xavier del Bac, and the town of Tucson. Fray Juan Maldonado was assigned to Oquitoa, whence he visited Ati, Santa Teresa, Tubutama, and Saric. Fray Faustino González stayed in Caborca, attending Pitiquito and Bisani. Manuel Escalante y Arvizu to the state governor, Arizpe, January 13, 1830, AGES, Fondo Ejecutivo, vol. 62, exp. 9.

Allowing the Franciscans to once again manage mission holdings in an attempt to help those communities return to their former economic self-sufficiency and to increase settler numbers was by no means motivated by philanthropy. Grande, the man who had supervised the civil administration of mission temporalities knew this better than anyone else. In spite of his personal differences with the head of the Queretaran missionaries in Sonora, he respected the work of the Franciscans and praised the dedication of the four priests who persevered in Sonora in 1830. However, as he explained in a lengthy report to the state governor in that same year, conserving the mission regime in Pimería Alta was "politically convenient" for the state, which benefited from maintaining settlers along the frontier with the Apaches.[32]

Hence, the desire to maintain the buffer zone convinced the governor of the Estado de Occidente to decree, on January 22, 1830, that the administration of mission holdings in Pimería Alta was to be returned to the four Queretarans remaining in Sonora (Pérez Llera, Díaz, Maldonado, and González).[33] However, the return of temporalities to missionary administration was much less appealing than expected because of the poor management by previous civil administrators. Shortly before arriving to resume control of mission assets, Pérez Llera wrote to the state governor to protest the negligence and abuses of those administrators. "The *temporalidades* and furnishings . . . have been thoroughly looted," affirmed the Franciscan, "whether due to the ineptitude of those in charge, to their excessive salaries, [and/or] to total neglect[,] all activities have been left paralyzed."

The list of abuses committed by the administrators was a long one. Pérez Llera mentioned the liberties those men had taken in paying their own salaries with the best of the cattle and grain stores on the missions without taking the least interest in caring for livestock, crops, or goods. As a result of this disorder, the friar alleged, the 2,000 head of cattle that the administrators received had been reduced to just 600 by early 1830.[34] In contrast to earlier periods in which secular administrators managed mission temporalities, the return of the properties in 1830 to missionary control was not accompanied by the missions'

---

[32] Fernando Grande to the state governor, Cucurpe, May 25, 1830, AGES, Fondo Ejecutivo, vol. 62, exp. 9.

[33] This order was communicated to the president of the Queretarans in March of that year. Fernando Grande to Fray José María Pérez Llera, Cucurpe, March 1, 1830, BL, M-A 25:4, document 49. The missions were received by president Pérez Llera with their furnishings, and sacramental and account books between April 29 and May 19, 1830. AGES, Fondo Ejecutivo, vol. 62, exp. 9.

[34] BL, M-A 25:4, document 60.

economic recovery.[35] The new political realities in Sonora, suspension of stipend payments to the missionaries, and, above all, the government's recognition of mission residents' rights to decide whether to abandon the "regime of the bell" (*el regimen de campana*) constituted basic differences compared to the earlier periods.

Although the government recognized the need for missionaries to exploit mission property, the Indians were no longer under any obligation to work in mission towns, and anyone, including the Franciscans, who desired to employ Indians "is in that case obliged to negotiate with them for their wages and work day."[36]

Once the Estado de Occidente split into the autonomous states of Sonora and Sinaloa in 1831, the Sonoran government decided to reexamine the situation of the Indian towns in Pimería Alta. Decree 19 preserved the mission regime in that region and ordered the annual election of a *juez económico* and an *alguacil* in each town. This decree also established that in addition to fulfilling the primary objectives of their religious ministry, the missionaries were also "obliged to guide the Indians in everything that concerns their well-being and prosperity."[37] This decree seemed to hold out the promise of mission economic recovery, but for many people involved, prolonging the mission regime was a burden they no longer wished to bear. Therefore, public demands for rescinding Decree 19 began to appear on the election day of the first communal authorities in mission towns. For instance, in late July 1831, in the Caborca meeting house when local elections were being held, an Indian named Alejo Neblina and five other residents asserted that they would not vote for anyone because the town already had an *alcalde*, and that what they wanted was to "free themselves from the servitude and authority of the [Indian] governors."[38]

In September 1831, this and other complaints about Indians' subordinate status led the state government to offer Indians and mestizos residing in mission towns the chance to abandon the mission regime without leaving their

---

[35] This is the most important point to keep in mind with respect to the topic of the management of temporalities. It has traditionally been thought that the embezzlement of mission properties by the royal administrators in 1767 was one of the main causes of the "mission crisis," but this is incorrect, as after 1767 the missions in Pimería Alta reactivated their economies, allowing the reconstruction of all the churches there. The opposite occurred in 1830, when mission residents ceased to work under Franciscan control.

[36] BL, M-A 25:5, document 49.

[37] Leonardo Escalante, governor of Sonora, Decree 19, June 11, 1831, Hermosillo, Sonora, BL, M-A 25:5, document 68.

[38] José Cañedo to Fray José María Pérez Llera, Caborca, August 4, 1831, BL, M-A 25:5, document 41.

homes. Decree 32 opened the door for the Indians of Pimería Alta to obtain from the state government a "letter of security and separation" from the mission regime, which obliged them "henceforth to subject themselves to the [civil] judges and constitutional authorities." Those who opted for this separation might receive a piece of land that the government judged sufficient for their sustenance. Also, they would be considered equal to "the rest of the citizens of the State" in terms of their rights and obligations.[39]

These kinds of disputes made it clear that demographic changes in Pimería Alta conflicted in a major way with the viability of the mission regime.[40] In the view of mission residents, the continuity of this form of social organization restricted personal liberty to possess and exploit resources individually. The missionary perspective was that this transition to other forms of governance ensured the ruin of the missions and endangered the existence of the buffer zone between themselves and the Pápago and Apache Indians. According to Pérez Llera, "[T]he time has come in which we are missionaries in name only and manage the temporalities only in appearance."[41] As a result, in 1834 Pérez Llera offered to turn the missions over to the state government, taking advantage of the nationwide decree dated April 16 of that year to secularize the missions in Mexico.[42] The Sonoran government resisted Pérez Llera's suggestion, arguing that nothing could be done until the federal government resolved whether the missions in Pimería Alta could be exempted from the decree.

Despite the fact that the missionaries' desires were now distinct from those of the Pimería Alta's inhabitants, the government of Sonora insisted upon the need to maintain a line of settlements along the frontier with the Pápago nation to serve as a refuge for that group and to create a buffer against the Apache threat. Hence, the government searched for a way to sustain the mission regime in Pimería Alta. It promised the missionaries that it would seek mechanisms to

[39] Leonardo Escalante, governor of Sonora, Decree 32, September 27, 1831, Hermosillo, Sonora, BL, M-A 25:5, document 69.

[40] See Chapter 2. The arrival of new, non-Indian settlers around the missions led authorities in such places as Tucson, San Ignacio, and Cocóspera to distribute land to the *vecinos*, a measure that awoke among the mission Indians the desire to hold their own lands as private property; BL, M-A 25:5, document 61. For an analysis of the process of mission land redistribution in Sonora, see Jerónimo Romero, *De las misiones.*

[41] BL, M-A 25:5, document 24.

[42] AGES, Fondo Ejecutivo, vol. 62, exp. 10. On April 16, 1834, Valentín Gómez Farías—then vice-president of Mexico—decreed the secularization of all missions in Mexico. However, President Santa Anna abrogated this law later in 1834. Manuel Dublán and José María Lozano, *Legislación mexicana o Colección completa de las disposiciones legislativas expedidas desde la independencia de la República*, vol. 2 (Mexico City: Imprenta del Comercio, 1876), 689–90.

pay more than 30,000 pesos in overdue stipends[43] and offered payment of 1,000 pesos to hold them over while the government found a solution to the problem.[44] However, no middle ground between the missionaries' projects and the increasingly varied forms of social organization of the Indians and Spanish settlers in Pimería Alta could be reached in the short term. The reality was, as the state governor eventually explained to the Queretarans, that in the midst of so many urgent demands to be addressed, the Sonoran government was unable to resolve such highly controversial matters. Thus, he suggested that "as the problems have no solution," the Franciscans "should let them be."[45]

In 1837, Pérez Llera undertook a final measure to attempt to sustain the socioreligious project in Pimería Alta. Upon appointing Fray Faustino González as commissary of the Pimería Alta missions, and after a brief stay at the Colegio de Querétaro, Pérez Llera arrived in Mexico City to speak personally with Mexican President Anastasio Bustamante, whom he informed as to the situation of the missions and suggested measures needed to restore them. To Pérez Llera's great misfortune, the commission appointed by Bustamante to consider this matter opted to take advantage of the fact that the recently elected bishop of Sonora, Lázaro de la Garza, was also staying in Mexico City, and decided to consult with him. Full of optimistic intentions and totally unfamiliar with his diocese, the new bishop was inclined to staff his diocese with young priests capable of making up for the Franciscans' shortcomings. With this, Pérez Llera's petition for support was summarily canceled. Added to this rebuff were conflicts over control of the Sonoran government that pitted José Urrea against Manuel María Gándara, situations that convinced Pérez Llera to remain at the Querétaro seminary, where he soon assumed the office of guardian.

Meanwhile, back in Sonora, by mid-1841 Fray Faustino González had died and Father Maldonado had rejoined the Xalisco province, leaving the mission administration of Pimería Alta—comprised of sixteen towns and four presidios—in the hands of only two Franciscans (Rafael Díaz and Ángel Arroyo).[46]

In these conditions, which were further complicated by the Colegio de Querétaro's severe staffing problems, the most viable way out for all concerned

---

[43] In January 1825, calculations were made of the amounts owed to the Queretarans for unpaid stipends since 1814. The resulting balance was 33,642 pesos. One of the reasons for this situation was that authorities at the state and federal level refused to cover this outlay that had previously been made by the royal treasury. BL, M-A 25:4, document 13; BL, M-A 25:5, document 21.

[44] BL, M-A 25:5, document 15.

[45] Pérez Llera, *Apuntes*, AFPM, AQ, Letter Q, no. 20.

[46] After González's death in early 1841, Fray Rafael Díaz was named president of the missions by the then guardian of Querétaro, Fray José María Pérez Llera. BL, M-A 25:4, document 123.

seemed to be to turn the Pimería Alta missions over to the Diocese of Sonora.[47] All that was needed was an excuse to allow the Queretarans a decorous withdrawal. That pretext arose in 1841, when a small child in Sonora reached the age to receive the sacrament of confirmation in one of the diocese's parishes. By that time, the bishop of Sonora was residing in Culiacán, in the extreme southern area of the diocese.[48] Given the impossibility of the bishop making the arduous journey to Pimería Alta to perform this ceremony, one of the missionaries agreed to confirm the child in the belief that—as had been the accepted practice since the sixteenth century—he was fully authorized to do so. When Bishop de la Garza learned about the incident, he believed that his spiritual jurisdiction had been ignored by the missionaries in Pimería Alta and began an angry polemic concerning the faculties of various ecclesiastical groups and how the status of the mission towns in Pimería Alta was henceforth to be understood. The Queretarans' defense consisted in demonstrating the privileges and faculties conferred upon the Franciscans since the sixteenth century to impart all sacraments in mission territory and arguing that they had not violated the bishop's authority. De la Garza, in turn, informed the Queretarans that since the secularization of the missions in 1834, those towns had become true parishes that only preserved the title of "missions" due to habit, and that it was only because of the shortage of diocesan priests that they were still in the hands of the Franciscans.[49]

To resolve this conflict, the guardian of the Colegio de Querétaro informed the bishop that it would be best for his institution to abandon the missions. Moreover, only two friars were left in Querétaro, so the return of their fellows in Pimería Alta was a pressing need for the college. Given the scarcity of priests there, and their ongoing problems with the bishop, Pérez Llera concluded, "I should no longer maintain the missions as I cannot, I do not wish to, and it is not convenient." Pérez Llera bid farewell to Sonora in January 1842. In his resignation he stated: "[I]f the missions belong to the

---

[47] As a result of the expulsion of the Spaniards in 1828, the Colegio de Querétaro suffered a severe human resources crisis, as most of its members were peninsular Spaniards. Beginning in that year, and in an attempt to survive as an autonomous institute, the colegio found itself obliged to receive most of its clergy from other Franciscan colegios and provinces in Mexico who wished to join it. By the same token, rules for admittance of the few young men who wished to don the gray robe of the college became less strict, with the result that in the 1830s disciplinary problems became the institute's main concerns. In order to curtail these problems, the colegio's discretorium was obliged to reduce the number of friars there, to such a degree that by 1840 the colegio was no longer able to assist the missions in Pimería Alta. Pérez Llera, *Apuntes.*

[48] The modern-day state of Sinaloa.

[49] BL, M-A 25:4, documents 123–26.

bishop, [then] I attended them as long as I could; and now His Lordship will see how he attends them. And if they are mine, then I give them to him absolutely."[50]

Secularism and Mission Secularization in Pimería Baja and Opatería

By 1830, the general situation of the Franciscan missions in Sonora had become extremely complicated from all perspectives. In Pimería Baja and Opatería, several decades had passed since the missionaries had been legally separated from the organization and government of Indian towns. Although Franciscan influence in those communities had by no means disappeared (in fact, it continued to be evident in several areas, especially land disputes), offices in most communities such as the "general of the Ópata nation" and "protector of Indians" provided alternative secular symbols of internal security and cohesion.[51] In addition, the social relations of mission residents in the towns in Pimería Baja and Opatería were more clearly secular. By the early nineteenth century, merchants and ranchers had endowed mission towns with a new socioeconomic orientation, which would later be transformed into political loyalties during rebellions and faction-based uprisings after Mexican independence.[52]

Perhaps the best example of this budding clientelism and growing secularism among the indigenous peoples of central Sonora is the complexity of land disputes between the Indians of Opodepe and Tuape (*visita* of Cucurpe) brought before the Audiencia de Guadalajara in 1817.[53] Both towns claimed possession of an area known as the Merisichi, a strip of fertile land some 100 *cordeles* long and 14 *cordeles* wide, located on the boundary between Opodepe and Tuape. At the time, Indians from Tuape occupied the site, denounced as squatting by Indians residing in Opodepe. Both towns alleged that the site had been theirs "from time immemorial" and each requested that its land survey be

---

[50] Fray José María Pérez Llera, Querétaro, January 15, 1842, BL, M-A 25:5, document 126.

[51] De la Torre Curiel, "Un mecenazgo fronterizo," 185–212.

[52] In this sense, towns in both regions experienced processes similar to those that characterized the late colonial period in central New Spain. In his study of the parishes of the Archdiocese of Mexico and the Diocese of Guadalajara, William Taylor shows that in the late eighteenth century certain personages began to stand out in some towns and came to exercise notable power at the local level thanks to their ability to negotiate with different instances of government on behalf of their communities. Identified by Taylor and other authors as *caciques*, these figures played a fundamental role in the history of rural Mexico in the nineteenth century. Taylor, *Magistrates*, 384–94.

[53] *Instancia promovida por los indios de Opodepe contra los de Tuape sobre posesión de terrenos*, ARAG, Ramo Civil, 424-1-6888.

recognized. The Indians of Opodepe argued that the Merisichi had always belonged to their community, but because they could not occupy the land for several years, they loaned it to Tuape residents, who in turn based their claims on this occupation. At the time of the hearing, Opodepe spokespersons said that their town was growing and thus needed more land. They asked that their right to possession of the Merisichi be honored.

Up to this point, the dispute between Tuape and Opodepe would have been one among many examples of growing competition for land among Indian towns in New Spain at the end of the colonial period. But this particular dispute eventually involved several civil and ecclesiastical authorities and triggered additional litigation in which various actors delivered low blows to adversaries.[54]

The dispute discussed here began in June 1817 with a suit brought by José Vázquez, Indian governor of Opodepe, to the local justice of Cucurpe, Fernando Grande. On that occasion, Vázquez sent Grande a letter outlining Opodepe's claim to Merisichi lands with annexed documents showing town boundaries. After dismissing Opodepe's suit, Grande gave the documents on Opodepe's boundaries to the missionary at Cucurpe, Fray Fernando Madueño. The Opodepe plaintiffs interpreted this act as proof that Grande and the missionary were conspiring to defend Tuape's usurpation of the site. The case was immediately taken to a higher authority, the intendant of Sonora, where the Opodepans reiterated their case for the recovery of the Merisichi and denounced Grande and Madueño.

When informed of the matter in August 1817, Intendant Antonio Cordero commissioned Severino Varela (who was from Opodepe but lived in El Realito), to undertake an investigation into both plaintiff and defendant accusations. When the commissioner ordered that representatives of the two sides go to Merisichi and resolve the issue by examining the documents that supported respective allegations, Tuapeans declined to attend because their protector, Tomás Escalante, was not available. They also alleged that the Indians of Opodepe had sought a resolution through their governor and not through their protector (Juan de Gándara), as they should.[55] The Opodepe Indians

[54] As in central and western Mexico, this type of conflict was related to the demographic recovery that took place in the late eighteenth century. De la Torre Ruiz, "Mojoneras," 75–108.

[55] In 1805, the Indian towns of the province of Sonora were divided into three groups (*partidos*) for these objectives, each with its own *protector partidario*. The *partido* of Arizpe comprised Arizpe, Oposura, Cucurpe, Batuco, Bacerac, Huachinera, Huásavas, Bacadehuachi, Oputo, Chinapa, Sinoquipe, Banamichi, Huepaca, Aconchi, Babiacora, Cucurpe, Tuape, Babispe, Cuquiarachi, Bacoachi, Caborca, Ati, Tubutama, Saric, San Xavier del Bac, Tumacácori, Cocospera, San Ignacio, Tubac, Tucson, and Santa María Suamca. The *partido* of Sonora included

were convinced that Fray Madueño had planned this maneuver so that interested parties would not view the Opodepe documents, and told the commissioner as much.[56] The Opodepe litigants reached the conclusion that Madueño
was the "spring that cleverly moves the machinery of this suit. . . . [H]e is committing a horrible prevarication, [simultaneously] playing . . . the role[s] of
minister, . . . *teniente de justicia* and . . . Indian governor."[57]

Having failed to reconcile the two parties, Varela resigned from his commission and, in December of that year, Intendant Cordero appointed his
replacement, Don Ignacio Elías González, commander of the Pima company
stationed in Tubac. In this new phase, protagonists in the dispute over property lines between Opodepe and Tuape were the town's respective protectors.
Perhaps confident in the way that Fray Madueño was handling the affair in
Tuape, the protector, Don Tomás de Escalante, only sent a statement to the
intendant in which he claimed to have in his possession a copy of the official
land survey (*fundo legal*) of Tuape, which showed that they were missing sev-
enty-eight *cordeles* of land that would complete their parcel, as only 322 of the
original 400 *cordeles* had been given to the town.[58]

Nacameri, Opodepe, Ures, Santa Rosalía, San José de Pimas, Cumuripa, Tecoripa, Suaqui, Mátape,
Nacori, Álamos, Cocori, Bacum, Torim, Vicam, Potam, Raum, Huirivis, and Belem. Included in the
partido of Álamos were Batacosa, Tepaguí, Conicari, Macoyagui, Nuri, Maicoba, Yecora, Mobas,
Onavas, Tonichi, Arivechi, Bacanora, Ponida, Sahuaripa, Santo Tomás, Taraichi, Camoa, Navojoa,
Cuiximpo, Hechojoa, Tagueria, Santa Cruz, Baimena, Chois, Huiris, Baca, Toro, Charay, San
Miguel, Mochicague, and Ahome. ARAG, Ramo Criminal, 64-19-1035. Although the post of protector of Indians was eliminated after independence when the Indians were declared "citizens," the
state government of Sonora reestablished it in decree no. 61, issued June 11, 1835. BL, M-M,
285:409. One example of the application of this decree in Sonora is found in Rafael Elías González's
role as protector of the Indians from Sinoquipe, Banamichi, Huepaca, Aconchi, and Baviácora in the
redistribution of communal lands in 1836. AGES, Fondo Ejecutivo, vol. 84, exp. 9.

[56] In this part of the process, Opodepe Indians seem to have had right on their side, as an
analysis of the dates of the documents signed by the commissioner Varela and of the responses "by
the people" of Tuape confirms that it would have been impossible for Asencio Bichama, the governor of Tuape, to have responded to the citation issued by the commissioner. The people from
Opodepe proved that they had arrived at Cucurpe the night of August 2 to show Madueño the
citation from commissioner Varela and to ask him for the documents that he had been given by
Fernando Grande. They alleged that it was impossible for the Indians of Tuape to have left
Cucurpe for Tuape, to have met with Bichama and the rest of the community, to have discussed
the issue, and then to have drafted a document such as the one they were impugning, and still have
time to reach El Realito (near Opodepe) to deliver that document to commissioner Varela before
the afternoon of August 3.

[57] ARAG, Ramo Civil, 424-1-6888, f. 20.

[58] Escalante suggests that handing Merisichi over to the people of Tuape would have completed
that town's land endowment and resolved the boundary problem. Tomás de Escalante to Intendant
Antonio Cordero, Arizpe, December 17, 1817, ARAG, Ramo Civil, 424-1-6888, ff. 44–45.

The Opodepe protector decided to try a different tack. A few days after Commissioner Elías González arrived in Tuape, Gándara appeared with a document in which he asked González to acknowledge Opodepe property lines as stated in the transcription of an old survey that he had recently discovered in a dossier. González had many reasons to be suspicious of the urgency with which Gándara pressed him to check those survey measurements, and thus excused himself, saying that he could not do so unless the Tuape protector was also present. After studying this situation and other testimonies, González decided against Opodepe.

A conversation with the governor of Opodepe had convinced González that the Indians were interested in receiving lands only in Merisichi. Their claims of "immemorial possession" could be dismissed because they had no original documents proving the same. The only certainty, he concluded in a report to the intendant of Sonora, was that the Indians of Opodepe

> from time immemorial had never made use of that terrain . . . as pasture [or] . . . cropland, [but that] some 20 years ago certain Spanish settlers began to enter the site, and with great zeal and much individual labor began to plant [and] initiate irrigation works. When these Indians saw [these advances], they attempted to make it appear that the terrain belonged to them [and] began to charge [the Spaniards] rent. . . . [T]hen the Indians from Tuape, some 20 years ago, began to . . . deforest lands farther up and cultivate them with immense work and when those fields were . . . in cultivation, [the Indians from Opodepe] began to try to displace them, not for purposes of cultivating on their own, as they had never done so, but out of their desire to gain . . . by renting those lands [to the Spanish settlers].[59]

Commissioner Elías González's conclusion—later ratified by the intendant—was to dismiss the claims presented by the plaintiffs and proceed to take new measurements to complete the *fundo legal* of each town.

Gándara opposed the decisions by the commissioner and intendant and managed to prolong the litigation by demanding that measures be taken according to the documents he had discovered. González then decided to resign his commission, and in April 1818 a new commissioner arrived, Don José Esteban, captain of the presidio at Bacoachi.[60] Esteban arranged to bring

[59] Ignacio Elías González to Intendant Antonio Cordero, Opodepe, December 24, 1817, ARAG, Ramo Civil, 424-1-6888, f. 69.

[60] The official letter authorizing José Esteban's commission is dated April 1, 1818. On that same date Esteban was charged with determining whether it was true that the Indians from Opodepe were taking up arms to attack those of Tuape. I discuss this matter in greater detail below.

Gándara and the protector of Tuape, Don Fernando Lino de Cárdenas (who represented Tomás de Escalante), together in May 1818 to survey both towns in accordance with Gándara's petition. Thanks to the astuteness of the protector of Opodepe, the new boundaries favored his party and the conflict was resolved with Merisichi being assigned to Opodepe. At this juncture, however, the dispute took a completely unexpected turn: with Opodepe's ownership of Merisichi having been recognized, Gándara "donated" forty-one *cordeles* of the area to Tuape, while holding the other fifty-nine *cordeles* for Opodepe.[61] The objective of this donation, which came to light later, was to ask that the *fundo legal* of Opodepe be amended with lands from around El Realito, a settlement whose inhabitants lived primarily from the products of the lands that they rented from Opodepe.

These new events prompted irate reactions on several fronts. In an attempt to reverse the course that the boundary conflict between Tuape and Opodepe had taken, in March 1818 the *teniente de justicia* of Cucurpe, Fernando Grande, accused Opodepe and its protector, Gándara, of the crime of high treason.[62] Portraying the townspeople of Opodepe as rebels in the midst of the Mexican Independence struggles seemed a bit far-fetched, although it was clear to all that the charges stemmed from the land dispute between the two towns.[63] Fernando Grande argued that the proof of the crime lay in the discovery of "an armory of bows and lances that [they] are attempting to set up in the town of Opodepe," and attributed responsibility to Gándara, the alleged organizer of this armory among the Indians of Opodepe.[64] Aware that this accusation was related to the dispute over Merisichi, the intendant of Sonora asked Commissioner Esteban to look into the charges while proceeding to survey the lands of both communities. Esteban's inquiry found that the Indian governor of Opodepe had sent two Indians to a site near Cucurpe to cut tree

[61] ARAG, Ramo Civil, 424-1-6888, ff. 120–40.

[62] ARAG, Ramo Civil, 264-5-3600.

[63] In 1822, the *fiscal* of the Audiencia de Guadalajara remembered this case as a conspiracy against the Indians of Opodepe organized by Fernando Grande and Father Madueño. He wrote, "concerning the accusation [at hand], lodged by the aforementioned *teniente* and Father Fray Fernando Madueño for the purpose of interrupting the course of events concerning lands, this superior tribunal was informed [and became convinced] that the calumny and posture of the accuser could not harm the persecuted Indians of Opodepe, [and] that the conduct of the latter was irreprehensible and their patriotism unquestioned." ARAG, Ramo Civil, 424-1-6888, f. 190.

[64] Fernando Grande to Intendant Antonio Cordero, Cucurpe, March 30, 1818, *Diligencias practicadas a consecuencia de representación del Teniente de Justicia de Cucurpe sobre que los indios de Opodepe habían provisión extraordinaria de arcos y flechas*, ARAG, Ramo Civil, 427-11-6947, ff. 3–4.

branches to make bows and lances for Gándara. Several additional testimonies confirmed those events and revealed that Cucurpe residents were fearful of the "improper use" to which the Indians of Opodepe might put those weapons.[65]

Other testimonies, however, indicated that while Gándara had indeed asked the missionary at Opodepe, Fray Luis Romero, for a certain number of bows and lances, his purpose was to arm the Indians working for him on his ranch at Santa Rita (Ures) so that they could defend themselves against attacks by the Seri Indians. Romero, a merchant named Ramón Agudo, and the Indian governor of Opodepe, José Vázquez, had decided to give the weapons to Gándara. The missionary had given the woodcutters supplies, the governor had sent two mission Indians to transport the wood, and the merchant had provided the mules to carry the wood.[66]

In view of the evidence, Commissioner González concluded that Cucurpe had no reason to fear aggression from the Indians of Opodepe. He duly informed Intendant Antonio Cordero, who, upon discussing the matter with Alejo García Conde, Internal Provinces commander general, identified two individuals as being responsible for the situation. Cordero wrote that upon taking up duties as intendant, he had found "the Indians of Tuape and Opodepe bitterly engaged in a land dispute." Shortly thereafter he realized that the missionaries of both towns "were those who fomented discord." Hence, Cordero thought, the objective of the new denunciation was to "deceive the government and make it an instrument of a sorry vengeance" that would have been carried out had he not asked the commissary of the Xaliscans to remove both missionaries.[67]

The reader will recall that in 1818 the blame for the disquiet among the residents of Opodepe was attributed—not without cause—to Father Luis Romero. It must also be considered that José Vázquez initially championed Opodepe's cause, and the protector Gándara had the good fortune of "finding" the document that gave possession of Merisichi to Opodepe. Finally, Gándara donated part of the Merisichi site in exchange for some lands that belonged to El Realito. Now, in 1818, it became known that Father Romero had accused Vázquez of enticing the Opodepe Indians into immoral conduct and disobedience against the missionary. The Indians, in turn, accused

---

[65] ARAG, Ramo Civil, 427-11-6947, f. 28.

[66] *Ibid.*, ff. 18–40.

[67] Antonio Cordero to Alejo García Conde, Durango, July 30, 1818, ARAG, Ramo Civil, 427-11-6947, ff. 46–48. The bad news for Intendant Cordero was that around the same time, Father Fernando Madueño was elected commissary of the Xaliscan missions in Sonora.

Father Romero of separating a woman and her husband and prohibiting them from living together. In order to put an end to these discussions, Romero initiated the process of electing new local authorities, an act that Severino Varela, the *teniente de justicia* of Opodepe who resided in El Realito, immediately seconded.

In early 1819, Varela arrived in Opodepe to oversee the election of the new governor, but this caused great discontent among the Indians because they knew he would use the opportunity to express the resentment he held against them. The Indians opposed Vázquez's removal and, in fact, reelected him as governor. This affair came to the attention of Juan de Gándara, who immediately asked the intendant of Sonora to launch a judicial investigation into Father Romero's role in those events.[68] The testimony of the Indians interviewed in the case, as well as the actions of José Vázquez and Juan de Gándara during the inquiry, shifted Father Romero to a rather secondary role in the community life of Opodepe. In fact, this particular episode would ultimately convince the authorities in Sonora that the inhabitants of Opodepe might even confront their minister if necessary, as they "recognized no other superior than their protector Don Juan de Gándara."[69]

These confrontations between towns of the same ethnic group, between the conflicting interests of Spanish settlers and Indian residents, and between communities and secular and ecclesiastical authorities, all confirm two processes of change that characterized the life of Indian towns in the early nineteenth century. First, by the nineteenth century the integrating element of the socioeconomic life of towns such as those in Opatería and Pimería Baja was no longer the mission. Instead, the agricultural enterprises of a group of prominent ranchers and merchants began to dominate in that period. In the Opodepe area, one individual taking this role was Juan de Gándara, who appeared in all of the abovementioned cases litigating in favor of the townsfolk, offering employment to local Indians on his ranches, and supplying them with weapons as a means of securing his own interests and those of the people he protected.

Second, recent studies have shown that in Indian towns, collective expressions of protest, violence, or political cooperation with other social actors were emerging through those communities' forms of consensus making on issues affecting group interests.[70] In the cases discussed above, the changing attitude

---

[68] ARAG, Ramo Criminal, 147-11-2227.
[69] *Ibid.*, f. 19.
[70] Mallon, *Peasant and Nation*, 319; Guardino, *Peasants*, 147–68.

of the townspeople of Opodepe toward their missionary and the durable alliances with the Gándara family seem to have meshed with this new way of understanding the political negotiations of the nineteenth century.

However, another factor frequently ignored in such bottom-up analyses of political history is that the cement allowing such alliances to endure was expressed materially in the benefits accruing to the towns through their representatives' efforts. By the early decades of the nineteenth century, the missions in Opatería could no longer offer an alternative model of security and labor self-sufficiency. It is probable that thanks to the mechanisms of luring laborers away, described in earlier chapters, individuals such as Juan de Gándara succeeded in retaining significant numbers of Indians on their ranches, as was the case in Opodepe. Determining whether personal charisma of one or more persons involved and the internal negotiating mechanisms of those communities were more powerful than the mechanisms of economic coercion described previously is a task that goes beyond the scope of the present study. However, it is clear that in these regions the linkages between prominent members of the Sonoran elite and indigenous communities became increasingly consolidated as the nineteenth century wore on. The factional war between Manuel María Gándara and José Urrea and the later one involving Gándara and Pesqueira cannot be understood if the historical antecedents allowing the Gándara family to cultivate multiple networks of aid and reciprocity over the course of several decades are not taken into account. Without this context, one cannot explain why the indigenous towns of central Sonora threw their weight so decidedly behind the Gándara family, one of the "three kinship networks dominating the political scene in Sonora," during the struggles for political power after 1831.[71]

As the nineteenth century advanced, financial shortages increasingly affected missions in Pimería Baja and Opatería, but, more importantly, the missions were decaying from within as they could no longer offer their residents the spiritual attention or the models of social organization of earlier times. The sixteen missionaries assigned by the Xalisco province to Sonora in 1820 were reduced just a decade later to eleven. By 1850 only one missionary remained, a sixty-two-year-old friar who served seven towns (Table 6.1).

The mission regime in Pimería Baja and Opatería had quickly grown "old" after 1820. For several years, the Xalisco province had experienced problems in attracting new recruits and renewing its religious personnel. Despite this, in

[71] Ignacio Almada, *Breve historia de Sonora* (Mexico City: Fondo de Cultura Económica, 2000), 124–34.

TABLE 6.1. Xaliscan missionaries in Sonora, 1820–1855

	1820	1831	1834	1850–1855
Cumuripa	Salvador Castillo	Diego García		
Tecoripa	Ignacio Dávalos	Ignacio Dávalos	Ignacio Dávalos	Antonio Flores
Sahuaripa	Dionisio Oñederra	Antonio Encinas	Dionisio Camberos	
Arivechi	José Rico	Jose Maria Pérez	José María Pérez	
Taraichi	Antonio Encinas	Antonio Flores		
Huásavas	Luis Temblet	Juan Esterlic	Juan Esterlic	Attended by Flores
Bacadehuachi	Lorenzo Simó	Francisco Frias	Miguel Tellechea	Attended by Flores
Basarac	José Manuel Portillo	Luis Temblet	Luis Temblet	Attended by Flores
Bacoachi	Diego García	Mariano Nieto	Mariano Nieto	Attended by Flores
Cucurpe	Fernando Madueño	Agustin Zaldúa	Agustín Zaldúa	Attended by Flores
Seris del Pitic	José Llobregat	Dionisio Camberos		
San José de Pimas	Dionisio Camberos		Antonio Encinas	Attended by Flores
Opodepe	Antonio Flores			

Note: In 1820 the following missionaries were also in Sonora: Martín Pérez in the parish of Ures, Patricio Quezada at the presidio of Pitic, and Francisco Robles at the Fronteras presidio. BPEJ, CM, libro 33, ff. 121–23.

Source: AHZPFSFSM, *Tablas capitulares de la Provincia de Xalisco.*

1828 three young friars (Antonio Encinas, Mariano Nieto, and Juan Maldonado) were sent to Sonora in an attempt to support the missionaries already stationed there. This infusion was insufficient, as illness and advanced age of most Sonoran missionaries left many towns entrusted to the Xaliscans without religious services.[72]

While the mission enterprise grew old due to the Xalisco province's incapacity to send new missionaries to Sonora, it is also evident that it had

[72] A list of the six Spanish missionaries that the province of Xalisco maintained in Sonora suggests the following panorama: Father Juan Bautista Esterlic, the missionary in Huásavas, was "habitually ill with hemorrhoids." Fray Diego García, Esterlic's companion in Huásavas, was an invalid, "tremulous and unable to celebrate Mass." Fray Luis Temblet, Tellechea's companion in Basarac, "has very poor eyesight." Fray Dionisio Oñederra, who lived on the Arivechi mission with Father José María Pérez, was over sixty years of age and was "crippled in one leg that had been fractured." Fray Ignacio Dávalos, *Lista de religiosos Españoles que subsisten en las Misiones de Pimería baja en esta Sonora,* Nacori, May 17, 1833, BPEJ, CM, book 45, f. 71.

reached the age of maturity. Local communities had changed and were now demanding freedoms and forms of socialization that the mission regime either prohibited or was unable to offer. The secularization of the mission at Pitic in 1833 was the clearest expression of this maturation process, as this measure turned out to be the only possible means of resolving "certain difficulties that have been invincible for some time," according to the priest in Hermosillo, in alluding to the close relationship between his parishioners and mission residents and the constant jurisdictional conflicts between parish and mission.[73]

In subsequent years, the maturation process affecting the mission towns and the missionaries themselves forced the Xaliscans to abandon additional sites. On April 16, 1834, the national government decreed the secularization of all missions in the Mexican Republic. The government of Sonora responded to the decree with an official document affirming that the orders would be carried out only with great difficulty in the "missions that exist in name only in the interior of the state," as the missions lacked sufficient priests.[74] For this reason, the state government asked the Franciscans to remain in those towns, despite the fact that the missions in Pimería Baja and Opatería were formally secularized in the same year. The Franciscans still living in those places did, in fact, remain in charge of those missions even after secularization. When these friars died, they were not replaced because in the face of its own lack of personnel the Xalisco province could not supply friars to parishes in the Diocese of Sonora.

---

[73] To the north of the Sonora River, across from the mission at Pitic (also called *San Pedro de la Conquista de los Seris* or *pueblo de los Seris del Pitic*), a *villa* also called Pitic had been established, though it changed its name to Hermosillo in 1828. The "ongoing competition for jurisdiction" between the priest and the missionary was the reason to promote the secularization of Pitic "so that in the future it be recognized as, and be subject to, the bishop." The fact that this secularization had been presented to the state government of Sonora by the diocese as of February 1833, and that the Franciscans turned it over on August 24 of the same year—well before the government of Sonora had decided whether it would approve the change—is indicative of the transformation of that society and of the disposition of the Franciscans to attempt to improve the distribution of their personnel. The petition for secularization can be seen in Francisco de Orrantia to the government of Sonora, Villa del Fuerte, February 26, 1833, AGES, Fondo Ejecutivo, vol. 87, exp. 4. The Franciscans' decision to turn this mission over was communicated by Fray Ignacio Dávalos to Minister Provincial Fray Antonio Galindo, Tecoripa, September 14, 1833, BPEJ, CM, book 45, f. 131. The change of the *villa* of Pitic's name was established in decree no. 77 (September 5, 1828) of the Estado de Occidente congress, BL, M-M 285:108.

[74] *Iniciativa que la Honorable Legislatura de Sonora dirige a las Augustas Cámaras de la Unión, impetrando no sean comprendidas las misiones de la Pimería Alta en el decreto de 16 de abril del presente año*, Arizpe, May 27, 1834, AGES, Fondo Ejecutivo, vol. 87, exp. 4.

In 1855, at the age of sixty-seven, Fray Antonio Flores's departure from Sonora marked the end of relations between the Franciscans and towns in Opatería and Pimería Baja. The Xalisco province finally and formally relinquished those missions, several decades after it had lost the capacity to influence the social organization of those towns.[75]

[75] AHZPFSFSM, *Tablas capitulares*, n.d. The last available record about Flores in Sonora indicates that in May 1855 he continued administering the Xaliscan missions there. BPEJ, CM, book 26, f. 39. In a report to Bishop Clemente Munguía, dated July 1855, the minister provincial of Santiago de Xalisco does not mention the missions of Sonora anymore, which would indicate that by that date the province had turned over those missions. Fray Luis Ojeda, *Informe que da el prelado provincial de esta de franciscanos de Santiago de Jalisco*, Guadalajara, July 7, 1855, BPEJ, book 26, ff. 303–304.

CONCLUSIONS

Standard narratives on the transformation of New Spain's northern frontier identify the expulsion of the Jesuits in 1767 as the turning point in mission history, due in large part to the subsequent misuse of the missions' wealth by royal administrators. After that date, according to the conventional wisdom, the missions' limited resources were unattractive to the Indian population and kept the missionaries from participating in the market economy as actively as they had previously.

From a different perspective, the dissolution of mission life took place when politicians and local elites at the time of the Spaniards' expulsion from Sonora (1828) struggled for control of mission assets. Reflecting on this episode, McCarty commented that "the beginning of the end of the mission economy in the Pimería Alta had nothing to do with religion. . . , but everything to do with money and politics."[1] The symbolic quality of the latter is obviously not in dispute. What has been at issue in these pages is the long process of decline of mission towns, the factors involved in their decay, and the various ways in which the people affected experienced the deterioration of mission life.

Not long ago, David Sweet stated that "the effect of the missions can be seen *only* in the experience of the peoples they were established to serve."[2] This approach responds to new attempts to uncover the histories of those whose lives were affected by the missions in various epochs in ways that are only recently being understood. The case presented here offers an alternative approach by inquiring precisely into the ways that diverse groups of actors influenced the settlement process creating the missions. The missions can no longer be understood as enterprises devoted to one or two specific goals. On the contrary, they should be conceived of as spaces invested with different meanings, and as processes experienced in different ways depending on the functions they performed for individual actors. These perspectives were per-

---

[1] McCarty, *A Frontier Documentary. . .* , 16–17.
[2] Sweet, "The Ibero-American Frontier. . . ," 8.

ceptible in the series of structural changes analyzed herein: (1) demographic transformation, (2) cultural transfers between Indian and Spanish/Mexican populations, (3) consolidation of a captive market and deterioration of the mission regime's economic structures, and (4) administrative differences between and within the Franciscan groups in charge of the Sonoran missions.

The changes in Sonora's demographic structure during the second half of the eighteenth century show that not all mission districts experienced the same rates of decline of the Indian population, as seen in the contrast between the Pimería Baja-Opatería districts and the towns located in Pimería Alta. In the latter region, the frequent migration of Pápago Indians from their homeland in the most arid zones of northern Sonora to the mission towns, allowed the mission regime to recover from epidemics and high mortality rates that had diminished the original Pima population in those districts. In contrast, the Pima Bajo, Ópata, Eudeve, and Jova groups gradually came to be outnumbered by the Spanish population, mainly because of intermarriage with non-Indian residents of Pimería Baja and Opatería. These demographic trends partially explain the survival of the mission regime in Pimería Alta until the early decades of the nineteenth century, as well as the increasing pressure that the Indians and Spanish settlers exerted upon the missionaries in the Pimería Baja and Opatería districts to eliminate the regime.

The middle ground among Indians, missionaries, Spanish—and later Mexican—settlers constitutes another area involved in the transformation of the mission communities in Sonora. The mission experience was a dynamic process in which people in these groups participated as cultural mediators. By moving between indigenous and Spanish societies, those groups accelerated the reception of cultural, ideological, and material elements, and later modified their respective forms of coexistence and means of subsistence.

By understanding transculturation as the relationships characterized by exchanges allowing autonomous, asymmetrical participant systems to assert themselves and acquire elements from "the other," I have approached the transformation of Indian religious practices in Sonora, adaptations of the material culture of both Indians and Spaniards, evolution of patterns of indigenous mobility, and creation of new forms of socialization and interdependence in the mission communities of Sonora. These four processes offer several scenarios in which Indians and Spaniards act as cultural mediators and confirm the argument that the consolidation of Spanish settlements in Sonora altered the missions' social functions.

The analysis of religious conversion in Sonora, for instance, shows that in addition to the problems the missionaries faced as mediators instructing their catechumens, the active role of some Indians who assisted missionaries was also instrumental in the Indians' appropriation of Catholic rituals and beliefs on their own terms. Among the Pimas, native ceremonialism coexisted with Catholic rites, in an example of religious syncretism made possible by the congruence the Indians found between the new faith and their own forms of social organization. In Pimería Baja and Opatería, the Franciscans did not have as many problems as in Pimería Alta in terms of explaining Catholic doctrine to the Indians and were especially successful in preserving the social stratification that the Jesuits reinforced through the *cargos* system. In such areas, these indigenous assistants' functions were central to the propagation of the new doctrine, observance of the liturgical calendar, and control of local communities. Above all, they served as the moral authorities and spiritual specialists of these communities when the time came for the Xaliscans to leave Sonora.

Indian and Spanish societies were also intertwined as two types of horizontal mobility evolved in Sonora. During the period considered here, the Pápagos' ancient seasonal migrations from their desert homeland in search of alternative foodstuffs brought them to the mission districts of Pimería Alta, which became their primary place of residence. In this process, the Pima mission residents mediated the seasonal visitors' adaptation to life in the mission communities. Together with these patterns of early indigenous mobility, new conditions of frontier life among various Indian groups increased the mingling of mission Indians with the Spanish population of Sonora. Forced to leave the missions because of burdensome communal work, rejection of the missionaries' supervision, the need to escape from local secular authorities, or drawn to more attractive jobs among the Spanish population, many Sonoran Indians created new and firmer bonds with their non-Indian neighbors during the late eighteenth century. Hence, in time the mission as the locale structuring their day-to-day activities was replaced. The formation of pluriethnic bands that raided Sonoran towns and the displacement of workers to new job sites were typical of these patterns of emerging mobility.

Because of the limitations imposed on the mission regime in the late eighteenth and early nineteenth centuries, the missionaries' models of social organization no longer met the needs of the local indigenous population. The Indians then relied on the Spanish settlers around them to provide employment. This process was especially clear in Opatería, where diverse kinds of security and protection by local landowners replaced the missionary as the focal point of loyalty in Indian communities. In the context of growing disputes over land tenure, increasing demands for jobs outside the mission compound, and the evident need for legal protection against land encroachment and abuses by nonindigenous settlers, Indians and Spaniards developed new forms of socialization.

Departing from accepted interpretations that posit the consolidation of capitalist structures in Sonoran society in the late colonial period, the development of a market economy, and the primitive accumulation of agrarian capital by the Spaniards through the systematic acquisition of mission lands, this study shows that Sonora's economy was deeply conditioned by a captive market or trade system that allowed Sonoran merchants to manipulate prices, artificially alter the value of the *peso* in their transactions, defraud final consumers, and generate relations of subordination and dependence that tied people to a certain place of residence through debt peonage. These circumstances show clearly that on the eve of the nineteenth century this sector of Sonora's population was not moving toward a capitalist economy. On the contrary, what occurred is the reenactment of forms of coercion and surplus extraction typical of *ancien régime* societies, in which the strengthening of certain social groups or institutions contrasted with severe exploitation endured by the rest of the society.

During a time when the missions' economic power was declining due to the Crown's restrictions on the missionaries after 1767 (prohibitions on using Indian labor without wage compensation, restrictions on access to temporalities), this captive commercial system allowed Sonoran merchants and *hacendados* to secure the Indian workers needed for their estates (haciendas, ranches, or mines) through a form of debt peonage that forced people to either flee their communities to avoid compulsory unpaid work or spend their lives chained to their patrons' landholdings.

Four conditions facilitated the consolidation of this commercial system in the late eighteenth century: scarcity of currency, high freight costs, payment of wages in kind, and the inability of the missionaries to compete with Sonoran merchants as providers of foodstuffs and commodities for the local population. As this study shows, it is inaccurate to construe commercial activity in Sonora as constituting an articulated market because of the absence of currency and the circumstances that surrounded the payment of wages in kind. To begin with, the idea that certain kinds of clothes, foodstuffs, and personal belongings constituted a form of currency that activated local economies makes little sense since none of those objects possessed the characteristics of actual currency. It has been suggested that certain textiles, highly valued by Indians, were, in fact, used in place of currency in their barter operations. In this way, the use of such a "currency" supposedly activated local markets. However, the fact that those textiles did not have an accepted uniform value, together with the prerogative of the merchants and employers to set the rates of exchange of such means of payment, clearly worked to the disadvantage of consumers. Moreover, unlike hard currency, these textiles had a very limited useful life due to the weather conditions of Sonora, which meant that sooner rather than later this supposed form of currency simply disappeared (or at least became useless), thus causing a financial loss to its owner. The scarcity of currency, it must be concluded, was not compensated by this pseudo-money, and worked to the advantage of merchants and employers able to acquire and/or sell goods at advantageous prices for themselves and underpay the labor of the Sonoran population. As for considering wages to be a sign of the development of Sonora's economy, it must be considered that such payments hardly ever took the form of exchanging labor for fixed amounts of money, nor did they allow workers to freely spend the fruits of their labor. Quite the contrary, the wages "paid" in Sonora were but a symbolic marker of the merchandise and foodstuffs that employers would advance to their workers as a means of securing the labor force they needed. Since the employers had the prerogative of calculating the value of the goods thus distributed using an arbitrary exchange rate, the actual amount of merchandise "paid" to the workers did not match the nominal income they were supposed to earn. Given these circumstances, it is clear that the mechanisms activating Sonora's economy were designed to ensure maximum possible profits for the small group of people controlling the circulation of goods as well as mining, ranching, and farming activities. It is hardly surprising, then, that the fortunes of nineteenth-century Sonora's most prominent politicians, miners, and rancher-farmer entrepreneurs were amassed through these mechanisms. Family names such as Gándara, Pesqueira, and Elías González are prominent examples of the functioning of these *ancien régime* structures, which in the long run strengthened ties of dependence and mutual (but in no way equal) interest between Indians and Spanish/Mexican settlers in Sonora.

Finally, the differences among the Franciscans in charge of Sonora's mission districts constitute the fourth indicator in the transformation of the mission regime. The comparison between the mission districts entrusted to the Franciscans from the Colegio de Querétaro (Pimería Alta) and those under the care of the Franciscan Province of Xalisco (Pimería Baja and Opatería) shows that the Franciscan order's mission regimes did not possess the level of administrative unity, uniformity in evangelizing models, and economic prosperity that had characterized the Jesuit epoch. This is the reason why the author considers it more appropriate to refer to this enterprise as a *regime*—that is, an attempt to regulate day-to-day activities and control the moral conduct of mission residents—and not as a *system*, as has been the custom in the literature on mission history.

From the very beginnings of Franciscan administration in 1768, the Colegio de Querétaro issued a series of regulations that aimed to establish an ordered evangelization of their mission districts. Although such initiative did not include the elaboration of a comprehensive, uniform method of indoctrination, it at least represented an effort to inform the missionaries as to their obligations to the Crown and the Catholic Church, as well as the constraints they were to observe in their interaction with Indians and Spaniards. Furthermore, the Queretarans appointed a *padre presidente* chief to oversee the missionaries, and relied on direct communication between that prelate and the governing bodies of the colegio (the guardian and discretorium). The Colegio de Querétaro appointed a *procurador* who acquired the goods requested by the missionaries directly in Mexico City in an effort to avoid the excessive prices charged by Sonoran merchants. In contrast, the Xalisco province failed to elaborate a similar program and left the Sonoran enterprise to the best judgment of their *comisario de misiones*. It should not be assumed that such differences arose from the Xaliscans' incapacity or lack of commitment to conversion of the Indians. It must be recalled that those friars' religious activities focused mainly on the convents and *doctrinas* located in central and western Nueva Galicia, and that from 1753 to the end of the colonial period, the Franciscan Province of Xalisco dedicated most of its financial resources and energies to litigation against the secularization of its *doctrinas*. Thus, the friars from Xalisco devoted fewer resources to the missions than they otherwise would have done.

The specific histories of the two Franciscan missionary groups are fundamental components of the Sonora missionary districts' internal conflicts during the late colonial period, as they account for the loose Franciscan administration of the missions in Pimería Baja and Opatería, and the formation of the united front of Queretarans in Pimería Alta under Fray Francisco Antonio Barbastro and Fray Francisco Iturralde. The fact that as early as 1769 the Queretarans had a defined form of administering their missions (including the management of *temporalidades*) led them to oppose creation of the missionary custody of Sonora in 1783, a project designed by the first bishop of Sonora, Fray Antonio de los Reyes. Defense of the Queretarans' administration, or the "old method of government" as it came to be called, was aimed at keeping the missions outside the bishop's control. The Queretarans' refusal to obey the rules established upon the creation of the custody, the confrontations between "older missionaries" and followers of de los Reyes's projects, and the death of the bishop of Sonora, all contributed to the decision to dissolve the custody in 1791.

After this failed experiment, the ecclesiastical administration of the two Sonoran missionary areas parted ways once again. At this time, the differences in administering the two abovementioned Franciscan entities increased to such a degree that at the turn of the century the splendor of the mission churches in Pimería Alta contrasted with the ruin of the same kind of buildings in Pimería Baja and Opatería. Several reasons account for this stark difference: the Queretarans' right to administer missions' assets; their ability to attract funds for their missions through credits, donations, or sales of mission produce; the cooperation of both Pima and Pápago Indians in working the fields and in the construction of churches; and finally, the Xaliscans' lack of control over temporalities, together with their fruitless requests to Spanish authorities for financial assistance in order to continue their work and maintain mission buildings.

In this context, as the nineteenth century continued, the mission regime in Pimería Baja and Opatería became increasingly affected by financial shortages, but, more importantly, those missions were also decaying from within as they could no longer offer their residents the spiritual attention or the models of security and labor self-sufficiency that had characterized earlier times. By the early nineteenth century, the missions in Pimería Baja and Opatería had clearly ceased to fulfill the social functions once entrusted to them. The severe financial straits of the Xalisco province together with the steady decline in missionary numbers prevented the Xaliscans from reversing this trend in their missionary districts. An examination of the conditions under which the missionaries who remained in those districts coped with their situation in the early nineteenth century reveals a marked dependency on local elites for their daily sustenance. In return for this protection, the missionaries encouraged local populations to cooperate with such patrons, thus reinforcing the prominent role that certain individuals and new population centers—such as haciendas and Spanish towns—began to play as providers, protectors, and employers within a social order that the missions were no longer able to sustain.

On April 16, 1834, the Mexican government decreed the secularization of all the missions in the country, although in Sonora the missionaries were allowed to continue working in newly created parishes because inadequate numbers of diocesan priests kept the government from replacing the friars immediately. It is necessary to emphasize that although this decree *formally* ended the mission period in the Pimería Baja and Opatería regions, the mission regime had actually ceased to exist as such for several decades. By the time this decree was applied in Sonora, fewer than ten missionaries were still administering the sacraments in the Xaliscan missions. By 1850 the number of Franciscans in those regions had declined to just a single missionary, whose withdrawal from the missions in 1855 ended this episode in Sonoran history.

In Pimería Alta, in contrast, the mission regime entered the nineteenth century in much better shape. However, since the majority of the Queretaran missionaries were born in Spain, the mission regime in Pimería Alta was severely threatened by the laws of expulsion of Spaniards decreed during the 1820s and 1830s. Upon expulsion of the Spanish friars, the Sonoran government appointed local residents as commissaries entrusted with the temporary administration of mission assets. In this case, the expulsion marked the turning point in the Queretaran administration of these communities, not because of the misuse of the temporalities under the new arrangement, but because after that date the missionaries did not regain the ability to organize community life. In 1769 the temporalities had declined under royal administrators, although missionary activities did not collapse and the friars were able to restore the financial structures of those missions. After 1828, however, the expulsion of the Spanish friars and the lay administrators' takeover of temporalities coincided with a period in which most mission residents decided to change their legal status from "mission children" to citizens of equal status with others in Mexican society, a condition that was inconsistent with the communal tasks characteristic of mission life. Thus, the combination of these three factors was the cause of the ultimate demise of the mission regime in Pimería Alta in 1841.

In contrast to the mission system crisis paradigm, this study reveals that the decline varied by region and did not depend only on economic factors. Comparison of the two Franciscan missionary areas of Sonora demonstrates that in regions located closer to Spanish settlements, the mission regime began to deteriorate earlier. In the case of the Pimería Baja and Opatería regions, this regime changed drastically in *ca.* 1768, not because of the poor condition of mission assets, but because Indian residents were not obliged to provide personal services for the mission anymore. In contrast, the beginning of the missions' decline in Pimería Alta occurred in the 1820s, when mission residents were encouraged to exchange their status as mission Indians for that of Mexican citizens. In both cases, the transformation of the mission communities was a complex phenomenon that cannot be explained by a single cause. The gradual consolidation of Spanish colonization, manifested in demographic, cultural, economic, and institutional change, speaks of deep realignments in Sonoran society. In the case of the missions, this new epoch kept the Franciscan friars from performing the functions of protectors, producers, employers, providers, and "righters of wrongs" that their Jesuit predecessors had continuously performed. Far from being the result of an economic crisis, the transformation of the mission regime was the clearest result of the growing secularization of the life, culture, and society of New Spain.

GLOSSARY

Adscripticio: An individual assigned to the service of another person or bonded to the land that the former lives and works on. The term comes from feudal times, when the individual was considered to form part of the land he or she lived on, and therefore could be sold together with that estate. A person thus considered was "ascribed to the land" or *gleba adscriptae*.

Alcalde mayor: Chief magistrate in a political jurisdiction called *alcaldía mayor*.

Almud: Unit of dry measure equivalent to four quarts or 4.6 liters. It is also one-twelfth of a *fanega*.

Arroba: Measure of weight, equivalent to twenty-five pounds.

Audiencia: High court.

Bayeta: Woolen cloth.

Bretaña: British fine linen.

Cabecera: The administrative center of a mission or parish district. Also applied to the administrative center of a political jurisdiction comprised of two or more towns.

Caja real: Local dependency of the royal treasury, located in strategic villages and mines.

Commissary general: Within the Franciscan order, the delegate of the minister general for the governance of a specific jurisdiction. During the colonial period the commissary general in New Spain resided in Mexico City, and the commissary general of the Indies resided in Madrid.

Comisario de misiones: Mission administrator. Franciscan friar subordinate to the minister provincial, with authority over a missionary district.

Comisario real: Royal administrator. In the missions of northwestern New Spain, the person entrusted with the administration of mission assets after the expulsion of the Jesuits.

Cordel: Unit of linear measure equivalent to fifty *varas* or forty-two meters.

Consejo de Indias: Council of the Indies. Royal tribunal that discussed matters of government concerning the Spanish American territories, advised the king over the administration of the Indies, and ruled over certain issues.

Conversiones vivas: Recent conversions.

Custodia: Custody. A group of Franciscan convents and friars, governed by a *custos*, that has not been organized as a province.

Custos: Franciscan friar who presides over a custody.

275

Definitory: Council of Franciscan minister provincial.

Discretorium: Council or governing body of a Franciscan convent that assists respective guardian in governance of a community of friars. Its members are the convent's vicar and a group of friars acting as members of the discretorium.

Encomienda: Grant of the right to receive tribute or labor from one or various Indian towns.

Fanega: Unit of dry measure, equivalent to 46.025 kilograms or 1.5 bushels.

Fiscal: In a mission town, lay assistant to the missionary who served as church notary, undertaker, and assistant in all matters related to ecclesiastical services.

Fundo legal: Indian town's endowment of land.

Gachupín: Derogatory term for peninsular Spaniard (i.e., person born in Spain).

Gente de razón: People of reason; term used to designate non-Indian people and especially Spaniards.

Gobernación: Any political and administrative division of Spain's overseas dominions placed under a governor's authority.

Guardian: The superior of a Franciscan convent.

Habilitado: Person authorized by the viceregal authorities to act as official supplier of the goods required by the *presidios*, to stock local stores, and to pay soldiers' wages.

Intendente: Intendant. Chief officer of an intendancy.

Jacal: Wattle-and-daub house.

Justicia: Judicial officer of a given town or district.

Leyes de Indias: "Laws of the Indies." Compilation of all the regulations and decrees pertaining to Spanish America and the Philippines from the late fifteenth century to 1680.

Mador: Lay assistant to the parish priest or missionary.

Mestizo: Person of mixed Spanish and indigenous ancestry.

Minister provincial: The superior of the province, an ecclesiastical administrative division among regular orders.

Ornamentos: Priest vestments.

Paño: Woolen cloth.

Presidio: Garrisoned fortification located on the periphery of Spanish territories.

Procurador: Procurator. Delegate from a religious order who is typically appointed to deal with mission legal affairs and economic matters.

Province: (1) Ecclesiastical administrative division of a religious order, comprised of members living in a particular group of convents, missions, or parishes.(2) Administrative division of a kingdom or country.

Real: One-eighth of a *peso*.

Rectorate: Jesuit missionary district governed by a rector, comprised of several *cabecera* missions and respective *visitas* or mission stations.

Rescatador: A buyer or itinerant merchant who visited the missions or mining sites to acquire local products to sell or trade.

Royal fifths: Five-percent tax imposed on minted silver.

Ruan: Fine cotton cloth from Ruan, France.

Secularization: (1) Conversion of a proto-parish or mission administered by the regular clergy into a parish administered by the secular clergy. (2) Change from religious to secular use or ownership. (3) Term applied to the growing worldly spirit or views of a person, community, process, or epoch.

Temastián: Lay assistant to priest or missionary; sexton and catechist.

Temporalities: Ecclesiastical properties or revenues; mission assets.

Teniente de justicia: Lieutenant of an *alcalde mayor*.

Third Order: Congregation of laymen directed by a Franciscan friar, devoted to pious ends and to the salvation of their souls through penitence. Also called Third Order of Penitence.

Vara: Linear measure equivalent to thirty-three inches.

Vecino: Spanish or non-Indian resident, typically a landholder.

Visita: (1) Inspection tour by a bishop or his delegates to a diocese, by a member of any religious order to the convents or missions of a province or apostolic college, or by a royal official. (2) Individual village or settlement, part of the jurisdiction of a mission or parish town, *visited* or attended to on a regular basis by the missionary or priest in charge of said jurisdiction.

BIBLIOGRAPHY

Primary Sources

ANONYMOUS
  Relación de Sahuaripa (1778), Bancroft Library, Berkeley, California (BL), 99/380 m, 122:12.
ARRICIVITA, Juan Domingo de, O.F.M.
  Crónica seráfica y apostólica del Colegio de Propaganda Fide de la Santa Cruz de Querétaro, part two. Mexico City: F. de Zúñiga y Ontiveros, 1792.
BONILLA, Antonio
  Informe sobre la provincia de Sonora, August 14, 1774, AGN, *Provincias Internas*, vol. 88.
BRINGAS de Manzaneda y Encinas, Diego Miguel, O.F.M.
  Testimonio de la visita efectuada por el Pe. . . , a los catorce pueblos que componen las ocho misiones de la Pimería alta. . . , Archivo Franciscano de la Provincia de Michoacán, Fondo Archivo de Querétaro, Celaya, Mexico (AFPM, AQ), Letter K, leg. 18, no. 17.
———. *Friar Bringas Reports to the King. Methods of Indoctrination on the Frontier of New Spain, 1796–1797*, edited by Daniel S. Matson and Bernard L. Fontana. Tucson: University of Arizona Press, 1977.
———. *Sermon que en las solemnes honras celebradas en obsequio de los VV. PP. Predicadores apostólicos, Fr. Francisco Tomás Hermenegildo Garcés, Fr. Juan Marcelo Díaz, Fr. José Matías Moreno, Fr. Juan Antonio Barreneche, misioneros del Colegio de Propaganda Fide de la Santa Cruz de Querétaro. . . .* Madrid: Imprenta de Fermin Villalpando, 1819.
CALVO, Vicente
  Descripción política, física, moral y comercial del Departamento de Sonora en la República Mexicana, 1843, Biblioteca Nacional de Madrid (BNM), Mss 19637.
CAÑAS, Cristóbal de, S.J.
  Estado de la Provincia de Sonora (1730), Archivo General de la Nación (AGN), *Historia*, vol. 16.
CORBALÁN, Pedro
  Estado que manifiesta el no. de poblaciones correspondientes a esta jurisdicción, distancias y rumbos de la capital: Bienes que poseen sus habitantes, y lo demás que se expresa en las casillas, Álamos, September 30, 1778, Biblioteca Nacional de México, Fondo Franciscano, Mexico City (BNFF), 34/736.

DÍAZ, Juan, O.F.M.
Copia de la visita hecha este año . . . por el Padre . . . Presidente de las misiones de la Pimería baja, por mandado de el MRP fr. Antonio Fernández, (1775), Fray Marcellino da Civezza Collection, Bancroft Library (Fr. MCC) 201–5.

DUBLÁN, Manuel and José María Lozano
Legislación mexicana o Colección completa de las disposiciones legislativas expedidas desde la independencia de la República, vol. 2. Mexico City: Imprenta del Comercio, 1876.

ESPINOSA, Isidro Félix.
Crónica de los Colegios de Propaganda Fide de la Nueva España. Washington, DC: Academy of American Franciscan History, 1964.

GARCÉS, Francisco, O.F.M.
Diario de Exploraciones en Arizona y California (1775–1776), edited by John Galvin. Malaga: Editorial Algazara, 1996.

GÓMEZ Canedo, Lino
Sonora hacia fines del siglo XVIII. Guadalajara: Librería Font, 1971.

GONZÁLEZ, Diego, S.J.
Informe . . . sobre misiones de Sonora (1737), AGN, Provincias Internas, vol. 87, exp. 7.

GRIMAREST, Enrique
Informe ... al virrey Revillagigedo, Álamos, July 31, 1792, AGN, Historia, vol. 72.

JANUSKE, Daniel, S.J.
Breve informe del estado presente en que se hallan las misiones de esta Provincia [de Sonora] (1723), AGN, Archivo Histórico de Hacienda, vol. 278, exp. 2.

LORETO, George, O.F.M.
Informe en que se manifiesta el estado en que se halla en lo espiritual esta misión de Sta Ma. Basarac y sus pueblos de visita. . ., 1796, BL, 71/283m, folder 3.

MEMORIA en que el gobierno del Estado Libre de Sonora da cuenta de los ramos de su administración al congreso del mismo estado. . . . Ures: Imprenta del Gobierno del Estado a cargo de Jesús P. Siqueiros, 1850.

MIRANDA, Tomás, S.J.
Carta apologética al padre José Utrera de la compañía de Jesús, Visitador General de las misiones de la provincia de la nueva España, escrita por el padre. . ., Cumuripa, February 18, 1755, University of Arizona Library, Special Collections, Tucson, Arizona (UAL), MS 184.

MOYANO, Francisco, O.F.M.
Noticia de las misiones que ocupan los religiosos del colegio de la Santa Cruz de Querétaro en . . . [Sonora]. . . , Oquitoa, May 18, 1803, Archivo General de Indias, Seville, Spain (AGI), México 2736.

NENTUIG, Juan, S.J.
El rudo ensayo: Descripción geográfica, natural y curiosa de la provincia de Sonora, 1764. Mexico City: Instituto Nacional de Antropología e Historia, 1977.

NÚÑEZ, Ángel Antonio, O.F.M.
Carta edificante histórico-curiosa, escrita desde la misión de Sta Maria de Baserac en los fines de Sonora al MRP Fr. Manuel Riezu . . . Ministro Provincial de la Santa Provincia de Santiago de Xalisco. . ., Santa María de Basarac, March 31, 1777, UAL, MS 193.

OJEDA, Luis, O.F.M.
Informe que da el prelado provincial de esta de franciscanos de Santiago de Jalisco al. . . , Obispo de Michoacán, como Delegado y Visitador Apostolico de regulares en la República mejicana. . . , Guadalajara, July 7, 1855, Biblioteca Pública del Estado de Jalisco, Colección de Manuscritos, Guadalajara, Mexico (BPEJ, CM), book 26, 303–304.

ORTEGA, José, S.J.
"Maravillosa reducción y conquista de la provincia de San Joseph del Gran Nayar, Nuevo Reino de Toledo." In *Apostólicos Afanes de la Compañía de Jesús, escritos por un padre de la misma sagrada religión de su provincia de México*, edited by Francisco Javier Fluvia, 1–223. Barcelona: Pablo Nadal Impresor, 1754.

ORTIZ Parrilla, Diego
Informe general de Sonora. . . , 1753, BL, M-M 500.

PÉREZ Llera, José María, O.F.M.
Apuntes sobre los acontecimientos de las misiones que mantuvo este Colegio de la Sma Cruz de Querétaro en la alta pimería. . . , desde el año de 1821 hasta el de 1841. . . , AFPM, AQ, Letter Q, no. 20.

PFEFFERKORN, Ignaz
Descripción de la provincia de Sonora. Mexico City: Consejo Nacional para la Cultura y las Artes, 2008.

PINEDA, Juan de
Informe que en el año de 1763 hizo Don Juan de Pineda al virrey de Nueva España, RBP, II/2824, *Miscelánea de Ayala*, vol. X.

PÍO VI
Breve Apostólico . . . y estatutos generales para la erección y gobierno de las Custodias de misioneros franciscos observantes de Propaganda fide en las provincias internas de Nueva España. Madrid: Edición de D. Joachin Ibarra, 1781.

REGLAMENTO e instrucción para los presidios que se han de formar en la línea de frontera, de la Nueva España, resuelto por el Rey en cédula de 10 de [septiembre] de 1772, BL, M-M 379:1.

REVILLAGIGEDO, Conde de
Informe de las misiones, 1793. Mexico City: Editorial Jus, 1966.

REYES, Antonio María de los, O.F.M.
Noticia de la California, Sonora, Nueva Vizcaya, y Nuevo México, en cuyos territorios se han de fundar las Custodias de Misioneros de Propaganda Fide. . . , BNM, Ms. 2550.

———. *Copia del manifiesto estado de las provincias de Sonora,* Mexico City, April 20, 1772, AHMNAH, FF, vol. 66, ff. 52–61.

———. *Estado de la Provincia de Sonora,* Mexico City, July 6, 1772, Archivo Histórico del Museo Nacional de Antropología e Historia, Fondo Franciscano, Mexicy City (AHMNAH), FF, vol. 65, ff. 1–22.

———. (Attributed). *Descripción sucinta de las provincias de Culiacán, Sinaloa y Sonora,* November 19, 1772, BNM, Ms. 19266.

———. *Memorial y Estado Actual de las Misiones de la Pimería Alta y Baja: Presentado al Exmo. Sor. Virrey Frey Don Antonio María Bucareli y Ursua, en 6 de julio de 1774,* AGI, Guadalajara 586.

————. *Plan para arreglar el gobierno espiritual de los pueblos y misiones en las provincias septentrionales de Nueva España*. . . , San Ildefonso, September 16, 1776, AGI, Guadalajara 586.

————. *Relación clara y metódica de todas las misiones establecidas en la diócesis de Sonora*. . . , Sonora, September 15, 1784, BNFF, 34/759.

RIESGO, Juan Miguel, *et al.*
Memoria sobre las proporciones naturales de las provincias internas occidentales. Mexico City: Imprenta de D. José María Ramos Palomera, 1822.

RODRÍGUEZ Gallardo, José
Informe que el visitador general de la Sinaloa y Sonora hace en cumplimiento de su obligación. . . , 1750, AGN, *Provincias Internas*, vol. 29, exp. 6, ff. 396–440.

ROJAS, Carlos de, S.J.
Misión de Nra Sra de la Asunción de Arispe, BL, M-M 1716:41.

TAMARÓN y Romeral, Pedro
Viajes pastorales y descripción de la Nueva Vizcaya (1765), edited by Mario Hernández Sánchez-Barba. Madrid: Aguilar, 1958.

VELASCO, José Francisco
Noticias Estadísticas del Estado de Sonora [1850]. Hermosillo: Gobierno del Estado de Sonora, 1985.

VINIEGRA, Juan Manuel de
Varios papeles escritos despues de praticado el viaxe a Californias, Sonora, y Nueva Vizcaia por el visitador general del reino de México, Don José de Gálvez, 1773, BL, MSS 86/87 cm.

ZÚÑIGA, Ignacio
Rápida ojeada al estado de Sonora: Dirigida y dedicada al Supremo Gobierno de la Nación. . . , Mexico City: Imprenta de Juan Ojeda, 1835.

Secondary Sources

ABAD Pérez, Antolín
Los franciscanos en América. Madrid: Mapfre, 1992.

AGUIRRE Beltrán, Gonzalo
El proceso de aculturación. Mexico City: Universidad Nacional Autónoma de México, 1957.

ALESSIO Robles, Vito
Coahuila y Texas en la época colonial. Mexico City: Editorial Porrúa, 1978.

ALMADA, Francisco R.
Diccionario de Historia, Geografía y Biografía Sonorenses. Hermosillo: Gobierno del Estado de Sonora, 1983.

ALMADA Bay, Ignacio, José Marcos Medina Bustos, and María del Valle Borrero
"Hacia una nueva interpretación del régimen colonial en Sonora: Descubriendo a los indios y redimensionando a los misioneros," *Región y Sociedad* 19, special issue (2007): 237–65.

ALMADA Bay, Ignacio, *et al.*
Manifiesto de Eusebio Bentura Beleña, edited by Ignacio Almada Bay *et al.*, Zamora: El Colegio de Michoacán, Universidad de Guadalajara, El Colegio de Sonora, 2006.

ALMADA Bay, Ignacio

Breve historia de Sonora. Mexico City: Fondo de Cultura Económica, 2000.

————. "La descomposición de las misiones en las provincias de Sonora y Sinaloa, 1690–1767: Un acopio de factores internos y externos a la Compañía de Jesús." In *Misiones del Noroeste de México: Origen y destino 2005*, edited by José Rómulo Félix Gastelum and Raquel Padilla Ramos, 169–88. Hermosillo, Sonora: Fondo Regional para la Cultura y las Artes, Consejo Nacional para la Cultura y las Artes, 2007.

ALMARAZ, Félix D.

The San Antonio Missions and Their System of Land Tenure. Austin: University of Texas Press, 1989.

————. "San Antonio's Old Franciscan Missions: Material Decline and Secular Avarice in the Transition from Hispanic to Mexican Control." *The Americas* 44, no. 1 (1987): 1–22.

————. "Franciscan Evangelization in Spanish Frontier Texas: Apex of Social Contact, Conflict and Confluence, 1751–1761." *Colonial Latin American Historical Review* 2, no. 3 (1993): 253–87.

ÁLVAREZ, Salvador

"Colonización agrícola y colonización minera: la región de Chihuahua durante la primera mitad del siglo XVIII." In *El septentrión novohispano: Ecohistoria, sociedades e imágenes de frontera*, edited by Salvador Bernabéu Albert, 73–108. Madrid: Consejo Superior de Investigaciones Científicas, 2000.

————. "El pueblo de indios en la frontera septentrional novohispana." *Relaciones* 95 (2003): 115–64.

————. "La misión y el indio en el norte de la Nueva Vizcaya." In *Misiones para Chihuahua*, edited by Clara Bargellini, 23–67. Mexico City: Editorial México Desconocido, Grupo Cementos de Chihuahua, 2004.

ARNAL Simón, Luis

"Las fundaciones del siglo XVIII en el noreste novohispano." In *Arquitectura y urbanismo del septentrión novohispano*, edited by Luis Arnal Simón, 7–55. Mexico City: Universidad Nacional Autónoma de México, 1999.

ATONDO Rodríguez, Ana María and Martha Ortega Soto

"Entrada de colonos españoles en Sonora durante el siglo XVII." In *Historia general de Sonora*, vol. 2, edited by Sergio Ortega Noriega, 79–110. Hermosillo: Gobierno del Estado de Sonora, 1996.

AYALA, Manuel Josef de

Diccionario de Gobierno y Legislación de Indias, vol. 12. Madrid: Agencia Española de Cooperación Internacional, Ediciones de Cultura Hispánica, 1995.

AXTELL, James

The European and the Indian: Essays in the Ethnohistory of Colonial North America. Oxford and New York: Oxford University Press, 1981.

————. *The Invasion Within: The Contest of Cultures in Colonial North America*. New York: Oxford University Press, 1985.

BAHR, Donald M.

"Pima and Papago Medicine and Philosophy." In *Handbook of North American Indians. The Southwest*, vol. 10, edited by Alfonso Ortiz, 193–200. Washington, DC: Smithsonian Institution, 1983.

————. "Pima and Papago Social Organization." In *Handbook of North American Indians. The Southwest*, vol. 10, edited by Alfonso Ortiz, 178–92. Washington, DC: Smithsonian Institution, 1983.

BANCROFT, Hubert H.
History of the North Mexican States and Texas, vol. 1. New York: Bancroft Company, n.d.

BANNON, John Francis, S.J.
The Spanish Borderlands Frontier, 1513–1821. Albuquerque: University of New Mexico Press, 1974.

————. "The Mission as a Frontier Institution: Sixty Years of Interest and Research." *Western Historical Quarterly* 10 (1979): 303–22.

BARR, Juliana
Peace Came in the Form of a Woman: Indians and Spaniards in the Texas Borderlands. Chapel Hill: University of North Carolina Press, 2007.

BARRAGÁN López, Esteban
"Formas espaciales y procesos sociales en la Sierra del Tigre." *Relaciones* 85 (2001): 105–29.

BAYLE, Constantino
El protector de indios. Seville: Escuela de Estudios Hispanoamericanos, 1945.

BEEBE, Rose Marie and Robert M. Senkewicz
"Uncertainty on the Mission Frontier: Missionary Recruitment and Institutional Stability in Alta California in the 1790s." In *Francis in the Americas: Essays on the Franciscan Family in North and South America*, edited by John F. Schwaller, 295–322. Berkeley, CA: Academy of American Franciscan History, 2005.

BERMINGHAM, Ann
"System, Order, and Abstraction: The Politics of English Landscape Drawing around 1795." In *Landscape and Power*, edited by W.J.T. Mitchell, 77–101. Chicago: University of Chicago Press, 1994.

BERNABÉU Albert, Salvador
Expulsados del infierno: el exilio de los misioneros jesuitas de la península californiana, 1767–1768. Madrid: Consejo Superior de Investigaciones Científicas, 2008.

BOLTON, Herbert Eugene
"The Mission as a Frontier Institution in the Spanish-American Colonies." *American Historical Review* 23 (1917): 42–61.

————. *The Spanish Borderlands: A Chronicle of Old Florida and the Southwest*. New Haven, CT: Yale University Press, 1921.

————. *Rim of Christendom: A Biography of Eusebio Kino, Pacific Coast Pioneer*. New York: MacMillan Company, 1936.

BORRERO Silva, María del Valle
Fundación y primeros años de la gobernación de Sonora y Sinaloa, 1732–1750. Hermosillo: El Colegio de Sonora, 2004.

BOWEN, Thomas
"Seri." In *Handbook of North American Indians. The Southwest*, vol. 10, edited by Alfonso Ortiz, 230–49. Washington, DC: Smithsonian Institution, 1983.

BRADING, David A.
Church and State in Bourbon Mexico: The Diocese of Michoacán, 1749–1810.
Cambridge: Cambridge University Press, 1994.

BRANIFF, Beatriz, ed.
Sonora: antropología del desierto. Primera reunión de Antropología e Historia del Noroeste. Mexico City: Instituto Nacional de Antropología e Historia, 1976.

BRANIFF, Beatriz
La frontera protohistórica Pima-Ópata en Sonora, México, vol. 1. Mexico City: Instituto Nacional de Antropología e Historia, 1992.

BROOKS, James F.
Captives and Cousins: Slavery, Kinship and Community in the Southwest Borderlands. Chapel Hill and London: University of North Carolina Press, 2002.

BURRUS, Ernest J. and Félix Zubillaga, S.J., eds.
El Noroeste de México: Documentos sobre las misiones jesuíticas, 1600–1769. Mexico City: Universidad Nacional Autónoma de México, 1986.

BUSHNELL, Amy Turner and Jack P. Greene
"Peripheries, Centers, and the Construction of Early Modern American Empires."
In *Negotiated Empires: Centers and Peripheries in the Americas, 1500–1820,* edited by Christine Daniels and Michael V. Kennedy, 1–14. New York and London: Routledge, 2002.

CARBAJAL López, David
La población en Bolaños, 1740–1848: Dinámica demográfica, familia y mestizaje.
Zamora: El Colegio de Michoacán, 2009.

CÁRDENAS Ayala, Elisa, Erika Pani, and Alicia Salmerón
"Nuevas tendencias en la historia política." *Takwá. Revista de historia* 10 (2006): 103–26.

CARMAGNANI, Marcello
El regreso de los dioses: El proceso de reconstitución de la identidad étnica en Oaxaca.
Mexico City: Fondo de Cultura Económica, 1988.

CASTETTER, Edward F. and Willis H. Bell
Pima and Papago Indian Agriculture. Albuquerque: University of New Mexico Press, 1942.

CHARTIER, Roger
"The World as Representation." In *Histories: French Constructions of the Past,*
edited by Jacques Ravel and Lynn Hunt, 544–58. New York: New Press, 1995.

CLENDINNEN, Inga
Ambivalent Conquests: Maya and Spaniard in Yucatan, 1517–1570. Cambridge: Cambridge University Press, 1987.

COMMONS, Áurea
Las Intendencias de la Nueva España. Mexico City: Universidad Nacional Autónoma de México, 1993.

COOK, Sherburne F.
The Extent and Significance of Disease among the Indians of Baja California from 1697 to 1773. Berkeley, CA: University of California Press, 1935.

———. *The Conflict between the California Indians and White Civilization.* Berkeley, CA: University of California Press, 1976.

CRAMAUSSEL, Chantal
La provincia de Santa Bárbara en Nueva Vizcaya. Chihuahua: Universidad Autónoma de Ciudad Juárez, 1990.
———. "Los apaches en la época colonial." *Cuadernos del Norte* 21 (1992): 25–26.
———. *Poblar la frontera: La provincia de Santa Bárbara en Nueva Vizcaya durante los siglos XVI y XVII.* Zamora: El Colegio de Michoacán, 2006.
CRUZ Rangel, José Antonio
Chichimecas, misioneros, soldados y terratenientes: Estrategias de colonización, control y poder en Querétaro y la Sierra Gorda. Siglos XVI–XVIII. Mexico City: Secretaría de Gobernación, Archivo General de la Nación, 2003.
CUTTER, Charles R.
The Protector de Indios in Colonial New Mexico, 1659–1821. Albuquerque: University of New Mexico Press, 1986.
DEEDS, Susan M.
Defiance and Deference in Mexico's Colonial North: Indians under Spanish Rule in Nueva Vizcaya. Austin: University of Texas Press, 2003.
———. "Pushing the Borders of Latin American Mission History." *Latin American Research Review* 39, no. 2 (2004): 211–20.
DE LA TORRE Curiel, José Refugio
Vicarios en entredicho: Crisis y desestructuración de la provincia franciscana de Santiago de Xalisco. Zamora: El Colegio de Michoacán, 2001.
———. "El Crisol del Reformismo: Sonora en la víspera de la visita de Gálvez y Beleña." In *Manifiesto de Eusebio Bentura Beleña*, edited by Ignacio Almada Bay, *et al.*, 43–67. Zamora: El Colegio de Michoacán, Universidad de Guadalajara, El Colegio de Sonora, 2006.
———. "Comerciantes, precios y salarios en Sonora en el periodo colonial tardío: Caracterización de un circuito comercial cautivo." *Historia mexicana* 58, no. 2 (2008): 595–656.
———. "'Enemigos encubiertos': bandas pluriétnicas y estado de alerta en la frontera sonorense a finales del siglo XVIII." *Takwá* 14 (2008): 11–31.
———. "Decline and Renaissance Amidst the Crisis: The Transformation of Sonora's Mission Structures in the Late Colonial Period." *Colonial Latin American Review* 18, no. 1 (2009): 51–73.
———. "La frontera misional novohispana a fines del siglo XVIII: un caso para reflexionar sobre el concepto de misión." In *El Gran Norte Mexicano: Indios, misioneros y pobladores entre el mito y la historia*, edited by Salvador Bernabéu Albert, 285–330. Seville: Consejo Superior de Investigaciones Científicas, 2009.
———. "Un mecenazgo fronterizo: el protector de indios Juan de Gándara y los ópatas de Opodepe (Sonora) a principios del siglo XIX." *Revista de Indias* 248 (2010): 185–212.
———. "Franciscan Missionaries in Late-Colonial Sonora: Five Decades of Change and Conflict." In *Alta California: Peoples in Motion, Identities in Formation, 1769–1850*, edited by Steven W. Hackel, 47–75. Berkeley and Los Angeles: University of California Press, The Huntington Library, 2010.
DE LA TORRE Ruiz, Rosa Alicia
Cambios demográficos y de propiedad territorial en la provincia de Ávalos, siglos XVIII–XIX. Guadalajara, Mexico: Universidad de Guadalajara, 2012

DeLAY, Brian
War of a Thousand Deserts: Indian Raids and the U.S.–Mexican War. New Haven, CT, and London: Yale University Press, 2008.

DEL RÍO, Ignacio
"El noroeste novohispano y la nueva política imperial española." In *Tres siglos de historia sonorense (1530–1830),* edited by Sergio Ortega Noriega, 249–86. Mexico City: Universidad Nacional Autónoma de México, 1993.

———. *La aplicación regional de las reformas borbónicas en Nueva España: Sonora y Sinaloa, 1768–1787.* Mexico City: Universidad Nacional Autónoma de México, 1995.

———. *El régimen jesuítico de la Antigua California.* Mexico City: Universidad Nacional Autónoma de México, 2003.

DEVENS, Carol
"Separate Confrontations: Gender as a Factor in Indian Adaptation to European Colonization in New France." *American Quarterly* 38, no. 3 (1986): 461–480.

DOBYNS, Henry
Spanish Colonial Tucson: A Demographic History. Tucson: University of Arizona Press, 1976.

DUNNE, Peter Masten, S.J.
Pioneer Jesuits in Northern Mexico. Berkeley, CA: University of California Press, 1944.

DUNNIGAN, Timothy
"Lower Pima." In *Handbook of North American Indians. The Southwest,* vol. 10, edited by Alfonso Ortiz, 217–29. Washington, DC: Smithsonian Institution, 1983.

ECKHART, George
A Guide to the History of the Missions of Sonora, 1614–1826. Tucson, AZ: Author, 1961.

ELDERSVELD Murphy, Lucy
"Autonomy and the Economic Roles of Indian Women of the Fox-Wisconsin River Region, 1763–1832." In *Negotiators of Change: Historical Perspectives on Native American Women,* edited by Nancy Shoemaker, 72–89. New York and London: Routledge, 1995.

———. "To Live among Us: Accommodation, Gender, and Conflict in the Western Great Lakes Region, 1760–1832." In *Contact Points: American Frontiers from the Mohawk Valley to the Mississippi, 1750–1830,* edited by Andrew R. L. Cayton and Fredrika J. Teute, 270–303. Chapel Hill and London: University of North Carolina Press, 1998.

ELLIOTT, J. H.
Empires of the Atlantic World: Britain and Spain in America, 1492–1830. New Haven, CT, and London: Yale University Press, 2006.

ENGLEBERT, Omer, O.F.M.
The Last of the Conquistadors: Junípero Serra, 1713–1784. New York: Harcourt, Brace and Company, 1956.

ESCANDÓN, Patricia
"La nueva administración misional y los pueblos de indios." In *Tres siglos de historia sonorense (1530–1830),* edited by Sergio Ortega Noriega, 327–60. Mexico City: Universidad Nacional Autónoma de México, 1993.

————. "Los problemas de la administración franciscana en las misiones sonorenses, 1768–1800." In *Actas del IV Congreso Internacional sobre los Franciscanos en el Nuevo Mundo*, edited by Congreso Internacional sobre los Franciscanos en el Nuevo Mundo, 277–91. Madrid: DEIMOS, 1992.

EZELL, Paul H.
"History of the Pima." In *Handbook of North American Indians. The Southwest*, vol. 10, edited by Alfonso Ortiz, 149–60. Washington, DC: Smithsonian Institution, 1983.

FELGER, Richard
"Investigación ecológica en Sonora y localidades adyacentes en Sinaloa: una perspectiva." In *Sonora: Antropología del desierto. Primera reunión de Antropología e Historia del Noroeste*, edited by Beatriz Braniff, 21–62. Mexico City: Instituto Nacional de Antropología e Historia, 1976.

FLETCHER, Yolanda
Transculturación, historia y literatura en América Latina, La Paz, Bolivia: Facultad de Humanidades y Ciencias de la Educación, Universidad Mayor de San Andrés, 1999.

FLORESCANO, Enrique and Isabel Gil Sánchez
"La época de las reformas borbónicas y el crecimiento económico, 1750–1808." In *Historia General de México*, vol. 1, edited by Daniel Cosío Villegas, 471–589. Mexico City: El Colegio de México, 1976.

FONTANA, Bernard L.
"History of the Papago." In *Handbook of North American Indians. The Southwest*, vol. 10, edited by Alfonso Ortiz, 137–48. Washington, DC: Smithsonian Institution, 1983.

————. "Pima and Papago: Introduction." In *Handbook of North American Indians. The Southwest*, vol. 10, edited by Alfonso Ortiz, 125–36. Washington, DC: Smithsonian Institution, 1983.

————. *Of Earth and Little Rain: The Papago Indians*. Tucson: University of Arizona Press, 1989.

————. "The O'Odham." In *The Pimería Alta. Missions and More*, edited by James Officer, Mardith Schuetz-Miller, and Bernard L. Fontana, 19–27. Tucson, AZ: Southwestern Mission Research Center, 1996.

FRANCO Carrasco, Jesús
El Nuevo Santander y su arquitectura, vol. 1. Mexico City: Universidad Nacional Autónoma de México, 1991.

FRANK, Ross
From Settler to Citizen: New Mexican Economic Development and the Creation of Vecino Society, 1750–1820. Berkeley and London: University of California Press, 2000.

GANSON, Barbara
The Guaraní under Spanish Rule in the Río de la Plata. Stanford, CA: Stanford University Press, 2003.

GARAVAGLIA, Juan Carlos and Juan Carlos Grosso
"Indios, campesinos y mercado: La región de Puebla a finales del siglo XVIII." *Historia mexicana* 46, no. 2 (1996): 245–78.

GARCÍA Martínez, Bernardo
Los pueblos de la sierra: El poder y el espacio entre los indios del norte de Puebla hasta 1700. Mexico City: El Colegio de México, 1987.

GARNER, Richard L.
"Exportaciones de circulante en el siglo XVIII (1750–1810)." *Historia mexicana* 31, no. 4 (1982): 544–98.
———. "Price Trends in Eighteenth-Century Mexico." *Hispanic American Historical Review* 65, no. 2 (1985): 279–325.

GARNER, Richard and S. E. Stefanou
Economic Growth and Change in Bourbon Mexico. Gainesville: University Press of Florida, 1993.

GEERTZ, Clifford
The Interpretation of Cultures. New York: Basic Books, 1973.

GERHARD, Peter
La frontera norte de la Nueva España. Mexico City: Universidad Nacional Autónoma de México, 1996.

GIBSON, Charles
The Aztecs under Spanish Rule: A History of the Indians of the Valley of Mexico, 1519–1810. Stanford, CA: Stanford University Press, 1964.

GIL Pujol, Xavier
Tiempos de política: perspectivas historiográficas sobre Europa Moderna. Barcelona: Edicions Universitat de Barcelona, 2006.

GONZÁLEZ y González, Luis
La ronda de las generaciones: los protagonistas de la Reforma y la Revolución Mexicana. Mexico City: Secretaría de Educación Pública, 1984.

GONZÁLEZ H., Carlos
Civilizar o exterminar: Tarahumaras y apaches en Chihuahua, siglo XIX. Mexico City: CIESAS, Instituto Nacional Indigenista, 2000.

GONZÁLEZ Rodriguez, Luis
Etnología y misión en la Pimería Alta, 1715–1740. Mexico City: Universidad Nacional Autónoma de México, 1977.
———. *El noroeste novohispano en la época colonial.* Mexico City: Miguel Ángel Porrúa, Universidad Nacional Autónoma de México, 1993.

GRIFFEN, William B.
Indian Assimilation in the Franciscan Area of Nueva Vizcaya. Tucson: University of Arizona Press, 1979.

GRIFFITH, James S. and Francisco Javier Manzo Taylor
The Face of Christ in Sonora. Tucson, AZ: Rio Nuevo Publishers, 2007.

GRIFFITH, James S.
"Kachinas and Masking." In *Handbook of North American Indians. The Southwest,* vol. 10, edited by Alfonso Ortiz, 764–77. Washington, DC: Smithsonian Institution, 1983.
———. *Beliefs and Holy Places: A Spiritual Geography of the Pimería Alta.* Tucson: University of Arizona Press, 1992.
———. "Saints, Stories, and Sacred Places." In *The Pimería Alta: Missions and More,* edited by James Officer, Mardith Schuetz-Miller, and Bernard L. Fontana, 97–103. Tucson, AZ: Southwestern Mission Research Center, 1996.

GRIFFITHS, Nicholas
The Cross and the Serpent: Religious Repression and Resurgence in Colonial Peru. Norman and London: University of Oklahoma Press, 1995.

GUARDINO, Peter
Peasants, Politics, and the Formation of Mexico's National State: Guerrero, 1800–1857. Stanford, CA: Stanford University Press, 1996.

GUTIÉRREZ, Ramón A.
When Jesus Came, the Corn Mothers Went Away: Marriage, Sexuality and Power in New Mexico, 1500–1846. Stanford, CA: Stanford University Press, 1991.

GUY, Donna J. and Thomas Sheridan, eds.
Contested Ground: Comparative Frontiers on the Northern and Southern Edges of the Spanish Empire. Tucson: University of Arizona Press, 1998.

HAAS, Lisbeth
Conquests and Historical Identities in California, 1769–1936. Berkeley, CA: University of California Press, 1995.

HACKEL, Steven W.
"Land, Labor and Production: The Colonial Economy of Spanish and Mexican California." In *Contested Eden: California before the Gold Rush*, edited by Ramón Gutiérrez and Richard J. Orsi, 111–46. Berkeley, CA: University of California Press, 1998.

———. *Children of Coyote, Missionaries of Saint Francis: Indian–Spanish Relations in Colonial California, 1769–1850.* Chapel Hill: University of North Carolina Press, 2005.

HACKENBERG, Robert A.
"Pima and Papago Ecological Adaptations." In *Handbook of North American Indians. The Southwest*, vol. 10, edited by Alfonso Ortiz, 161–77. Washington, DC: Smithsonian Institution, 1983.

HAGEDORN, Nancy L.
"'Faithful, Knowing, and Prudent': Andrew Montour as Interpreter and Cultural Broker, 1740–1772." In *Between Indian and White Worlds: The Cultural Broker*, edited by Margaret Connell Szasz, 44–60. Norman and London: University of Oklahoma Press, 1994.

HARLEY, J. B.
The New Nature of Maps: Essays in the History of Cartography. Baltimore: Johns Hopkins University Press, 2001.

HART, William B.
"Black 'Go-Betweens' and the Mutability of 'Race': Status and Identity on New York's Pre-Revolutionary Frontier." In *Contact Points: American Frontiers from the Mohawk Valley to the Mississippi, 1750–1830*, edited by Andrew R. L. Cayton, 88–113. Chapel Hill and London: University of North Carolina Press, 1998.

HASKETT, Robert
"Coping in Cuernavaca with the Cultural Conquest." In *The Indian in Latin American History: Resistance, Resilience, and Acculturation*, edited by John E. Kicza, 93–138. Wilmington, DE: Scholarly Resources, 2000.

HAUSBERGER, Bernd and Antonio Ibarra, eds.
Comercio y poder en América colonial: los consulados de comerciantes, siglos XVII–XIX. Madrid: Iberoamericana, Vervuert, Instituto Mora, 2003.

HAUSBERGER, Bernd
"La vida cotidiana de los misioneros jesuitas en el noroeste novohispano." *Estudios de Historia Novohispana* 17 (1997): 63–106.

HELSINGER, Elizabeth
"Turner and the Representation of England." In *Landscape and Power*, edited by W.J.T. Mitchell, 103–25. Chicago: University of Chicago Press, 1994.

HERNÁNDEZ Sánchez-Barba, Mario
La última expansión española en América. Madrid: Instituto de Estudios Políticos, 1957.

HESPANHA, Antonio Manuel
"Las estructuras del imaginario de la movilidad social en la sociedad del Antiguo Régimen." In *Poder y movilidad social: cortesanos, religiosos y oligarquías en la península ibérica, (siglos XV–XIX)*, edited by Francisco Chacón Jiménez and Nuno Gonçalo Monteiro, 21–42. Madrid: Consejo Superior de Investigaciones Científicas, Universidad de Murcia, 2006.

HINTON, Thomas B.
"Southern Periphery: West." In *Handbook of North American Indians. The Southwest*, vol. 10, edited by Alfonso Ortiz, 315–28. Washington, DC: Smithsonian Institution, 1983.

Hu-DeHART, Evelyn
Missionaries, Miners and Indians: Spanish Contact with the Yaqui Nation of Northwestern New Spain, 1533–1820. Tucson: University of Arizona Press, 1981.

HURT, R. Douglas
The Indian Frontier, 1763–1846. Albuquerque: University of New Mexico Press, 2002.

IBARRA, Antonio
"Mercado colonial, plata y moneda en el siglo XVIII novohispano: comentarios para un diálogo con Ruggiero Romano, a propósito de su nuevo libro." *Historia mexicana* 49, no. 2 (1999): 279–308.
———. "El Consulado de Comercio de Guadalajara: entre la modernidad institucional y la obediencia a la tradición, 1795–1818." In *Mercaderes, comercio y consulados de Nueva España en el siglo XVIII*, edited by Guillermina del Valle Pavón, 310–33. Mexico City: Instituto Mora, 2003.

JACKSON, John Brinckerhoff
A Sense of Place, a Sense of Time. New Haven, CT, and London: Yale University Press, 1994.

JACKSON, Robert
"Demographic Change in Northwestern New Spain." *The Americas* 41, no. 4 (1985): 462–79.
———. *Indian Population Decline: The Missions of Northwestern New Spain, 1687–1840*. Albuquerque: University of New Mexico Press, 1994.
———. *Missions and the Frontiers of Spanish America: A Comparative Study of the Impact of Environmental, Economic, Political, and Socio-Cultural Variations on the Missions in the Rio de la Plata Region and on the Northern Frontier of New Spain*. Scottsdale, AZ: Pentacle Press, 2005.

JACOBS, Wilbur R.
Wilderness Politics and Indian Gifts: The Northern Colonial Frontier, 1748–1763. Lincoln: University of Nebraska Press, 1966.

JANSEN, Andre
"El virrey Charles de Croix y la expulsión de los jesuitas de Mejico en 1767." *Hispania: Revista Española de Historia* 36 (1976): 321–54.

JENKINS, Richard
Social Identity. London and New York: Routledge, 1996.

JERÓNIMO Romero, Saul
De las misiones a los ranchos y las haciendas: la privatización de la tenencia de la tierra en Sonora, 1740–1860. Hermosillo: Gobierno del Estado de Sonora, 1995.

JOHNSON, Jean B.
The Opata: An Inland Tribe of Sonora. Albuquerque: University of New Mexico Press, 1950.

JOHNSON, Lyman and Enrique Tandeter, eds.
Economías coloniales: precios y salarios en América Latina, siglo XVIII. Buenos Aires: Fondo de Cultura Económica, 1992.

JONES, Oakah L.
Nueva Vizcaya: Heartland of the Spanish Frontier. Albuquerque: University of New Mexico Press, 1988.

KESSELL, John L.
Friars, Soldiers, and Reformers: Hispanic Arizona and the Sonora Mission Frontier, 1767–1856. Tucson: University of Arizona Press, 1976.

———. *Kiva, Cross and Crown: The Pecos Indians and New Mexico, 1540–1840.* Washington, DC: National Park Service, 1979.

———. "The Ways and Words of the Other: Diego de Vargas and Cultural Brokers in Late Seventeenth-Century New Mexico." In *Between Indian and White Worlds: The Cultural Broker,* edited by Margaret Connell Szasz, 25–43. Norman and London: University of Oklahoma Press, 1994.

———. *Spain in the Southwest: A Narrative History of Colonial New Mexico, Arizona, Texas and California.* Norman: University of Oklahoma Press, 2002.

KICZA, John E.
"El crédito mercantil en Nueva España." In *El crédito en Nueva España,* edited by María del Pilar Martínez and Guillermina del Valle Pavón, 33–60. Mexico City: Instituto Mora, 1998.

———. *The Indian in Latin American History: Resistance, Resilience, and Acculturation.* Wilmington, DE: Scholarly Resources, 2000.

KUBLER, George
The Religious Architecture of New Mexico: In the Colonial Period and Since the American Occupation. Albuquerque: University of New Mexico Press, 1972.

KIDWELL, Clara Sue
"Indian Women as Cultural Mediators." *Ethnohistory* 39, no. 2 (1992): 97–107.

LAMPHERE, Louise
"Southwestern Ceremonialism." In *Handbook of North American Indians. The Southwest,* vol. 10, edited by Alfonso Ortiz, 743–63. Washington, DC: Smithsonian Institution, 1983.

LANGER, Erick and Robert H. Jackson, eds.
The New Latin American Mission History. Lincoln and London: University of Nebraska Press, 1995.

LANGER, Erick D.
"Debt Peonage and Paternalism in Latin America." *Peasant Studies* 13, no. 2 (1986): 121–27.

LEJEUNE, Louis
La guerra apache en Sonora. Hermosillo: Gobierno del Estado de Sonora, 1984.

LEÓN PORTILLA, Miguel
"El periodo de los franciscanos, 1768–1771." In *Panorama histórico de Baja California*, edited by David Piñera Ramírez, 117–25. Tijuana: Universidad Autónoma de Baja California, Instituto de Investigaciones Históricas, Universidad Nacional Autónoma de México, 1983.

LIGHTFOOT, Kent G.
Indians, Missionaries, and Merchants: The Legacy of Colonial Encounters on the California Frontier. Berkeley, CA: University of California Press, 2005.

LIZÁRRAGA García, Benjamín
Templo de San Diego del Pitiquí. Hermosillo: Gobierno del Estado de Sonora, 1996.

MacCORMACK, Sabine
Religion in the Andes: Vision and Imagination in Early Colonial Peru. Princeton, NJ: Princeton University Press, 1991.

MAGAÑA Mancillas, Mario Alberto
Población y misiones de Baja California: estudio histórico-demográfico de la misión de Santo Domingo de la Frontera, 1775–1850. Tijuana: El Colegio de la Frontera Norte, 1998.

MALLON, Florencia
Peasant and Nation: The Making of Postcolonial Mexico and Peru. Berkeley, CA: University of California Press, 1995.

MANCALL, Peter C. and James H. Merrell, eds.
American Encounters: Natives and Newcomers from European Contact to Indian Removal, 1500–1850. New York and London: Routledge, 2000.

MARTÍNEZ, María del Pilar and Guillermina del Valle Pavón
"Los estudios sobre el crédito colonial: problemas, avances y perspectivas." In *El crédito en Nueva España*, edited by María del Pilar Martínez and Guillermina del Valle Pavón, 13–32. Mexico City: Instituto Mora, 1998.

MAZÍN, Oscar
Entre dos Majestades: el obispo y la Iglesia del Gran Michoacán ante las reformas borbónicas. 1758–1772. Zamora: El Colegio de Michoacán, 1987.

———. *El cabildo catedral de Valladolid de Michoacán*. Zamora: El Colegio de Michoacán, 1996.

McCARTY, Kieran, O.F.M.
A Spanish Frontier in the Enlightened Age: Franciscan Beginnings in Sonora and Arizona, 1767–1770. Washington, DC: Academy of American Franciscan History, 1981.

———. *A Frontier Documentary: Sonora and Tucson, 1821–1848*. Tucson: University of Arizona Press, 1997.

McCREERY, David, and Murdo J. MacLeod
  "Debt Peonage." In *Encyclopedia of Latin American History and Culture*, edited
  by Barbara Tenenbaum, 2:360–62. New York: Charles Scribner's Sons, 1996.
MEDINA Bustos, José Marcos
  *Vida y muerte en el antiguo Hermosillo, 1773–1828: Un estudio demográfico y social
  basado en los registros parroquiales.* Hermosillo: Gobierno del Estado de Sonora,
  1997.
MENEGUS, Margarita
  Los indios en la historia de México. Siglos XVI al XIX: balance y perspectivas. Mexico
  City: Fondo de Cultura Económica, Centro de Investigaciones y Docencia
  Económicas, 2006.
MERRILL, William L.
  Raramuri Souls: Knowledge and Social Process in Northern Mexico. Washington,
  DC: Smithsonian Institution Press, 1988.
  ———. "Conversion and Colonialism in Northern Mexico: The Tarahumara Response
  to the Jesuit Mission Program, 1601–1767." In *Conversion to Christianity:
  Historical and Anthropological Perspectives on a Great Transformation*, edited by
  Robert W. Hefner, 129–63. Berkeley and Los Angeles: University of California
  Press, 1993.
  ———. "Cultural Creativity and Raiding Bands." In *Violence, Resistance, and Survival
  in the Americas: Native Americans and the Legacy of Conquest*, edited by William
  Taylor and Franklin Pease G.Y., 124–52. Washington, DC, and London:
  Smithsonian Institution Press, 1994.
MEYER, Jean
  "Las misiones jesuitas del Gran Nayar, 1722–1767: Aculturación y predicación del
  Evangelio." *Trace* 22 (1992): 86–101.
MIRAFUENTES Galván, José Luis
  Movimientos de resistencia y rebeliones indígenas en el norte de México (1680–1821).
  Mexico City: Universidad Nacional Autónoma de México, 1989.
MITCHELL, W.J.T.
  Landscape and Power. Chicago: University of Chicago Press, 1994.
MOORHEAD, Max L.
  *The Apache Frontier: Jacobo Ugarte and Spanish–Indian Relations in Northern New
  Spain, 1769–1791.* Norman and London: University of Oklahoma Press, 1968.
  ———. *The Presidio: Bastion of the Spanish Borderlands.* Norman and London:
  University of Oklahoma Press, 1975.
MÖRNER, Magnus
  The Expulsion of the Jesuits from Latin America. New York: Knopf, 1965.
MUNDY, Barbara
  *The Mapping of New Spain: Indigenous Cartography and the Maps of the Relaciones
  Geográficas.* Chicago: University of Chicago Press, 1996.
MUNK, Joseph Amasa
  Southwest Sketches. New York: G.P. Putnam's Sons, 1920.
NAVARRO García, Luis
  *Don José de Gálvez y la Comandancia General de las Provincias Internas del Norte
  de Nueva España.* Seville: Consejo Superior de Investigaciones Científicas, 1964.

NOLASCO, Margarita
Conquista y dominación del noroeste de México: El papel de los jesuitas. Mexico City: Instituto Nacional de Antropología e Historia, 1998.
OFFICER, James, Mardith Schuetz-Miller and Bernard L. Fontana, eds.
The Pimería Alta: Missions and More. Tucson, AZ: Southwestern Mission Research Center, 1996.
O'GORMAN, Edmundo
La idea del descubrimiento de América. Mexico City: Universidad Nacional Autónoma de México, 1976.
ORTEGA Noriega, Sergio, ed.
Tres siglos de historia sonorense (1530–1830). Mexico City: Universidad Nacional Autónoma de México, 1993.
ORTEGA Noriega, Sergio
"El sistema de misiones jesuíticas, 1591–1699." In *Tres siglos de historia sonorense (1530–1830),* edited by Sergio Ortega Noriega, 41–94. Mexico City: Universidad Nacional Autónoma de México, 1993.
ORTEGA Soto, Martha
"La colonización española en la primera mitad del siglo XVIII." In *Tres siglos de historia sonorense (1530–1830),* edited by Sergio Ortega Noriega, 187–245. Mexico City: Universidad Nacional Autónoma de México, 1993.
———. *Alta California: Una frontera olvidada del noroeste de México, 1769–1846.* Mexico City: Universidad Autónoma Metropolitana Iztapalapa, Plaza y Valdés Editores, 2001.
ORTELLI, Sara
"¿Apaches hostiles, apóstatas rebeldes o súbditos infidentes? Estado borbónico y clasificaciones etnopolíticas en la Nueva Vizcaya de la segunda mitad del siglo XVIII." In *Hegemonías, clasificaciones etnopolíticas y protagonismo indígena, siglos XVII–XX,* edited by Guillaume Boccara and Sara Ortelli, 79–94. Tandil, Argentina: Instituto de Estudios Histórico Sociales, 2007.
———. *Trama de una guerra conveniente: Nueva Vizcaya y la sombra de los apaches (1748–1790).* Mexico City: El Colegio de México, 2007.
ORTIZ, Alfonso, ed.
Handbook of North American Indians. The Southwest, vol. 10. Washington, DC: Smithsonian Institution, 1983.
ORTIZ, Fernando
Contrapunteo cubano del tabaco y el azúcar. Havana: J. Montero, 1940.
OUWENEEL, Arij and Cristina Torales Pacheco, eds.
Empresarios, indios y Estado: perfil de la economía mexicana (siglo XVIII). Amsterdam: Centro de Estudios y Documentación Latinoamericanos, 1988.
PATWARDHAN, S.
"Aspects of Social Mobility among Scheduled Castes in Poona." In *Urban Sociology in India: Reader and Sourcebook,* edited by M.S.A. Rao, 300–31. New Delhi: Orient Longman, 1974.
PENNINGTON, Campbell W.
The Pima Bajo of Central Sonora, México. Salt Lake City: University of Utah, 1989.

PERDUE, Theda
"Women, Men and American Indian Policy: The Cherokee Response to 'Civilization.'"
In *Negotiators of Change: Historical Perspectives on Native American Women*, edited by
Nancy Shoemaker, 90–114. New York and London: Routledge, 1995.
———. *Cherokee Women: Gender and Culture Change, 1700–1835*. Lincoln: University
of Nebraska Press, 1998.

PÉREZ Herrero, Pedro
Plata y libranzas: la articulación comercial del México borbónico. Mexico City: El
Colegio de México, 1988.

PICKENS, Buford, ed.
The Missions of Northern Sonora: A 1935 Field Documentation. Tucson: University
of Arizona Press, 1993.

PIETSCHMANN, Horst
"Agricultura e industria rural indígena en el México de la segunda mitad del siglo
XVIII." In *Empresarios, indios y Estado: perfil de la economía mexicana (siglo
XVIII)*, edited by Arij Ouweneel and Cristina Torales Pacheco, 71–85. Amster-
dam: Centro de Estudios y Documentación Latinoamericanos, 1988.

POLZER, Charles
Kino. A Legacy: His Life, His Works, His Missions, His Monuments. Tucson, AZ:
Jesuit Fathers of Southern Arizona, 1998.

PORRAS Muñoz, Guillermo
Iglesia y Estado en Nueva Vizcaya (1562–1821). Mexico City: Universidad Nacional
Autónoma de México, 1980.

POWELL, Philip W.
Soldiers, Indians and Silver: North America's First Frontier War. Berkeley:
University of California Press, 1952.

PRADEAU, Alberto Francisco
La expulsión de los jesuitas de las provincias de Sonora, Ostimuri y Sinaloa en 1767.
Mexico City: Antigua Librería Robredo, 1959.

PRATT, Mary Louise
Imperial Eyes: Travel, Writing and Transculturation. London and New York:
Routledge, 1992.

PRIESTLEY, Herbert Ingram
José de Gálvez: Visitor-General of New Spain (1765–1771). Berkeley: University of
California Press, 1916.

PRUCHA, Francis Paul
*American Indian Policy in the Formative Years: The Indian Trade and Intercourse
Acts, 1790–1834*. Lincoln: University of Nebraska Press, 1970.

RADDING, Cynthia
"The Function of the Market in Changing Economic Structures in the Mission
Communities of Pimería Alta, 1768–1821." *The Americas* 34, no. 2 (1977): 155–70.
———. *Las estructuras socioeconómicas de las misiones de la Pimería Alta, 1768–1850*.
Hermosillo, Sonora: Instituto Nacional de Antropología e Historia, 1979.
———. *La acumulación originaria de capital agrario en Sonora: la comunidad indígena
y la hacienda en Pimería Alta y Opatería, 1768–1868*. Hermosillo, Sonora:
Instituto Nacional de Antropología e Historia, 1981.

————. "Crosses, Caves, and Matanchines: Divergent Appropriations of Catholic Discourse in Northwestern New Spain." *The Americas* 55, no. 2 (1988): 177–203.

————. *Entre el desierto y la sierra: Las naciones o'odham y tegüima de Sonora, 1530–1840.* Mexico City: CIESAS, Instituto Nacional Indigenista, 1995.

————. *Wandering Peoples: Colonialism, Ethnic Spaces, and Ecological Frontiers in Northwestern Mexico, 1700–1850.* Durham, NC: Duke University Press, 1997.

————. "Cultural Boundaries between Adaptation and Defiance: The Mission Communities of Northwestern New Spain." In *Spiritual Encounters: Interactions between Christianity and Native Religions in Colonial America*, edited by Nicholas Griffiths, 116–35. Lincoln: University of Nebraska Press, 1999.

————. "From the Counting-House to the Field and Loom: Ecologies, Cultures, and Economies in the Missions of Sonora (Mexico) and Chiquitanía (Bolivia)." *Hispanic American Historical Review* 81, no. 1 (2001): 45–88.

————. *Landscapes of Power and Identity: Comparative Histories in the Sonoran Desert and the Forests of Amazonia from Colony to Republic.* Durham, NC, and London: Duke University Press, 2005.

RAMÍREZ Zavala, Ana Luz, and Abby Valenzuela Rivera
"De misiones a parroquias: la empresa de secularización en Sonora." In *Misiones del noroeste de México: origen y destino 2005*, edited by José Rómulo Félix Gastelum and Raquel Padilla Ramos, 41–51. Hermosillo, Sonora: Fondo Regional para la Cultura y las Artes, Consejo Nacional para la Cultura y las Artes, 2007.

REDFIELD, Robert, Ralph Linton, and Melville J. Herskovits
"Memorandum for the Study of Acculturation." *American Anthropologist* 38, no. 1 (1936): 149–52.

REFF, Daniel T.
Disease, Depopulation and Culture Change in Northwestern New Spain, 1518–1764. Salt Lake City: University of Utah Press, 1991.

RODRÍGUEZ-Sala, María Luisa
Los gobernadores de la Provincia de Sonora y Sinaloa, 1733–1771. Culiacán: Universidad Autónoma de Sinaloa, 1999.

ROMANO, Ruggiero
Moneda, seudomonedas y circulación monetaria en las economías de México. Mexico City: El Colegio de México, Fondo de Cultura Económica, 1998.

————. "Respuesta a los comentarios de Antonio Ibarra." *Historia mexicana* 49, no. 2 (1999): 309–12.

————. *Mecanismo y elementos del sistema económico colonial americano, siglos XVI–XVIII.* Mexico: Fondo de Cultura Económica, 2004.

RONDA, James P.
"Generations of Faith: The Christian Indians of Martha's Vineyard." In *American Encounters: Natives and Newcomers from European Contact to Indian Removal, 1500–1850*, edited by Peter C. Mancall and James H. Merrell, 138–60. New York and London: Routledge, 2000.

ROZAT, Guy
Indios imaginarios e indios reales en los relatos de la conquista de México. Mexico: Tava Editores, 1993.

————. *América, imperio del demonio.* Mexico City: Universidad Iberoamericana, 1995.

SÁIZ, Félix
"La expansión misionera en las fronteras del imperio español: colegios misioneros franciscanos en Hispanoamérica." In *Franciscanos en América*, edited by Francisco Morales, 187–94. Mexico City: Conferencia Franciscana de Santa María de Guadalupe, 1993.

SANDOS, James
Converting California: Indians and Franciscans in the Missions. New Haven, CT, and London: Yale University Press, 2004.

SAUER, Carl Ortwin
The Distribution of Aboriginal Tribes and Languages in Northwestern Mexico. Berkeley: University of California Press, 1934.

———. *Aboriginal Population of Northwestern Mexico.* Berkeley: University of California Press, 1935.

SEMPAT Assadourian, Carlos
El sistema de economía colonial. El mercado interior: regiones y espacio económico. Mexico City: Nueva Imagen, 1983.

SHERIDAN, Thomas E.
Empire of Sand: The Seri Indians and the Struggle for Spanish Sonora, 1645–1803. Tucson: University of Arizona Press, 1999.

———. "The Columbian Exchange." In *The Pimería Alta: Missions and More*, edited by James Officer, Mardith Schuetz-Miller, and Bernard L. Fontana, 55–59. Tucson, AZ: Southwestern Mission Research Center, 1996.

SHOEMAKER, Nancy
"Kateri Tekakwitha's Tortuous Path to Sainthood." In *Negotiators of Change. Historical Perspectives on Native American Women*, edited by Nancy Shoemaker, 49–71. New York and London: Routledge, 1995.

SILVA Riquer, Jorge, and Antonio Escobar Ohmstede, eds.
Mercados indígenas en México, Chile y Argentina, siglos XVIII–XIX. Mexico City: Instituto Mora, CIESAS, 2000.

SILVA Riquer, Jorge, Juan Carlos Grosso, and Carmen Yuste, eds.
Circuitos mercantiles y mercados latinoamericanos, siglos XVIII–XIX. Mexico City: Instituto Mora, Instituto de Investigaciones Históricas, Universidad Nacional Autónoma de México, 1995.

SILVA Riquer, Jorge
"La participación indígena en el abasto de la villa de Zamora, 1792." *Secuencia* 29 (1994): 101–25.

———. *Mercado regional y mercado urbano en Michoacán y Valladolid, 1778–1809.* Mexico City: El Colegio de México, 2008.

SIMS, Harold D.
The Expulsion of Mexico's Spaniards, 1821–1836. Pittsburgh, PA: University of Pittsburgh Press, 1990.

SOROKIN, Pitirim A.
Social Mobility. London and New York: Routledge, 1998.

SPICER, Edward H.
"Spanish-Indian Acculturation in the Southwest." *American Anthropologist* 56, no. 4 (1954): 663–78.

————. "Types of Contact and Processes of Change." In *Perspectives in American Indian Culture Change*, edited by Edward Spicer, 517–44. Chicago: Chicago University Press, 1961.

————. *Cycles of Conquest: The Impact of Spain, Mexico and the United States on the Indians of the Southwest, 1533–1960.* Tucson: University of Arizona Press, 1962.

————. *Los yaquis, historia de una cultura.* Mexico City: Universidad Nacional Autónoma de México, 1994.

STAGG, Albert
The First Bishop of Sonora: Antonio de los Reyes, OFM. Tucson: University of Arizona Press, 1976.

STEIN, Stanley J. and Barbara H. Stein
Apogee of Empire: Spain and New Spain in the age of Charles III, 1759–1789. Baltimore: Johns Hopkins University Press, 2003.

SUÁREZ Arguello, Clara Elena
"El parecer de la élite de comerciantes del consulado de la ciudad de México ante la operación del libre comercio (1791–1793)." In *Comercio y poder en América colonial: los consulados de comerciantes, siglos XVII–XIX*, edited by Bernd Hausberger and Antonio Ibarra, 103–29. Madrid: Iberoamericana, Vervuert, Instituto Mora, 2003.

————. "Las compañías comerciales en la Nueva España a fines del siglo XVIII: el caso de la compañía de Juan José de Oteyza y Vicente Garviso (1792–1796)." *Estudios de historia novohispana* 28 (2003): 103–39.

SUÑE Blanco, Beatriz
"Evolución de la figura del protector de indios en la frontera norte de Nueva España." In *Estudios sobre América: siglos XVI–XX*, edited by Antonio Gutiérrez Escudero and María Luisa Laviana Cuetos, 727–43. Seville: Asociación Española de Americanistas, 2005.

SWEET, David
"The Ibero-American Frontier Mission in Native American History." In *The New Latin American Mission History*, edited by Erick Langer and Robert H. Jackson, 1–48. Lincoln and London: University of Nebraska Press, 1995.

SZASZ, Margaret Connell, ed.
Between Indian and White Worlds: The Cultural Broker. Norman and London: University of Oklahoma Press, 1994.

TABANICO, Dora
"De Tuape a la Basílica de Guadalupe." In *Memorias del IV Simposio de la Sociedad Sonorense de Historia A.C.*, edited by Juan José Gracida, 133–38. Hermosillo: Instituto Sonorense de Cultura, 1993.

TAJFEL, Henri, ed.
Social Identity and Intergroup Relations. Cambridge: Cambridge University Press, 1982.

TAYLOR, William B.
Landlord and Peasant in Colonial Oaxaca. Stanford, CA: Stanford University Press, 1972.

————. *Magistrates of the Sacred: Priests and Parishioners in Eighteenth-Century Mexico.* Stanford, CA: Stanford University Press, 1996.

————. "Short Journeys to Sacred Places: Devotional Landscapes and Circulation in Colonial Mexico." Travis-Merrick Lecture presented at the University of Oklahoma, Norman, October 27, 2005.

TePASKE, John J. and Herbert S. Klein
    Ingresos y egresos de la Real Hacienda de Nueva España, vol. I. Mexico City: Instituto Nacional de Antropología e Historia, 1986.

TURGEON, Laurier
    "From Acculturation to Cultural Transfer." In *Transferts culturels et métissages. Amérique / Europe, XVIe–XXe siècle*, edited by Laurier Turgeon, 33–54. Québec: Les Presses de l'Université Laval, 1996.

TURNER, Frederick Jackson
    "The Significance of the Frontier in American History." In *Where Cultures Meet: Frontiers in Latin American History*, edited by David Weber and Jane M. Rausch, 1–18. Wilmington, DE: Scholarly Resources, 1994. Originally published in *Annual Report of the American Historical Association* (Washington, DC: Government Printing Office, 1894), 199–227.

TURNER, John C.
    Rediscovering the Social Group: A Self-Categorization Theory. Oxford: Basil Blackweel Ltd., 1987.

TUTINO, John
    From Insurrection to Revolution in Mexico: Social Bases of Agrarian Violence, 1750–1940. Princeton, NJ: Princeton University Press, 1986.

UNDERHILL, Ruth
    Papago Indian Religion. New York: Columbia University Press, 1939.
    ————. *Biografía de una mujer pápago.* Mexico City: Secretaría de Educación Pública, 1975.

VALLE, Ivonne del
    Escribiendo desde los márgenes: colonialismo y jesuitas en el siglo XVIII. Mexico City: Siglo XXI, 2009.

VALLE Pavón, Guillermina del
    "Apertura comercial del imperio y reconstitución de facciones en el consulado de México: el conflicto electoral de 1787." In *Mercaderes, comercio y consulados de Nueva España en el siglo XVIII*, edited by Guillermina del Valle, 259–90. Mexico City: Instituto Mora, 2003.

VAN YOUNG, Eric, ed.
    Mexico's Regions: Comparative History and Development. San Diego: Center for U.S.-Mexican Studies, University of California Press, 1992.

VELÁZQUEZ, María del Carmen
    "Los apaches y su leyenda." *Historia mexicana* 24, no. 2 (1974): 161–76.

VIDARGAS del Moral, Juan Domingo
    "Sonora y Sinaloa como provincias independientes y como Estado Interno de Occidente: 1821–1830." In *Tres siglos de historia sonorense (1530–1830)*, edited by Sergio Ortega Noriega, 421–66. Mexico City: Universidad Nacional Autónoma de México, 1993.

WEBER, David J.
"John Francis Bannon and the Historiography of the Spanish Borderlands: Retrospect and Prospect." In *Myth and the History of the Hispanic Southwest*, edited by David Weber, 55–88. Albuquerque: University of New Mexico Press, 1988.

———. *The Spanish Frontier in North America*. New Haven, CT, and London: Yale University Press, 1992.

———. *Bárbaros: Spaniards and Their Savages in the Age of Enlightenment*. New Haven, CT, and London: Yale University Press, 2005.

WEBER, David J. and Jane M. Rausch, eds.
Where Cultures Meet: Frontiers in Latin American History. Wilmington, DE: Scholarly Resources, 1994.

WEBER, Max
Economy and Society: An Outline of Interpretive Sociology. Edited by Guenther Roth and Claus Wittich. 2 vols. Berkeley and Los Angeles: University of California Press, 1978.

WEST, Robert C.
Sonora: Its Geographical Personality. Austin: University of Texas Press, 1993.

YUSTE López, Carmen and Matilde Souto Mantecón, eds.
El comercio exterior de México, 1713–1850: Entre la quiebra del sistema imperial y el surgimiento de una nación. Mexico City: Instituto Mora, Universidad Nacional Autónoma de México, Universidad Veracruzana, 2000.

ZAHINO Peñafort, Luisa
Iglesia y sociedad en México, 1765–1800. Mexico City: Universidad Nacional Autónoma de México, 1995.

ZEMON Davis, Natalie
"Iroquois Women, European Women." In *American Encounters: Natives and Newcomers from European Contact to Indian Removal, 1500–1850*, edited by Peter C. Mancall and James H. Merrell, 97–118. New York and London: Routledge, 2000.

INDEX

Abalza, Fray José, 191
Acapulco: and commerce in Sonora, 163
Acatzingo: and commerce in Sonora, 164–65
acculturation, xxvi, xxx
Aconchi, 42 n.83, 167, 191, 217–19, 258 n.55; and commerce in Sonora, 169; as target of José Reyes Pozo's band, 138; Barbastro's death, 241; mission district, 72–74; opposing Bishop de los Reyes's reforms, 209; population estimates 1765–1850, 72–74; secularization, 96, 213; Third Order chapel, 238–39; under Arizpe's *protector de indios*, 257 n.55
Act of Tepupa, 143
adaptation, xxvi
Agorreta, Fray Juan José, 191
Aguaje: and Apache attacks, 121
Agudo, Ramón, 142, 261
Aguilar, Victores de: debtor of Fagoaga-Ximénez company, 166
Agustín, José: Oquitoa mission worker, 182
Ahome: under Álamos's *protector de indios*, 258 n.55
Ahumada, Fray Antonio: member of the custody's definitory, 204
Aivino River, 24
Akai O'odham, *See* Pima Alto
Álamos, 24, 26, 166, 194; and commerce in Sonora, 161; Bishop de los Reyes at, 208; *Caja real*, 31 n.57; population estimates 1765–1850, 72–74; de los Reyes-Barbastro meeting, 210; under Sonora's *protector de indios*, 258 n.55; Yaqui workers, 153
alcaldes mayores, 11, 33
alguacil, 252

Alias, Fray Juan, 239
Allende, Pedro de: debtor of Fagoaga-Ximénez company, 166; presidio captain, 56
Almela, Miguel, 153
Alta California: and commerce in Sonora, 161; communication with New Mexico, 39 n.78; communication with Sonora, 41
Altar Desert, 3, 5
Altar River, 3, 12
Altar Valley, 5
Altar, 167; as destination for Spanish missionary after 1828, 248 n.21; contract for merchandise supply, 179; presidio, 54
Amorós, Pedro, 237 n.124
Anza, Juan Bautista de, 121
Apaches, 25, 139, 253; alliances with Navajos, 129; and U.S. society, 5; as barbarous savages, 133; as enemies, 18; as generic term for pluriethnic bands, 125, 125 n.153; as members of pluriethnic bands, 124, 135; as potential threat, 15, 24, 39 n.78, 42, 44, 150, 251, 253; attacks, 71, 121, 128–39, 152; attack on Janos, 1776, 124; attacks as means of securing food and provisions, 135 n.195; attacks in Nueva Vizcaya, 130 n.176; attempts to exterminate them, 127; forming interethnic alliances, 132; in Franciscan narratives, 8; in Ópata ritual games, 94; leaving Bacoachi, 138; peace treaties with Spanish authorities, 57; raiding San Xavier de Bac, 231 n.104; raids in Pimería Alta, 57; setting in Bacoachi, 128–29; southward expansion, 126–29; surrounding missions, 41; U.S. army against, 5

303

Leiva, José María, 249 n.26

León, José Blas de, 249 n.26

Linaz, Fray Antonio: and Propaganda Fide, 229–30 n.54

Llobregat, Fray José, 264

Llorens, Juan Bautista: against Indians' political freedoms, 244–45; as missionary, 235; building church in San Xavier de Bac, 214 n.78

Loaiza, Francisco: commerce with Spanish vecinos, 153

López Murto, Fray Antonio, 202 n.42

López, Buenaventura, 249 n.26

López, Ramón, 237 n.124

Lorenzana, Francisco: and native languages, 98

Lorenzo: Oquitoa mission worker, 182

Loreto, Fray George: as author, 103 n.80

Loreto, 167

Louisiana: intendancies in, 36 n.71; silver from New Spain, 154

Lower California, See Baja California

Loyola, Marcos de, 16

Luz Núñez, Francisco: debtor of Fagoaga-Ximénez company, 166

Mababi: and Apache attacks, 121

Macarulla, Antonio de: secularization of Pimería Baja missions, 198

Macoyagui: under Álamos's protector de indios, 258 n.55

mador, 86, 97–98, 103; after 1825, 101; description of office, 97 n.60

Madrid, 126, 202; Barbastro filing complaints at, 211

Madueño, Fray Fernando: as commissary of Xaliscans, 261 n.67; as missionary, 257–58, 264; supplying goods to missionaries, 217–19

maestro mayor, 96 n.57

Magdalena, 45, 54–55; after 1828, 248 n.22; in 1830, 250 n.31; mission church remodeled, 111 n.107; Pima adobe houses, 112; Saint Francis Xavier feast day, 90–91

Maicoba: under Álamos's protector de indios, 258 n.55

Maldonado, Fray Juan, 251; as missionary by 1830, 250 n.31, 264; joining

Queretarans after 1828, 249; joining Xaliscans after 1841, 254

Marcial, José: captain of Ópata Indians, 140 n.205; financing local missionary, 140 n.205, 219

Maricopas: and Apaches, 125 n.153

mariscadas, 56

Martín, Pedro: debtor of Fagoaga-Ximénez company, 166

Martínez, Fray Juan Felipe: 1797 visit to Pimería Baja, 224–25

Martinez, Miguel: debtor of Fagoaga-Ximénez company, 167

Mata y Viñolas, Pedro de: debtor of Fagoaga-Ximénez company, 166

Mata, Pablo, 237 n.124

matachines: among Pima Bajo and Yaqui, 95

Mátape, 13, 23, 166, 191, 217–19; as target of José Reyes Pozo's band, 138; commerce with Spanish vecinos, 153; mission district, 23–24, 72–74; opposing Bishop de los Reyes's reforms, 209; population estimates 1765–1850, 72–74; river, 13; secularization, 96, 213; under Sonora's protector de indios, 258 n.55; valley, 3

Mayo River, 1

Mayorga, Martín de, 202 n.42

Mazatlán, 23

measles, 49; 1728 epidemic, 14

Medina, Fray Antonio, 191

Medina, Fray José, 191

Medina, Roque, 136 n.199; debtor of Fagoaga-Ximénez company, 166

Medrano, Francisco: Ópata governor of Basarac, 109

Mendoza, Francisco, 249 n.26

Merino y Moreno, Manuel: debtor of Fagoaga-Ximénez company, 166

Merisichi: disputed by Tuape and Opodepe, 256–62

Mexican population: cultural transfers, 268

Mexico: expulsion of Spaniards, 247; secularization of missions, 253 n.42; trade networks, xxx, 1

Mexico City, 190; and commerce in Sonora, 161, 163; and mission supplies, 108, 151, 216–21; Barbastro filing com-

Sonora, 161; as part of the Estado de Occidente, 100, 247 n.16, 247; geographical descriptions, 31; Jesuit inspectors in, 79; José Rodriguez Gallardo's visit, 157–59; lack of currency, 155

síndico, 168

sínodo, 151, 160, 191; for payment of merchandise, 170; regional differences, 192

Sinoquipe, 258 n.55; under Arizpe's *protector de indios,* 257 n.55

smallpox, 49; in Pimería Baja, 64

Sobaipuri: responses to Christianity, 79–80

Society of Jesus: *See* Jesuits

Sola, Esteban: debtor of Fagoaga-Ximénez company, 166

Soler, Fray José, 191; describing Queretaran preaching methods, 87 n. 25; usage of temporalities, 231

Sombrerete: mines, 11

Sonoitac, 54–55

Sonora River, 3, 13

Sonora State, 113; protector of Indians, 141 n.206; vagrancy laws, 125

Sonora Valley, 31

Sonora, xxviii, xxx, 3, 39; after the dissolution of Franciscan custody, 213; and Apache threat, 253; and *protectores de indios,* 257 n.55; appraisal system, 157–59; arrival of Bishop de los Reyes, 208; arrival of Franciscans in, 188–95; as autonomous state, 252; as part of the Estado de Occidente, 100, 247, 247 n.16; attacks by pluriethnic bands, 123; captive commerce, 160–86; cattle market, 23; changes in war against Apaches, 134; colonization projects, 19–20, 26; commerce with New Mexico, 154; credit sales, 177; cultural change, 11; cultural exchanges, xxvii, 78; cultural mediators, 268; description 1772–1774, 23–36; diocese of 36, 37 n.72, 190 n.12, 211, 232, 255–56, 265; ecology, 1–5; economy, xxx, 11, 18, 145, 150; ethnic territories, 5; explorations in, 38; expulsion of Jesuits, 190; Fagoaga-Ximénez company, 160–86; Franciscans in, xviii; foundation of diocese, 202 n.43; frontier, xxvii, geography, 25; in geographical descriptions, 8,

12–14, 31; *gobernación,* 1, 17; Indians and Spaniards relations, 47, 106; Indian population decline, 50–76; Indian responses to Christianity 82–96; Indian uprisings, 17; intendancy of, 37 n.71; interethnic contacts, 105; Jesuit inspector, 79; Jesuit rectorates, 10; José Rodriguez Gallardo's visit, 157–59; jurisdiction of *protector de indios,* 257 n.55; lack of currency, 155, 176; landscape, xxix, 6–7, 36; land tenure, 17 n.30, 20, 147, 188; linked to New Spain's economy, 148; methods of government, 44; military complaints against Apaches, 127; missions, xvii, 195; mission churches, 220; mission frontier, xviii, 48; on mission secularization, 265; northern frontier, xxvi; official reports on Indian raids, 131–35; policies on personal services in missions, 102–103; political alliances, 263; problems after Mexican Independence, 4; province, xxix, 1, 83, 152; Queretaran expansion to Papaguería, 243; Queretarans leaving missions, 255; silver remittances, 154; Sonoran Catholicism, 99–100; Spanish settlements, 21; state policies concerning missions, 101; temporalities by 1830, 250; transculturation processes, 106 n.92

South America: silver from New Spain, 154

Southwest: recollections of Apache raids in, 131

Soyopa, 23, 26, 62–63; ethnic composition, 65

Spain: intendancies in, 36 n.71; missionary recruitment in, 206; silver from New Spain, 154; reforms on mission administration, 222

Spaniards: and colonial economy, 150; and Indians, xxvi, xxviii; cultural transfers, 268; in Sonora, xxix; living in missions, 198

Spanish borderlands, xxvi n.34

Spanish empire: and frontier institutions, xx; frontier societies, xxiii

Suamca, 54–55, 191; and Apache attacks, 121; under Arizpe's *protector de indios,* 257 n.55